Essentials of Computer Architecture

This easy-to-read textbook provides an introduction to computer architecture, focusing on the essential aspects of hardware that programmers need to know. Written from a programmer's point of view, *Essentials of Computer Architecture, Third Edition* covers the three key aspects of architecture: processors, physical and virtual memories, and input-output (I/O) systems.

This third edition is updated in view of advances in the field. Most students only have experience with high-level programming languages, and almost no experience tinkering with electronics and hardware. As such, this text is revised to follow a top-down approach, moving from discussions on how a compiler transforms a source program into binary code and data, to explanations of how a computer represents data and code in binary.

Additional chapters cover parallelism and data pipelining, assessing the performance of computer systems, and the important topic of power and energy consumption. Exclusive to this third edition, a new chapter explains multicore processors and how coherence hardware provides a consistent view of the values in memory even though each core has its own cache.

Suitable for a one-semester undergraduate course, this clear, concise, and easy-to-read textbook offers an ideal introduction to computer architecture for students studying computer programming.

Douglas Comer is a Distinguished Professor of Computer Science at Purdue University with a courtesy appointment in Purdue's Electrical and Computer Engineering Department. He has created and taught courses for undergraduate students, graduate students, engineers, and non-technical audiences on a variety of topics including computer architecture, operating systems, computer networks, the Internet, digital literacy, and cloud computing. Prof. Comer has authored seventeen textbooks. His books have been translated into sixteen languages, and widely used in industry as well as academia. In addition to teaching at Purdue, Prof. Comer continues to lecture at companies and industry conferences. He is the recipient of multiple teaching awards and a Fellow of the ACM. An internationally recognized authority on computer networking, the Internet, and the TCP/IP protocols, he is a member of the Internet Hall of Fame.

Essentials of Computer Architecture
Third Edition

Douglas Comer

CRC Press
Taylor & Francis Group
Boca Raton London New York

CRC Press is an imprint of the
Taylor & Francis Group, an **informa** business

A CHAPMAN & HALL BOOK

Third edition published 2024
by CRC Press
2385 NW Executive Center Drive, Suite 320, Boca Raton FL 33431

and by CRC Press
4 Park Square, Milton Park, Abingdon, Oxon, OX14 4RN

CRC Press is an imprint of Taylor & Francis Group, LLC

© 2024 Douglas Comer

First Edition published by Pearson 2004
Second Edition published by CRC Press 2017

ISBN: 978-1-0327-2719-6 (hbk)
ISBN: 978-1-0327-2720-2 (pbk)
ISBN: 978-1-0034-1014-0 (ebk)

DOI: 10.1201/9781003410140

Typeset in Times Roman
by KnowledgeWorks Global Ltd.

Publisher's note: This book has been prepared from camera-ready copy provided by the authors.

To Chris, who makes all the
bits of life meaningful

Contents

Chapter 4   A High-Level Overview Of Processors   **53**

Chapter 5   Instruction Sets And Operands   71

Chapter 6   Operand Addressing And Operand Types   97

Chapter 11   Storage: File Systems, Blocks, And SSDs   209

Chapter 12   A Programmer's View Of Devices, I/O, And Buffering   223

Chapter 13   Buses And Bus Architectures   239

Chapter 14   Programming Devices And Interrupt-Driven I/O   263

Chapter 15   Data Paths And Instruction Execution   285

Chapter 21   Power And Energy   391

Chapter 22   Building Blocks: Transistors, Gates, And Clocks   407

Chapter 23   Hardware Modularity   **441**

Appendix 1   Rules For Boolean Algebra Simplification   **451**

Preface

Hardware engineering has shifted the use of discrete electronic components to the use of programmable devices. Consequently, programming has become much more important. Programmers who understand how hardware operates and a few basic hardware principles can construct software systems that are more efficient and less prone to errors. Consequently, a basic knowledge of computer architecture allows programmers to appreciate how software maps onto hardware and to make better software design choices. A knowledge of the underlying hardware is also a valuable aid in debugging because it helps programmers pinpoint the source of problems quickly.

The text is suitable for a one-semester undergraduate course. In many Computer Science programs, a course on computer architecture or computer organization is the only place in the curriculum where students are exposed to fundamental concepts that explain the structure of the computers they program. Unfortunately, most texts on computer architecture are written by hardware engineers and are aimed at students who are learning how to design hardware. This text takes a different approach: instead of focusing on hardware design and engineering details, it focuses on programmers by explaining the essential aspects of hardware that a programmer needs to know. Thus, topics are explained from a programmer's point of view, and the text emphasizes consequences for programmers.

Over the past twenty years, the background and interests of Computer Science undergrads have shifted, and the new edition addresses the shift. Many students enter a computer architecture course with little or no experience with low-level programming languages, such as C, and no intuition about data items stored in memory. To address the change, the text has been completely reorganized, switching from a bottom-up to a top-down approach. Instead of starting with transistors and logic gates, the new edition starts with computer programs and describes how a compiler translates a computer program from code written in a high-level programming language into binary code and binary data items. It then explains the data representations computers use, and goes on to cover the fundamentals of processors, memory, and I/O devices. Later chapters cover more advanced topics, including parallelism, data pipelining, performance, and the important topic of power and energy. A new chapter on multicore processors includes a description of cache coherence. The final chapters cover digital logic and hardware modularity.

Appendices provide additional information. Appendix 1 contains the rules used for Boolean Algebra. Appendix 2 provides a quick introduction to x86 assembly language, x86 registers, the x86 calling sequence, and the x64 extensions. Appendix 3 covers the ARM registers and calling sequence. Appendix 4 describes a hands-on lab where students can learn by doing. Although most lab problems focus on programming, students should spend the first few weeks in lab wiring a few gates on a breadboard. The equipment is inexpensive (we spent less than fifteen dollars per student on permanent equipment; students purchase their own set of chips for under twenty dollars).

We use the text and lab exercises at Purdue; students have been extremely positive about both, sending notes of thanks for the course. For many students, the course is a first introduction to hardware.

My thanks to the many individuals who contributed to the latest edition. George Adams suggested using a top-down approach, and Andre Fonteles provided comments on earlier chapters.

Finally, I thank my wife, Chris, for her patient and careful editing and valuable suggestions that improve and polish the text.

Douglas E. Comer

About The Author

Dr. Douglas E. Comer, PhD, has an extensive background in computer systems, and has worked with both hardware and software. Comer's work on software spans most aspects of systems, including compilers and operating systems. He created a complete operating system, including a process manager, a memory manager, and device drivers for both serial and parallel interfaces. Comer has also implemented network protocol software and network device drivers for conventional computers and network processors. Both his operating system, Xinu, and TCP/IP protocol stack have been used in commercial products.

Comer's experience with hardware includes work with discrete components, building circuits from logic gates, and experience with basic silicon technology. He has written popular textbooks on network processor architectures, and at Bell Laboratories, Comer studied VLSI design and fabricated a VLSI chip.

Comer is a Distinguished Professor of Computer Science at Purdue University, where he develops and teaches courses and engages in research on computer organization, operating systems, networks, and Internets. In addition to writing a series of internationally acclaimed technical books on computer operating systems, networks, TCP/IP, and computer technologies, Comer has created innovative laboratories in which students can build and measure systems such as operating systems and IP routers; all of Comer's courses include hands-on lab work.

While on leave from Purdue, Comer served as the inaugural VP of Research at Cisco Systems. He continues to consult and lecture at universities, industries, and conferences around the world. For twenty years, Comer served as the editor-in-chief of the journal *Software — Practice and Experience*. He is a Fellow of the Association for Computing Machinery (ACM), a Fellow of the Purdue Teaching Academy, and a recipient of numerous awards, including a USENIX Lifetime Achievement Award. Comer is a member of the Internet Hall of Fame.

Additional information can be found at:

www.cs.purdue.edu/people/comer

Chapter Contents

1

Introduction And Overview

1.1 The Importance Of Architecture

Programmable processors have taken over. In addition to tablets, laptops, desktops, and high-end servers, programmable processors operate cell phones, video games, HVAC systems, household appliances, and vehicles. Software tools, such as compilers, hide most of the hardware details, making it easy to build software without understanding the hardware, which brings up an important question: why should someone interested in building software study computer architecture? The answer is that understanding the hardware makes it possible to write smaller, faster code that is less prone to errors. A basic knowledge of architecture also helps programmers appreciate the relative cost of operations, such as the time required for an I/O operation, which allows a software engineer to structure software in a way that optimizes overall performance. Finally, understanding the hardware can be essential in debugging because some bugs arise from a misunderstanding of hardware operations. In short, the more a software engineer understands about the underlying hardware, the better they will be at designing software.

1.2 Learning The Essentials

As a hardware engineer will tell you, digital hardware used to build computer systems is incredibly complex. In addition to myriad technologies and intricate sets of electronic components that constitute each technology, hardware engineers must master design rules that dictate how the components can be constructed and how they can be interconnected to form systems. Furthermore, the technologies continue to evolve, and newer, smaller, faster components appear continuously.

3

Fortunately, as this text demonstrates, it is possible to understand architectural components without knowing low-level technical details. The text focuses on essentials, and explains computer architecture in broad, conceptual terms — it describes each of the major components and examines their role in the overall system. Thus, readers do not need a background in electronics or electrical engineering to understand the subject.

1.3 The Cycle Of New Hardware And New Software

Since electronic computers first appeared, the computer architectures and computer hardware have changed dramatically. It may seem that after many decades of research and commercial development, industry would have settled on an optimal design for computing equipment. However, change continues, and we still are discovering new ways to architect and design computers and new ways to build software that uses computers.

To understand why change continues, one must appreciate a fundamental cycle: new hardware technologies make it possible to use computers in new ways and new uses of computers create demand for new hardware technologies. For example, in the middle of the last century, large mainframe computers consumed huge amounts of power. Using a battery to power a mainframe computer was unthinkable. The invention of new hardware technologies that take much less power enabled industry to devise portable, battery-powered laptop computers. The popularity of portable devices spurred work on technologies that could result in even smaller portable devices. More important, portable devices spurred new ways to use computers, such as the creation of software to play digital music.

The point is that new hardware technologies spur software engineers to create new ways to use the hardware, and the popularity of new applications spurs hardware engineers to create new and better hardware that runs the applications. In some cases, the new hardware designs force software engineers to make significant changes. For example, hardware for digital signal processing eliminates the software pieces that convert microphone input to digital values or digital values into audio output.

As you read the text, keep in mind that change is inevitable:

> *The creation of new hardware technologies results in the creation of new computer architectures which, in turn, result in new or better ways to build software and new applications. The demand for new applications spurs the creation of new and improved hardware technologies, and the cycle of change continues.*

1.4 What We Will Cover

What should someone who builds software know? Anyone who has purchased a computer has heard about the four main components that must be chosen. Figure 1.1 lists the components.

Figure 1.1 The four main components of a computer system.

Processor. One of the key areas of architecture, processing, concerns both computation (e.g., arithmetic) and control (e.g., executing a sequence of steps). We will learn about the basic hardware pieces used in a processor, and see how the pieces are interconnected to form a modern *Central Processing Unit (CPU)*.

Memory. A second key area of architecture, memory, focuses on the system that holds programs and data when a computer program runs. We will examine both physical and virtual memory systems, and understand one of the most important concepts in computing: memory caching.

I/O Devices. The third key area of architecture, input and output, focuses on the interconnection of computers and devices such as microphones, keyboards, mice, displays, storage devices, and computer networks. We will learn about bus technology, see how a processor uses a bus to communicate with a device, and understand the role of device driver software.

Storage. A fourth key area of architecture, storage, focuses on mechanisms and technologies that provide long-term non-volatile data storage for a computer's file system. We will learn about the block-oriented interface such devices provide and how they transfer data over a bus directory to and from memory.

In addition to the four items in Figure 1.1, the text covers two additional aspects of architecture: underlying components and advanced topics. The underlying hardware components section introduces the basics of digital logic, data representation, and the way seemingly simplistic electronic components can be interconnected to build complex electronic mechanisms that store and process digital information. The advanced topics section explains techniques that hardware engineers use to improve performance: pipelining and parallelism. We will see that both play important roles in computing systems.

1.5 What We Will Omit

Paring a topic down to essentials means choosing items to omit. In the case of this text, we have chosen breadth rather than depth — when a choice is required, we have chosen to focus on concepts instead of details. Thus, the text covers the major topics in architecture, but omits lesser-known variants and low-level engineering details. For example, instead of details about the exact internal structure of logic gates or an analysis of how a gate dissipates the electrical current that flows into it, we will focus on the general idea of using gates to build circuits that accept a set of inputs and deliver as outputs Boolean combinations of the inputs. Similarly, our discussion of processors and memory systems avoids many technical details and the quantitative analysis of performance that a hardware engineer must learn.

1.6 What We Will Emphasize

The text places the greatest emphasis on aspects of the underlying computer hardware that have the most relevance to software engineers — professionals who design, implement, test, and debug software. Thus, instead of surveying hardware technologies and their characteristics, the text presents overall hardware features and then considers the consequences for programmers. In short, software engineers will find the text helpful in their career. The point is:

> *Instead of diving into hardware design and the details of hardware technologies, the text emphasizes topics with the greatest relevance and importance to software engineers.*

1.7 Architecture, Design, and Implementation

How can computer hardware be specified? As in most engineering disciplines, multiple levels of specification exist, with the amount of detail increasing in successively lower levels. Figure 1.2 lists three primary levels of specification and the terms used to describe them.

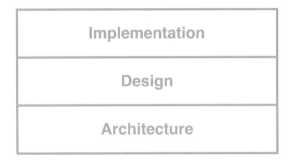

Figure 1.2 Three levels of specification used with computer hardware.

Architecture. The term *architecture* refers to the overall organization of a system, and forms the base for the system. In software engineering, the architecture specifies the major modules, and specifies the functionality that each module provides as well as which other modules a given module uses. In hardware engineering, an architecture also specifies the major components, the functionality of each, and the interconnections among them. In both cases, the architecture specifies the functionality a component supplies without giving details about how the functionality can be realized.

Design. Before a system can be built, engineers must translate the overall architecture into a practical *design* that fills in some of the details that the architectural specification omits. In software engineering, a design specifies the set of functions (or methods) that the module supples and, for each function, an algorithm the function uses, the arguments the function takes, and the value(s) the function returns. Similarly, in hardware engineering, a design specifies how to achieve the functionality for each component and the component's hardware interfaces, including the input signals a component receives and the output signals the component generates. For example, a hardware design may specify the technology used for a component, how the component is built from chips, how components are grouped onto circuit boards, and the interconnections among components.

Implementation. Eventually, a design must be implemented, which entails making choices for all remaining details that the design omits. In software engineering, implementation requires choosing a programming language, specifying data structures and variable names to be used, and writing code for each function. Similarly, in hardware engineering, implementation requires choosing exact components from which the system will be constructed and specifying all details.

Note that the progression from architecture to design to implementation represents successive *levels of abstraction*. An architecture gives a high-level specification for a system without specifying many details. A design specifies additional details, and an implementation fills in the remaining details. Many designs can be used to satisfy a given architectural plan, and many implementations can be used to realize a given design. The point is:

> *Each step in moving from an architecture to an implementation requires choosing how to fill in additional details. A design represents one possible way to realize a given architecture, and an implementation represents one possible way to realize a given design.*

1.8 Hardware Designs And Unexpected Constraints

Creating a design requires knowing both a set of *design goals* and a set of *constraints*. Software and hardware engineers share the basic design goals of functionality and performance: a design must provide the functionality described in the architectural plan, and the resulting system must meet a set of performance goals. However, hardware designers face additional constraints that a software designer may find unexpected. For example, a hardware designer may face limits on the amount of power that the overall system or specific components may draw, the physical size of the system, the temperature and humidity ranges over which the system must operate, limits on the type and amount of cooling required, the amount of electromagnetic radiation the system must tolerate, and the electromagnetic radiation the system may generate.

Interestingly, few hardware design choices remain independent. For example, increasing the speed of hardware circuits also increases the power consumed and the cooling required. Similarly, adding shielding to prevent radiation from affecting a circuit may increase the physical size. Thus, hardware designers understand that no design can optimize all goals.

The point is:

> *Many designs result because hardware design contends with multiple, conflicting goals, and a design that does better at achieving one goal may do worse at achieving another.*

1.9 Summary

The text covers the essentials of computer architecture without requiring a background in electrical engineering. It focuses on concepts and topics pertinent to software engineers, and concentrates on architectural specifications, without covering the details of hardware design or implementation.

Chapter Contents

2

Program Interpretation And Transformation

2.1 Introduction

Later chapters of the book explain various types of processors and their characteristics. In each case, we will see that a processor does not perform computation on its own. Instead, a processor must be given a detailed set of instructions that specify steps to take; the processor merely follows the instructions.

We use the term *computer program* to describe the set of instructions given to a processor. This chapter introduces two basic ideas about computer programs. First, the steps needed for a computation can be expressed at various levels of abstraction. Second, software systems exist that can transform a program from a high level of abstraction convenient for humans into a compact, low-level form efficient for use with computer hardware.

2.2 Specification Of Computation

To understand levels of abstraction and program transformation, consider a trivial problem: computing the sum of the integers 1 through 10. When they communicate ideas to others, humans use natural languages. Consequently, the highest level of abstraction consists of using a natural language to express computation. We use the term *algorithm* to refer to such a high-level abstraction. For example, Figure 2.1 shows an algorithm that outlines the steps needed to compute the sum of the integers from 1 to 10.

Start a total at 0
Perform the following step for each integer from 1 through 10
        Add the integer to the total
Announce the total as the answer

Figure 2.1 An algorithm to compute the sum of integers from 1 through 10.

Although they suffice for human communication, natural languages contain many ambiguities. To express computer programs precisely, software engineers use *programming languages*. A programming language represents a slightly lower level of abstraction that specifies more details. Figure 2.2 shows code in the C programming language for the algorithm in Figure 2.1.

```
#include <stdio.h>        /* Use C's standard I/O functions */
int      total = 0;       /* Start the total at zero */

/* Iterate through integers from 1 to 10 and add each to the total */

for(int value_to_add = 1; value_to_add<=10; value_to_add++)
        /* Increment the total for this value */
        total += value_to_add;

/* Announce total as the answer */
printf("The answer is %d\n", total);
```

Figure 2.2 C code to compute the sum of integers from 1 through 10.

2.3 Automated Program Interpretation

For centuries, mathematicians, scientists, and engineers have worked to devise programmable machines that perform computation automatically; the work has culminated in modern electronic digital computers. We say that a computer *interprets* or *runs* a program. Interpretation can be handled in many ways. For example, it is possible to write a computer program called an *interpreter* that takes the code in Figure 2.2 as input data and performs the computation. The program would scan the input until it reached the keyword *int*, and scan further until it found the name *sum* along with the assignment of zero. It would then store the variable *sum* with the value zero. The interpreter would go on to evaluate each line in the program.

Can we build a more efficient interpreter? The answer is yes. One obvious optimization uses a two-step process. In step 1, the interpreter transforms the input to a more compact form. In step 2, the interpreter scans the compact form. To understand the idea, observe that, like most computer programs, the code in Figure 2.2 contains *comments* and whitespace intended for software engineers who need to read and modify the code. It takes time to scan past whitespace and comments. For a trivial program, the wasted time is insignificant, but for a long, complex program, the time can be substantial. Furthermore, comments and whitespace can be removed without affecting the computation. In addition, software engineers use variable names that have meaning to humans, such as *value_to_add*. The program can be shortened by replacing each long name with a short name (e.g., *v* instead of *value_to_add*) and eliminating unneeded line breaks. For example, Figure 2.3 shows a shortened version of the code in Figure 2.2 that takes less than one-third as many bytes. Transforming a program to a short version moves the code to a lower level of abstraction.

```
#include <stdio.h>
int total=0;int v;for(v=1;v<=10;v++)total+=v;printf(
"The answer is %d\n",total);
```

Figure 2.3 A shorter version of the code from Figure 2.2.

2.4 What Level Of Abstraction Should Be Used For Programs?

The question has been studied extensively. Although there is no absolute optimum for all cases, a few general principles have emerged.

- Using hardware to interpret computer programs results in a mechanism that runs orders of magnitude faster than one that uses software. The principle should not surprise anyone who understand computers because a software-based interpreter must run on some underlying hardware system, which means a software-based interpreter runs much slower. We say that a software-based interpreter imposes additional *overhead* that reduces performance.

- Using hardware to interpret computer programs takes less energy than using a software-based interpreter because there is less overhead.

- To make hardware efficient, a computer program must be transformed to a much lower-level abstraction than the shortened form in Figure 2.3. In place of statements, such as a *for* loop, found in high-level languages, computation must be transformed into a set of *machine instructions* (also known as *machine language*), symbolic variable names must be replaced by numeric memory addresses, and the entire program along with data values must be represented in binary.

2.5 Transforming A Source Program To Machine Language

We use the term *source program* to refer to a program written in a high-level language, and *object program* to refer to a program transformed into binary machine instructions suitable for the hardware to execute. To transform a source program into machine language, a user invokes a tool known as a *compiler*, such as *gcc*. The compiler reads a file containing source code, transforms the program into an equivalent *exe-*

cutable binary program, and places the result in an output file. We say the source program has been *compiled* into an *executable object program* that can be run on the
hardware.

Because compilation requires several complex steps, designers divide the task into
multiple pieces that each run independently. When a user invokes a compiler (e.g., invokes *gcc*), the user actually invokes a program that runs each of the pieces and sends
the output from one piece to the input of the next piece. Figure 2.4 illustrates the pieces
and the form of a program passed from one piece to the next..

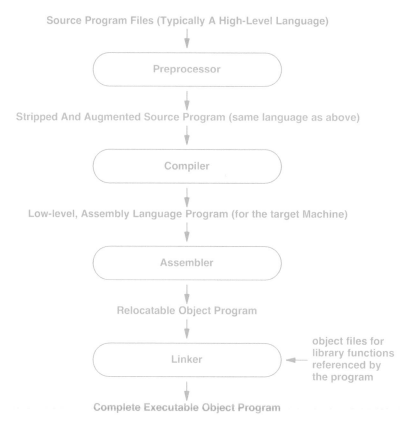

Figure 2.4 The four pieces of software that run when a user compiles a program, and the form of the program passed from one to another.

The C preprocessor handles three tasks. First, it *strips* (i.e., removes) comments
and extra white space from the source program. Second, it parses include files, and extracts pertinent type definitions and function prototypes. Third, it raises the level of
abstraction by providing a parameterized macro facility that allows a programmer to define sequences of code that can be invoked by name. Unlike a conventional function
that must be called at run-time, the preprocessor *expands* macros by inserting a copy of

the code into the source program. For example, consider a macro that rounds a non-negative integer to the nearest multiple of five.

$$\#define \ rnd5(x) \ (\ ((x)+4)/5 \ * \ 5)$$

Once the macro has been defined, a programmer can use it in arithmetic expressions. If the course code contains the line:

$$ans \ = \ z \ + \ rnd5(qqq);$$

the preprocessor expands the line to:

$$ans \ = \ z \ + \ (\ ((qqq)+4)/5 \ * \ 5);$$

The second piece, labeled *compiler*†, performs the most significant change by transforming a source program into an equivalent set of steps that the hardware can perform. The transformation depends on the hardware for which the program is being compiled, called the *target machine*, because the machine language to be generated depends on the design of the processor, and may even depend on the exact model of the processor.

Despite the translation into a low-level abstraction, the compilation step does not produce binary values. Instead, a compiler generates *assembly language* code that a human can read. An assembler reads the assembly language form of the program and converts it to a *relocatable object program*, which contains *machine instructions* in binary form.

The term *relocatable object program* arises because the resulting file contains information that allows the object program to be combined with others. Once a source program has been transformed into one or more relocatable object programs, a final step occurs in which a *linker* combines the relocatable object program(s) to form an *executable object program*. When it links the object program produced by the assembler, a linker may incorporate additional object programs as needed, usually from libraries. For example, if a program references library function *printf*, the linker will search libraries, find a library file containing the *printf* object program, and include the printf function in the executable object program being created.

2.6 Using Memory Addresses Instead Of Variable Names

When a program runs, variables and instructions reside in memory. Each variable and each instruction resides in a unique physical memory location. Instead of referencing a variable by the name used in the source file, the hardware uses the memory address of the variable. We can imagine that when an instruction references a variable, x, the instruction contains a pointer to the memory location where variable x resides. Similarly, when it executes a function call, the hardware instruction that makes the call does not use the function's name. Instead, the instruction must specify the location in memory where the function resides. The point is:

---

†Although a user thinks that all four pieces together constitute a compiler, compiler designers reserve the

*Machine instructions do not use the abstractions of names for vari-
ables or functions. Instead, hardware instructions reference data
items and functions by specifying their address in memory.*

2.7 Global And Local Variables

Programming languages divide variables into two groups: *global variables* and *local variables*. A global variable can be accessed from any function, while a local variable can only be accessed from the function for which it has been defined. Each
language offers a way to specify whether a given variable is local or global. In the C
programming language, a global variable must be declared outside any function,
whereas any variable declared inside a function is interpreted as local to the function.
For example, Figure 2.5 shows a C program with labels indicating local and global variables.

```
/* An example C program */
int total = 0;  ◄——————— initialized global variable
int temp;       ◄——————— uninitialized global variable
main(int argv, char[]* argv) {
    int    i;   ◄——————— local variable (local to main)
    for(i=0; i<10; i++) {
        temp = i*i;
        total += temp;
    }
    printf("The total is %d0, total);
    exit(0);
}
```

Figure 2.5 An example C program with global and local variables.

A compiler allocates space for each local variable on a *run-time stack* in memory,
which is also known as the *function call stack*. Each time a function is called, the code
pushes items on the top of the run-time stack, including a copy of all local variables for
the function. Later, when the function returns, the code removes all items that were
pushed onto the stack when the function was called (i.e., it restores the stack to exactly
the same condition as it was before the function call).

2.8 Segments And Their Location In Memory

A linker must plan the exact memory layout that will be used when the program runs, including memory locations for the code in each function, locations for global variables, and initial values for the locations when needed. Once the plan is complete, the linker writes the information to an executable file. Later, when a user launches the program, the operating system uses the information in the file to load the program into memory and start it running.

The linker groups similar items together, and uses the term *segment* to describe a group. For example, the linker places the code for all functions into a *text segment*. The linker divides global variables into two segments: a *data segment* contains all global variables that were assigned initial values, and the *bss† segment* contains all uninitialized global variables. For example, look again at the program in Figure 2.5. Because the program assigns variable *total* an initial value of zero, the linker plans space for *total* in the data segment. Because the program does not assign an initial value to global variable *temp*, the linker plans space for *temp* in the bss segment.

Figure 2.6 illustrates how the segments occupy memory when the program runs.

Figure 2.6 The memory assigned to a program divided into four segments.

The *text* segment, which starts at the lowest memory address, contains all the compiled machine instructions for the main program and the functions the program calls. The *data* segment contains global variables that are declared with an initial value, and the *bss* segment contains global variables that are declared with no initial value. Finally, the stack segment holds the run-time stack for the program.

The stack starts at the highest memory address and grows downward. When the program starts, the stack only contains local variables for the *main* function. We say that the unused memory locations between the bss segment and the lowest address in the stack constitute *free memory*. If the program calls *malloc* to allocate a block of memory, the system takes the block from the bottom (i.e., lowest address) of free memory. Thus, we can think of the heap growing upward from the bss. At the other end of free memory, the run-time stack grows downward, taking part of free memory as needed. In particular, whenever the program calls a function, the call pushes a copy of the function's local variables on the stack. Later, when a called function returns, the return pops the local variables from the stack, returning the stack to its previous size. Figure 2.7 illustrates how a stack grows and shrinks as a program calls functions and the functions return.

---

†The term *bss* comes from an early assembly language in which *bss*, an abbreviation for *block stated by symbol*, specified an uninitialized global data item.

Main program begins:				main's locals
Main calls function A:			A's locals	main's locals
A returns:				main's locals
Main calls function B:			B's locals	main's locals
B calls function C:		C's locals	B's locals	main's locals
C returns:			B's locals	main's locals
B returns:				main's locals

Figure 2.7 The run-time stack growing and shrinking as a program makes function calls and the functions return.

Unlike the stack, the program can allocate heap dynamically by calling *malloc*. Once malloc allocates a block of memory, the block remains allocated until the program calls *free* to return the block to the free memory pool. The system allocates heap memory from the lowest part of the free memory, which starts just beyond the bss segment. Figure 2.8 illustrates the allocation for three calls of *malloc*.

program begins:	text	data	bss			
1st call to malloc:	text	data	bss	m1		
2nd call to malloc:	text	data	bss	m1	m2	
3rd call to malloc:	text	data	bss	m1	m2	m3

Figure 2.8 Illustration of malloc allocating heap memory from the free memory beyond the bss segment. Heap allocation proceeds upward and stack allocation proceeds downward.

2.9 Relocation And Memory Addresses

The important idea is that the text, data, and bss segments each contain items from the main program and all the functions. To make a plan, the linker examines each of the relocatable object programs that must be included in the final program. It extracts the code from each object file, and plans a single, large text segment that contains all the code. It extracts the data segment items from each object file, and plans a single, large data segment that contains all the data items. Finally, it extracts the bss items from each object file, and plans a single, large bss segment that contains all the bss items.

When it creates a plan, the linker assigns each object a unique memory address. We say the linker *relocates* objects. An example will clarify how relocation works. Suppose the linker is given three object files that Figure 2.9 lists†: one file for a main program and two files for two functions the program calls.

Object File	Instruction Bytes	Data Bytes	Bss Bytes
prog.o	1000	50	100
fcn_a.o	500	200	100
fcn_b.o	500	100	40
Totals	2000	350	240

Figure 2.9 An example of three relocatable files to be linked into executable object program.

The linker assigns instructions from *prog.o* to locations *0* through *999*, instructions from *fcn_a.o* to locations *1000* through *1499*, and instructions from *fcn_c.o* to locations *1500* through *1999*. Once it knows that the combined text segment contains *2000* bytes, the linker can assign data items to the next memory locations. Figure 2.10 lists the resulting assignments.

Starting Location	Ending Location	Object File	Segment Type
0	999	prog.o	text
1000	1499	fcn_a.o	text
1500	1999	fcn_b.o	text
2000	2049	prog.o	data
2050	2249	fcn_a.o	data
2250	2349	fcn_b.o	data
2350	2449	prog.o	bss
2450	2549	fcn_a.o	bss
2550	2589	fcn_b.o	bss

Figure 2.10 Memory locations in the combined object file for the relocatable object files in Figure 2.9.

The linker must plan a memory location for each variable. An object program contains two pieces of information that the linker uses. First, a *symbol table* lists each global variable's name and size along with an initial value, if the variable has an initial value. Second, *relocation information* lists which instructions reference functions and global variables along with the exact variable or function that each one references. The linker uses the symbol table to plan a memory address for each variable. For example, if the first three initialized variables in the main program consist of 4-byte integers

---
†The sizes in the table are unrealistically small, and have been chosen to simplify the example.

named q, r, and s, the linker will assign q locations 2000 through 2003, r locations 2004 through 2007, and t locations 2008 through 2011. As it plans the memory layout, the linker creates a new symbol table that records the memory location assigned to each variable.

Once it has planned where to place each function and variable in memory, the linker uses the relocation information to modify each instruction that calls another function or references a global variable. For example, an instruction in the main program that stores a value into variable r will be modified to use address 2004 because variable r will be at location 2004 when the program runs. Similarly, if the main program contains an instruction to call function A, the instruction will be modified to use address 1000 because function A will reside at location 1000 when the program runs.

After it completes the plan, the linker creates an output file that contains the executable object program. The file contains the instructions and variables to be loaded when the program runs. When a user launches the executable object file, the operating system allocates memory space for the program and loads initial values exactly as the linker planned.

To summarize:

> When it creates an executable object program, a linker modifies instructions that reference global variables or functions so each instruction will use the memory address the variable or function will have when the program runs. The names of variables and functions do not appear in the machine instructions.

2.10 The ELF Standard for Storing Object Programs

What file formats should be used to store relocatable and executable object programs? Interestingly, a single standard has been created that handles both forms. The standard is known as *ELF*, which stands for *Executable and Linkable Format*†. In fact, the ELF standard handles much more than object files. It can also be used for shared libraries and core dumps.

As mentioned above, in addition to storing machine instructions and initial values for global data, an ELF file may contain a symbol table and relocation information. If present, the symbol table lists the names of all variables, functions, and other external objects that were used to create the file. The relocation information specifies which instructions reference global objects. In the case of a relocatable object file, the relocation information must specify the name of the variable or function the instruction references.

Is there any reason to include a symbol table in an ELF file that contains an executable object? Yes. The operating system does not need to know the names and locations of variables or functions because the instructions have already been modified to contain the address of global objects. However, debuggers and diagnostic tools can use the symbol table in an executable file to help identify problems when a program crashes

---

†Although Unix and Linux systems use ELF, Windows, and MacOS use other binary format standards.

or misbehaves. For example, if a program crashes at a certain address in the text segment, the symbol table in the executable file can be used to identify the function that was running when the crash occurred. Similarly, a debugger can use the symbol table to find the location of variables and display their contents. Consequently, most programmers leave the symbol table in executable object files even though the operating system does not need the symbol table to launch the executable program.

2.11 Translation Of An Example C Program

To illustrate how variable and function names become translated into memory addresses during the steps of Figure 2.4†, consider a C program. Our example consists of a program that prints the sum of integers for each integer from 1 through a maximum value given by constant *MAXINT*. The code is neither elegant nor efficient. It contains variables that would normally be unnecessary, and merely have been inserted to illustrate the binding times for variable names during translation.

To illustrate compilation and linking, the code has been divided into two files: file *example.c* contains a main program and file *addval.c* contains function, *addval*. Figure 2.11 lists the command line arguments used to compile and link the program using *gcc*.

```
# Step 1 — run the C preprocessor to generate two .i files
gcc -E example.c > example.i
gcc -E addval.c > addval.i

# Step 2 — run the C compiler to produce two assembly (.s) files
gcc -S example.i
gcc -S addval.i

# Step 3 — run the C assembler to produce two object (.o) files
gcc -c example.s
gcc -c addval.s

# Step 4 — run the linker to produce an executable object file
gcc -o example example.o addval.o
```

Figure 2.11 The commands used to preprocess, compile, assemble, and link
the two example files.

Figure 2.12 shows the contents of file *example.c*, which defines a global integer *ncalls* and the main program for the example.

---

†Figure 2.4 can be found on page 14.

```
/* example.c - main program to sum integers from 1 to MAXINT */

extern  int      printf(char *, ...);
extern  int      f1(int), sum;
int     ncalls = 0;
#define MAXINT  10
int     main(int argc, char *argv[]) {
        int      temp, ctr;

        for (ctr=1; ctr<=MAXINT; ctr++) {
                temp = addval(ctr);
                if (temp > 0 ) printf("sum is now %d\n", sum);
        }
        printf("done: number of calls was %d\n", ncalls);
        return 0;
}
```

Figure 2.12 The source code in file *example.c*.

Figure 2.13 shows the contents of file *addval.c*, which defines global integers *called* and *sum*. The function uses a convoluted way to initialize *sum*. The first time *addval* is called, global variable *called* will be zero. The code sets *called* to 1 and sets *sum* to zero.

```
/* addval.c - function to add a value to the sum  */
int     called = 0;
int     sum;
extern  int      ncalls;
int     addval(int arg1) {

        if (called == 0) { /* initialize the sum to zero*/
                called = 1;
                sum = 0;
        }
        ncalls++;
        sum += arg1;
        return 1;
}
```

Figure 2.13 The source code in file *addval.c*.

During step 1, the preprocessor replaces the defined constant *MAXINT* with the value 10, which means the identifier *MAXINT* does not appear in the .i file. During step 2, the compiler replaces references to local variables and arguments with locations, which means the names *ctr*, *temp*, and *arg1* do not appear in the .s files. During step 3, the assembler assigns initialized global variables *called* and *ncalls* to the *data* segment, and assigns uninitialized global variable *sum* to the *bss* segment. Finally, during step 4, the linker produces a single executable object file that contains the instructions and global variables for both the main program and function addval. The linker assigns variables to successive locations in each segment†. On one computer, for example, integers each occupy 32 bits (four bytes). The linker assigns variable *ncalls* to memory locations 134776 through 134779, assigns variable *called* to locations 134780 through 134783, and assigns variable *sum* to location 134784 through 134787.

Note that although the executable object file includes a symbol table with all global variable names, a user can run the *strip* command to remove the symbol table. The resulting stripped file will still be able to execute because references to global variables and functions have been converted to addresses.

EXERCISES

2.1 Start with a trivial C program that calls *printf* to print "program ran" and returns. Instead of entering *printf* in the code, define a preprocessor macro named *PF* that has a value of *printf*, and then use *PF* in the code. Compile the program four times, stopping after preprocessing (-E to get a .i file), compiling (-S to get a .s file), generating a relocatable object program (-c to get a .o file), and generating an executable object program (known as an a.out file). Compare the sizes of the resulting files.

2.2 Use the *file* command on each of the four files generated in the previous exercise. Which ones use the ELF format?

2.3 Use the *nm* command to print the symbol table in the executable ELF file in Exercise 2.1, and find the memory address assigned to the *printf* function.

2.4 Use the *strip* command to strip the executable ELF file from Exercise 2.1, and then run *nm* on the stripped file. Explain what has been removed.

2.5 Extend the previous exercise to compare the size of the stripped file to the original.

2.6 Write function A, function B, and a main program, place each in a file, and compile each of the three files to produce three relocatable object files (i.e., .o files). Arrange for the main program to call each function, and have a function merely print its name (e.g., "function A called"). Compile and link all three files, and run *nm* on the resulting executable object file. What addresses have been assigned to the main program and the two functions.

2.7 Extend the previous exercise by adding initialized global variables to each file. Add the declaration *int aa=1;* to function A, *int bb=2;* to function B, and *int mm=3;* to the main program. When the files are compiled a linked, what addresses are assigned to *aa*, *bb*, and *mm*?

---

†As an optimization, some compilers place data items that are initialized to zero in the bss segment because Unix systems set the bss segment to zero when the program is loaded.

Chapter Contents

3

Data And Program Representation

3.1 Introduction

The previous chapter describes the transformation of a high-level programming language into a low-level, binary form that allows efficient computation by the underlying hardware. In particular, to allow the hardware to perform calculations and storage at high speed, all data items must be stored in binary. This chapter examines the binary representations that computers use for data, including integers, characters, and floating point values. We will see that representing data in binary has consequences for software engineers.

3.2 Definitions Of Bit And Byte

All data representations that hardware uses build on an abstraction known as a *bit*, which abbreviates *binary digit*. A bit can have two possible values. Hardware engineers often use two voltage levels to represent the two values, and may label the values *high* and *low* or *true* and *false*. When software engineers think about the meaning of a bit, they think of data, and use the mathematical values of *0* and *1*.

Although individual bits may be useful in special cases, most computation requires a larger range of values. To handle large ranges, hardware engineers build hardware units that each include a string of bits. For example, we define a *byte* to be a string of eight bits†. The underlying hardware mechanism that holds a byte contains eight hardware units that each hold one bit. All eight units operate in parallel to deliver all

---

†Before the byte size was standardized, early computer designers experimented with a variety of byte sizes.

eight bits of a byte at the same time, making it appear that a single hardware unit handles a byte as a single entity.

3.3 Possible Values In A Byte

The number of bits in a byte determines the range of numerical values that the byte can hold, just as the number of digits in a decimal number determines the range of values the number can hold. For example, a decimal number with two digits can represent one hundred values, 0 through 99. If we write leading zeros, the range is 00 through 99. In general, a decimal number with k digits can represent a range of 10^k because each digit can represent ten possible values. Similarly, because each bit can represent two possible values, a byte with eight bits can represent a range of $2^8 = 256$ values (0 through 255). In general, a data item that occupies k bits can represent 2^k possible values. That is, there are exactly 2^k unique strings of k bits. As an example, consider the eight possible combinations that can be achieved with three bits. Figure 3.1 illustrates the combinations.

```
000         010         100         110
001         011         101         111
```

Figure 3.1 The eight unique combinations that can result from assigning
zeros and ones to three bits.

What does a given pattern of bits represent? The most important thing to understand is that the bits themselves have no intrinsic meaning — the interpretation of the value is determined by the way hardware and software use the bits. For example, a string of bits could represent an alphabetic character, a string of more than one character, an integer, a floating point number, an audio recording (e.g., a song), a video, or instructions in a computer program.

In addition to items a computer programmer understands, computer hardware sometimes uses bits to represent the status of hardware devices. For example, a string of three bits might be used as follows:

- The first bit has the value 1 if a keyboard is connected.
- The second bit has the value 1 if a camera is connected.
- The third bit has the value 1 if a printer is connected.

Alternatively, hardware can be designed in which a set of three bits can be used to represent the current status of three pushbutton switches: the ith bit is 1 if a user is currently pushing switch i.

The point is:

> *Bits have no intrinsic meaning — all meaning is imposed by the way bits are interpreted.*

3.4 Binary Weighted Positional Representation

One of the most common abstractions used to associate a meaning with a string of bits interprets them as a numeric value. For example, an integer interpretation is taken from mathematics: bits are values in a positional number system that uses base two. To understand the interpretation, remember that in base ten, the possible digits are 0, 1, 2, 3, 4, 5, 6, 7, 8, and 9, each position represents a power of 10, and the number 123 represents 1 times 10^2 plus 2 times 10^1 plus 3 times 10^0. In the binary system, the possible digits are 0 and 1, and each bit position represents a power of two. That is, the positions represent successive powers of two: 2^0, 2^1, 2^2, and so on. Figure 3.2 illustrates the positional concept for binary numbers.

Figure 3.2 The value associated with each of the first six bit positions when using a positional interpretation in base two.

As an example, consider the bit string:

$$0\ 1\ 0\ 1\ 0\ 1$$

According to the figure, the value of the string is:

$$0\ 1\ 0\ 1\ 0\ 1\ =\ 0 \times 2^5 + 1 \times 2^4 + 0 \times 2^3 + 1 \times 2^2 + 0 \times 2^1 + 1 \times 2^0\ =\ 21$$

Similarly, the value of 111100 is:

$$1\ 1\ 1\ 1\ 0\ 0\ =\ 1 \times 2^5 + 1 \times 2^4 + 1 \times 2^3 + 1 \times 2^2 + 0 \times 2^1 + 0 \times 2^0\ =\ 60$$

We will discuss more about specific forms of integer representation (including negative numbers) later in the chapter. For now, it is sufficient to observe an important consequence of conventional positional notation: the binary numbers that can be represented in k bits are all positive and start at zero instead of one. If we use the positional interpretation illustrated in Figure 3.2, the binary numbers that can be represented with three bits range from zero through seven. Similarly, the binary numbers that can be represented with eight bits range from zero through two hundred fifty-five. We can summarize:

A set of k bits can be interpreted to represent a binary integer. When conventional positional notation is used, the values that can be represented with k bits range from 0 through $2^k - 1$.

Because it is an essential skill in the design of both software and hardware, anyone working in those fields should know the basics. Figure 3.3 lists the decimal equivalents of binary numbers that hardware and software designers should know. Modern hardware usually supports data items that occupy thirty-two bits (four bytes) and sixty-four bits (eight bytes). Therefore, the table includes entries for 2^{32} and 2^{64} (an incredibly large number). Although smaller values in the table should be memorized, hardware and software designers only need to know the order of magnitude of the larger entries. Fortunately, it is easy to remember that 2^{32} contains ten decimal digits and 2^{64} contains twenty.

Power of 2	Decimal Value	Decimal Digits
0	1	1
1	2	1
2	4	1
3	8	1
4	16	2
5	32	2
6	64	2
7	128	3
8	256	3
9	512	3
10	1024	4
11	2048	4
12	4096	4
15	16384	5
16	32768	5
20	1048576	7
30	1073741824	10
32	4294967296	10
48	281474976710656	15
64	18446744073709551616	20

Figure 3.3 Decimal values for commonly used powers of two.

3.5 Bit Ordering

The positional notation in Figure 3.2 may seem obvious. After all, when writing decimal numbers, we always write the least significant digit on the right and the most significant digit on the left. Therefore, when writing binary, it makes sense to write the *Least Significant Bit* (*LSB*) on the right and the *Most Significant Bit* (*MSB*) on the left. When digital hardware stores an integer, however, the concepts of "right" and "left" no longer make sense. Therefore, a computer architect must specify exactly how bits are stored, and which are the least and most significant.

The idea of bit ordering is especially important when bits are transferred from one location to another. For example, when a numeric value is moved between a register in the processor and memory, the bit ordering must be preserved. Similarly, when sending data across a network, the sender and receiver must agree on the bit ordering. That is, the two ends must agree whether the LSB or the MSB will be sent first.

3.6 Hexadecimal Notation Used By Humans

Software engineers sometimes need to specify and examine the binary values stored in a computer system. Although a numeric value can be specified in decimal, decimal digits do not show the individual bits. For example, if a programmer needs to examine the fifth bit from the right, using the binary value 10000 makes the intention much clearer than the equivalent decimal constant 16 does.

Unfortunately, long strings of bits can be unwieldy and difficult to understand. For example, to determine whether the sixteenth bit is set in the following binary number, a human needs to count individual bits:

1 1 0 1 1 1 1 0 1 1 0 0 1 0 0 1 0 0 0 0 1 0 0 1 0 1 0 0 1 0 0 1

To aid humans in expressing binary values, programming languages and software tools offer a compromise: a positional numbering system with a larger base. If the base is chosen to be a power of two, translation to binary is trivial. Base eight (known as *octal*) has been used, but base sixteen (known as *hexadecimal*) has become especially popular.

Hexadecimal representation offers three advantages. First, the representation is substantially more compact than binary. Second, because sixteen is a power of two, conversion between binary and hexadecimal is straightforward and does not involve a complex arithmetic calculation. Third, hexadecimal matches the hardware well because each pair of hex digits specifies the eight bits in one byte.

Hexadecimal encodes each group of four bits as a single hex† "digit" that has a value between zero and fifteen. To express each hex digit as a single character, programming languages use six alphabetic characters, adding *A* though *F* to the set of decimal digits. Figure 3.4 lists the sixteen hex digits along with the binary and decimal equivalent of each. The figure and the examples that follow use uppercase letters *A*

---

†Programmers use the term *hex* as an abbreviation for *hexadecimal*.

through F to represent hex digits above nine. Some programming languages use lower-case letters a through f instead; both have the same meaning and programmers should be prepared to use whichever form a language requires.

Hex Digit	Binary Equivalent	Decimal Value
0	0000	0
1	0001	1
2	0010	2
3	0011	3
4	0100	4
5	0101	5
6	0110	6
7	0111	7
8	1000	8
9	1001	9
A	1010	10
B	1011	11
C	1100	12
D	1101	13
E	1110	14
F	1111	15

Figure 3.4 The sixteen hexadecimal digits and their equivalent binary and decimal values. Each hex digit encodes four bits of a binary value.

As an example of hexadecimal notation, Figure 3.5 illustrates how a binary string corresponds to its hexadecimal equivalent.

Figure 3.5 Illustration of the relationship between binary and hexadecimal. Each hex digit denotes four bits.

3.7 Notation For Hexadecimal And Binary Constants

Because the digits used in binary, decimal, and hexadecimal notations overlap, constants can be ambiguous. To solve the ambiguity, programming languages use a notation that makes the base clear. Mathematicians and some textbooks add a subscript to denote a base other than ten (e.g., 135_{16} specifies that the constant is hexadecimal). Software engineers follow programming language notation: hex constants begin with prefix $0x$, and binary constants begin with prefix $0b$. Thus, to denote 135_{16}, a programmer writes $0x135$. Similarly, to specify the 32-bit constant from Figure 3.5, a programmer writes:

0xDEC90949

3.8 Character Sets

We said that strings of bits have no intrinsic meaning, and that hardware or software must determine what each bit represents. More important, a given string of bits can be interpreted multiple ways — a string can be created using one interpretation and interpreted another way later.

As an example, consider characters entered from a keyboard. Each computer system defines a *character set* to be a set of symbols that the computer and I/O devices agree to use. A typical western character set contains uppercase and lowercase letters, digits, and punctuation marks, and is defined such that each character fits into a single byte (i.e., the numeric value assigned to a character requires at most eight bits). If a character set uses all possible combinations of eight bits, the character set can contain at most two hundred fifty-six (2^8) possible characters. The historic relationship between the byte size and the character set is so strong that many programming languages refer to a byte as a *character* (*char*).

What bit values are used to encode each character? Whoever designs the character set must decide. In the 1960s, for example, IBM Corporation chose the *Extended Binary Coded Decimal Interchange Code* (*EBCDIC†*) representation as the character set used on IBM computers. Other computer companies chose their own character sets, and the choices are completely incompatible.

As a practical matter, separate companies started to appear that manufactured peripheral I/O devices such as keyboards, printers, and modems. It became obvious that the industry would benefit if everyone agreed to use the same character set. To encourage the industry to build compatible equipment, the *American National Standards Institute* (*ANSI*) defined a character representation known as the *American Standard Code for Information Interchange* (*ASCII*). The ASCII character set specifies the representation of one hundred twenty-eight characters, including the usual letters, digits, and punctuation marks; ASCII defines additional values in the eight-bit byte for special symbols, such as the *Escape* key, the *Delete* key, and other control keys. The standard became widely accepted, and is still used.

Figure 3.6 lists the ASCII representation of characters by giving two hexadecimal digits and the corresponding symbolic character. Of course, the hexadecimal notation is merely a shorthand notation for a binary string. For example, the lowercase letter *a* has hexadecimal value $0x61$, which corresponds to the binary value $0b01100001$. Some of the ASCII values correspond to "special" characters, such as *space* ($0x20$), *horizontal tab* ($0x09$), *backspace* ($0x08$), and *escape* ($0x1B$).

The figure only lists one hundred twenty-eight characters, which means only seven bits are needed to represent an ASCII character. When ASCII is used on a conventional computer, one-half of the possible values of a byte (decimal values 128 through 255)

---

†Names of character sets are pronounced, not spelled out. For example, EBCDIC is pronounced *ebb'se-*

remain unassigned. How are the additional values used? In some cases, they are not —
some applications and devices leave the eighth bit in each byte set to zero. In other
cases, an application programmer uses the eighth bit to extend the possible characters
(e.g., by using some of the values to represent symbols or punctuation marks in alternate languages).

00	nul	01	soh	02	stx	03	etx	04	eot	05	enq	06	ack	07	bel
08	bs	09	ht	0A	lf	0B	vt	0C	np	0D	cr	0E	so	0F	si
10	dle	11	dc1	12	dc2	13	dc3	14	dc4	15	nak	16	syn	17	etb
18	can	19	em	1A	sub	1B	esc	1C	fs	1D	gs	1e	rs	1F	us
20	sp	21	!	22	"	23	#	24	$	25	%	26	&	27	'
28	(	29	)	2A	*	2B	+	2C	,	2D	–	2E	.	2F	/
30	0	31	1	32	2	33	3	34	4	35	5	36	6	37	7
38	8	39	9	3A	:	3B	;	3C	<	3D	=	3E	>	3F	?
40	@	41	A	42	B	43	C	44	D	45	E	46	F	47	G
48	H	49	I	4A	J	4B	K	4C	L	4D	M	4E	N	4F	O
50	P	51	Q	52	R	53	S	54	T	55	U	56	V	57	W
58	X	59	Y	5A	Z	5B	[	5C	\	5D	]	5E	^	5F	_
60	`	61	a	62	b	63	c	64	d	65	e	66	f	67	g
68	h	69	i	6A	j	6B	k	6C	l	6D	m	6E	n	6F	o
70	p	71	q	72	r	73	s	74	t	75	u	76	v	77	w
78	x	79	y	7A	z	7B	{	7C			7D	}	7E	~	7F	del

Figure 3.6 The ASCII character set. Each entry shows a hexadecimal value
and the graphical representation for printable characters and the
meaning for others.

3.9 Unicode

Although English and most European languages have fewer than two hundred
fifty-six possible symbols in their character set, some languages have more. For example, Chinese defines thousands of symbols and glyphs. To accommodate such
languages, extensions and alternative ways of representing characters have been created.

One of the widely accepted standards for extended character sets is named *Uni-
code†*. Unicode extends ASCII, and is intended to accommodate character sets of all
languages, including those from Asia. Originally designed as a sixteen-bit character set,
later versions of Unicode have been extended to accommodate larger representations.
In fact, the current standard defines approximately 150,000 symbols. Some applications
use Unicode instead of ASCII. For example, text applications that allow a user to include emojis use Unicode.

---

†The Unicode standard is defined by the *Unicode Consortium*.

3.10 Unsigned Integers And Endianness

The positional representation of binary numbers illustrated in Figure 3.2† produces *unsigned integers* because each possible combination of k bits produces a nonnegative numeric value‡. How should the bits be numbered and stored? If we view the set as an unsigned binary number, it makes sense to start numbering from the right (i.e., from the numerically least significant bit). However, if we view the set of bits as a string, it makes sense to start numbering from the left because strings are usually read from left to right. Bit ordering is especially important when transferring data over a computer network because the sending and receiving sides must agree on whether the least-significant or most-significant bit of an integer will be transferred first.

The issue of numbering becomes more complicated if we consider data items that span multiple bytes. For example, consider an unsigned integer that spans thirty-two bits (i.e., four bytes). The bytes can be transferred starting with the least-significant or the most-significant byte.

We use the term *little endian* to characterize a system that stores and transmits bytes of an integer from least significant to most significant, and the term *big endian* to characterize a system that stores and transmits bytes of an integer from most significant to least significant. Similarly, we use the terms *bit little endian* and *bit big endian* to characterize systems that transfer bits within a byte starting at the least-significant bit and most-significant bit, respectively. To understand endianness, think of the bytes of an integer as being stored in an array. The endianness determines the direction of the integer in memory. Figure 3.7 uses an example integer to illustrate the two byte orders, showing positional representation and the arrangement of bytes in memory using both little endian order and big endian order.

00011101 10100010 00111011 01100111

(a) Integer 497,171,303 in binary positional representation

least significant byte

	loc. i	loc. i+1	loc. i+2	loc. i+3	
· · ·	01100111	00111011	10100010	00011101	· · ·

(b) The integer stored in little endian order

most significant byte

	loc. i	loc. i+1	loc. i+2	loc. i+3	
· · ·	00011101	10100010	00111011	01100111	· · ·

(c) The integer stored in big endian order

Figure 3.7 An illustration of the arrangement of bytes in memory when storing an integer in little endian and big endian order.

---

†Figure 3.2 can be found on page 29.

‡We will learn later that the number of bits in an unsigned integer is the *word size* of the computer.

The big endian representation may seem appealing because it mimics the order humans use to write numbers, whereas little endian order seems to store the integer backward. Surprisingly, little endian order has several advantages for computing. For example, little endian allows a programmer to use a single memory address to refer to all four bytes of an integer, the two low-order bytes, or only the lowest-order byte.

3.11 Signed Binary Integers

Because the positional representation used in unsigned integers only provides a way to represent non-negative values, an alternate must be used to represent negative numbers. Three representations have been created for *signed integers*.

- *Sign Magnitude*. For an integer of k bits, the sign-magnitude representation interprets the most significant bit as a sign bit (1 if the number is negative and 0 otherwise), and uses the remaining $k-1$ bits as an unsigned integer that specifies the absolute value of the integer (i.e., the magnitude).
- *One's Complement*. A positive integer uses the same positional representation as an unsigned integer, making the maximum positive value of a k-bit integer $2^{k-1}-1$ (because the most significant bit is zero). To form the negative of any value, invert each bit (i.e., change from 0 to 1 or vice versa).

- *Two's Complement*. A k-bit two's complement integer uses the same positional representation used in an unsigned integer, with exception that the most significant bit has the value -2^k. To form a negative number, start with the positive value, subtract one, and invert each bit. Figure 3.8 illustrates the representation.

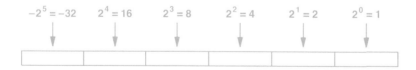

Figure 3.8 The value associated with each of the bits of a six-bit two's complement integer.

As an example, consider the bit string:

$$0\ 1\ 0\ 1\ 0\ 1$$

Because the high-order bit is zero, two's complement value is 21, the same as the unsigned value:

$$0\ 1\ 0\ 1\ 0\ 1\ =\ 0\times-2^5+1\times2^4+0\times2^3+1\times2^2+0\times2^1+1\times2^0\ =\ 21$$

Now consider the string:

$$1\ 1\ 1\ 1\ 0\ 0$$

When interpreted as an unsigned integer, the value is 60. Because the high-order bit is one, however, the two's complement value is negative:

$$1\ 1\ 1\ 1\ 0\ 0 = 1 \times -2^5 + 1 \times 2^4 + 1 \times 2^3 + 1 \times 2^2 + 0 \times 2^1 + 0 \times 2^0 = -4$$

3.12 Quirks Of Signed Representations

Interestingly, all three representations for signed integers share some characteristics. For example, the most significant bit of the integer will be 1 if the number is negative. In addition, for positive values, the remaining bits will be the same; only the representation of negative values differs.

Each interpretation has interesting quirks. For example, the sign-magnitude interpretation makes it possible to create a value of *negative zero*, even though negative zero does not make sense mathematically. The one's complement interpretation provides two values for zero: all zero bits and the complement, all one bits. Finally, the two's complement interpretation includes one more negative value than positive values (think of zero being in the positive half).

Which interpretation is best? Programmers can debate the issue because each interpretation works well in some cases. However, programmers cannot choose because computer architects make the choice and build hardware accordingly. Each of the three representations has been used in at least one computer. Modern hardware architectures use the two's complement representation for two reasons. First, two's complement makes it possible to build low-cost, high-speed hardware to perform arithmetic operations, such as addition and subtraction. Second, as the next section explains, hardware for two's complement arithmetic can also handle unsigned integer arithmetic.

3.13 An Example Of Two's Complement Numbers

We said that k bits can represent 2^k possible combinations. Unlike the unsigned representation in which the combinations correspond to a continuous set of integers starting at zero, two's complement divides the combinations in half. Each combination in the first half (zero through $2^{k-1}-1$) is assigned the same value as in the unsigned representation. Combinations in the second half, each of which has the high-order bit equal to one, correspond to negative integers. Thus, at exactly one-half of the way through the possible combinations, the value changes from the largest possible positive integer to the negative integer with the largest absolute value.

An example will clarify the two's complement assignment. To keep the example small, we will consider a four-bit integer. Figure 3.9 lists the sixteen possible bit combinations and the decimal equivalent when using unsigned, sign magnitude, one's complement, and two's complement representations.

Binary String	Unsigned (positional) Interpretation	Sign Magnitude Interpretation	One's Complement Interpretation	Two's Complement Interpretation
0000	0	0	0	0
0001	1	1	1	1
0010	2	2	2	2
0011	3	3	3	3
0100	4	4	4	4
0101	5	5	5	5
0110	6	6	6	6
0111	7	7	7	7
1000	8	-0	-7	-8
1001	9	-1	-6	-7
1010	10	-2	-5	-6
1011	11	-3	-4	-5
1100	12	-4	-3	-4
1101	13	-5	-2	-3
1110	14	-6	-1	-2
1111	15	-7	-0	-1

Figure 3.9 The decimal value assigned to each combination of four bits when using unsigned, sign-magnitude, one's complement, and two's complement interpretations.

As noted above, unsigned and two's complement have the advantage that the same hardware operations work for both representations. For example, adding one to the binary value 1001 produces 1010. In the unsigned interpretation, adding one to nine produces ten; in the two's complement interpretation, adding one to negative seven produces negative six.

The important point is:

> *A computer can use a single hardware circuit to perform both unsigned and two's complement integer arithmetic; software running on the computer can choose an interpretation for the resulting bit strings.*

3.14 Sign Extension

Although Figure 3.9 shows four-bit binary strings, the ideas can be extended to an arbitrary number of bits. Many computers include hardware for multiple integer sizes (e.g., a single computer can offer sixteen-bit, thirty-two-bit, and sixty-four-bit representations), and allow a programmer to choose one of the sizes for each integer data item.

For example, consider the following C code when run on a computer that defines an *int* to be thirty-two bits and a *short* to be sixteen bits. Assume the computer uses the two's complement interpretation for signed integers (the most widely used form).

```
short  a = 1,  b = -1; int c, d;
       c = a;  d = b;
```

Variables *a* and *b* each occupy sixteen bits. Variable *a* has the value +1, which in two's complement has fifteen 0 bits and the low-order bit set to 1. Variable *b* has the value −1, which is represented by sixteen 1 bits. When it finds the assignment *c* = *a*, the compiler arranges to *promote* the sixteen-bit value of *a* to a thirty-two-bit value. How does promotion work? Two's complement hardware copies the sixteen-bit value into the low-order sixteen bits of the thirty-two-bit integer. What about the upper sixteen bits? The upper sixteen bits of *c* should be zero to make the value +1. However, after promotion, the upper sixteen bits of *d* must all be 1s to make the value −1.

In the two's complement interpretation, the most significant bit of an integer is interpreted to be a *sign bit* because the most significant bit is 1 in negative integers and 0 otherwise. To preserve the numeric value when promoting to an integer with more bits, the extra high-order bits must each be set to the most significant bit of the original integer. We use the term *sign extension* to specify that the hardware uses the sign bit to fill the extra bits. If the original value is negative, sign extension fills the extra bits with 1s; otherwise, sign extension fills the high-order bits with 0s. In either case, the integer with more bits will have the same numeric value as the original integer that had fewer bits†.

We can summarize:

> *Two's complement hardware uses* sign extension *when promoting a k-bit integer, Q, into an integer of more than k bits. Sign extension sets the additional bits to the sign bit from Q. Extending the sign bit ensures that the numeric value will remain the same if each is interpreted as a two's complement value.*

3.15 Casting Integers

In addition to requiring a program to declare the type of each variable, many modern languages allow a programmer to override the variable's type when the variable appears in an expression. We use the term *cast* to refer to the notation used to specify an override, and the term *casting* to refer to the process. A cast merely changes the way a compiler interprets the bits in a value without actually changing any of the bits. For example, consider the following C code that declares an unsigned short variable *v* with an initial value of 60000, and then assigns *v* to an *int* and uses a cast in two assignments.

---

†Because division and multiplication by powers of two can be implemented with shift operations, sign extension occurs during a right-shift operation, which results in the correct value. Thus, shifting integer −14

```
unsigned short  v = 60000;  /* 0xea60 in hex */
int x, y, z;
x = v;            /* allow the compiler to promote v */
y = (int)v;      /* cast v to type int */
z = (short)v;    /* cast v to type short */
printf("x in hex=%x in decimal=%d\n", x,x);
printf("y in hex=%x in decimal=%d\n", y,y);
printf("z in hex=%x in decimal=%d\n", z,z);
```

Casting can be tricky because the compiler follows a set of rules to promote integer types. A cast overrides the type at one point in the expression, but the compiler still applies the rules to decide how to interpret the entire expression. For example, when the above code runs, the program outputs:

```
x   in hex=ea60 and in decimal=60000
y   in hex=ea60 and in decimal=60000
z   in hex=ffffea60 and in decimal=−5536
```

In the assignment to x, the compiler promotes v to a 32-bit unsigned value and takes steps to remove the sign-extended bits. The assignment to y has an explicit cast, and the compiler behaves the same way as with x. In the assignment to z, the cast specifies that v should first be interpreted as a signed, sixteen-bit value. Interpreting the bits as a signed value means the value is −5536. The compiler applies the rules for promotion, which specify leaving the sign extension in place. As a result, z has the appropriate negative value.

The point is:

> *Although it does not change the value of bits, casting changes the way a compiler processes a data item. The rules for casting and the rules for integer promotion interact.*

3.16 Floating Point

In addition to hardware that performs signed and unsigned integer arithmetic, general-purpose computers provide hardware that performs arithmetic on *floating point* values that include fractional amounts. Because they think of decimal fractions, humans use notation in which a *decimal point* separates an integer part and a fractional part. Each successive digit to the right of the decimal point specifies a value multiplied by a smaller power of 10: 10^{-1}, 10^{-2}, 10^{-3}, and so on. For example, 3.5 denotes 3 plus 5/10 (i.e., 5×10^{-1}).

Because they work with binary values, computers represent fractions using binary. That is, successive digits to the right of the *binary point* represent 2^{-1}, 2^{-2}, 2^{-3}, and so on. For example, the decimal value 3.5 can be written in binary as 11.1 because in binary 11 represents the integer 3 and the binary fraction .1 represents $1{\times}2^{-1}$ (i.e., one-half). Similarly, the binary value 101.110 represents $5 + 2^{-1} + 2^{-3}$ (i.e., 5 + 1/2 + 1/8 which comes to 5.625 in decimal).

Floating point representation used in computers derives from *scientific notation* in which each value is represented by two values: a *mantissa* and an *exponent*. For example, scientific notation expresses the value -0.012345 as $-1.2345{\times}10^{-2}$. Similarly, a chemist might write a well-known constant, such as Avogadro's number, as:

$$6.023 \times 10^{23}$$

Early computer vendors each defined their own floating point hardware schemes, which led to incompatibilities and inconsistent results. Researchers studied the situation, and in 1985, *IEEE*† combined the results of research and defined standard number 754 for floating point. The IEEE standard became widely adopted, and most floating point hardware now follows the standard.

Unlike conventional scientific notation, the floating point representation used in computers is based on binary‡. a.. Thus, a floating point value uses the sign-magnitude approach in which the value consists of a bit string divided into three fields: the first consists of a single bit that stores the sign of the number, the second field consists of bits that store a mantissa, and a third field consists of bits that store an exponent without using an explicit sign bit. Unlike conventional scientific notation, everything in floating point is based on powers of two. For example, the mantissa uses a binary positional representation to represent a value, and the exponent is an integer that specifies a power of 2 rather than a power of 10. In scientific notation, we think of an exponent as specifying how many digits to shift the decimal point; in floating point, the exponent specifies how many bits to shift the binary point.

To increase the precision that can be obtained from a fixed group of bits, IEEE floating point includes three optimizations:

- The value is normalized.

- The most significant bit of the mantissa is implicit.

- The exponent is biased to simplify magnitude comparison.

The first two optimizations are related. A floating point number is *normalized* by adjusting the exponent to eliminate leading zeros from the mantissa. In decimal, for example, $0.003{\times}10^4$ can be normalized to $3{\times}10^1$. Normalizing a binary floating point number always produces a leading bit of 1 (except in the special case of the number zero). Therefore, to increase the number of bits of precision in the mantissa, floating point representations do not need to store the most significant bit of the mantissa when a value is stored in memory. Instead, when a floating point number computation is required, the hardware inserts a 1 bit at the beginning of the mantissa.

---

†IEEE stands for the *Institute of Electrical and Electronics Engineers*, an organization that creates standards used in electronic digital systems.

‡Although the standard includes a specification for decimal floating point, most systems use binary.

How large are the mantissa and exponent fields? The IEEE standard specifies two sizes for floating point values: *single-precision* and *double-precision* floating point numbers. According to the standard, a single-precision value occupies a total of thirty-two bits, and a double-precision value occupies a total of sixty-four bits. In each case, the IEEE floating point representation uses three fields arranged as a sign bit field, an exponent field, and a mantissa field. Figure 3.10 illustrates how the IEEE standard divides a floating point number into three fields and the sizes of the files for both single-precision and double-precision values.

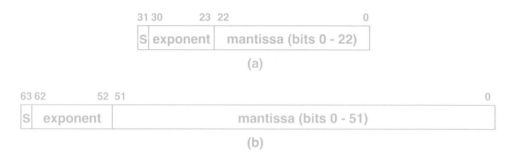

Figure 3.10 The format of (a) a single-precision and (b) a double-precision floating point number according to IEEE Standard 754, with the lowest and highest bit in each field labeled. Both precisions define a sign bit, exponent, and mantissa.

Bit numbering in the figure follows the IEEE standard, in which the least significant bit is assigned bit number zero. In single-precision, for example, the twenty-three rightmost bits, which constitute a mantissa, are numbered zero through twenty-two. The next eight bits, which constitute an exponent, are numbered twenty-three through thirty, and the most significant bit, which contains a sign, is bit number thirty-one. For double-precision, the mantissa occupies fifty-two bits and the exponent occupies eleven bits.

3.17 Range Of IEEE Floating Point Values

The IEEE standard for single-precision floating point allows normalized values in which the exponent ranges from negative one hundred twenty-six through one hundred twenty-seven. Thus, the approximate range of values that can be represented is:

$$2^{-126} \text{ to } 2^{127}$$

which, in decimal, is approximately:

$$10^{-38} \text{ to } 10^{38}$$

The IEEE standard for double-precision floating point provides an enormously larger range than single-precision. The range is:

$$2^{-1022} \text{ to } 2^{1023}$$

which, in decimal, is approximately:

$$10^{-308} \text{ to } 10^{308}$$

3.18 Biased Exponent Values

To express both small and large numbers, a standard must allow an exponent to be a signed integer. Because comparing two's complement integers takes extra time, the IEEE standard uses a *biased* representation for exponents. The exponent field stores the exponent (a power of two) plus a *bias constant*. The bias constant used with single-precision is one hundred twenty-seven, and the bias constant used with double-precision is one thousand twenty-three. The bias constant is always $2^{k-1}-1$, where k is the number of bits in the exponent field. The single-precision floating point format allocates eight bits to the exponent, making the bias 127. To represent an exponent of three, the biased exponent field contains one hundred thirty, and to represent an exponent of negative five, the biased exponent field contains one hundred twenty-two. Before it performs a computation, the floating point unit subtracts the bias value from the stored exponent.

To understand how the bias works, remember the goal: allow positive and negative values, but use a representation similar to unsigned integers that keeps the numbers easy to compare. Exponent values 0 (all 0s) and 255 (all 1s) are special cases. Of the remaining values, approximately half represent negative exponents. Instead of storing a value in the range –126 through 127, adding a bias of 127 shifts the range, and results in storing a value in the range 1 through 254.

3.19 An Example Floating Point Number

As an example of floating point, consider how 6.5 is represented. In binary, 6 is 110, and .5 is a single bit following the binary point, giving us 110.1 (binary). If we use binary scientific notation and normalize the value, 6.5 can be expressed:

$$1.101 \times 2^2$$

To express the value as an IEEE single-precision floating point number, the sign bit is zero, and the exponent must be biased by 127, making it 129. In binary, 129 is:

$$10000001$$

To understand the value in the mantissa, recall that the leading 1 bit is not stored, which means that instead of 1101 followed by zeros, the mantissa is stored as:

Figure 3.11 shows how the fields combine to form a single-precision IEEE floating point representation of 6.5.

S	exponent (23 – 30)	mantissa (bits 0 – 22)																				
0	1 0 0 0 0 0 0 1	1 0 1 0 0 0 0 0 0 0 0 0 0 0 0 0 0 0 0 0 0 0 0

Figure 3.11 The value 6.5 (decimal) represented as a single-precision IEEE floating point constant.

3.20 Special Values And NaN

Recall that the IEEE floating point standard specifies that a mantissa is assumed to have a leading one bit that is not stored. If the IEEE standard strictly enforced the assumption of an implicit leading one bit, the standard would be useless because it could not represent zero. To handle zero, the IEEE standard makes an exception — when all bits are zero, the implicit leading bit assumption is ignored, and the stored value is taken to be zero. The sign bit means it is possible to represent both positive and negative zeros, which does not make sense mathematically, but allows computations that approach zero from either side,

The IEEE standard includes many other special values. For example, if the exponent contains all ones and the mantissa contains all zeros, the value is either interpreted to be positive or negative infinity, depending on the sign bit. The motivation for including infinity is that some digital systems do not have facilities to handle errors such as arithmetic overflow. On such systems, it is important that a value be reserved so that the software can determine that a floating point operation failed.

In addition to the special values mentioned above, the IEEE format classifies any other value with an exponent of all ones to be a *NaN* (*Not A Number*). NaN values can be used to indicate indeterminate results, such as the logarithm or square root of a negative number, zero divided by zero, positive infinity minus positive infinity, negative infinity minus negative infinity, and so on. A NaN value can be used to initialize a variable to an "undefined" value in a way that cannot be confused with a valid floating point value. Furthermore, the rules for computation specify that a NaN value is propagated, so the result of a complex computation will be a NaN if a NAN occurs in the computation. For example, adding 1 to a NaN results in a NaN.

It may seem that having 2^{23} NaN values for single-precision is wasteful. However, designating a specific exponent value to cover all NaN values makes it faster for floating point hardware to detect and process the values, which is important because:

Despite the optimizations that improve performance, floating point computation and computation using floating point numbers takes significantly more time than computation using integers.

3.21 Binary Coded Decimal Representation

Most computers employ the binary representations for integers and floating point numbers described above. Because the underlying hardware uses digital logic, binary digits of 0 and 1 map directly onto the hardware. As a result, hardware can compute binary arithmetic efficiently and all combinations of bits are valid. However, two disadvantages arise from the use of binary representations. First, the range of values is a power of two rather than a power of ten (e.g., the range of an unsigned 32-bit integer is zero to 4,294,967,295). Second, floating point values are rounded to binary fractions rather than decimal fractions.

The use of binary fractions has some unintended consequences, and their use does not suffice for all computations. For example, consider a bank account that stores U.S. dollars and cents. We represent cents as hundredths of dollars, writing 5.23 to denote five dollars and 23 cents. Surprisingly, one hundredth (i.e., one cent) cannot be represented exactly as a binary floating point number because it turns into a repeating binary fraction. If banks use binary floating point arithmetic, individual pennies will be rounded, making the totals inaccurate. In a scientific sense, the inaccuracy is bounded, but humans demand that banks keep accurate records — they become upset if a bank preserves significant digits of their account but gains or loses pennies.

To accommodate banking and other computations where decimal is required, a *Binary Coded Decimal* (*BCD*) representation is used. Some computers (notably on IBM mainframes) have hardware to support BCD arithmetic; on other computers, software performs all arithmetic operations on BCD values.

Although a variety of BCD formats have been used, they each represent a value as a string of decimal digits. The simplest case consists of a character string in which each byte contains the character for a single digit. However, the use of character strings makes computation inefficient and takes more space than needed. As an example, if a computer uses the ASCII character set, the integer 123456 is stored as six bytes with values†:

0x31 0x32 0x33 0x34 0x35 0x36

If a character format is used, each ASCII character (e.g., 0x31) must be converted to an equivalent binary value (e.g., 0x01) before arithmetic can be performed. Furthermore, once an operation has been performed, the digits of the result must be converted from binary back to the character format. To make computation more efficient, modern BCD systems represent digits in binary rather than as characters. Thus, 123456 could be represented as:

0x01 0x02 0x03 0x04 0x05 0x06

---

†Although our examples use ASCII, BCD is typically used on IBM computers that employ the EBCDIC

Although the use of a binary representation has the advantage of making arithmetic faster, it also has a disadvantage: a BCD value must be converted to character format before it can be displayed or printed. The general idea is that because arithmetic is performed more frequently than I/O, keeping a binary form will improve overall performance.

3.22 Signed, Fractional, And Packed BCD Representations

Our description of BCD omits many details found in commercial systems. For example, an implementation may limit the size of a BCD value. To handle fractions, BCD must either include an explicit decimal point or the representation must specify the location of the decimal point. Furthermore, to handle signed arithmetic, a BCD representation must include a sign. Interestingly, one of the most widely used BCD conventions places the sign byte at the right-hand end of the BCD string. Thus, −123456 might be represented by the sequence:

0x01   0x02   0x03   0x04   0x05   0x06   0x2D

where 0x2D is a value used to indicate a minus sign. The advantage of placing the sign on the right arises because no scanning is required when arithmetic is performed — all bytes except the last byte of the string correspond to decimal digits.

The final detail used with BCD encodings arises from the observation that using a byte for each digit is inefficient. Each digit only requires four bits, so placing one digit in each eight-bit byte wastes half of each byte. To reduce the storage space needed for BCD, a *packed* representation is used in which each digit occupies a *nibble*† (i.e., four bits). With a packed version of BCD, the integer −123456 can be represented in four bytes:

0x01   0x23   0x45   0x6D

where the last nibble contains the value 0xD to indicate that the number is negative‡.

3.23 Data Aggregates

So far, we have only considered the representation of individual data items such as characters, integers, and floating point numbers. Most programming languages allow a programmer to specify *aggregate* data structures that contain multiple data items, such as *arrays*, *records*, or *structs*. How are such values stored? In general, an aggregate value occupies contiguous bytes. Thus, a data aggregate that consists of three *short* (i.e., sixteen-bit) integers occupies six contiguous bytes as Figure 3.12 illustrates.

†Nibble is sometimes spelled *nybble*, *nyble*, or *nybl*.
‡To aid with BCD arithmetic, the x86 architecture has a condition code bit that indicates whether 4-bit

Figure 3.12 A data aggregate consisting of three short integers arranged in successive bytes of memory numbered 0 through 5.

Because it contains three identical data items, the data aggregate in the figure could either be declared to be an array or a struct with three fields:

```
                                      struct {
                                            short    a;
            short   x[3];                   short    b;
                                            short    c;
                                      } x;
```

No matter how they are declared, computer hardware does not understand or process data aggregates. Instead, when a program accesses or manipulates a data aggregate, a compiler generates machine instructions that access and manipulate the individual data items that constitute the data aggregate. The point is:

> *The hardware remains unaware of data aggregates, such as arrays and structs. When a program defines and uses data aggregates, a compiler generates instructions that access and manipulate individual items in the aggregate.*

Our simplistic description of data aggregates states that they occupy contiguous bytes in memory. We will see later that some memory systems require data items to be *aligned* on memory boundaries, which means the items in a data aggregate may not be contiguous. We will revisit the topic of data aggregates and learn more about their implementation when we discuss memory architecture.

3.24 Instructions And Their Representation

Modern computers are classified as *stored program computers* because instructions reside in memory during program execution. An instruction is a string of bits, usually multiple bytes. Computer architects have studied how to design instructions that the hardware can execute efficiently. Many early computers used *variable-length instructions* in which some instructions occupied more bits than others. Hardware to execute variable-length instructions is large and complex. To ensure that execution can proceed at high speed, modern computers use *fixed-length instructions* in which every instruction occupies exactly the same number of bits (e.g., each instruction occupies four bytes or thirty-two bits). Using fixed-length means the hardware is less complex and can operate faster, but each instruction has limited functionality, which may result in more instructions being needed to perform a given computation. Interestingly, modern computers that still offer the same variable-length instructions from the past do not have a separate hardware circuit for each instruction. Instead, they use two levels of hardware: a small engine inside the processor uses fixed-length instructions to perform the processing required for each variable-length instruction.

Both variable-length and fixed-length instructions employ the same general format that specifies an operation to be performed followed by the operands to use. We use the term *op code* to refer to the bits that represent an operation. For example, the op code might specify *add* and the operands might specify the two values to add together. Figure 3.13 illustrates the format.

Figure 3.13 The general format of an instruction that starts with an op code that specifies an operation to perform and is followed by operands that specify the values to use.

As we will learn later, the number of operands and the sizes of fields in an instruction depend on the hardware architecture. In addition, the exact contents of an operand field depend on the architecture. For example, an operand may specify a memory address that gives the location of a variable in memory, it may specify an internal hardware unit called a *register* that the processor uses to hold values for arithmetic operations, or it may contain the value itself (if the value can fit into the number of bits in the operand field). In addition to specifying where to obtain values for the operation to use, one or more operands may specify where to store the result(s) of the operation. For now, it is sufficient to understand that an instruction occupies successive bytes in memory, starts with an op code that specifies the operation, and contains operands that the operation will use.

3.25 Summary

Digital computers use binary digits (bits) to represent data and instructions. Bits are organized into eight-bit bytes, and a given data item can occupy multiple bytes. Bits have no intrinsic meaning; they can be interpreted as a character from the computer's character set, a signed or unsigned integer, a single- or double-precision floating point value, or instructions in a computer program. A computer architect chooses data representations carefully to maximize the flexibility and speed of the hardware while keeping the cost low. The two's complement representation for signed integers is particularly popular because a single piece of hardware can be constructed that performs operations on either two's complement integers or unsigned integers. The IEEE 754 standard for floating point, which defines both single-precision and double-precision formats has become widely used. To handle decimal arithmetic, some computers offer Binary Coded Decimal values in which a number is represented by a string of bits that specifies individual decimal digits.

Organizations, such as ANSI and IEEE, have created standards for representation. Such standards allow hardware manufactured by two separate companies to interoperate and exchange data.

EXERCISES

3.1 Give a mathematical proof that a string of k bits can represent 2^k possible values (hint: argue by induction on the number of bits).

3.2 What is the hexadecimal notation for the following binary string?

1101 1110 1010 1101 1011 1110 1110 1111

3.3 Write a function that determines whether the computer on which it is running uses big endian or little endian representation for integers. Hint: use a character pointer to treat the integer as an array of bytes.

3.4 Write a function that prints 1s and 0s for the individual bits of an integer. Add a space between bytes.

3.5 Write a function that takes an unsigned integer as an argument and shows the value if the integer is interpreted as a one's complement integer, a two's complement integer, or as four ASCII characters.

3.6 Write a C program that prints a table of all possible eight-bit binary values and the two's complement interpretation of each.

3.7 Write a computer program that adds one to the largest possible positive integer and uses the result to determine whether the computer implements two's complement arithmetic.

3.8 Write a computer program to display the value of a byte in hexadecimal, and apply the program to an array of bytes. Add an extra space after every four bytes to make the output easier to read.

3.9 Extend the hexadecimal dump program in the previous exercise to also print the character representation of any byte that corresponds to a printable character. For bytes that do not have a printable representation, arrange for the program to print a period.

3.10 A programmer computes the sum of two unsigned 32-bit integers. Can the resulting sum be less than either of the two values? Explain.

3.11 Suppose you are given a computer with hardware that can only perform 32-bit arithmetic, and are asked to create functions that add and subtract 64-bit integers. How can you perform 64-bit computations with 32-bit hardware? (To simplify the problem, limit your answer to unsigned arithmetic.)

3.12 The C programming language allows a programmer to specify constants in decimal, binary, hexadecimal, and octal. Write a program that declares 0, 5, 65, 128, –1, and –256 in decimal, binary, hexadecimal, and octal, and uses printf to show that the values are correct. Which is the easiest representation?

3.13 Create a function that takes as input two integers in the Binary Coded Decimal format described in the chapter, and computes the sum in a binary coded decimal as output. Test the computation on two integers of length twelve digits.

3.14 Extend the previous program to include multiplication.

3.15 The financial industry uses a "bankers" rounding algorithm. Read about the algorithm, and implement a program that uses decimal arithmetic to compute the sum of two decimal values with both bankers rounding and conventional rounding.

3.16 Show the bit string that results when you convert –17.25 into an IEEE 754 single-precision floating point value.

3.17 Print the values of byte that contain instructions. Write a program that declares a variable *char *o;* and then assigns *p* the address of *printf*. Repeat twenty times: print the value of the byte to which *p* points in hexadecimal and then increment *p*.

3.18 Write a computer program that defines a double-precision floating point variable. Assign the variable .01 (one hundredth). Then print the value of each byte of the variable in hexadecimal, and explain each of the resulting bits.

3.19 Write a function *ispower2* that takes an *unsigned int* as an argument, and returns 1 if the argument is a power of two and zero otherwise. Hint: in binary, a number is a power of two if it has a single one bit and all other bits are zero.

Chapter Contents

4

A High-Level Overview Of Processors

4.1 Introduction

This chapter provides an overview of one of the four main components of a computer and a key element of computer architecture, the processor. The chapter introduces the general concept, describes a range of processors, explains the basic building blocks inside a general-purpose CPU, and discusses the difference between clock rate and processing rate. Later chapters expand the discussion by explaining the internal structure of a processor, including data paths.

4.2 The Two Basic Architectural Approaches

Early in the history of computers, architects experimenting with new designs considered how to organize the hardware. Two basic approaches emerged that are named for the groups who proposed them:

- Harvard Architecture
- Von Neumann Architecture

We will see that the two share ideas, and only differ in how programs and data are stored and accessed.

4.3 The Harvard And Von Neumann Architectures

The term *Harvard Architecture*† refers to a computer organization with four principal components: a processor, an instruction memory, a data memory, and I/O facilities, organized as Figure 4.1 illustrates.

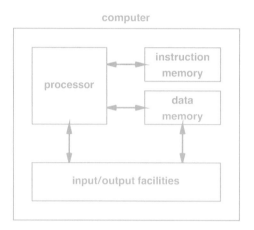

Figure 4.1 Illustration of the Harvard Architecture that uses two memories, one to hold programs and another to store data.

Although it includes the same basic components, a *Von Neumann Architecture*‡ uses a single memory to hold both programs and data. Figure 4.2 illustrates the approach.

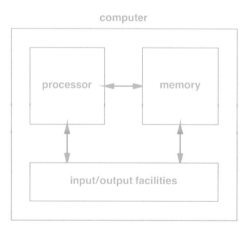

Figure 4.2 Illustration of the Von Neumann Architecture. Both programs and data can be stored in the same memory.

---

†The name arises because the approach was first used on the *Harvard Mark I* relay computer.
‡The name is taken from John Von Neumann, a mathematician who first proposed the architecture.

The chief advantage of the Harvard Architecture arises from its ability to have the hardware of one memory unit optimized to store programs and the hardware of another memory unit optimized to store data. The chief disadvantage arises from inflexibility: when purchasing a computer, an owner must choose the size of the instruction memory and the size of data memory. Once the computer has been purchased, an owner cannot use part of the instruction memory to store data nor can the owner use part of the data memory to store programs. Although it has fallen out of favor for general-purpose computers, the Harvard Architecture is still sometimes used in small embedded systems and other specialized designs.

Unlike the Harvard Architecture, the Von Neumann Architecture offers complete flexibility: at any time, an owner can change how much of the memory is devoted to programs and how much to data. The approach has proven to be so valuable that it has become widely adopted.

Because it offers flexibility, the Von Neumann Architecture, which uses a single memory to hold both programs and data, has become pervasive: almost all computers follow the Von Neumann approach.

We say a computer that follows the Von Neumann Architecture employs a *stored program* approach because a program is stored in memory. More important, programs can be loaded into memory just like other data items.

Except when noted, the remainder of the text implicitly assumes a Von Neumann Architecture. There are two primary exceptions in Chapters 15 and 10. Chapter 15, which explains data paths, uses a simplified Harvard Architecture in the example. Chapter 10, which explains caching, discusses the motivation for using separate instruction and data caches.

4.4 Definition Of A Processor

The remainder of this chapter considers the processor component present in both the Harvard and Von Neumann Architectures. The next sections define the term and characterize processor types. Later sections explore the subcomponents of complex processors.

Although programmers tend to think of a conventional computer and often use the term *processor* as a synonym for the *Central Processing Unit* (*CPU*), computer architects have a much broader meaning that includes the processors used to control the engine in an automobile, processors in hand-held remote-control devices, and specialized video processors used in graphics equipment. To an architect, a *processor* refers to a digital device that can perform a computation involving multiple steps. Individual processors are not complete computers; they are merely one of the building blocks that an architect uses to construct a computer system. Thus, although it can compute more than the combinatorial Boolean logic circuits we examine in Chapter 22, a processor need not be large or fast. In particular, some processors are significantly less powerful than the general-purpose CPU found in a typical laptop. The next sections help clarify the definition by examining characteristics of processors and explaining some of the ways they can be used.

4.5 The Range Of Processors

Because processors span a broad range of functionality and many variations exist, no single description adequately captures all the properties of processors. Instead, to help us appreciate the many designs, we need to divide processors into categories according to functionality and intended use. For example, we can use four categories to explain whether a processor can be adapted to new computations. The categories are listed in order of flexibility:

- Fixed logic
- Selectable logic
- Parameterized logic
- Programmable logic

A *fixed logic processor*, which is the least flexible, performs a single task. More important, all the functionality needed to perform the operation is built in when the processor is created, and the functionality cannot be altered without changing the underlying hardware†. For example, a fixed logic processor can be designed to compute a function, such as $sine(x)$, or to perform a graphics operation needed in a video game.

A *selectable logic processor* usually forms a subpart of a more powerful processor (e.g., a later section describes an Arithmetic-Logic Unit as part of a CPU). The selectable processor contains hardware to perform more than one function, and control lines specify which function to perform at a given time. For example, if a selectable logic processor can compute either $sine(x)$ or $cosine(x)$, a single control input (i.e., a single wire) can specify 0 to select sine and 1 to select cosine.

A *parameterized logic processor* adds additional flexibility. Although it only computes a predetermined function, the processor accepts a set of parameters that control the computation. For example, consider a parameterized processor that computes a hash function, $h(x)$. The hash function uses two constants, p and q, and computes the hash of x by computing the remainder of x when multiplied by p and divided by q. For example, if p is 167 and q is 163, $h(26729)$ is the remainder of 4463743 divided by 163, or 151‡. A parameterized processor for such a hash function allows constants p and q to be changed each time the processor is invoked. That is, in addition to the input, x, the processor accepts two additional parameters, p and q, that control the operation.

A *programmable logic processor* offers the most flexibility because it allows the sequence of steps to be changed each time the processor is invoked. The processor can be given a program to run, typically by placing the program in memory.

†Engineers use the term *hardwired* for functionality that cannot be changed without altering the underlying wiring.

‡Hashing is often applied to strings by converting the string to an integer value. In the example, number

4.6 Hierarchical Structure And Computational Engines

A large processor, such as a modern, general-purpose CPU, is so complex that no human can understand the entire processor as a single unit. To control the complexity, computer architects use a hierarchical approach in which subparts of the processor are designed and tested independently before being combined into the final design.

Some of the independent subparts of a large processor are so sophisticated that they fit our definition of a processor — the subpart can perform a computation that involves multiple steps. For example, a general-purpose CPU that has instructions for *sine* and *cosine* might be constructed by first building and testing a trigonometry processor, and then combining the trigonometry processor with other pieces to form the final CPU.

How do we describe a subpiece of a large, complex processor that acts independently and performs a computation? Some engineers use the term *computational engine*. The term *engine* usually implies that the subpiece fills a specific role and is less powerful than the overall unit. For example, Figure 4.3 illustrates a CPU that contains several engines interconnected inside the CPU.

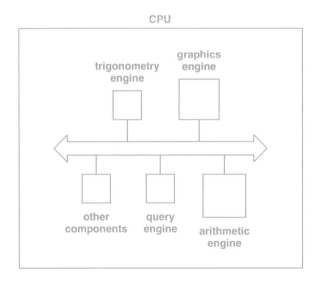

Figure 4.3 An example of a CPU that includes multiple components. The large arrow in the center of the figure indicates a central interconnect mechanism that the components use to coordinate.

The CPU in the figure includes a special-purpose *graphics engine*. Graphics engines, sometimes called *graphics accelerators*, are common because video game software is popular and many computers need a graphics engine to drive the graphics display at high speed. For example, a graphics engine might include facilities to repaint the surface of a graphical figure after it has been moved (e.g., in response to a joystick movement).

The CPU illustrated in Figure 4.3 also includes a *query engine*. Query engines and closely related *pattern engines* are used in database processors. A query engine examines a database record at high speed to determine if the record satisfies the query; a pattern engine examines a string of bits to determine if the string matches a specified pattern (e.g., to test whether a document contains a particular word). In either case, a CPU has enough capability to handle the task, but a special-purpose processor can perform the task much faster.

4.7 Structure Of A Conventional Processor

Although the imaginary CPU described in the previous section contains many engines, most processors do not. Two questions arise. First, what engine(s) are found in a conventional processor? Second, how are the engines interconnected? This section answers the questions broadly, and later sections give more detail.

Although a practical processor contains many subcomponents with complex interconnections among them, we can view a processor as having five conceptual units:

- Controller
- Arithmetic Logic Unit (ALU)
- Local data storage (typically, registers)
- Internal interconnection(s)
- External interface(s) (I/O buses)

Figure 4.4 illustrates the concept.

Controller. The controller forms the heart of a processor. Controller hardware has overall responsibility for program execution. That is, the controller steps through the program and coordinates the actions of all other hardware units to perform the specified operations.

Arithmetic Logic Unit (ALU). We think of the ALU as the main computational engine in a processor. The ALU performs all computational tasks, including integer arithmetic, operations on bits (e.g., left or right shift), and Boolean (logical) operations (e.g., Boolean *and*, *or*, *exclusive or*, and *not*). However, an ALU does not perform multiple steps or initiate activities. Instead, the ALU only performs one operation at a time, and relies on the controller to specify exactly what operation to perform on the operand values.

Local Data Storage. A processor must have at least some local storage to hold data values such as operands for arithmetic operations and the result. As we will see, local storage usually takes the form of hardware *registers* — values must be loaded into the hardware registers before they can be used in computation.

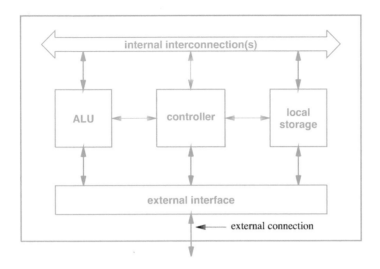

Figure 4.4 The five major units found in a conventional processor. The external interface connects to the rest of the computer system.

Internal Interconnection(s). A processor contains one or more hardware mechanisms that are used to transfer values between the other hardware units. For example, the interconnection hardware is used to move data values from the local storage to the ALU or to move results from the ALU to local storage. Architects sometimes use the term *data path* to describe an internal interconnection.

External Interface(s). The external interface unit handles all communication between the processor and the rest of the computer system. In particular, the external interface manages communication between the processor and external memory and I/O devices.

4.8 Processor Categories And Roles

Understanding the range of processors is especially difficult for someone who has not encountered hardware design because processors can be used in a variety of roles. It may help if we consider the ways that hardware devices use processors and how processors function in each role. Here are four examples:

- Coprocessors
- Microcontrollers
- Embedded system processors
- General-purpose processors

Coprocessors. A coprocessor operates in conjunction with and under the control of another processor. Usually, a coprocessor consists of a special-purpose processor that performs a single task at high speed. For example, some CPUs use a coprocessor known as a *floating point accelerator* to speed the execution of arithmetic operations — when a floating point operation occurs, the CPU automatically passes the necessary values to the coprocessor, obtains the result, and then continues execution. In some designs, the main processor uses a coprocessor to handle I/O or network communication, thereby increasing performance by offloading some tasks. In architectures where a running program does not know which operations are performed directly by the CPU and which operations are performed by a coprocessor, we say that the operation of a coprocessor is *transparent* to the software. Typical coprocessors use fixed or selectable logic, which means that the functions the coprocessor can perform are determined when the coprocessor is designed.

Microcontrollers. A microcontroller consists of a programmable device dedicated to the control of a physical system. Microcontrollers often run physical systems such as the engine in a modern automobile, the landing gear on an airplane, and the automatic door in a grocery store. In many cases, a microcontroller performs a trivial function that does not require much traditional computation. Instead, a microcontroller tests sensors and sends signals to control devices. Figure 4.5 lists an example of the steps a typical microcontroller can be programmed to perform:

```
do forever {
    wait for the sensor to be tripped;
    turn on power to the door motor;
    wait for a signal that indicates the
        door is open;
    wait for the sensor to reset;
    delay ten seconds;
    turn off power to the door motor;
}
```

Figure 4.5 Example of the steps a microcontroller performs. In most cases, microcontrollers are dedicated to trivial control tasks.

Embedded System Processors. An embedded system processor runs a sophisticated electronic device, such as a wireless router or the infotainment system in a vehicle. The processors used for embedded systems are usually more powerful than the processors that are used as microcontrollers, and often run a protocol stack used for communication. However, the processor may not contain all the functionality found on more general-purpose CPUs.

General-purpose Processors. General-purpose processors are the most familiar and need little explanation. For example, the CPU in a laptop or smart phone is a general-purpose processor.

4.9 Processor Technologies

How are processors created? In the 1960s, processors were created by connecting individual transistors or small electronic components that contained multiple transistors (known as logic gates) on a circuit board. The board plugged into a chassis where wires interconnected it with other boards to form a working computer. By the 1970s, large-scale integrated circuit technology arrived, which meant that the smallest and least powerful processors — such as those used for microcontrollers — could each be implemented on a single integrated circuit. As integrated circuit technology improved and the number of transistors on a chip increased, a single chip became capable of holding more powerful processors. Today, many of the most powerful general-purpose processors consist of a single integrated circuit.

4.10 Stored Programs

Recall that a processor performs a computation that involves multiple steps. Although some processors have the series of steps built into the hardware, most do not. Instead, they are *programmable* (i.e., they rely on a mechanism known as *programming*). That is, the sequence of steps to be performed comprise a program that is placed in a location the processor can access; the processor accesses the program and follows the specified steps.

Computer programmers are familiar with conventional computer systems that use main memory as the location that holds a program. The program is loaded into memory each time a user runs the application. The chief advantage of using main memory to hold programs lies in the ability to change the program. The next time a user runs a program after it has been changed, the altered version will be used.

Although our conventional notion of programming works well for general-purpose processors, other types of processors use alternative mechanisms that are not as easy to change. For example, the program for a microcontroller usually resides in hardware known as *Read Only Memory* (*ROM*†). In fact, a ROM that contains a program may reside on an integrated circuit along with a microcontroller that runs the program. For example, the microcontroller used in an automobile may reside on a single integrated circuit that also contains the program the microcontroller runs.

The important point is that programming is a broad notion:

> *To a computer architect, a processor is classified as programmable if, at some level of detail, the processor is separate from the program it runs. To a user, it may appear that the program and processor are integrated, and it may not be possible to change the program without replacing the processor.*

†Chapters 8 and 9 describe memory in more detail.

4.11 The Fetch-Execute Cycle

How does a programmable processor access and perform steps of a program? Although the details vary among processors, all programmable processors follow the same fundamental paradigm. The underlying mechanism is known as the *fetch-execute cycle*.

To implement fetch-execute, a processor has an instruction pointer that automatically moves through the program in memory, performing each instruction. That is, each programmable processor executes two basic steps repeatedly. Algorithm 4.1 presents the two fundamental steps†.

Algorithm 4.1

Repeat forever {

      Fetch: retrieve the next instruction of the program from the
           location in which the program has been stored.

      Execute: perform the instruction.

}

Algorithm 4.1 The Two Fundamental Steps Of The Fetch-Execute Cycle

The important point is:

> *At some level, every programmable processor implements a fetch-execute cycle.*

Several questions arise. Exactly how are the instructions of a program represented in memory? How does a processor identify the *next* step of a program? What are the possible operations that can be performed during the execution phase of the fetch-execute cycle? How does the processor perform a given operation? Where is the result of a computation stored?

Later chapters answer each of these questions in more detail. The remainder of this chapter considers a few basic ideas, including how instructions are represented in memory, why hardware engineers favor making all instructions the same number of bytes, how fast a processor operates, how a processor begins with the first step of a program, and what happens when the processor reaches the end of a program.

---

†Note that the algorithm presented here is a simplified form; when we discuss I/O, we will see how the algorithm is extended to handle device interrupts.

4.12 Instructions In Memory

When a processor fetches an instruction from memory, exactly what does it fetch? Later chapters explain that various approaches have been used to define instructions and their meaning. For now, we will only focus on conventional processors and only consider a few basics.

As Chapter 3 notes, each instruction occupies a set of sequential bytes in memory. The compiler that generates the bits to be stored in an instruction and the hardware that interprets the instruction must agree on all the details. Thus, when it compiles a program, a compiler must generate instructions for a specific type of processor.

In general, the processor divides the bits of an instruction into separate *fields*. The most important field in the instruction, known as an *opcode* (short for *operation code*) specifies the operation to be performed. Other fields specify the *operands* to use when the processor executes the instruction. On one type of processor, for example, an opcode field spans four bits, and the four-bit opcode 0b0100 specifies addition. An addition instruction contains three operand fields which specify where to obtain the two values to add and where to place the result.

4.13 Variable-length and Fixed-length Instructions

Are all instructions exactly the same size? It depends on the processor. Many early computers used *variable-length instructions* in which some instructions occupied more bytes than others. Variable length seems to make sense because some operations need more operands than others. For example, an instruction that increments a value only needs one operand to specify the location of the value to increment, but an instruction that performs subtraction needs two operands. Consequently, early computer architects specified that instructions with fewer operands would occupy fewer bytes than instructions with more operands.

Many modern processors used fixed-length instructions because doing so allows a processor to operate faster. To understand why, consider the difference between software engineering and hardware engineering. When they think about processing variable-length instructions, software engineers imagine an algorithm:

Fetch the byte of the instruction that contains the opcode
Use the opcode to compute N, the number of additional bytes
Repeat N times
    Fetch an additional byte of the instruction
Use the opcode to decide how to perform the instruction

Hardware engineers take a different approach because an iterative algorithm does not work well in hardware. To make hardware operate at high speed, the hardware must work in parallel. Therefore, when they think about fetching an instruction, hardware engineers imagine hardware working in parallel:

> Build an instruction decoder with hardware for each bit of the instruction
> Fetch all bits of the instruction from memory in parallel
> Use the opcode to choose an internal unit to execute the instruction
> Transfer all bits of the instruction to the unit in parallel

For example, if the opcode specifies an arithmetic operation, the hardware will transfer the instruction to the Arithmetic-Logic Unit, which performs the operation. If each instruction is exactly the same size as other instructions, a single piece of hardware can handle any instruction. Figure 4.6 illustrates parallel hardware and parallel transfers.

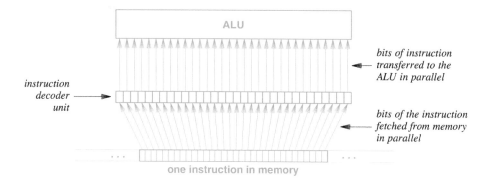

Figure 4.6 Two conceptual transfers performed by parallel hardware when fetching and executing an arithmetic instruction.

The point is that instead of using iteration, hardware systems have a separate piece of hardware for each bit and perform operations on all bits in parallel. To capture the concept, we say that hardware is *iterated in space*. Making instructions a uniform size means a single piece of hardware can be designed that accommodates any instruction.

We can summarize:

> *Unlike software, hardware is iterated in space which means a separate piece of hardware handles each bit, allowing the hardware to transfer and process all bits at the same time. As a consequence, hardware works best with fixed-length instructions.*

4.14 Clock Rate And Instruction Rate

One of the primary questions about processors concerns speed: how fast does the fetch-execute cycle operate? The answer depends on the hardware technology used to create the processor, the speed of the memory from which the processor must fetch instructions, the internal processor design, the type of computation the processor can perform, the use of coprocessors and hardware accelerators, and the speed of the hardware that interconnects the processor to memory and other hardware units. On the one hand, a processor used as a microcontroller to actuate a physical device (e.g., an electric door) can be relatively slow because a response time under one-tenth of a second seems fast to a human. On the other hand, a processor used in the highest-speed computers must run as fast as possible because the goal is maximum performance.

Digital hardware systems, including processors, use a mechanism known as a *clock* to control the rate at which the underlying digital logic operates. A hardware engineer defines a clock to be a circuit that pulses at a regular rate. The signal from a clock travels across wires to all parts of a circuit, and can be used to coordinate the operation of all the pieces. Anyone who has purchased a computer knows that sales personnel push customers to purchase a fast clock with the argument that a higher clock rate will result in higher performance.

A higher clock rate means the internal circuits of the processor run at higher speed, and many basic instructions can complete in one clock cycle. However, the clock rate does not give the rate at which the fetch-execute cycle handles all operations because the time required for the *execute* portion of the cycle depends on the instruction being performed. Operations that require memory access or I/O may take more than one clock cycle, execution time even varies among arithmetic operations because floating point arithmetic usually requires more clock cycles than integer arithmetic. Floating point multiplication and division stand out as especially costly — a single floating point division can require many more clock cycles than an integer addition. Thus, the number of instructions executed per second depends on the computation an application performs. For now, it is sufficient to remember the general principle:

> *The fetch-execute cycle may not proceed at a fixed rate because the time taken to execute an instruction depends on the operation being performed. An operation, such as floating point multiplication, may require more clock cycles than integer operations.*

4.15 Control: Getting Started And Stopping

So far, we have discussed a processor running a fetch-execute cycle without giving details. We now need to answer two basic questions. How does the processor start running the fetch-execute cycle? What happens after the processor executes the last step in a program?

The issue of program termination is the easiest to understand: processor hardware is not designed to stop. Instead, the fetch-execute cycle continues indefinitely. Of course, a processor can be permanently halted, but such a sequence is only used to power down a computer — in normal operations, the processor continues to execute one instruction after another.

In some cases, a program uses a loop to delay. For example, a microcontroller may need to wait for a sensor to indicate an external condition has been met before proceeding. The processor does not merely stop to wait for the sensor. Instead, the program contains a loop that repeatedly tests the sensor. Thus, from a hardware point of view, the fetch-execute cycle continues.

The notion of an indefinite fetch-execute cycle has a direct consequence for programming: software must be planned so a processor always has a next step to execute. In the case of a dedicated system such as a microcontroller that controls a physical device, the program consists of an infinite loop — when it finishes the last step of the program, the processor starts again at the first step. In the case of a general-purpose computer, an operating system is always present. The operating system can load an application into memory, and then direct the processor to run the application. To keep the fetch-execute cycle running, the operating system must arrange to regain control when the application finishes. When no application is running, the operating system enters a loop to wait for input (e.g., from a touch screen, keyboard, or mouse).

To summarize:

> Because a processor runs the fetch-execute cycle indefinitely, software must be designed to ensure that there is always a next step to execute. In a dedicated system, the same program executes repeatedly; in a general-purpose system, an operating system runs when no application is running.

4.16 Starting The Fetch-Execute Cycle

How does a processor start the fetch-execute cycle? The answer is complex because it depends on the underlying hardware. For example, some processors have a hardware *reset* mechanism. On such processors, engineers arrange for a combinatorial circuit to apply voltage to the reset line until all system components are ready to operate. When voltage is removed from the reset line, the processor begins executing a program from a fixed location. Some processors start executing a program found at location zero in memory once the processor is reset. In such systems, the designer must guarantee that a valid program is placed in location zero before the processor starts.

The steps used to start a processor are known as a *bootstrap*. In an embedded environment, the program to be run usually resides in *Read Only Memory* (*ROM*) or *Non-Volatile RAM* (*NVRAM*). On a conventional computer, the hardware starts running bootstrap code. The bootstrap program reads a copy of the operating system from an I/O device, such as a disk, places the copy into memory, and branches to the copy. In either case, a hardware signal must be passed to the processor that causes the processor to start the fetch-execute cycle to begin the bootstrap sequence.

Many devices have a *soft power switch*, which means that the power switch does not actually turn power on or off. Instead, the switch acts like a sensor — the processor can interrogate the switch to determine its current position. Booting a device that has a soft power switch is no different than booting a computer with a traditional power switch. When power is first applied (e.g., when a battery is installed), the hardware enters an initial state in which the hardware monitors the soft power switch, but does not otherwise start. Once the user presses the soft power switch, the hardware enters the bootstrap sequence.

4.17 Summary

A processor is a digital device that can perform a computation involving multiple steps. Processors can use fixed, selectable, parameterized or programmable logic. The term *engine* identifies a processor that is a subpiece of a more complex processor.

Processors are used in various roles, including coprocessors, microcontrollers, embedded processors, and general-purpose processors. Although early processors were created from discrete logic, a modern processor is implemented as a single VLSI chip.

A processor is classified as programmable if at some level, the processor hardware is separate from the sequence of steps that the processor performs; from the point of view of the end user, however, it might not be possible to change the program without replacing the processor. All programmable processors follow a fetch-execute cycle; the time required for one cycle depends on the operation performed. Because fetch-execute processing continues indefinitely, a designer must construct a program in such a way that the processor always has an instruction to execute.

A processor executes instructions from memory. Although early processors used variable-length instructions, making all instructions the same size allows parallel hardware to fetch and execute instructions at high speed.

EXERCISES

4.1 Neither Figure 4.1 nor Figure 4.2 has *storage* as a major component. Where does storage (e.g., a solid-state disk) fit into the figures?

4.2 Consult Wikipedia to learn about early computers. How much memory did the Harvard Mark I computer have, and what year was it created? How much memory did the IBM 360/20 computer have, and what year was it created?

4.3 Although CPU manufacturers brag about the graphics accelerators on their chips, some video game designers choose to keep the graphics hardware separate from the processor. Explain one possible motivation for keeping it separate.

4.4   Imagine a smart phone that employs a Harvard Architecture. If you purchase such a phone, what would you need to specify that you do not normally specify?

4.5   What aspect of a Von Neumann Architecture makes it more vulnerable to hackers than a Harvard Architecture?

4.6   A programmable logic processor can perform any function. Why would a designer use a fixed, selectable, or parameterized logic processor instead of a programmable logic processor. Hint: think of portable devices.

4.7   Suppose a CPU offers an instruction that computes the *tangent* function. What engine might you expect to find in the CPU?

4.8   If you visit the Computer History Museum and look at a computer from the 1950s, the CPU will not consist of a single computer chip. How do you expect the CPU to appear?

4.9   Find out whether the processor on your laptop uses fixed-length or variable-length instructions.

4.10 What is the clock rate of the processor on your laptop computer?

4.11 When you are purchasing a laptop, the sales person shows you a model with a clock rate of 2.5 gigahertz. Does that mean the laptop always performs 2.5 billion instructions per second? Explain.

4.12 Write a computer program that compares the difference in execution times between an integer division and a floating point division. To test the program, execute each operation 100,000 times, and compare the difference in running times.

Chapter Contents

5

Instruction Sets And Operands

5.1 Introduction

The previous chapter introduces various types of processors and explains the fetch-execute cycle that programmable processors use. This chapter continues the discussion by focusing on the set of operations that a processor can perform and the form of operands instructions use. The chapter explains some of the approaches computer architects have chosen, and discusses the advantages and disadvantages of each.

5.2 Mathematics, Convenience, And Cost

What operations should a processor offer? From a mathematical point of view, a wide variety of computational models provide equivalent computing power. In theory, as long as a processor offers a few basic operations, the processor has sufficient power to compute any computable function†.

Software engineers understand that although only a minimum set of operations are absolutely necessary, such a set does not result in a usable computer. To see why, consider arithmetic. It is possible to compute a quotient by repeated subtraction and to compute a product by repeated addition. Using repeated addition or subtraction results in horribly slow performance. Instead, modern CPUs have instructions for both multiplication and division, and use a built-in hardware unit that can perform the operations efficiently.

---

†In a mathematical sense, only three operations are needed to compute any computable function: add one, subtract one, and branch if a value is nonzero.

To a computer architect, choosing a set of operations that the processor will perform represents a tradeoff. On the one hand, adding additional operations along with hardware to execute the instructions can improve performance. On the other hand, each additional operation takes space on the chip that could be used for other operations, and the processor will consume more power (and generate more heat). As a result, processors for smart phones and other battery-powered devices do not usually offer as many instructions as the processors used in high-performance data center servers.

The point is that when considering the set of operations a given processor provides, we need to remember that the choice represents a complex tradeoff:

> *The set of operations a processor provides represents a tradeoff among the cost of the hardware, the performance of the processor, and engineering considerations such as power consumption.*

5.3 Instruction Sets

When an architect designs a programmable processor, the architect must make two key decisions:

- Instruction set — the set of operations the processor provides
- Instruction representation — the format for each instruction

We use the term *instruction set* to refer to the set of operations the hardware recognizes, and refer to each operation as an *instruction*. We assume that on each iteration of its fetch-execute cycle, a processor *fetches* and *executes* one instruction.

The definition of an instruction set specifies all details about each instruction, including an exact specification of actions the processor takes when it executes the instruction. Thus, the instruction set defines values on which each instruction operates and the results the instruction produces. The definition specifies allowable values (e.g., the division instruction requires the divisor to be nonzero) and error conditions (e.g., what happens if an addition results in an overflow).

The term *instruction representation* (*instruction format*) refers to the binary representation that the hardware uses for instructions. The instruction representation is important because it defines a key interface: the interface between software that generates instructions and places them in memory and the hardware that executes the instructions. The software (e.g., the compiler, assembler, linker, and loader) must create an image in memory that uses exactly the same instruction format that the processor hardware expects.

5.4 Instruction Set Architecture

When the computer industry was first starting in the 1950s, a vendor designed each model independently. The vendor started with overall design goals, such as the memory size, processing speed, target applications, and cost. Hardware engineers then created a design by choosing, among other things, an instruction set. If a vendor offered two computers, the instruction set on the vendor's smaller computer often differed completely from the instruction set on the vendor's larger computer.

In the 1960s, IBM Corporation noticed the downside of incompatibility among its models: IBM customers who started with a small IBM computer could not move up easily to a large IBM computer without rewriting all their software. It was just as easy for a customer to rewrite their software for another vendor's large computer, which meant IBM was missing potential sales.

To solve the problem, IBM decided to offer a range of computers that all used the same instruction set. IBM used the name *System/360* to refer to the general design, and then gave each computer a specific model number (e.g., the System/360 model 20). With minor exceptions, all System/360 computers ran the same instructions. Although they remained compatible, individual models differed widely in other details, with approximately a 1:30 ratio in the sizes of memory, processor speeds, and cost†.

Having a range of products allowed a customer to start with a smaller, inexpensive computer. Once the computer became overloaded, IBM could offer the customer an easy upgrade to a larger, faster computer that ran the customer's existing programs without any change. We say that the specification of an instruction set and the corresponding representation defines an *Instruction Set Architecture (ISA)*. That is, an ISA defines both format and meaning of an instruction set, but does not specify the hardware implementation or speed.

Modern CPU vendors use the same approach as IBM. They define an Instruction Set Architecture, and then offer a series of processor chips that each implement the same ISA but differ in speed, power consumption, and physical size. For example, Intel Corporation has defined the *Intel Architecture*, popularly known as *x86 architecture* because it is based on an 8086 chip designed in the 1980s, and the Arm Corporation has defined an ISA known as *ARM Architecture* that is widely used in mobile devices.

To summarize:

> *Modern CPU architects follow the approach of defining an Instruction Set Architecture and then offering a range of chips that all implement the same ISA but differ in details, such as physical size, speed, and power consumption.*

---

†We use the term *cost* rather than *price* because customers usually leased mainframe computers instead of purchasing them.

5.5 Opcodes, Operands, And Results

Recall that each instruction contains fields that specify the operation to be performed (the opcode), a set of value(s) to use for the operation (operands), and
location(s) to place the result(s). Each field is a bit string. Depending on the operation
being performed, the field may be interpreted as a number or possibly as a memory address. The following paragraphs refine the definitions.

Opcode. The opcode field specifies the exact operation to be performed. When an
architect designs an instruction set, the architect assigns a unique opcode to each operation. For example, integer addition might be assigned the four-bit opcode 0100, and integer subtraction might be assigned the four-bit opcode 0010.

Operands. The term *operand* refers to a value that is needed to perform an operation. The definition of an instruction set specifies the exact number of operands for
each instruction, and the possible values (e.g., the addition operation takes two signed
integers).

Results. In some architectures, one or more of the operand fields specify where the
processor should place results of an instruction (e.g., the result of an arithmetic operation); in other architectures, the location of the result is determined automatically.

5.6 Typical Instruction Format

Each instruction is represented as a binary string. Many architectures specify that
an instruction begins with the opcode field followed by fields that specify the operands.
The opcode value specifies how many operands follow, and may specify the size of
each operand. Figure 5.1 illustrates the general format.

Figure 5.1 The general instruction format that many processors use. The opcode at the beginning of an instruction determines which
operands follow.

5.7 General-Purpose Registers

When a program runs, all variables the program uses must reside in memory.
However, accessing memory introduces delay — a processor can execute an operation
faster than it can access memory. Thus, if a processor always fetched operands from
memory and always placed results back in memory, execution would take a long time.
To speed computation, processors use a small, high-speed storage mechanism when performing computation. The mechanism consists of a small set of hardware units called

general-purpose registers†. Each register has a fixed size. For example, on a processor that provides 32-bit arithmetic, each general-purpose register will be 32 bits wide.

Instead of fetching operands from memory for each instruction, registers can be used to achieve higher speed. A copy of each value needed for the computation must be fetched from memory and placed in a register. An instruction uses values in the registers, and places the result in a register. To make a general-purpose register available for use with a subsequent instruction, code may need to save the results of computation in a variable in memory.

In many architectures, general-purpose registers are numbered from 0 through N−1. The processor provides instructions that can access the value(s) in specified registers as well as instructions that can store a value in a general-purpose register. Each general-purpose register has the same semantics as memory: an access always returns the last value *stored* into the register.

5.8 Floating Point Registers And Register Identification

Processors that support floating point arithmetic often use a separate set of registers to hold floating point values. Confusion can arise because both general-purpose registers and floating point registers are usually numbered starting at zero. The opcode in the instruction tells whether an operand refers to a general-purpose register or a floating point register. For example, if registers 3 and 6 are specified as operands for an integer subtraction instruction, the processor will extract the operands from the general-purpose registers; if the opcode specifies a floating point subtraction, the processor will extract the operands from the floating point registers.

5.9 Programming With Registers

In addition to requiring each of the operands that an instruction uses to be stored in a general-purpose register, the instruction may require another operand to specify one or more general-purpose registers that will hold the result(s) of the instruction. For example, to compute $Z = X + Y$, the values from variables X and Y must be placed into registers, and the result of the addition must be placed in a register. To use registers *3*, *6*, and *7*, a program might contain four instructions that:

- Fetch a copy of variable X from memory and place into register 3
- Fetch a copy of variable Y from memory and place into register 6
- Add the value in register 3 to the value in register 6, and place the result into register 7
- Store a copy of the value in register 7 to variable Z in memory

Figure 5.2 Steps taken to compute $Z = X + Y$ using registers.

---

†As the term *general-purpose* implies, a processor contains additional special-purpose registers that have other uses. We will see examples later.

Moving a value between memory and a register takes time. So, if a later computation will use a variable, leaving the variable in a register temporarily rather than storing it back in memory immediately will save time. Eventually, when the value will no longer be needed, it must be stored in memory. Because a processor only contains a small number of registers, a compiler (or a programmer) must decide which values to keep in registers at any time and which values to store in memory†. The process of choosing which values the registers contain is known as *register allocation*.

Many details complicate register allocation. One of the most common arises if an instruction generates a large result, called an *extended value*. For example, integer multiplication can produce a result that contains twice as many bits as either operand. Some processors offer facilities for *double-precision* arithmetic (e.g., if a standard integer is thirty-two bits wide, a double-precision integer occupies sixty-four bits).

To handle extended values, the hardware may treat two consecutive registers as a single large register. On such processors, for example, an instruction that loads a double-precision integer into register 4 will place half the integer in register 4 and the other half in register 5 (i.e., the value of register 5 will change even though the instruction contains no explicit reference). When choosing registers to use, a programmer must plan for instructions that place extended data values in consecutive registers.

5.10 Register Banks

An additional hardware detail complicates register allocation: some architectures divide registers into multiple *banks*, and require the operands for an instruction to come from separate banks. For example, on a processor that uses two register banks, an integer *add* instruction may require the two operands to be from separate banks.

To understand register banks, we must examine the underlying hardware. In essence, register banks allow the hardware to operate faster because each bank has a separate physical access mechanism and the two mechanisms can operate simultaneously. Thus, when the processor executes an instruction that accesses two operands, placing the operands in separate banks means both operands can be obtained at the same time, speeding access. Figure 5.3 illustrates the concept.

Register banks have an interesting consequence for programmers: it may not be possible to keep a given data value in a given register permanently. To understand why, consider the following assignment statements that are typical of those used in a conventional programming language, and assume we want to implement the statements on a processor that has two register banks as Figure 5.3 illustrates.

$$R \leftarrow X + Y$$
$$S \leftarrow Z - X$$
$$T \leftarrow Y + Z$$

---

†We use the term *register spilling* to refer to moving a value from a register back into memory to make the register available for a new value.

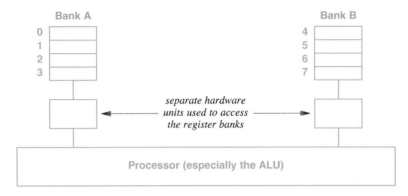

Figure 5.3 Illustration of eight registers divided into two banks. Hardware allows the processor to access both banks at the same time.

To perform the first addition, X and Y must be in separate register banks. Let's assume X is in a register in bank A, and Y is in a register in bank B. For the subtraction, Z must be in the opposite register bank from X (i.e., Z must be in a register in bank B). For the third assignment, Y and Z must be in different banks. Unfortunately, the first two assignments mean that Y and Z are located in the same bank. Thus, there is no possible assignment of X, Y, and Z to registers that works with all three instructions. We say that a *register conflict* occurs.

What happens when a register conflict arises? A compiler (or a programmer, if they are programming in assembly language) must insert an instruction to copy a value into another register bank. For the example above, the extra instruction could copy the value of Z into a register in Bank A before the final addition is performed.

5.11 Terminology: Complex And Reduced Instruction Sets

Instruction sets can be divided into two broad categories†:

- CISC (Complex Instruction Set Computer)
- RISC (Reduced Instruction Set Computer)

A CISC instruction set usually includes many instructions (often hundreds), and each instruction can perform an arbitrarily complex computation‡. Intel's x86 instruction set is classified as CISC because it includes hundreds of instructions, some of which require a long time to execute (e.g., one instruction manipulates graphics in memory and others compute the *sine* and *cosine* functions).

In contrast to CISC, a RISC instruction set is small. Instead of arbitrary instructions, a RISC design strives for a minimum set of instructions that is sufficient for all computation (e.g., a total of thirty-two instructions). Instead of allowing a single instruction to compute an arbitrary function, each RISC instruction performs a basic com-

---

†The acronyms are pronounced *sisk* and *risk*.

‡The next chapter explains that, in addition to complex instructions, complex operand types have been

putation. To achieve the highest possible speed, RISC designs constrain instructions to be a fixed size. Finally, as the next section explains, a RISC processor is designed to execute an instruction in one clock cycle†. Arm and MIPS Corporations have each created RISC architectures in which one instruction can be completed every clock cycle. The Arm designs are especially popular for use in smart phones and other battery-powered devices.

We can summarize:

> *An instruction set is classified as CISC if the instruction set contains instructions that perform complex computations that can require long times; an instruction set is classified as RISC if it contains a small number of instructions that can each execute in one clock cycle.*

Early in the history of computers, programmers wrote code in assembly language. On such systems, CISC designs were popular because a CISC instruction set includes powerful and complex instructions, which means a programmer could specify a computation with fewer lines of code. By the 1970s, most programmers used high-level languages, and emphasis shifted from finding an instruction set that was convenient for human programmers to finding instructions hardware could execute quickly. In 1980, IBM release the IBM 801, often considered to be the first RISC computer chip. Within a few years, Sun Microsystems developed a RISC chip named *Sparc*.

Interestingly, most modern computers contain a RISC design, even if they offer a CISC instruction set. Buried in the processor, a RISC engine performs the actual computation. An additional layer of hardware on top of the RISC engine decodes each CISC instruction and then uses the RISC engine to perform the steps needed to execute the instruction. We will learn more about CPUs that have a lower-level engine built in when we discuss microcode.

5.12 RISC Design And The Execution Pipeline

We said that a RISC processor executes one instruction per clock cycle. In fact, a more accurate version of the statement is: a RISC processor is designed so the processor can *complete* one instruction on each clock cycle. To understand the subtle difference, it is important to know how the hardware works. We said that a processor performs a fetch-execute cycle by first fetching an instruction and then executing the instruction. In fact, the processor divides the fetch-execute cycle into several steps, typically:

- Fetch the next instruction
- Decode the instruction and fetch operands from registers
- Perform the operation specified by the opcode
- Perform memory read or write, if needed
- Store the result back to the registers

†Chapter 22 describes how a hardware clock, which pulses at regular intervals, controls the processor and

To enable high speed, RISC processors contain parallel hardware units that each perform one step listed above. The hardware is arranged in a *multistage pipeline†*, which means the results from one hardware unit are passed to the next hardware unit. Figure 5.4 illustrates a pipeline.

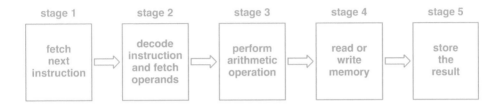

| stage 1 | stage 2 | stage 3 | stage 4 | stage 5 |

| fetch next instruction | decode instruction and fetch operands | perform arithmetic operation | read or write memory | store the result |

Figure 5.4 An example pipeline of the five hardware stages that are used to perform the fetch-execute cycle.

In the figure, an instruction moves left to right through the pipeline. The first stage fetches the instruction, the next stage examines the opcode, and so on. Whenever the clock ticks, all stages simultaneously pass the instruction to the right. Thus, instructions move through the pipeline like an assembly line: at any time, the pipeline contains five instructions.

The speed of a pipeline arises because all stages operate in parallel — while the fourth stage executes an instruction, the third stage fetches the operands for the next instruction. Thus, a stage never needs to delay because an instruction is always ready on each clock cycle. Figure 5.5 illustrates how a set of instructions pass through a five-stage pipeline.

	clock	stage 1	stage 2	stage 3	stage 4	stage 5
Time	1	inst. 1	—	—	—	—
	2	inst. 2	inst. 1	—	—	—
	3	inst. 3	inst. 2	inst. 1	—	—
	4	inst. 4	inst. 3	inst. 2	inst. 1	—
	5	inst. 5	inst. 4	inst. 3	inst. 2	inst. 1
	6	inst. 6	inst. 5	inst. 4	inst. 3	inst. 2
	7	inst. 7	inst. 6	inst. 5	inst. 4	inst. 3
	8	inst. 8	inst. 7	inst. 6	inst. 5	inst. 4

Figure 5.5 Instructions passing through a five-stage pipeline. Once the pipeline is filled, each stage is busy on each clock cycle.

The figure clearly illustrates that although a RISC processor cannot perform all the steps needed to fetch and execute an instruction in one clock cycle, parallel hardware allows the processor to finish one instruction per clock cycle. We can summarize:

†The terms *instruction pipeline* and *execution pipeline* are used interchangeably to refer to the multistage

Although a RISC processor cannot perform all steps of the fetch-execute cycle in a single clock cycle, an instruction pipeline with a parallel hardware unit for each stage provides approximately the same performance: once the pipeline is full, one instruction completes on every clock cycle.

5.13 Pipelines And Instruction Stalls

We say that the instruction pipeline is *transparent* to programmers because the instruction set does not contain any explicit references to the pipeline. That is, the hardware is constructed so the results of a program are the same whether or not a pipeline is present. Although transparency can be an advantage, it can also be a disadvantage: a programmer who does not understand the pipeline can inadvertently introduce inefficiencies.

To understand the effect of programming choices on a pipeline, consider a program that contains two successive instructions that perform an addition and subtraction on operands and results located in registers that we will label A, B, C, D, and E:

$$\text{Instruction K:} \quad \text{C} \leftarrow \text{add A B}$$
$$\text{Instruction K+1:} \quad \text{D} \leftarrow \text{subtract E C}$$

Although instruction K can proceed through the pipeline from beginning to end, instruction K+1 encounters a problem because operand C is not available in time. That is, the hardware must wait for instruction K to finish before fetching the operands for instruction K+1. We say that a stage of the pipeline *stalls* to wait for the operand to become available. Figure 5.6 illustrates what happens during a pipeline stall.

The figure shows a normal pipeline running until clock cycle 3, when Instruction K+1 has reached stage 2. Recall that stage 2 fetches operands from registers. In our example, one of the operands for instruction K+1 is not available, and will not be available until instruction K writes its results into a register. The pipeline must stall in cycle 4 until instruction K completes. In the code above, because the value of C has not been computed, stage 2 cannot fetch the value for C. Thus, stages 1 and 2 remain stalled during clock cycles 5 and 6. During clock cycle 7, stage 2 can fetch the operand, and pipeline processing continues.

The rightmost column in Figure 5.6 shows the effect of a stall on performance: the final stage of the pipeline does not produce any results during clock cycles 6, 7, and 8. If no stalls had occurred, instruction K+1 would have completed during clock cycle 6; the stall means the instruction does not complete until clock cycle 9.

To describe the delay between the cause of a stall and the time at which output stops, we say that a *bubble* passes through the pipeline. Of course, the bubble is only apparent to someone observing the pipeline's performance because correctness is not affected. That is, an instruction always passes directly to the next stage as soon as one stage completes, which means all instructions are executed in the order specified.

	clock	stage 1 fetch instruction	stage 2 fetch operands	stage 3 ALU operation	stage 4 access memory	stage 5 write results
	1	inst. K	inst. K-1	inst. K-2	inst. K-3	inst. K-4
Time	2	inst. K+1	inst. K	inst. K-1	inst. K-2	inst. K-3
	3	inst. K+2	(inst. K+1)	inst. K	inst. K-1	inst. K-2
	4	(inst. K+2)	(inst. K+1)	—	inst. K	inst. K-1
	5	(inst. K+2)	(inst. K+1)	—	—	inst. K
	6	(inst. K+2)	inst. K+1	—	—	—
	7	inst. K+3	inst. K+2	inst. K+1	—	—
	8	inst. K+4	inst. K+3	inst. K+2	inst. K+1	—
	9	inst. K+5	inst. K+4	inst. K+3	inst. K+2	inst. K+1
	10	inst. K+6	inst. K+5	inst. K+4	inst. K+1	inst. K+2

Figure 5.6 Illustration of a pipeline stall. Instruction K+1 cannot proceed until an operand from instruction K becomes available.

5.14 Other Causes Of Pipeline Stalls

In addition to waiting for operands, a pipeline can stall when the processor executes any instruction that delays processing or disrupts the normal flow. For example, a stall can occur when a processor:

- Accesses external storage
- Invokes a coprocessor
- Branches to a new location
- Calls a subroutine

The most sophisticated processors contain additional hardware to avoid stalls. For example, to handle branching, some processors contain two copies of a pipeline, which allows the processor to start decoding the instruction that will be executed if a branch is taken as well as the instruction that will be executed if a branch is not taken. The two copies operate until a branch instruction can be executed. At that time, the hardware knows which copy of the pipeline to follow; the other copy is ignored. Other processors contain special shortcut hardware that passes a copy of a result back to a previous pipeline stage.

5.15 Consequences For Programmers

To achieve maximum speed, a program for a RISC architecture must be written to accommodate an instruction pipeline. For example, a programmer should avoid introducing unnecessary branch instructions. Similarly, instead of referencing a result register immediately in the following instruction, the reference can be delayed. As an example, Figure 5.7 shows how code can be rearranged to run faster.

```
C ← add A B              C ← add A B
D ← subtract E C         F ← add G H
F ← add G H              M ← add K L
J ← subtract I F         D ← subtract E C
M ← add K L              J ← subtract I F
P ← subtract M N         P ← subtract M N

     (a)                      (b)
```

Figure 5.7 (a) A list of instructions, and (b) the instructions reordered to run
          faster in a pipeline. Reducing pipeline stalls increases speed.

In the figure, the optimized program separates references from computation. For example, in the original program, the second instruction references value C, which is produced by the previous instruction. Thus, a stall occurs between the first and second instructions. Moving the subtraction to a later point in the program allows the processor to continue to operate without a stall.

Of course, a programmer can choose to view a pipeline as an automatic optimization instead of a programming burden. Fortunately, most programmers do not need to perform pipeline optimizations manually. Instead, compilers for high-level languages perform the optimizations automatically.

> *Rearranging code sequences can increase the speed of processing when the hardware uses an instruction pipeline; a compiler may reorder instructions to increase speed, provided the new order does not affect correctness.*

5.16 Programming, Stalls, And No-Op Instructions

In some cases, the instructions in a program cannot be rearranged to prevent a stall. In such cases, programmers can document stalls so anyone reading the code will understand that a stall occurs. Such documentation is especially helpful if a program is modified later because the programmer who performs the modification can reconsider the situation and attempt to reorder instructions to prevent a stall.

How should programmers document a stall? One technique is obvious: insert a comment that explains the reason for a stall. However, most code is generated by compilers and is only read by humans when problems occur or special optimization is required. In such cases, another technique can be used: in places where stalls occur, insert extra instructions in the code. The extra instructions show where items can be inserted without affecting the pipeline. Of course, an extra instruction must be innocuous — it must not change the values in registers or otherwise affect the program. In most cases, the hardware provides the solution: a *no-op*. That is, an instruction that does absolutely nothing except occupy time. The point is:

> Most processors include a no-op instruction that does not reference data values, compute a result, or otherwise affect the state of the computer. No-op instructions can be inserted to document locations where an instruction stall occurs.

5.17 Forwarding

As mentioned above, some hardware has special facilities to improve instruction pipeline performance. For example, an ALU can use a technique known as *forwarding* to solve the problem of successive arithmetic instructions passing results.

To understand how forwarding works, consider the example of two instructions where operands A, B, C, D, and E are in registers:

$$\text{Instruction K:} \quad C \leftarrow \text{add } A \ B$$
$$\text{Instruction K+1:} \quad D \leftarrow \text{subtract } E \ C$$

We said that such a sequence causes a stall on a pipelined processor. However, a processor that implements forwarding can avoid the stall by arranging for the hardware to detect the dependency and automatically pass the value for C from instruction K directly to instruction $K + 1$. That is, a copy of the output from the ALU in instruction K is forwarded directly to the input of the ALU in instruction $K + 1$. As a result, instructions continue to fill the pipeline, and no stall occurs.

5.18 Types Of Operations

When computer architects discuss instruction sets, they divide the instructions into a few basic categories. Figure 5.8 lists one possible division.

- Integer arithmetic instructions

- Floating point arithmetic instructions

- Logical instructions (also called Boolean operations)

- Data access and transfer instructions

- Conditional and unconditional branch instructions

- Processor control instructions

- Graphics instructions

Figure 5.8 An example list of instruction categories; a general-purpose processor includes instructions in all the categories.

5.19 Program Counter, Fetch-Execute, And Branching

Recall from Chapter 4 that every processor implements a basic fetch-execute cycle. During the cycle, control hardware in the processor automatically moves through instructions — once it finishes executing one instruction, the processor automatically moves past the current instruction in memory before fetching the next instruction. To implement moving through instructions, the processor uses a special-purpose hardware register known as an *instruction pointer* or *program counter*†.

When a fetch-execute cycle begins, the program counter contains the memory address of the instruction to be executed. After an instruction has been fetched, the program counter must be updated to the address of the next instruction, which means that when it finishes executing the current instruction, the processor automatically moves to the next successive instruction in memory. Algorithm 5.1 specifies how the fetch-execute cycle moves through successive instructions.

The algorithm allows us to understand branch instructions. There are two cases: absolute and relative. An *absolute branch* computes a memory address, and the address specifies the location of the next instruction to execute. Some instruction sets use the term *jump instruction* to refer to an absolute branch. During the execution step of a jump instruction, the processor loads a new value into the internal register *A* that Algorithm 5.1 describes. At the end of the fetch-execute cycle, the hardware copies the value into the program counter, which means the processor will use the new address as the location from which to fetch the next instruction. For example, the absolute branch instruction:

jump 0x05DE

causes the processor to load *0x05DE* into the internal address register, which is copied into the program counter before the next instruction is fetched. In other words, the next instruction fetch will occur at memory location *0x05DE*.

---

†The two terms are equivalent.

Algorithm 5.1

Assign the program counter an initial program address. Repeat forever {

   Fetch: access the next step of the program from the location given by the program counter.

   Set an internal address register, A, to the address beyond the instruction that was just fetched.

   Execute: Perform the step of the program.

   Copy the contents of address register A to the program counter.

}

Algorithm 5.1 The Fetch-Execute Cycle

Unlike an absolute branch instruction, a *relative branch instruction* does not specify an exact memory address. Instead, a relative branch computes a positive or negative increment for the program counter. For example, the instruction:

```
br +8
```

specifies branching to a location that is eight bytes beyond the current location (i.e., beyond the current value of the program counter).

To implement relative branching, a processor adds the operand in the branch instruction to the program counter, and places the result in internal address register *A*. For example, a relative branch operand *–12* means the next instruction the processor will execute will be at an address twelve bytes *before* the current instruction. A compiler might use a relative branch to implement a loop.

5.20 Condition Codes And Conditional Branching

A computer program does not always execute the same set of instructions. Instead, the computation depends on the input data. For example, a program may perform one series of steps when given a positive integer as input and another series of steps when given a negative integer. We say that a processor implements *conditional execution*. To allow a program to select among alternative computations, a processor offers a *con-*

ditional branch instruction. Unlike a normal branch instruction that always makes the processor start executing instructions at a new location, a conditional branch instruction uses current conditions to decide whether to branch to the new location or allow the processor to ignore the branch and continue with the next instruction in memory.

The hardware mechanism that provides the basis for conditional branching consists of a special-purpose, internal hardware register that holds a set of *condition codes*. The idea is straightforward: when an instruction performs a computation, the hardware produces two values: the result of the computation, and a status. An operand in the instruction specifies where to store the result of the computation (usually, a register); the processor sets condition code bits to record the status.

The easiest status values to understand arise from arithmetic instructions. When it performs an arithmetic operation, the ALU sets condition code bits to specify whether the result of the computation is positive, negative, zero, or an arithmetic overflow has occurred. A *conditional branch* instruction that follows the arithmetic operation can test one or more of the condition code bits, and use the test to determine whether to branch.

As an example of using condition codes, consider a program that performs an addition and then branches to the memory location given by *lab1* if the result of the addition is nonzero†. Figure 5.9 shows that the addition and conditional branch only require two instructions. The first instruction adds the contents of register *2* plus the contents of register *4*, and places the result in register *6*.

```
add    r2, r4, r6   # perform addition and set the condition code bits
bnz    lab1         # branch to lab1 if condition code bits specify nonzero
          ← the instruction here will be executed if the result is zero

   . . .

lab1:    ← the instruction here will be executed if the result is nonzero
```

Figure 5.9 An example of a conditional branch using condition code bits. The ALU sets the condition code bits when it executes the *add* instruction; the conditional branch instruction tests them.

5.21 Subroutine And Function Calls

High-level languages offer programming constructs that allow a program to invoke a subroutine, allow the subroutine to execute, and then allow control to return to the calling program. We say that a program *calls* a subroutine, and the subroutine *returns* to the caller. Programming languages use various terms for subroutines, including *subprograms*, *functions*, and *methods*.

Processors use specialized forms of branch instructions to invoke subroutines. Unlike a normal branch instruction, an instruction used to implement a subroutine call must save the address of the caller before branching to the subroutine. When it "re-

†Chapter 7 explains how a compiler uses conditional branching to implement loops and other constructs from high-level programming languages.

turns" to the caller, the subroutine extracts the saved address and branches to it. In fact, the processor saves the address of the instruction *following* the instruction used to invoke the subroutine. Thus, when control "returns" to the caller, the processor branches to the instruction *following* the call, and execution continues from there.

How does a processor implement a subroutine call? Although details vary among processors, two general approaches have been used. In each case, the processor includes a special instruction to call a subroutine. The difference lies in where the instruction saves the return address:

- The subroutine call instruction pushes the return address on the stack
- The subroutine call instruction saves the return address in a register

Early computers pushed the return address on the stack in memory. In assembly language, subroutine call instructions that push the return address on the stack often have names *jsr* (*jump to subroutine* or *call*). Because accessing memory takes more time than accessing a register, saving the return address in a register results in higher performance. In particular, in a processor that employs a pipeline, saving the return address in a register avoids unnecessary pipeline stalls. Consequently, processors that use an instruction pipeline save the return address in a register, and often use the name *bl* (*branch and link*) for the instruction that makes a subroutine call. For example, Arm architecture designates one of the general-purpose registers to be a *link register*, and uses the register to hold the return address during a subroutine call.

In terms of how a processor computes the return address when executing an instruction that calls a subroutine, Algorithm 5.1 explains that the return address does not require additional computation†. According to the algorithm, the hardware always computes the address of the next instruction beyond the instruction being executed. The processor saves the address in an internal register, *A*. When it executes an instruction that calls a subroutine, saving a return address only requires the processor to save the current contents of internal register A.

5.22 Argument Passing And Return Values

High-level languages offer *parameterized* subroutines. When it makes a function call or method invocation, the calling code supplies a set of *arguments*. We say that the caller *passes* arguments to the subroutine. In addition, many high-level languages provide a way for a subroutine to return one or more *result* values to the caller.

One of the principal differences among computer architectures arises from the way the underlying hardware passes arguments to a subroutine. We use the term *calling sequence* to describe the steps taken when calling a subroutine. On some architectures, the calling sequence uses the stack in memory for arguments — the calling program pushes arguments on the stack before the call, and the subroutine code extracts the values from the stack when the arguments are referenced. In other architectures, the calling sequence specifies that arguments must be placed in registers. Although some

---

†Algorithm 5.1 can be found on page 85.

early architects used special-purpose hardware registers, using general-purpose registers has become more popular†.

Using registers to pass arguments makes argument references much faster than using a stack in memory. Unfortunately, general-purpose registers cannot be devoted exclusively to argument passing because other computation also uses registers (e.g., to hold operands for arithmetic operations). If a register already contains a value that will be needed, the value must be saved (e.g., on the stack in memory) before the register can be used to hold an argument. Thus, an architect faces a tradeoff. On the one hand, using general-purpose registers to pass arguments can increase the speed of a subroutine call, but on the other hand, using general-purpose registers to hold the data values needed for computation can increase the speed with which the computation can be performed. The ARM architecture offers an interesting compromise: a caller places the first three arguments passed to a subroutine in general-purpose registers, and then pushes additional arguments into the stack in memory. The compromise works well because many subroutines have fewer than four arguments.

5.23 An Example Instruction Set

An example instruction set will help clarify the concepts described above. We have selected the MIPS processor as an example for two reasons. First, the MIPS instruction set is small and easily understood. Second, the MIPS instruction set includes sufficient instructions to illustrate important concepts. Figure 5.10 lists the instructions in the MIPS instruction set.

A MIPS processor contains thirty-two general-purpose registers, and most instructions require the operands and results to be in registers. For example, the *add* instruction takes three operands that are registers: the instruction adds the contents of the first two registers and places the result in the third.

In addition to the integer instructions that are listed in Figure 5.10, the MIPS architecture defines a set of floating point instructions for both single-precision (i.e., thirty-two-bit) and double-precision (i.e., sixty-four-bit) floating point values. The hardware provides a set of thirty-two floating point registers. Although they are numbered from zero to thirty-one, the floating point registers are completely independent of the general-purpose registers.

To handle double-precision values, the floating point registers operate as pairs. That is, only an even-numbered floating point register can be specified as an operand or target in a floating point instruction — the hardware uses the specified register plus the next odd-numbered register as a combined storage unit to hold a double-precision value. Figure 5.11 summarizes the MIPS floating point instruction set.

---

†Appendices 2 and 3 illustrate the difference. Appendix 2 describes the calling sequence used with an x86 architecture, and Appendix 3 explains how an ARM architecture passes some arguments in registers.

Instruction	Meaning
Arithmetic	
add	integer addition
subtract	integer subtraction
add immediate	integer addition (register + constant)
add unsigned	unsigned integer addition
subtract unsigned	unsigned integer subtraction
add immediate unsigned	unsigned addition with a constant
move from coprocessor	access coprocessor register
multiply	integer multiplication
multiply unsigned	unsigned integer multiplication
divide	integer division
divide unsigned	unsigned integer division
move from Hi	access high-order register
move from Lo	access low-order register
Logical (Boolean)	
and	logical *and* (two registers)
or	logical *or* (two registers)
and immediate	*and* of register and constant
or immediate	*or* of register and constant
shift left logical	shift register left N bits
shift right logical	shift register right N bits
Data Transfer	
load word	load register from memory
store word	store register into memory
load upper immediate	place constant in upper sixteen bits of register
move from coproc. register	obtain a value from a coprocessor
Conditional Branch	
branch equal	branch if two registers equal
branch not equal	branch if two registers unequal
set on less than	compare two registers
set less than immediate	compare register and constant
set less than unsigned	compare unsigned registers
set less than immediate	compare unsigned register and constant
Unconditional Branch	
jump	go to target address
jump register	go to address in register
jump and link	procedure call

Figure 5.10 An example instruction set. The table lists the instructions offered by the MIPS processor.

Instruction	Meaning

Arithmetic

FP add	floating point addition
FP subtract	floating point subtraction
FP multiply	floating point multiplication
FP divide	floating point division
FP add double	double-precision addition
FP subtract double	double-precision subtraction
FP multiply double	double-precision multiplication
FP divide double	double-precision division

Data Transfer

load word coprocessor	load value into FP register
store word coprocessor	store FP register to memory

Conditional Branch

branch FP true	branch if FP condition is true
branch FP false	branch if FP condition is false
FP compare single	compare two FP registers
FP compare double	compare two double-precision values

Figure 5.11 Floating point (FP) instructions defined by the MIPS architecture; double-precision values occupy two consecutive registers.

5.24 The Principle Of Minimalism

It may seem that the instructions listed in Figure 5.10 are insufficient and that additional instructions are needed. For example, the MIPS architecture does not include an instruction that copies the contents of a register to another register, nor does the architecture include instructions that can add a value in memory to the contents of a register. The MIPS instruction set has two goals: speed and minimalism. First, the basic instruction set has been designed carefully to ensure high speed, especially when the processor uses a pipeline. Second, the instruction set is *minimalistic* — it contains the fewest possible instructions that handle standard computation.

Limiting the number of instructions forms a key piece of the design. To understand the motivation, recall that hardware must be iterated in space. Thus, each instruction will require a hardware circuit. Even when it is not in use, the circuit consumes standby power. Thus, minimalism is especially important for battery-operated devices, which explains why the processors chosen for smart phones and other portable devices use a minimalistic approach.

An interesting feature of the MIPS architecture, which has been used in other processors, helps achieve minimalism: fast access to the value zero. In the case of MIPS, register 0 provides the mechanism — the register is reserved and always contains the value zero. Thus, to test whether a register contains zero, the register can be compared to register zero. To copy a value from one register to another, an instruction can add 0 to the source register contents and place the result in the destination register.

5.25 The Principles Of Elegance And Orthogonality

In addition to the technical aspects of instruction sets discussed above, an architect must consider the aesthetic aspects of a design. In particular, an architect strives for *elegance*. Elegance relates to human perception: how does the instruction set appear to a programmer? How do instructions combine to handle common programming tasks? Are the instructions balanced (if the set includes *right-shift*, does it also include *left-shift*)? Elegance calls for subjective judgment. However, experience with a few instruction sets often helps engineers and programmers recognize and appreciate elegance.

Known as the principle of *orthogonality*, a second principle concentrates on eliminating unnecessary duplication and overlap among instructions. We say that an instruction set is *orthogonal* if each instruction performs a unique task. An orthogonal instruction set has an important advantage: because only one instruction performs a given computation, neither a programmer nor a compiler designer needs to choose among multiple instructions that perform the same task. Making such a choice can be difficult. One aspect focuses on performance: among the multiple instructions that handle a given task, which will perform better? Interestingly, the answer can depend on the model of the processor that implements a given architecture, the instructions that will be executed immediately before a given instruction in question, and the instructions that will be executed immediately after the instruction in question. To avoid such problems, architects have adopted orthogonality as a general principle of processor design. We can summarize:

> *The* principle of orthogonality *specifies that each instruction must perform a unique task without duplicating or overlapping the functionality of other instructions.*

5.26 Summary

Each processor defines an instruction set that consists of operations the processor supports; the set is chosen as a compromise between programmer convenience and hardware efficiency. In some processors, each instruction is the same size, and in other processors size varies among instructions.

Most processors include a small set of general-purpose registers that are high-speed storage mechanisms. To program using registers, one loads values from memory into registers, performs a computation, and stores the result from a register into memory. To optimize performance, a programmer leaves values that will be used again in registers. On some architectures, registers are divided into banks, and a programmer must ensure that the operands for each instruction come from separate banks.

Processors can be classified into two broad categories of CISC and RISC depending on whether they include many complex instructions or a minimal set of instructions. RISC architectures use an instruction pipeline to ensure that one instruction can complete on each clock cycle. Programmers can optimize performance by rearranging code to avoid pipeline stalls.

To implement conditional execution (e.g., an *if-then-else*), many processors rely on a condition code mechanism — an ALU instruction sets the condition code, and a later instruction (a conditional branch) tests the condition code.

EXERCISES

5.1   When debugging a program, a programmer uses a tool that allows them to show the contents of memory. When the programmer points the tool to a memory location that contains an instruction, the tool prints three hex values with labels:

OC=0x43 OP1=0xff00 OP2=0x0324

What do the labels abbreviate?

5.2   If the arithmetic hardware on a computer requires operands to be in separate banks, what instruction sequence will be needed to compute the following?

$$A \leftarrow B - C$$
$$Q \leftarrow A * C$$
$$W \leftarrow Q + A$$
$$Z \leftarrow W - Q$$

5.3   Assume you are designing an instruction set for a computer that will perform the Boolean operations *and*, *or*, *not*, and *exclusive or*. Assign opcodes and indicate the number of operands for each instruction. When your instructions are stored in memory, how many bits will be needed to hold the opcode?

5.4   If a computer can add, subtract, multiply, and divide 16-bit integers, 32-bit integers, 32-bit floating point values, and 64-bit floating point values, how many unique opcodes will be needed? (Hint: assume one opcode for each operation and each data size.)

5.5   A computer architect boasted that they were able to design a computer in which every instruction occupied exactly thirty-two bits. What is the advantage of such a design?

5.6   Classify the following as RISC or CISC instruction sets: the ARM architecture owned by ARM Limited, the SPARC architecture owned by Oracle Corporation, and the Intel Architecture owned by Intel Corporation.

5.7 Consider a pipeline of N stages in which stage *i* takes time t_i. Assuming no delay between stages, what is the total time (start to finish) that the pipeline will spend handling a single instruction?

5.8 Insert *nop* instructions in the following code to eliminate pipeline stalls (assume the pipeline illustrated in Figure 5.5).

```
loadi   r7, 10          # put 10 in register 7
loadi   r8, 15          # put 15 in register 8
loadi   r9, 20          # put 20 in register 9
addrr   r10, r7, r8     # add registers 7 8; put the result in register 10
movr    r12, r9         # copy register 9 to register 12
movr    r11, r7         # copy register 7 to register 11
addri   r14, r11, 27    # add 27 plus register 11; put the result in register 14
addrr   r13, r12, r11   # add registers 11 and 12; put the results in register 13
```

5.9 Consider an instruction set S that does not use the principle of orthogonality and a compiler that compiles a high-level language into S. If a vendor offers five processor models that implement S, might the compiler generate slightly different code for one model than another? Explain.

5.10 Some computers keep the instruction pointer in a general-purpose register. On such computers, what would happen if a program stores *0x8A00FF* into the register that holds the instruction pointer?

5.11 One instruction set had a single instruction named *bc* that handled all conditional branching. The first operand of the instruction specified a set of bits to test, and the second operand was an address for the branch. Explain how the instruction worked.

5.12 Using a high-level language, a programmer writes a function that takes a single integer argument and returns the absolute value of the argument. Suppose the compiler the programmer uses allows the programmer to choose whether to pass arguments on the stack or in registers. Which choice will result in higher performance. Explain.

5.13 A smart phone manufacturer decides to design a new processor, and one of the engineers working for the company suggests a list of 37 new instructions that could be added to the instruction set. The engineer claims that the new instructions will make apps run faster. What tradeoff must be considered before adding the new instructions?

Chapter Contents

6

Operand Addressing And Operand Types

6.1 Introduction

The previous chapter discusses processors and instruction sets. This chapter focuses on the operands that instructions use. It discusses the ways operands can be specified and the tradeoffs associated with each. We will see that the forms of operands human programmers favor may not result in high performance when implemented by hardware.

6.2 Zero-, One-, Two-, And Three-Address Designs

Recall that an instruction contains an opcode followed by zero or more operands. Also recall that the operation being performed dictates the number of operands needed. For example, an integer subtraction instruction needs at least two operands because subtraction involves two quantities. Similarly, a Boolean *not* instruction needs one operand because logical inversion only involves a single quantity. In the example MIPS instruction set in Chapter 5, each instruction includes an extra operand that specifies the location for the result of the instruction. Thus, in the MIPS instruction set, a subtraction instruction requires three operands: two that specify integer values to be subtracted and a third that specifies a location for the result.

What about the maximum number of operands? Most software engineers prefer an instruction set in which a given instruction can have as many operands as needed, analogous to creating functions in a high-level programming language, where each function can have as many arguments as needed. However, hardware designers do not favor such an approach. To understand why, recall that hardware is iterated in space. To allow the number of operands to vary among instructions means allowing variable length, which results in slower execution and more power consumption, as Chapter 5 explains.

It may seem that parallel hardware could overcome the inefficiency. Imagine, for example, parallel hardware units that each fetch one operand of an instruction. If an instruction has two operands, two units operate simultaneously; if an instruction has four operands, four units operate simultaneously. However, parallel hardware will consume more power, Thus, parallel hardware is not an attractive option in many cases.

Can an instruction set be designed without allowing arbitrary operands? If so, what is the smallest number of operands that can be useful for general computation? Early computers answered the question by using a scheme in which each instruction only had one operand. Later computers introduced instruction sets that limited each instruction to two or three operands. Surprisingly, computers have been created in which instructions have no operands in the instruction itself.

6.3 Zero Operands Per Instruction

An architecture in which instructions have no operands is known as a *0-address* architecture. How can an architecture allow instructions that do not specify any operands? The answer is that operands must be *implicit*. A 0-address architecture is also called a *stack architecture* because operands are kept on a stack in memory; an internal hardware register contains the address of the top of the stack, and when the processor executes an instruction, the stack address changes. For example, an *add* instruction extracts the two values on the top of the stack, adds them together, and places the result back on the stack. As exceptions to the 0-address rule, a *push* instruction that specifies pushing a value onto the stack and a *pop* instruction that removes the top value on the stack and places it into a memory location each have an operand that specifies a memory address. Figure 6.1 lists a sequence of instructions used to add seven to variable X.

The chief disadvantage of a stack architecture arises because it takes much longer to fetch operands from a stack in memory than from registers in the processor. A later section discusses the concept; for now, it is sufficient to understand that the computer industry has moved away from stack architectures.

```
push X
push 7
add
pop  X
```

Figure 6.1 An example of instructions used on a stack computer to add seven to a variable X. The architecture is known as a zero-address architecture because the operands for an instruction such as *add* are found on the stack.

6.4 One Operand Per Instruction

An architecture that limits each instruction to a single operand is classified as a *1-address* design. In essence, a 1-address design relies on an *implicit* operand for each instruction: a special register known as an *accumulator*†. The instruction contains one operand, and the processor uses the value in the accumulator as a second operand. Once the operation has been performed, the processor places the result back in the accumulator. We think of each instruction as operating on the value in the accumulator. For example, consider arithmetic operations. Suppose an addition instruction has operand *X*:

$$\text{add} \quad X$$

When it encounters the instruction, the processor performs the following operation:

$$\text{accumulator} \leftarrow \text{accumulator} + X$$

Of course, the instruction set for a 1-address processor must include instructions that allow a programmer to load a constant or the value from a memory location into the accumulator and store the current value of the accumulator into a memory location.

6.5 Two Operands Per Instruction

Although it works well for arithmetic-logic operations, a 1-address design does not allow instructions to specify two values. For example, consider copying a value from one memory location to another. A 1-address design requires two instructions that load the value into the accumulator then store the value in the new location; the design is especially inefficient for moving graphics objects in display memory.

To overcome the limitations of 1-address systems, designers invented processors that allow each instruction to have two addresses. The approach is known as a *2-address* architecture. With the 2-address approach, an operation can be applied to a specified value instead of merely to the accumulator. Thus, in a 2-address processor,

$$\text{add} \quad X \quad Y$$

specifies that the value of X is to be added to the current value of Y:

$$Y \leftarrow Y + X$$

Because it allows an instruction to specify two operands, a 2-address processor can offer data movement instructions that treat the operands as a *source* and *destination*. For example, a 2-address instruction can copy data directly from location Q to location R‡:

$$\text{move} \quad Q \quad R$$

---

†The general-purpose registers discussed in Chapter 5 can be considered an extension of the original accumulator concept.

‡Some architects reserve the term *2-address* for instructions in which both operands specify a memory location, and use the term *1 1/2-address* for situations where one operand is in memory and the other operand is in a register.

6.6 Three Operands Per Instruction

Although a 2-address design handles data movement, further enhancement is possible, especially for processors that have multiple general-purpose registers: allow each instruction to specify three operands. Unlike a 2-address design, the key motivation for a *3-address* architecture does not arise from operations that require three input values. Instead, the point is that the third operand can specify a destination. For example, an addition operation can specify two values to be added as well as a destination for the result:

$$\text{add} \quad X \quad Y \quad Z$$

specifies an assignment of:

$$Z \leftarrow X + Y$$

6.7 Operand Sources And Immediate Values

The discussion above focuses on the number of operands that each instruction can have without specifying the exact details of an operand. We know that an instruction has a bit field for each operand, but questions arise about how the bits are interpreted. How is each type of operand represented in an instruction? Do all operands use the same representation? What semantic meaning is given to a representation?

To understand the issue, observe that the data value used as an operand can be obtained in many ways. Figure 6.2 lists some of the possibilities for operands†.

Operand used as a source (item used in the operation)

- A signed constant in the instruction
- An unsigned constant in the instruction
- The contents of a general-purpose register
- The contents of a memory location

Operand used as a destination (location to hold the result)

- A general-purpose register
- A contiguous pair of general-purpose registers
- A memory location

Figure 6.2 Examples of items an operand can reference in a 3-address processor. A source operand specifies a value and a destination operand specifies a location.

---

†To increase performance, modern 3-address architectures often limit operands so that at most one of the operands in a given instruction refers to a location in memory; the other two operands must specify registers.

As the figure indicates, architectures often allow an operand to be a constant. That is, the processor interprets bits in the operand field to be a binary integer. Although the operand field is small, having a way to represent a constant value can be important because programs use small constants frequently (e.g., to increment a loop index by 1); encoding a constant in the instruction is faster and requires fewer registers.

We use the term *immediate value* to refer to an operand that is a constant. Some architectures interpret immediate values as signed, some interpret them as unsigned, and others allow a programmer to specify whether the value is signed or unsigned.

6.8 The Von Neumann Bottleneck

Recall that conventional computers employ a *Von Neumann Architecture* which means the computer stores both programs and data in memory. Operand addressing exposes the central weakness of a Von Neumann Architecture: memory access can become a bottleneck. Because instructions reside in memory, a processor must make at least one memory reference per instruction. If one or more operands reside in memory, the processor must make additional memory references to fetch or store values. To optimize performance and avoid waiting for memory accesses, instructions must be designed to access operands in registers instead of memory.

The point is:

> *On a computer that follows the Von Neumann Architecture, the time spent accessing memory can limit the overall performance. Architects use the term* Von Neumann bottleneck *to characterize the situation, and avoid the bottleneck by choosing designs that access operands in registers.*

6.9 Implicit And Explicit Operand Encoding

How should an operand be represented in an instruction? The instruction contains a bit field for each operand, and an architect must specify exactly what the bits mean (e.g., whether they contain an immediate value, the number of a register, or a memory address). Computer architects have used two ways to represent operands: *implicit* and *explicit*. The next sections describe each of the approaches.

6.9.1 Implicit Operand Encoding

An *implicit operand encoding* is easiest to understand: the opcode specifies the types of operands. That is, a processor that uses implicit encoding contains multiple opcodes for a given operation — each opcode corresponds to one possible combination of operands. For example, Figure 6.3 lists three instructions for addition that each specify the types of the operands.

Opcode	Operands	Meaning
Add register	R1 R2	R1 ← R1 + R2
Add immediate signed	R1 I	R1 ← R1 + I
Add immediate unsigned	R1 UI	R1 ← R1 + UI
Add memory	R1 M	R1 ← R1 + memory[M]

Figure 6.3 An example of addition instructions for a 2-address processor that uses implicit operand encoding. Each combination of operands requires its own opcode.

As the figure illustrates, not all operands need to have the same interpretation. For example, consider the *add immediate signed* instruction. The instruction takes two operands: the first operand is interpreted to be a register number, and the second is interpreted to be a signed integer (i.e., an immediate value).

6.9.2 Explicit Operand Encoding

Figure 6.3 highlights the chief disadvantage of implicit encoding: multiple opcodes for a given operation. In fact, implicit encoding requires a unique opcode for each combination of operands. If an instruction set includes many operand types, the set of opcodes can become extremely large. As an alternative, an *explicit operand encoding* associates type information with each operand. Figure 6.4 illustrates the format of two *add* instructions for an architecture that uses explicit operand encoding.

opcode	operand 1		operand 2	
add	register	1	register	2

opcode	operand 1		operand 2	
add	register	1	signed integer	−93

Figure 6.4 Examples of operands on an architecture that uses explicit encoding. Each operand specifies a type as well as a value.

As the figure shows, each operand field contains two subfields: the first specifies the type of the operand and the second specifies a value. For example, an operand that references a register begins with a type field that specifies that the remaining bits must be interpreted as a register number.

6.10 Operands That Combine Multiple Values

The discussion above implies that each operand consists of a single value extracted from a register, memory, or the instruction itself. Some processors do indeed restrict each operand to a single value. However, other processors provide hardware that can compute an operand value by extracting and combining values from multiple sources. Typically, the hardware computes a sum of several values.

An example will help clarify how hardware handles operands composed of multiple values. One approach is known as a *register-offset* mechanism. The idea is straightforward: instead of two subfields that specify a type and value, each operand consists of three fields. The first specifies the type *register-offset*, the second contains a *register* number, and the third contains an *offset*. When it creates the operand value, the processor adds the contents of the offset field to the contents of the specified register, and then uses the result as the operand. That is, the hardware performs an extra addition in the step that fetches the operand. Figure 6.5 shows an example subtraction instruction with register-offset operands.

opcode	operand 1			operand 2		
sub	register-offset	2	−17	register-offset	4	76

Figure 6.5 An example of an *add* instruction in which each operand consists of a register plus an offset. During operand fetch, the hardware adds the offset to the specified register to obtain the value of the operand.

In the figure, the first operand specifies the contents of register 2 plus the constant −17, and the second operand specifies the contents of register 4 plus the constant 76. When we discuss memory, we will see that allowing an operand to specify a register plus an offset is especially useful when referencing a data aggregate such as a C language *struct* because a pointer to the structure can be left in a register and offsets used to reference individual items.

6.11 Tradeoffs In The Choice Of Operands

The discussion above seems unsatisfying — it lists many design possibilities but does not state which has been the most successful. Although each design has been used, none is considered best. Why hasn't one particular form of operand emerged as optimal? The answer is simple: each form represents a tradeoff among multiple design goals. The next paragraphs explain how design goals relate to the choice of operands.

Ease Of Programming. Complex forms of operands make programming easier. For example, allowing an operand to specify a register plus an offset makes data aggregate references efficient. Similarly, a 3-address approach that provides an explicit target means a programmer does not need an extra instruction to copy results into a final destination. Of course, to optimize ease of programming, an architect needs to trade off other aspects.

Fewer Instructions. Increasing the expressive power of operands reduces the number of instructions in a program. For example, allowing an operand to specify both a register and an offset means that the programmer does not need to insert an extra instruction to add an offset to a register. Increasing the number of addresses per instruction also lowers the count of instructions (e.g., a 3-address processor requires fewer instructions than a 2-address processor). Unfortunately, fewer instructions produce a tradeoff in which each instruction is larger.

Smaller Instruction Size. Limiting the number of operands, the set of operands types, and the maximum size of an operand keeps each instruction small because fewer bits are needed to identify the operand type or represent an operand value. In particular, an operand that specifies only a register will be smaller than an operand that specifies a register and an offset. As a result, some of the smallest, least powerful processors limit operands to registers — except for *load* and *store* operations, each value used in a program must come from a register. Unfortunately, making each instruction smaller decreases the expressive power, and therefore increases the number of instructions needed.

Larger Range Of Immediate Values. Recall from Chapter 3 that a string of k bits can hold 2^k possible values. Thus, the number of bits allocated to an operand determines the numeric range of immediate values that can be specified. Increasing the range of immediate values results in larger instructions.

Faster Operand Fetch And Decode. Limiting the number of operands and the possible types of each operand allows hardware to operate faster. For example, restricting each operand to be a register number allows hardware to operate faster than more complex operand forms.

Decreased Hardware Size And Complexity. Recall that the power a processor consumes depends on the number of transistors. Decoding complex forms of operands requires more power because it requires more hardware than decoding simpler forms. Consequently, limiting the complexity of operands helps reduce power consumption. As a tradeoff, programs become larger.

The point is:

> *Processor architects have created a variety of operand types. No single form is optimal for all processors because the choice represents a compromise among functionality, program size, complexity of the hardware required to fetch values, performance, and ease of programming.*

6.12 Direct And Indirect Operands In Memory

A processor must provide a way to access values in memory. A least one instruction must have an operand that the processor interprets as a memory address. When an operand specifies a location in memory, we say that the memory access is *direct*. Some processors extend memory references by permitting various forms of *indirection*. For example, an operand that specifies indirection through register 6 causes a processor to perform two steps:

- Obtain A, the current value from register 6
- Interpret A as a memory address, and fetch the operand from memory

Another form of operand indirection (sometimes called *double indirection*) uses two memory locations. The processor first computes a memory address M. Instead of merely loading or storing a value at address M, the processor assumes M contains a pointer to the value (i.e., the memory address of the value). In such cases, a processor performs the following steps:

- Obtain M, the value in the operand itself
- Interpret M as a memory address, and fetch the value A from memory location M
- Interpret A as another memory address, and fetch the operand from memory at location A

Such indirection allows an instruction to follow a linked list in memory. However, extra indirection imposes high performance cost because interpreting a single operand entails multiple memory references. Modern processors tend to avoid indirection and instead require a sequence of two instructions to follow an indirect reference.

6.13 Illustration Of Operand Addressing Modes

A processor usually contains a special internal hardware register, called an *instruction register*, that is used to hold an instruction while the instruction is being decoded. The possible types of operand addresses and the cost of each can be envisioned by considering the location of the operand and the references needed to fetch the value. An immediate value is the least expensive because the value is located in the instruction register (i.e., in the instruction itself). A general-purpose register reference is slightly more expensive than an immediate value. A reference to memory is more expensive than a reference to a register. Finally, double indirection, which requires two memory references, is the most expensive. Figure 6.6 lists the possibilities, and illustrates the hardware units involved in resolving each. A compiler or a human programmer must remain aware of performance costs when choosing operand types.

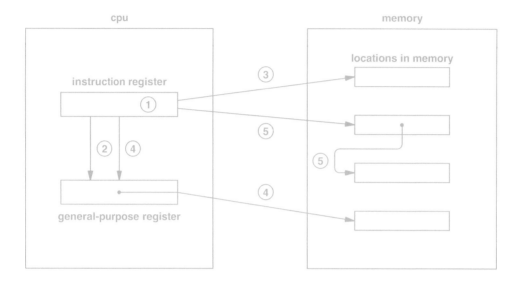

Figure 6.6 Illustration of the hardware units accessed when fetching an operand in various addressing modes. Indirect references take longer than direct references.

In the figure, modes 3 and 5 each require the instruction to contain a memory address. Although they were available on earlier computers, such modes have become unpopular because they require an instruction to be quite large.

6.14 Summary

When designing a processor, an architect chooses the number of operands and the operand types for each instruction. To make operand handling efficient, many processors limit the number of operands for a given instruction to three or fewer.

An immediate operand specifies a constant value; other possibilities include an operand that specifies using the contents of a register or a value in memory. Indirection allows a register to contain the memory address of the operand. Double indirection means the operand specifies a memory address and the value at the address is a pointer to another memory location that holds the value. The type of the operand can be encoded implicitly (i.e., in the opcode) or explicitly.

Many variations exist. The choice of operand number and type represents a trade-off among functionality, ease of programming, and engineering details such as the speed of processing.

EXERCISES

6.1 Suppose a computer architect is designing a processor for a computer that has an extremely slow memory. Would the architect choose a zero-address architecture? Why or why not?

6.2 Consider the size of instructions in memory. If an instruction set uses a six-bit opcode, uses a three-address architecture, and allows each immediate operand value to be sixty-four bits, how many bytes will an instruction occupy in memory? Why?

6.3 Assume a stack machine keeps the stack in memory. Also assume variable p is stored in memory. How many memory references will be needed to increment p by seven?

6.4 Assume two integers, x and y, are stored in memory, and consider an instruction that sets z in memory to the sum of $x+y$. How many memory references will be needed on a two-address architecture? Hint: remember to include instruction fetch.

6.5 How many memory operations are required to perform an *add* operation on a 3-address architecture if each operand specifies an indirect memory reference?

6.6 If a programmer increments a variable by a value that is greater than the maximum immediate operand, an optimizing compiler may generate two instructions. For example, on a computer that only allows immediate values of 127 or less, incrementing variable x by 140 results in the sequence:

```
load  r7, x
add_immediate  r7, 127
add_immediate  r7, 13
store  r7, x
```

Why doesn't the compiler store the constant 140 in a memory location and add the value to register 7?

6.7 Assume a memory reference takes twelve times as long as a register reference, and assume a program executes N instructions on a 2-address architecture. Compare the running time of the program if all operands are in registers to the running time if all operands are in memory. Hint: instruction fetch requires a memory operation.

6.8 Consider each type of operand that Figure 6.6 illustrates, and make a table that contains an expression for the number of bits required to represent the operand. Hint: the number of bits required to represent values from zero through N is:

$$\left\lfloor \log_2 N \right\rfloor$$

6.9   Name an advantage of a two-address architecture over a zero-address architecture.

6.10 Consider a two-address architecture that uses implicit operands. Suppose one of the two
          operands can be any of the five operand types in Figure 6.6, and the other can be any ex-
          cept an immediate value. List all the *add* instructions the computer needs.

6.11 Most compilers contain optimization modules that choose to keep frequently used variables
          in registers rather than writing them back to memory. What term characterizes the problem
          that such an optimization module is attempting to overcome?

Chapter Contents

7

Assembly Languages And Programming Paradigm

7.1 Introduction

Previous chapters describe processor instruction sets and operand addressing. This chapter discusses assembly languages used to specify instructions and operands. The chapter does not focus on the assembly language for a specific brand or model of processor. Instead, it provides a general discussion of how assembly language differs from high-level programming languages. Most important, it explains how assembly language implements common high-level language constructs, such as if-then-else and loops.

7.2 The Reason To Learn Assembly Language

Why should a software engineer learn about assembly language, and what should they learn? Early in the history of computers writing a program meant writing in assembly language. Once high-level languages had been invented, programming changed. Except for special cases, such as the low-level parts of an operating system and programs for the smallest embedded systems, programmers now write code in high-level languages and use compilers to translate the programs into assembly language.

If they do not write programs in assembly language, why should software engineers learn about it? The answer: understanding assembly language may be essential when debugging. On the one hand, if a compiler contains a flaw that causes the compiler to generate incorrect assembly code, a software engineer must examine the assembly code to identify the problem. On the other hand, even if a compiler translates a program into a correct sequence of assembly language instructions, the instructions may not have optimal performance. A software engineer cannot assess the reason for poor performance without examining the assembly code the compiler generates.

The point is:

> *Although software engineers do not usually write assembly code, understanding assembly language basics provides an important skill because reading the assembly language that a compiler generates may be the only way to find the source of errors or poor performance.*

7.3 Characteristics Of High-Level And Low-Level Languages

Programming languages can be divided into two broad categories: *high-level languages* and *low-level languages*. Assembly languages fit into the low-level category, and conventional programming languages, such as Python, Java, and C, fit into the high-level category. Figure 7.1 compares the properties of the two categories.

High-Level Language	Low-Level Language
One-to-many translation	One-to-one translation
Hardware independent	Hardware dependent
Application orientation	Systems orientation
General-purpose	Special purpose
Powerful abstractions	Few abstractions

Figure 7.1 A comparison of high-level and low-level programming language characteristics.

One-to-many vs. one-to-one translation. A compiler translates each statement in a high-level language into multiple machine instructions. An assembler translates each statement in an assembly language program into a single machine instruction.

Hardware independence vs. hardware dependence. A high-level language allows a software engineer to create a program without knowing most details of the underlying hardware. For example, a high-level language allows a programmer to specify addition of two variables without knowing the exact machine instruction that performs addition. Assembly language requires a programmer to know the instruction set and specify the exact instruction to use for the addition.

Application vs. systems orientation. A high-level language allows software engineers to create application programs. Assembly language provides direct access to all machine instructions, including those needed to build operating systems and low-level device drivers.

General-purpose language. special-purpose language. A high-level language makes it convenient for a software engineer to build arbitrary applications. Assembly language makes it difficult to build applications, but provides facilities needed for special-purpose system code.

Abstractions. A high-level language provides abstractions, such as functions (methods), that allow a software engineer to structure large and complex programs and express complex tasks succinctly. Assembly language provides almost no abstractions.

7.4 Assembly Languages

We use the term *assembly language* to describe a low-level language in which statements correspond to individual machine instructions. We use the term *assembler* for a piece of software that takes an assembly program as input and produces an output file with machine instructions in binary form.

It is important to understand that the term *assembly language* differs from names of programming languages (e.g., *Python* or *C*) because assembly language does not refer to a single language. Instead, a given assembly language defines statements for the instructions and operands from a single instruction set. Thus, many assembly languages exist, one for each instruction set. Consequently, software engineers might talk about an *ARM assembly language* or *Intel x86 assembly language*. To summarize:

> *Because a given assembly language defines statements for the instructions and operands of a specific instruction set, many assembly languages exist, one per instruction set.*

When a software engineer moves from a processor that uses one instruction set to a processor that uses another, the software engineer must learn a new language. The bad news: many details differ, including the names of instructions, the types of operands and the syntax used to express the types, and even the names of general-purpose registers. The good news: despite the differences, most assembly languages use the same basic approach. Therefore, once a programmer learns one assembly language, the programmer can learn others by mastering details rather than mastering new programming styles. More important, if a programmer understands the basic assembly language paradigm, they will be able to read the assembly language code that a compiler generates. The point is:

> *Despite their differences, many assembly languages follow the same fundamental approach. Consequently, a programmer who understands the assembly programming paradigm can learn a new assembly language quickly.*

To help programmers understand assembly language concepts, the next sections focus on general features and programming paradigms that apply to most assembly languages. In particular, sections describe how control statements in high-level languages translate into assembly language.

7.5 Assembly Language Syntax And Opcodes

7.5.1 Statement Format

Recall that each assembly language statement specifies a single machine instruction. In an assembly file, each line of input contains one statement. The line starts with an optional label, and contains an opcode and a set of operands separated by commas:

label: opcode   operand, operand, ...

The optional *label* gives a name to the statement that can be used for branching. The *opcode* specifies an instruction, and determines how many operands must follow; whitespace separates the opcode from other items. To make the code more readable, compilers and human programmers indent the opcode so that all opcodes align vertically. To further aid in readability, assemblers allow the label for a statement to appear on a separate line by itself before the statement.

7.5.2 Opcode Names

The assembly language for a given instruction set defines a symbolic name for each instruction. Although the symbolic names are intended to help a programmer remember the purpose of the instruction, most assembly languages use extremely short abbreviations instead of long names. Thus, a branch instruction might be assigned the opcode *br*.

Unfortunately, assembly languages do not agree on opcode abbreviations for common instructions. For example, an instruction that copies the contents of one register to another may have the opcode *mov* in one assembly language and the opcode *ld* in another†.

7.5.3 Commenting Conventions

Short opcodes tend to make assembly language easy to write but difficult to read. Furthermore, because it is a low-level language, assembly language tends to require many instructions to achieve a straightforward task. Thus, to ensure that assembly language programs remain readable, programmers add two types of comments: block comments that explain the purpose of each major section of code and a detailed comment on each individual line to explain the purpose of the line.

---

†Although some assembly languages use the name *mov* as an abbreviation for "move," the instruction merely makes a copy of the value and leaves the original unchanged.

To make it easy for programmers to add comments, assembly languages often allow comments to extend until the end of a line. That is, the language only defines a character (or sequence of characters) that starts a comment. One commercial assembly language defines the pound sign character (#) as the start of a comment, a second uses a semicolon to denote the start of a comment, and a third has adopted the C++ comment style and uses two adjacent slash characters. Human programmers often add additional characters to surround a block comment. For example, if a pound sign signals the start of a comment, the block comment below explains that a section of code searches a list to find a memory block of a given size:

```
###################################################################
#                                                                 #
#  Search linked list of free memory blocks to find a block  #
#  of size N bytes or greater.  A pointer to the list must   #
#  be in register 3, and N must be in register 4.  The code  #
#  destroys the contents of register 5, which is used to     #
#  walk the list.                                            #
#                                                                 #
###################################################################
```

Most programmers place a comment on each line of assembly code to explain how the instruction fits into the algorithm. For example, the code to search for a memory block might begin:

```
        ld      r5,r3     # load the address of list into r5
loop_1: cmp     r5,r0     # test to see if at end of list
        bz      notfnd    # if reached end of list go to label notfnd
        . . .
```

Although details in the example above may seem obscure, the point is relatively straightforward: a block comment before a section of code explains *what* the code accomplishes, and a comment on each line of code explains *how* that particular instruction contributes to the result.

7.6 Operand Order

One frustrating difference among assembly languages causes subtle problems for programmers who move from one assembly language to another: the order of operands. A given assembly language chooses a consistent operand order. For example, consider a load instruction that copies the contents of one register to another register. In the example code above, the first operand represents the *target* register (i.e., the register into which the value will be placed), and the second operand represents the *source* register (i.e., the register from which the value will be copied). Under such an interpretation, the statement:

```
        ld      r5,r3    # load the address of list into r5
```

copies the contents of register 3 into register 5. As a mnemonic aid to help them remember the right-to-left interpretation, programmers are told to think of an assignment statement in which the expression is on the right and the target of the assignment is on the left.

As an alternative to the example code, some assembly languages specify the opposite order — the source register is on the left and the target register is on the right. In such assembly languages, the code above is written with operands in the opposite order:

```
        ld      r3,r5    # load the address of list into r5
```

As a mnemonic aid to help them remember the left-to-right interpretation, programmers are told to think of a computer reading the instruction. Because text is read left to right, we can imagine the computer reading the opcode, picking up the first operand, and depositing the value in the second operand. Of course, the underlying hardware does not process the instruction left-to-right or right-to-left — the operand order is only a feature of the assembly language syntax.

Several other factors complicate operand ordering. First, unlike the examples above, many assembly language instructions have three operands, even if an instruction has two operands, the notions of source and destination may not apply (e.g., a comparison instruction). Therefore, someone reading assembly language may need to consult documentation to learn the meaning and order of operands for a given opcode.

Note that the order of operands in assembly language may differ from the order of operand fields in the binary form of an instruction. Basically, assembly languages choose notation convenient for a programmer to understand; an assembler may reorder operands during translation. For example, the author once worked on a computer that had two assembly languages, one created by the computer's vendor and another created by researchers at Bell Labs. Although both languages produced the same binary forms of instructions, one assembly language used a left-to-right interpretation of the operands, and the other used a right-to-left interpretation.

7.7 Register Names

Because many operands refer to registers, assembly languages tend to use short abbreviations for register names. Instead of names *register5* or *reg10*, an assembly language uses *r5* and *r10*. Unfortunately, short register abbreviations vary among assembly languages. In one assembly language, all register references begin with a dollar sign followed by digits (e.g., *$10* for register 10).

Some assemblers are more flexible regarding names: in addition to pre-defined names, the assembler allows a programmer to add their own definitions. To do so, a programmer inserts a series of declarations that define a specific name for each register. The chief advantage of allowing programmers to define register names arises from the ability to relate registers to their purpose in the program. For example, suppose a program manages a linked list. Instead of using numbers or names like *r6*, a programmer can give meaningful names to the registers.

```
#
#  Define register names for a linked list program
#
listhd   define  r6         # holds starting address of list
listptr  define  r7         # moves along the list
```

Although it can improve readability, choosing names for registers can also make programs more difficult to understand, modify, and debug. For example, if a programmer adds the above definitions to a program, someone reading code would need to remember that both *r6* and *listhd* refer to same register.

> *Because many operands refer to general-purpose registers, each assembly language provides short abbreviations for register names. Some assembly languages allow a programmer to assign a name to each register.*

7.8 Operand Syntax

As Chapter 6 explains, an instruction set may include multiple types of operands. The assembly language for the instruction set must include a syntax for each type. For example, suppose an instruction set allows an operand to specify an immediate value, the value in a register, or a value in a memory location where a register contains the address of the memory location. The assembly language needs a syntax for each type.

Many assembly languages interpret decimal strings as immediate constants. However, some assembly languages require a specific character (e.g., a dollar sign or pound sign) to denote a constant. In most assembly languages, using a register name as an operand means the contents of the register will be used as the operand value. Some assembly languages use parentheses around a register name to refer to an indirect memory reference. For example,

```
mov     r2,r1       # copy contents of reg. 1 into reg. 2
mov     r2,(r1)     # treat r1 as a pointer to memory and
                    # copy the item from memory to reg. 2
```

The point is:

> *An assembly language must provide a syntactic form for each possible operand type that the instruction set supports, such as a reference to a register, an immediate value, or an indirect reference to memory.*

7.9 Assembly Code For If-Then

High-level languages include an *if-then* construct to provide *conditional execution*; the body of the if-then may or may not be executed, depending on a specified condition. Because assembly language does not include an *if* statement, a compiler must generate a set of instructions that implement the functionality. Figure 7.2 shows how assembly language uses a conditional branch instruction to implement an if-then.

if (condition) {	code to test the condition and
body	set the condition code
}	branch to label if condition false
next statement;	code to perform body
	label: code for next statement
(a)	(b)

Figure 7.2 (a) Conditional execution as specified in a high-level language, and (b) the form of equivalent assembly language code.

As the figure shows, a compiler first generates code that tests the specified condition. It then generates a conditional branch instruction, code for the body, and a label for the code that follows the body. The conditional branch instruction takes the branch if the condition does *not* hold (i.e., the branch uses the inverse of the condition). For example, suppose a compiler receives the following input.

if (a == b) { x }

If we assume *a* has already been loaded into register five and *b* has been loaded into register six, a compiler might generate

```
        cmp     r5, r6      # compare the values of a and b and set cc
        bne     lab1        # branch if previous comparison not equal
        code for x . . .
lab1:   code for the next statement
```

7.10 Assembly Code For If-Then-Else

An *if-then-else* statement in a high-level language includes two sets of code, one to be executed if the specified condition is true, and the other to executed if the condition is false. Figure 7.3 shows how assembly language instructions implement if-then-else.

```
if (condition) {                    code to test the condition and
      then_part                         set the condition code
} else {                            branch to label1 if condition false
      else_part                     code to perform then_part
}                                   branch to label2
next statement;            label1:  code for else_part
                           label2:  code for next statement
```

          (a)   (b)

Figure 7.3 (a) An *if-then-else* statement in a high-level language, and (b) the
form of equivalent assembly language code.

As the figure shows, a compiler generates code to test the condition, a conditional
branch, code for the *then* part, an unconditional branch, a label and code for the *else*
part, and a label for the next instruction. The conditional branch instruction operates
similar to the conditional branch in Figure 7.2: it either falls through to the code for the
then part or branches to the code for the *else* part. Note that once the code for the *then*
part finishes, the compiler uses an unconditional branch to skip the *else* part and go on
to the next statement.

7.11 Assembly Code For Definite Iteration (For Loop)

High-level programming languages provide statements for *definite iteration*, which
means the program repeatedly executes a body of code a fixed number of times.
Languages typically use the keyword *for*, leading to the informal name *for loop*. Figure
7.4 shows how assembly instructions implement a for loop.

```
for (i=0; i<10; i++) {                   set r4 to zero
      body                      label1:  compare r4 to 10
}                                        branch to label2 if >=
next statement;                          code to perform body
                                         increment r4
                                         branch to label1
                            label2:      store r4 in variable i in memory
                                         code for next statement
```

          (a)   (b)

Figure 7.4 (a) A *for* statement used in a high-level language, and (b) the
form of assembly language code used to implement the loop.

7.12 Assembly Code For Indefinite Iteration (While Loop)

A high-level language offers *indefinite iteration* in which code is executed zero or more times, depending on a condition; software engineers use the informal term *while loop*. Figure 7.5 shows how assembly language instructions implement a while loop.

while (condition) {	label1: code to compute condition
body	branch to label2 if false
}	code to perform body
next statement;	branch to label1
	label2: code for next statement
(a)	(b)

Figure 7.5 (a) A *while* statement used in a high-level language, and (b) the form of assembly language code used to implement the loop.

7.13 Assembly Code For A Function Call

How does a compiler translate a function call into assembly language†? The answer has two parts. First, the processor vendor and/or the compiler designer define a set of *calling conventions* that specify the details of argument passing (e.g., whether the caller places arguments on the stack in memory or passes them in registers). Second, the instruction set includes an instruction that records the return address and makes the call (branches to the function). Figure 7.6 shows the general form of assembly instructions for a function and for two calls to the function.

The point is:

> *When reading the assembly language code for a function or a function call, one must know the calling conventions used by the processor and compiler as well as the instructions used to make the call and return.*

The figure omits one aspect of function invocation: a return value. As with argument passing, the exact details depend on the calling conventions. For example, the return value may be passed on the stack or in a register. In any case, the code generated for the calling function and the code generated for the called function must both adhere to the same calling conventions.

---

†Synonyms for *function call* include *subroutine call*, *procedure call*, and *method invocation*.

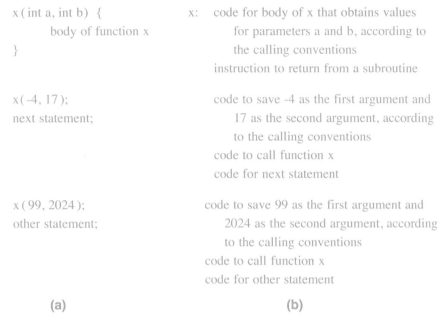

```
x ( int a, int b )  {              x:   code for body of x that obtains values
        body of function x                 for parameters a and b, according to
}                                          the calling conventions
                                        instruction to return from a subroutine

x ( -4, 17 );                           code to save -4 as the first argument and
next statement;                             17 as the second argument, according
                                            to the calling conventions
                                        code to call function x
                                        code for next statement

x ( 99, 2024 );                         code to save 99 as the first argument and
other statement;                            2024 as the second argument, according
                                            to the calling conventions
                                        code to call function x
                                        code for other statement
```

          (a)   (b)

Figure 7.6 (a) High-level language code for a declaration of function *x* and
two invocations of the function, and (b) the form of assembly
language a compiler generates when it translates the source code.

7.14 Variable Declarations In Assembly Code

In addition to statements that generate instructions, assembly languages permit a
programmer to define both initialized and uninitialized global data items. Data declarations use the same basic statement layout as an instruction. The label gives a name for
the data item, and in place of an opcode, the statement contains a *directive* that specifies
the size of the data item. For example, one assembly language uses the directive *.short*
to declare storage for a sixteen-bit item, and the directive *.long* to declare storage for a
thirty-two-bit item. An optional initial value follows the directive. Figure 7.7 shows
example declarations in a high-level language and the equivalent assembly code.

```
int     x = 139              x:    .long    139
int     y = 5000;            y:    .long    5000
int     z;                   z:    .long
                             w:    .short
short   w, q;                q:    .short

statement(s)                       code for statement(s)
```

          (a)   (b)

Figure 7.7 (a) Declaration of variables in a high-level language, and (b)
equivalent variable declarations in assembly language.

7.15 Example Assembly Language Code

An example will help clarify the concepts and show how items from a high-level language translate into assembly language. To compare assembly languages for x86 and ARM architectures, we will use the same example for both architectures. We begin with a small C program that illustrates a few basics: iteration and conditional execution. The example prints values from a *Fibonacci sequence*, where the first two values are each 1, and each successive value equals the sum of the preceding two values. Thus, the sequence begins 1, 1, 2, 3, 5, 8, 13, 21, 34.

7.15.1 The Fibonacci Example In C

Figure 7.8 shows a C program that generates and prints values in a Fibonacci sequence up to a limit. The program counts the number of Fibonacci values that are greater than 1000, and prints the count once the limit has been reached and the loop stops running. The code uses a trick to determine the limit: it assumes a two's complement computer and the loop keeps running until adding the two most recent Fibonacci values overflows the range of positive values in an *int*. When overflow occurs, the high-order bit of the integer will be set, the integer will be interpreted as negative, and the loop will terminate.

```
#include <stdlib.h>
#include <stdio.h>
#include <ctype.h>

int a = 1, b = 1, n, tmp;

void main(void) {

    n = 0;
    printf(" %10d\n", b);
    printf(" %10d\n", a);
    while ( (tmp = a + b) > 0 ) {
        b = a;
        a = tmp;
        if (a > 1000) {
            n++;
        }
        printf(" %10d\n", a);
    }

    printf("\nThe number of values greater than 1000 is %d\n", n);
    printf("Final values are: a=0x%08X b=0x%08X tmp=0x%08X\n",a,b,tmp);
    exit(0);
}
```

Figure 7.8 An example C program that computes and prints values in the Fibonacci sequence that fit into a thirty-two-bit signed integer.

The output begins as expected with lines containing 1, 1, 2, 3, 5, 8, 13, 21, 34, 55. Figure 7.9 shows the remaining lines of the output when the program runs on a 32-bit computer. Note that when the loop terminates, variable *tmp* has the hex value B11924E1, which means the high-order bit is set.

```
        55
        89
       144
       233
       377
       610
       987
      1597
      2584
      4181
      6765
     10946
     17711
     28657
     46368
     75025
    121393
    196418
    317811
    514229
    832040
   1346269
   2178309
   3524578
   5702887
   9227465
  14930352
  24157817
  39088169
  63245986
 102334155
 165580141
 267914296
 433494437
 701408733
1134903170
1836311903

The number of values greater than 1000 is 30
Final values are: a=0x6D73E55F b=0x43A53F82 tmp=0xB11924E1
```

Figure 7.9 The output that results from running the program in Figure 7.8.

7.15.2 The Fibonacci Example In x86 Assembly Language

Figure 7.10 shows x86 assembly code that generates the same output as the program in Figure 7.9. The code uses the gcc calling conventions to call *printf*.

```
        .data

a:      .long   1                   # initialized data (a and b)
b:      .long   1
        .comm   n,4,4               # uninitialized data (n and tmp)
        .comm   tmp,4,4

fmt1:   .string " %10d\n"
fmt2:   .string "\nThe number of values greater than 1000 is %d\n"
fmt3:   .string "Final values are: a=0x%08X b=0x%08X tmp=0x%08X\n"

        .text
        .globl  main
main:
        movl    $0, n               # n = 0

        movl    b, %esi             # set up args to print a
        movl    $fmt1, %edi
        movl    $0, %eax
        call    printf

        movl    a, %esi             # set up args to print b
        movl    $fmt1, %edi
        movl    $0, %eax
        call    printf

while:
        movl    a,%eax              # eax <- a
        addl    b,%eax              # eax <- eax + b
        movl    %eax,tmp            # tmp <- eax
        testl   %eax, %eax          # test eax
        jle     endwhile            # if <= 0 jump to endwhile

        movl    a, %eax             # eax <- a
        movl    %eax, b             # b <- eax
        movl    tmp, %eax           # eax <- tmp
        movl    %eax, a             # a <- eax

        cmpl    $1000, %eax         # compare 1000 to eax
        jle     endif               # if <= jump to endif
        movl    n, %ebx             # ebx <- n
        addl    $1, %ebx            # ebx <- ebx + 1
        movl    %ebx, n             # n <- ebx
```

```
endif:

        movl    a, %esi         # set up args to print a
        movl    $fmt1, %edi
        movl    $0, %eax
        call    printf
        jmp     while

endwhile:
        movl    n, %esi         # set up args to print n
        movl    $fmt2, %edi
        movl    $0, %eax
        call    printf

        movl    tmp, %ecx       # set up args to print a, b, and tmp
        movl    b, %edx
        movl    a, %esi
        movl    $fmt3, %edi
        movl    $0, %eax
        call    printf

        movl    $0, %edi        # exit with argument 0
        call    exit
```

Figure 7.10 An x86 assembly language program that implements the same functionality as the C program in Figure 7.8.

7.15.3 The Fibonacci Example In ARM Assembly Language

Figure 7.11 shows ARM assembly code that generates the same output as the x86 code in Figure 7.10. Neither the x86 nor the ARM code has been thoroughly optimized. In each case, instructions can be eliminated by keeping variables in registers. As an example, a small amount of optimization has been done for the ARM code: registers *r4* through *r8* are initialized to contain the addresses of variables *a*, *b*, *n*, *tmp*, and the format string *fmt1*. The registers remain unchanged while the program runs because called subprograms are required to save and restore values. Thus, when calling *printf* to print variable *a*, the code can use a single instruction to move the address of the format into the first argument register (*r0*):

$$mov \quad r0, r8$$

The code can also use a single instruction to load the value of *a* into the second argument register (*r1*):

$$ldr \quad r1, [r4]$$

Exercises suggest ways to improve the code.

```
        .text
        .align  4
        .global main
main:
        movw    r4, #:lower16:a         @ r4 <- &a
        movt    r4, #:upper16:a
        movw    r5, #:lower16:b         @ r5 <- &b
        movt    r5, #:upper16:b
        movw    r6, #:lower16:n         @ r6 <- &n
        movt    r6, #:upper16:n
        movw    r7, #:lower16:tmp       @ r7 <- &tmp
        movt    r7, #:upper16:tmp
        movw    r8, #:lower16:fmt1      @ r8 <- &fmt1
        movt    r8, #:upper16:fmt1

        mov     r0, #0
        str     r0, [r6]                @ n = 0

        ldr     r1, [r5]                @ r1 <- b
        mov     r0, r8                  @ r0 <- &fmt1
        bl      printf

        ldr     r1, [r4]                @ r1 <- a
        mov     r0, r8                  @ r0 <- &fmt1
        bl      printf

while:
        ldr     r3, [r4]                @ r3 <- a
        ldr     r2, [r5]                @ r2 <- b
        add     r1, r3, r2              @ r1 <- a + b
        str     r1, [r7]                @ tmp <- r1   (i.e., tmp <- a + b)
        cmp     r1, #0                  @ test tmp
        ble     endwhile                @ if tmp <= 0 go to endwhile

        str     r3, [r5]                @ b <- a
        str     r1, [r4]                @ a <- tmp

        cmp     r1, #1000               @ compare a and 1000
        ldrgt   r3, [r6]                @ if a>1000 r3 <- n
        addgt   r3, r3, #1              @ if a>1000 r3 <- r3 + 1
        strgt   r3, [r6]                @ if a>1000 n <- r3
        mov     r0, r8                  @ r0 <- &fmt1
        bl      printf                  @ r1 is still a

        b       while

endwhile:

        movw    r0, #:lower16:fmt2
```

```
         movt    r0, #:upper16:fmt2        @ r0 <- &fmt2
         ldr     r1, [r6]                  @ r1 <- n
         bl      printf

         ldr     r3, [r7]                  @ r3 <- tmp
         ldr     r2, [r5]                  @ r2 <- b
         ldr     r1, [r4]                  @ r1 <- a
         movw    r0, #:lower16:fmt3
         movt    r0, #:upper16:fmt3        @ r0 <- &fmt3
         bl      printf

         mov     r0, #0
         bl      exit                      @ exit with argument 0

         .align 4

         .comm   tmp,4,4                   @ uninitialized data
         .comm   n,4,4
         .data
         .align  4

b:       .word   1                         @ initialized data
a:       .word   1

fmt1:    .ascii  " %10d\012\000"
fmt2:    .ascii  "\012The number of values greater than 1000 is %d\012\000"
fmt3:    .ascii  "Final values are: a=0x%08X b=0x%08X tmp=0x%08X\012\000"
```

Figure 7.11 An ARM assembly language program that implements the same
functionality as the C program in Figure 7.8.

7.16 How An Assembler Works: Two-Pass Translation

Conceptually, an assembler performs the same task as a compiler. Each takes a source program as input and translates the program. However, a compiler has more freedom when choosing the translation. For example, a compiler can choose which values to keep in general-purpose registers at a given time, and can select among various sequences of instructions that handle a given computation. An assembler cannot make such choices because an assembly language program specifies all details. To summarize:

Although both a compiler and an assembler translate a program into a lower-level form, a compiler can choose which values to keep in registers and which sequence of instructions to use to implement the computation. An assembler merely provides a one-to-one translation of each statement in the source program to the equivalent binary form.

How does an assembler convert an assembly language program into a set of binary instructions? The assembler uses a *two-pass algorithm*, which means the assembler processes the source program two times. An assembler needs two passes before it can fill in the addresses in branch instructions. In particular, some branch instructions contain a *forward reference* to a label that has not yet appeared in the source file. When the assembler first reaches the statement, it cannot compute the address to which the instruction must branch. Therefore, during the first pass, the assembler does not generate code. Instead, it computes the number of bytes needed for each instruction and records the address that each label will have in the final program. It stores the information in a *symbol table*. During the second pass, the assembler generates code. If a branch instruction references a label, the label will either be in the symbol table along with its address (in which case the assembler can generate an instruction), or the program contains an error that prevents the assembler from completing the translation. Figure 7.12 illustrates the idea by showing a snippet of assembly language code and the relative locations assigned to each item during the first pass of assembly.

locations			assembly code		
0x00	–	0x03	x:	.long	
0x04	–	0x07	label1:	cmp	r1, r2
0x08	–	0x0B		bne	label2
0x0C	–	0x0F		jsr	label3
0x10	–	0x13	label2:	load	r3, 0
0x14	–	0x17		br	label4
0x18	–	0x1B	label3:	add	r5, 1
0x1C	–	0x1F		ret	
0x20	–	0x23	label4:	ld	r1, 1
0x24	–	0x27		ret	

Figure 7.12 A snippet of assembly language code and the addresses assigned to each item during the assembler's first pass.

To make two-pass processing possible, an assembly language must be designed carefully. In particular, it must be possible to compute the size of each instruction without filling in all the details. For example, the assembler must be able to compute the size of each branch instruction without knowing the address to which it will branch.

In the figure, the assembler knows that *label4* starts at location 0x20 (32 in decimal). During the second pass, the assembler can translate the branch to *label4* into the binary form with 0x20 as an immediate operand.

We can summarize:

> *To translate an assembly source program into binary instructions, an assembler makes two passes over the input. During the first pass, the assembler assigns a location to each instruction; during the second, the assembler generates code.*

Before the invention of assembly language, human programmers used binary to load instructions into a computer. A programmer had to perform assembly by hand, writing down instructions, counting how many bytes each occupied, and computing the addresses for branch instructions. Without an assembler to recompute addresses automatically, changing a program was tedious because a change required a programmer to recompute addresses by hand. Thus, the invention of assembly language and assemblers produced a significant advance in computing.

7.17 Assembly Language Macros

When human programmers wrote code in assembly language, the question arose of how to raise the level of the language. Programmers observed that they had to repeat sequences of instructions. As a first step toward higher-level languages, a *parameterized macro* facility was added to assemblers. The resulting language became known as *macro assembly*.

Similar to the C preprocessor, the macro facility in an assembler allows a programmer to insert a set of macro *definitions* and then invoke macros. Also similar to the C preprocessor, macro processing added an extra pass to the assembler that expands macro invocations before the normal first pass over the source program.

During the heyday of assembly language programming, macro facilities became quite sophisticated. The macro processor understood assembly language syntax, and could insert sequences of directives and instructions in a program. Programmers created libraries of macros to handle common tasks, such as walking along a linked list and performing a sequence of operations on each node. As computer programming moved to high-level languages, however, compilers generated assembly code, and interest in macro assembly languages faded. Now, many assembly languages use the C preprocessor or an equivalent to insert defined constants in assembly programs, but do not have an integrated macro facility.

7.18 Summary

Unlike a high-level language, each assembly language handles the instruction set, operand addressing modes, and hardware associated with a particular processor. Many assembly languages exist, one or more for each instruction set, and possibly for each model of a processor. A statement in an assembly language contains an optional label, an opcode, and zero or more operands. The statement corresponds to a single hardware instruction.

Assembly languages do not offer the same abstractions as high-level programming languages. Instead, abstractions such as conditional execution, iteration, and function invocation must be implemented with branch and conditional branch instructions.

An assembler is a piece of software that translates an assembly language source program into binary instructions that a processor can execute. Conceptually, an assembler makes two passes over the source program: one to assign addresses to items in the program and one to generate code. An assembler may include a macro facility to help programmers avoid tedious coding repetition. Because most human programmers use high-level languages, and because compilers do not need macros when they generate assembly code, interest in using an integrated macro facility has faded.

EXERCISES

7.1 State and explain the characteristics of a low-level assembly language.

7.2 A software engineer finds a piece of assembly language code that was written by a human, and remarks, "comments appear everywhere." Why would such a statement be made?

7.3 Look at the assembly language equivalent of an if-then-else statement. How many branch instructions will be performed if the condition is true? If the condition is false?

7.4 Show the form of assembly language that will be used to implement a *repeat-until* statement that executes a body of code and then repeatedly executes the body until a condition becomes true.

7.5 Write an assembly language function that takes two integer arguments, adds them, and returns the result. Test your function by calling it from C.

7.6 Write an assembly language program that declares four integer variables, assigns them values 10, 20, 30, and 40, and then calls printf to format and print the values.

7.7 Programmers sometimes mistakenly say *assembler language*. What have they confused, and what term should they use?

7.8 In Figure 7.12, if an instruction is inserted following label4 that jumps to label2, to what address will it jump? Will the address change if the new instruction is inserted before label1? Explain.

7.9 Look at the assembly code for the Fibonacci program in Figures 7.10 and 7.11. The code loads a value from a variable in memory whenever the value is needed. Choose one or the other, and rewrite the code to load values into registers, modify the values in the registers during the loop, and only write the values back to variables in memory after the loop runs.

7.10 Extend the previous exercise by compiling and running the code from the figure and your optimized version. How much faster does the optimized program run?

7.11 Compare the x86 and ARM versions of the Fibonacci program in Figures 7.10 and 7.11. Which version do you expect to require more instructions? Why?

7.12 Write a C function that takes one integer argument, uses a *while loop* to decrement the argument to zero, and returns. Compile the code in assembly language, and then identify the instructions that implement the while loop.

7.13 Write a C function that takes one integer argument, uses an if-then-else to set a temporary variable to -1 if the argument is negative and 1 otherwise. Return the temporary variable as the value of the function. Compile the code in assembly language, and then identify the instructions that implement the if-then-else.

7.14 When it translates a C program into assembly language, the assembly language program contains the same names for global variables and functions as the original C program contains. However, the code contains additional labels that the compiler generates. Explain why.

7.15 Use the -s option on gcc to generate assembly code for a C main program. For example, try the C program in Figure 7.8. How much extra code is generated beyond that needed for the statements in the program?

7.16 An assembly language macro can be defined that contains a sequence of instructions. Each time the macro is invoked, a copy of the instructions will be inserted into the program. To make the copies differ, the caller can specify values for defined constants and parameters that the macro uses. Thus, a macro invocation appears to be similar to a function call. Think carefully about the differences, and state the chief disadvantage of invoking a macro multiple times instead of calling a function multiple times.

Chapter Contents

8

Main Memory And Memory Addressing

8.1 Introduction

This chapter introduces one of the key topics of computer architecture: main memory. The chapter examines memory addresses and the concept of byte addressing. It describes the fetch-store paradigm, and explains how the underlying hardware organizes memory into words and provides a byte interface. Most important, the chapter describes consequences for software engineers. The next chapter expands the discussion to consider virtual memory.

8.2 Characteristics Of Computer Memory

Engineers use the term *Random Access Memory* (*RAM*) to denote the type of memory used as the primary memory system in most computers. RAM contains many locations that can each store an instruction or data. As the name implies, RAM allows a processor to access locations at random as opposed to sequentially. The processor can execute an instruction at one location and then branch to an arbitrary location, or can access data at a location and then access data at an arbitrary location. A processor can either fetch a copy of the bits in a location or store a new value to the location. Finally, current RAM technology is *volatile*, which means that values in RAM only persist as long as the memory hardware receives power. Once a computer is powered down, the values in RAM disappear. Thus, when a computer first starts, the memory does not contain any items from the previous time the computer was used.

8.3 Static And Dynamic RAM Technologies

Two basic technologies have been used to implement RAM: *Static RAM (SRAM†)* behaves as one might expect. At any time, the processor can write zeros and ones to bits in the memory. Once a value has been placed in the memory, the value stays in the memory as long as the memory stays powered on (i.e., as long as the computer stays powered on). Each bit in the memory consists of a miniature hardware unit that has three conceptual connections, as Figure 8.1 shows.

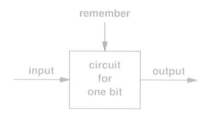

Figure 8.1 Illustration of a miniature SRAM circuit that stores one bit.

In the figure, the circuit has two inputs and one output. The output is either 1 or 0, and always has the last value stored into the bit. To change the value in the bit, hardware places the new value on the input connection, and temporarily sets the *remember* connection to 1, The circuit "remembers" whatever value was on the input connection, and the output changes accordingly. The hardware can then turn off the *remember* input (i.e., set it back to 0), and the circuit will ignore the input. Thus, to store a zero or one, the hardware places the value on the input, turns on the change enable line, and then turns the enable line off again.

Although it performs at high speed, SRAM has significant disadvantages: power consumption and heat generation. The power consumed by a circuit that stores an individual bit may seem trivial. However, a main memory can contain billions of bits.

Most computers use an alternative to SRAM, known as *DRAM‡ (Dynamic RAM)*, that consumes less power. The internal working of dynamic RAM is surprising and can be confusing. At the lowest level, to store information, DRAM uses a circuit that acts like a miniature rechargeable battery (or, if you understand electronic components, think of a capacitor). When a value is written to DRAM, the hardware charges or discharges the circuit to store a 1 or 0. Later, when a value is read from DRAM, the hardware examines the amount of charge that remains and reports whether it represents zero or one.

The surprising aspect of DRAM arises from the way the circuit works. Actually, the circuit doesn't work because it gradually loses its charge! In essence, a DRAM memory chip is an imperfect memory device — as time passes, the charge dissipates and a one becomes a zero. More important, DRAM loses its charge in a short time (e.g., in some cases, under a second).

†SRAM is pronounced "ess-ram."
‡DRAM is pronounced "dee-ram."

How can DRAM be used as a computer memory if values can quickly become zero? The answer lies in refresh. If one reads a value from DRAM before the charge has time to dissipate, the value will be correct. Writing the value back to DRAM refreshes the DRAM circuit (either by charging the circuit for a one or discharging the circuit for a zero). To keep the values correct, DRAM memory needs an extra hardware circuit, known as a *refresh circuit*, that performs the task of reading and then writing back each bit in memory repeatedly. Figure 8.2 illustrates the concept.

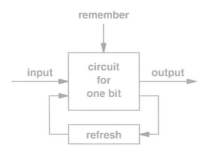

Figure 8.2 Illustration of a miniature DRAM circuit that stores one bit. An external refresh circuit must periodically read the data value and write it back again, or the charge will dissipate and the value will be lost.

In practice, a refresh circuit is more complex than the figure implies. To keep the refresh circuit small, architects do not build one refresh circuit for each bit. Instead, a single, small refresh mechanism is designed that can cycle through the entire memory. As it reaches a bit, the refresh circuit reads the bit, writes the value back, and then moves on. Complexity also arises because a refresh circuit must coordinate with normal memory operations. First, the refresh circuit must not interfere or delay normal memory operations. Second, the refresh circuit must ensure that a normal *write* operation does not change the bit between the time the refresh circuit reads the bit and the time the refresh circuit writes the same value back. Despite the need for a refresh circuit, the cost and power consumption advantages of DRAM are so beneficial that most computer memory uses DRAM rather than SRAM.

8.4 Memory Performance And Higher Data Rate Technologies

When they sell memory for computers and other digital devices, vendors do not merely sell DRAM. Instead, they sell variants of DRAM that give high performance. To understand performance, recall that a *clock* controls the digital circuits in the processor. Memory systems also use a clock to control exactly when a *read* or *write* operation begins. If the clocks in the processor and memory circuits do not agree, the processor may need to delay an extra clock cycle when it interacts with the memory hardware.

Although a single clock cycle may seem small, a delay on every memory operation accumulates, impacting performance.

To eliminate the delay, some memory technologies use a *synchronous* clock system in which the clocks running the processor and memory hardware are aligned. Consequently, a processor does not need to wait for memory references to complete. In
practice, synchronization has been effective; most computers now use synchronous
DRAM as the primary memory technology. To achieve higher speeds, many systems
run the clock for the memory system at a multiple of the processor clock rate (e.g., double or quadruple). Because the clock runs faster, the memory can deliver data faster.
The technologies are sometimes called *fast data rate* memories, typically *double data
rate* or *quadruple data rate*. Fast data rate memories have been successful, and are now
standard on most computer systems, including consumer smart systems, such as smart
phones and laptops.

Although we have covered highlights, our discussion of RAM memory technology
does not begin to illustrate the range of choices available to an architect or the detailed
differences among them. Some technologies optimize the time required to perform a
single memory operation, and others optimize the time required to perform a sequence
of memory operations, which is known as the *memory cycle time*. Figure 8.3 lists a few
commercially available RAM technologies:

Technology	Description
DDR-DRAM	Double Data Rate Dynamic RAM
DDR-SDRAM	Double Data Rate Synchronous Dynamic RAM
FCRAM	Fast Cycle RAM
FPM-DRAM	Fast Page Mode Dynamic RAM
QDR-DRAM	Quad Data Rate Dynamic RAM
QDR-SRAM	Quad Data Rate Static RAM
SDRAM	Synchronous Dynamic RAM
SSRAM	Synchronous Static RAM
ZBT-SRAM	Zero Bus Turnaround Static RAM
RDRAM	Rambus Dynamic RAM
RLDRAM	Reduced Latency Dynamic RAM

Figure 8.3 Examples of commercially available RAM technologies. Many
other technologies exist.

*A variety of memory technologies exist that optimize various aspects
of memory use. When choosing a technology, an architect considers
both the processor hardware and the expected ways memory will be
used.*

8.5 Memory Addresses For An Array Of Bytes

The description above focuses on the underlying memory hardware technologies that store bits. When they reference objects in memory, however, instructions cannot reference individual bits in the memory. Instead, memory appears to be an array of bytes. Each byte of memory is assigned an *address* starting at zero. We can think of an address as an unsigned integer that provides an index into the array of bytes. When an instruction references a byte in memory, an operand must supply the address of the byte. For a multi-byte object, such as an integer, the operand specifies the address of the lowest byte. For example, a four-byte integer will occupy contiguous bytes in memory, A, $A+1$, $A+2$, and $A+3$. An instruction that references the integer will use address A.

How many bits does a memory address require? In Chapter 3, we learned that an unsigned value of k bits can represent values from 0 through 2^k-1. On a 32-bit computer, a memory address occupies thirty-two bits (four bytes). Therefore, the computer cannot address more than 2^{32} bytes of memory, which is 4 Gigabytes or 4294967296 bytes. To accommodate larger memories, industry moved to a *64-bit computer* architecture in which each memory address occupies sixty-four bits (eight bytes). Using 64 bits for an address means a computer can have up to 17179869184 Gigabytes (18446744073709551616 bytes) of memory, more than any individual will ever need.

Increasing the size of memory addresses by one bit doubles the maximum memory size. Why would industry move from thirty-two bits to sixty-four bits instead of choosing a reasonable size, such as 40 or 48 bits? The answer lies in hardware. Remember that hardware is iterated in space. On a computer in which each general-purpose register holds thirty-two bits, the internal hardware units each contain thirty-two small hardware units that operate in parallel. Choosing 64-bit addresses means 32-bit hardware can be reused for an address: either a single 32-bit hardware unit can be used twice or two 32-bit hardware units can be used at the same time. For example, two adjacent 32-bit registers can be used to hold a 64-bit value, with half the value in each register†. The point is:

> *To accommodate memories of more than 4 Gigabytes, industry moved to using 64-bit memory addresses. Although much smaller addresses suffice for the foreseeable future, the choice allows 32-bit hardware units to be reused, such as two 32-bit registers used to hold a 64-bit address.*

8.6 The Fetch-Store Paradigm, Pointers, And Dereferencing

Memory hardware only supports two operations. An instruction can either *store* a value into a memory location or *fetch* the value last stored into the location. We use the term *fetch-store paradigm* to describe the hardware operations. We will learn later that a processor also uses the fetch-store paradigm to interact with I/O devices.

---

†Interestingly, Intel processors make each address sixty-four bits to accommodate hardware reuse, but

Recall that a compiler assigns a memory address to each variable in a program. When it generates code to store a value into a variable or obtain the value from a variable, the compiler inserts the address of the variable. When an instruction follows an address to a value in memory, we say that the instruction *dereferences* the address. High-level languages allow a programmer to declare variables that each hold a memory address. We use the term *pointer* to refer to such a variable, and say that the variable "points to" an object in memory.

In assembly language, all pointers are the same: a pointer is merely a memory address. Consequently, a pointer variable consists of contiguous bytes in memory sufficient to hold one memory address. Furthermore, performing an arithmetic operation on a pointer, such as incrementing the pointer, works exactly the same as performing the operation on an unsigned value. In a high-level language, however, each pointer has a *type* that specifies how the pointer will be used and how the compiler interprets operations. Specifically, the programmer must specify the type of the object that the pointer references. For example, the declarations

```
char    *p;
int     *q;
```

declare variable *p* to be a pointer to a character (i.e., a byte) and variable *q* to be a pointer to an integer.

From the hardware point of view, both *p* and *q* occupy the same number of bytes in memory, and they each hold an address of a byte in memory. So, how do *p* and *q* differ? The difference arises from the way the programming language interprets operations on the pointers and the code the compiler generates. First, to prevent unintended assignments, a compiler checks that the type of a value being assigned to a pointer matches the type of the pointer. Thus, a compiler will report an error if a programmer attempts to assign the address of a floating point variable to *p*. Second, the semantics of operations on the pointers depend on their type. Specifically, high-level languages implement *pointer arithmetic*, which means that incrementing a pointer increments the address by the number of bytes in the object to which it points. For example, if an integer occupies four bytes, a compiler will translate *q++* into code that increments the value of *q* by four.

The point is:

> *The hardware interprets each pointer variable to contain the address of a byte in memory and interprets arithmetic operations on a pointer to work as they work on any unsigned value. High-level languages impose a type on each pointer variable, and use the type to prevent unintended uses of the variable and to generate code that implements pointer arithmetic.*

8.7 Memory Dumps

An architecture that configures main memory to be an array of bytes offers an advantage for software engineers: at any time, a running program can observe the actual bits stored in arbitrary items in memory. If an error corrupts a data item, a software engineer can examine the values to help identify the source of the error. Furthermore, because the memory system does not understand whether the object being stored is an integer, a floating point number, a pointer (i.e., an address), an instruction, or a printable ASCII character, the bytes of an object can be accessed as if they are bytes in an array. Direct access to bytes can prove invaluable when debugging because the values in memory can be observed without performing operations that change the values (e.g., loading an integer into a register may reverse the bytes, depending on endianness).

Software engineers use the term *memory dump* to refer to output that shows the contents of successive locations in memory. Typically, a memory dump displays the hexadecimal value of each byte, which leads some engineers to call the output a *hex dump*.

A trivial example will help us understand a memory dump. The example assumes a 32-bit big-endian computer in which a memory address and an integer each occupy thirty-two bits (four bytes) of memory. To see the relationship between objects in a program and items in a memory dump, consider Figure 8.4, which shows a linked list of three nodes that each contain an integer value and a pointer to the next node on the list.

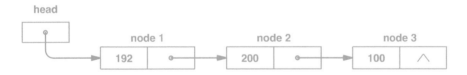

Figure 8.4 Example of a linked list. Each node contains a 32-bit integer and a 32-bit pointer to the next node on the list.

To define the shape of a node on the list in C, a programmer writes a *struct* declaration that contains two items:

```
struct  node  {
    int     value;
    struct node *next;
}
```

Similarly, a variable named *head* that serves as the head of the list is defined as:

```
struct  node  *head;
```

Because memory is an array of bytes, a node can be placed at any location†. Suppose the three nodes have been allocated in memory and linked together. The memory dump in Figure 8.5 shows one possible arrangement. Each line in the figure shows hex values for sixteen bytes of memory. For example, the first line shows bytes at addresses 0x0001bde0 though 0x0001bdef. The first node of the list starts at memory location 0x0001bdf8. In hexadecimal, the decimal integer 192 is 0x000000c0, and the address of the second node on the list is 0x0001be14. In hexadecimal, the value 200 in the second node, is 0x000000c8. The final node of the list starts at address 0x0001be00, and contains value 100 (0x00000064 in hex).

Address	Contents Of Memory			
0001bde0	00000000	0001bdf8	deadbeef	4420436f
0001bdf0	6d657200	0001be18	000000c0	0001be14
0001be00	00000064	00000000	00000000	00000002
0001be10	00000000	000000c8	0001be00	00000006

Figure 8.5 Illustration of a small portion of a memory dump that shows the hexadecimal values of sixty-four bytes in memory starting at address 0x0001bde0. Extra space has been inserted between groups of four bytes to improve readability.

In the figure, one group of four byes has the hexadecimal value 0xdeadbeef. To aid in debugging, programmers often initialize a region of memory to an unusual value before allocating linked lists or other objects. Using the value 0xdeadbeef makes it easy for a human to spot it in a hex dump.

Many memory dump programs include an extra field on each line that shows printable ASCII characters for the values in memory. If the memory holds readable strings, the extra field makes the dump easier to understand. The example memory dump in Figure 8.6 shows an area of memory that contains text.

Address	Contents Of Memory				Printable
00021190	54686973	20697320	61207374	72696e67	*This is a string*
000211a0	206f6620	7072696e	7461626c	65206368	* of printable ch*
000211b0	61726163	74657273	20616e64	20626c61	*aracters and bla*
000211c0	6e6b7320	666f6c6c	6f776564	20627920	*nks followed by *
000211d0	74686972	74792d74	776f2075	6e707269	*thirty-two unpri*
000211e0	6e746162	6c652062	79746573	203a2d29	*ntable bytes :-)*
000211f0	00010203	04050607	08090a0b	0c0d0e0f	*................*
00021200	10111213	14151617	18191a1b	1c1d1e1f	*................*

Figure 8.6 An example of a memory dump with an extra column showing the value for each printable character on the line. A period is used for each unprintable character.

---

†The next section considers *alignment* on address boundaries.

8.8 Aligned Memory Access And Aggregates In Memory

Although they treat memory as an array of bytes and use byte addressing, some computers require certain items to be *aligned* on specific memory boundaries. For example, an ARM architecture computer that uses 32-bit (i.e., 4-byte) integers may require that the starting memory address for each integer be a multiple of four. On such system, an integer may be stored at address 0x2fedc4 but not at address 0x2fedc5 because 0x2fedc4 (3141060 in decimal) is a multiple of four. If an instruction attempts to access an integer at an unaligned address, the instruction causes an *exception* similar to the way that attempting to divide by zero causes an exception. In addition to requiring that each integer be aligned, a computer that uses 32-bit instructions may also require each instruction to be aligned.

Even if a computer does not mandate alignment, the performance of memory operations may depend on where values are stored. For example, although the x86 architecture allows integers to start at arbitrary addresses, memory operations usually execute much faster if the values are aligned to multiples of four. Consequently, many compilers include alignment of items in memory as an optimization.

Two questions arise about aligning values in memory.

- Does a software engineer need to think about alignment, or does a compiler handle the alignment automatically?
- Why do some architectures mandate alignment, and why do others that allow unaligned access perform better when items are aligned?

In most cases, a compiler handles alignment automatically. However, a software engineer may need to be aware of alignment for two reasons: efficient use of memory and the format of data exchanged with other applications, especially when they run on other computers. Specifically, the way a compiler assigns memory locations to items in an aggregate data type depends on alignment. For example, Figure 8.7 shows a struct x that contains five items and the memory layouts for the struct when the items are unaligned and when they are aligned.

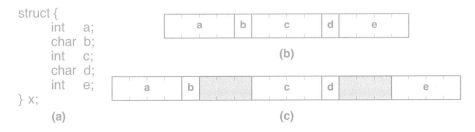

Figure 8.7 (a) A struct named x, (b) the memory layout for x when items are unaligned, and (c) the memory layout for x when items are aligned on a four-byte boundary.

The figure assumes that the struct begins on a 4-byte boundary, so the first integer, *a*, is aligned. If no further alignment is needed, *b* occupies a single byte, and integer *c* can follow *b* immediately. In the case where items must be aligned, a compiler inserts three bytes of *padding* after *b*, which aligns *c* on a 4-byte boundary. Similarly, the padding after *d* aligns *e* on a 4-byte boundary. The figure shows the padding in gray.

Suppose application *AL* has been compiled to use aligned integers. If application *AL* writes struct *x* into a file, the file will contain the padding. Similarly, if application *AL* transmits struct *x* over the Internet, the transmitted data will include the padding. Now suppose another application, *UL* has been compiled to use unaligned integers. If application *UL* reads struct *x* from the file that application *AL* wrote, the values will not be correct. Similarly, if application *UL* receives struct *x* over the Internet from application *AL*, the values will not be correct.

The point is:

> *Although compilers handle data alignment automatically, a software engineer may need to be aware of alignment when storing data in files that other applications read and when sending data over a computer network to another application.*

8.9 Ordering Items To Optimize Space With Aligned Access

Inserting padding to align items in memory wastes space, and the amount of waste can be significant. In Figure 8.7, for example, the aligned version of the struct takes over 40% more space than the unaligned version. The waste can become significant if a software engineer uses the struct as an element in a large array or as the layout of items written to a large file.

Fortunately, a technique exists that minimizes wasted space while still allowing a compiler to align memory access. More important, the technique provides an optimization that can avoid wasted space without any negative effect in the case where a compiler does not align access. To implement the optimization, a software engineer follows a straightforward rule for ordering items when declaring an aggregate data structure.

> *To avoid having a compiler leave wasted space in a data aggregate when aligning memory accesses, declare items in reverse order by the size of the item.*

For example, on a computer where each pointer takes 64 bits (8 bytes), each int takes 32 bits (4 bytes), each short takes 16 bits (2 bytes), and each char takes 8 bits (1 byte), following the rule means all pointers in a struct would appear first, then all ints, then all shorts, and finally all chars. Figure 8.8 illustrates how reordering items from Figure 8.7 reduces wasted space.

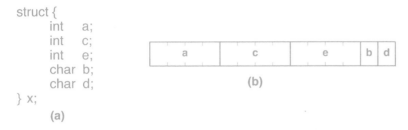

```
struct {
      int   a;
      int   c;
      int   e;
      char  b;
      char  d;
} x;
```

(a)

(b)

Figure 8.8 (a) The struct from Figure 8.7 with items reordered to reduce
wasted space, and (b) the memory layout, which is the same
whether items are aligned or unaligned.

As the figure shows, a compiler will not insert padding between items in the struct.
However, the resulting struct contains fourteen bytes, which is not a multiple of four
bytes. Therefore, if one declares an array of such structs, a compiler that enforces
alignment will pad each element of the array with two extra bytes to ensure alignment
of the next element.

8.10 Memory Organization And Aligned Memory Access

Why do some architectures mandate alignment, and why do others perform better
when accesses are aligned even though they allow unaligned access? The answer lies in
memory hardware. We used the term *memory organization* to describe the internal
structure of the memory hardware and the external addresses the memory hardware
presents to a processor. We will see why memory hardware favors aligned access.

Parallelism forms a key aspect of memory organization. A hardware unit known
as a *memory controller* provides an interface between the processor and the underlying
memory hardware†. To achieve high performance, the data path between the processor
and memory hardware consists of multiple wires that each can transfer one bit at any
time; the entire set of wires can be used to transfer multiple bits simultaneously. Figure
8.9 illustrates the conceptual organization.

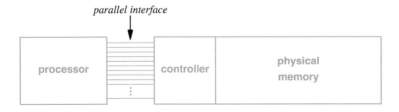

Figure 8.9 The conceptual interface between a processor and memory.

---

†Later chapters explain that I/O devices can also access memory through the memory controller; for now,
we will use a processor in the examples.

8.11 Memory Hardware, Words, And Word Operations

As Figure 8.9 illustrates, the memory hardware is iterated in space. Instead of accessing bits in memory sequentially, the hardware contains multiple units that work simultaneously to transfer multiple bits. The number of bits in the interface defines a *memory transfer size*. For example, if an architecture specifies that each instruction occupies thirty-two bits and each integer occupies thirty-two bits, many memory transfers will require thirty-two bits. Thus, if the data path between the processor and memory has thirty-two parallel wires, many memory accesses can be performed in one cycle.

To accommodate parallel memory transfers, the controller and underlying memory hardware must also support parallel operations. Conceptually, an architect chooses a *word size*, and organizes the underlying physical memory as a set of blocks that each hold one word. The hardware assigns each block a *word address*. Figure 8.10 illustrates the concept for a word size of four bytes (thirty-two bits).

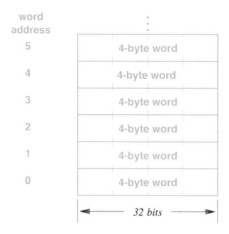

Figure 8.10 The conceptual organization of the underlying memory hardware as a set of words.

The figure makes memory appear to be an array. Furthermore, the hardware supports operations similar to an array — it is possible to store a 4-byte value into the ith word and to retrieve a 4-byte value from the ith word. However, it is important to understand that each element actually consists of a hardware unit that stores one word and responds to electrical signals that cause it to store a new value or retrieve the existing value. The hardware always operates in parallel: all bits of a word must be accessed (fetched or stored at the same time). The point is:

*The underlying memory hardware is organized into words, where the
word size is the same as the memory transfer size. Each fetch or
store operation accesses all bits of a word at the same time.*

8.12 Byte Addressing, Word Addressing, And Alignment

Understanding that memory hardware consists of units that each hold one word explains the motivation for alignment. On the one hand, the memory hardware presents
an array-of-bytes interface to instructions, and allows an instruction to reference an arbitrary byte address. On the other hand, the memory hardware can only access one word
at a time, and must translate each memory operation into one or more operations on
words. For example, if each word contains four bytes, word 0 will hold bytes 0, 1, 2,
and 3. Figure 8.11 illustrates byte addresses when the memory hardware uses a word
size of thirty-two bits.

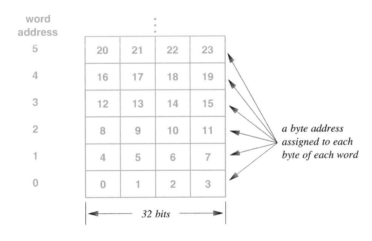

Figure 8.11 Example of a byte address assigned to each byte of each word in
a physical memory when a word contains four bytes.

Suppose an instruction tries to store a 4-byte integer in bytes 6 through 9. As the
figure shows, the bytes occupy areas in two separate words of memory. If the architecture mandates aligned memory accesses, the hardware will raise an exception when the
instruction runs. If the hardware does not mandate aligned access, the memory controller will need to perform two separate actions, changing bytes 6 and 7 in word 1, and
then changing bytes 8 and 9 in word 2. Because the underlying hardware only allows a
complete word to be stored, the memory controller will need to fetch word 1, replace
bytes 6 and 7 with the first two bytes of the integer being stored, and then store all four
bytes back into word 1. It will then need to read word 2, replace bytes 8 and 9 with the

new values, and write all four bytes back into word 2. Thus, even if the architecture permits unaligned memory accesses, operations on unaligned values take much longer.

8.13 Calculating A Word Address

When a memory controller receives a byte address, the controller must convert the address into a word address to use with the underlying hardware. For example, with 4-byte words, if the processor requests a *fetch* operation for byte address 17, the controller must access word 4. Mathematically, W, the word address, can be found by dividing B, the byte address, by N, the number of bytes per word, and ignoring the remainder. The controller must then compute O, the byte offset within the word, by finding the remainder of B divided by N. That is, the word address is given by:

$$W = \left\lfloor \frac{B}{N} \right\rfloor$$

and the offset is given by:

$$O = B \bmod N$$

As an example, consider the byte addresses in Figure 8.11, where $N=4$. A byte address of 11 translates to a word address of 2 and an offset of 3, which means that byte 11 is found in word 2 at byte offset 3†.

8.14 Calculating Word Addresses Using Powers of Two

Because a division or remainder computation takes time and requires additional hardware, architects avoid such computation. They instead use powers of two, which means an answer can be obtained without computation, merely by extracting bits. For example, for a word size of four bytes ($N = 2^2$), the offset can be computed by extracting the two low-order bits, and the word address can be computed by extracting everything except the two low-order bits. Figure 8.12 shows an example.

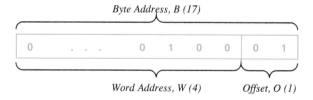

Figure 8.12 An example of using bit extraction to map byte address 17 to word address 4 and offset 1 on a computer with a word size of four (a power of two).

†The offset is measured from zero

We can summarize:

> *To avoid arithmetic calculations, such as division or remainder, architects choose the number of bytes per word to be a power of two, which means the translation from a byte address to a word address and offset can be performed by extracting bits from a byte address.*

8.15 Multiple Memories With Separate Controllers

The discussion above assumes a single physical memory and a single memory controller. In practice, some architectures contain multiple physical memories. One motivation for multiple memories arises from higher performance achieved through hardware parallelism. Multiple memory controllers can operate in parallel, as Figure 8.13 illustrates.

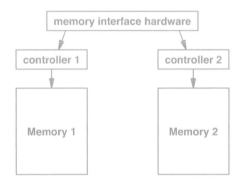

Figure 8.13 The conceptual organization of two memories, each with its own controller.

In the figure, the *memory interface*† receives requests from the processor. The interface uses the address in each request to decide which memory should handle the request. It then passes the request to the appropriate memory controller.

How does having multiple memories, each with their own controller, improve performance? After memory has been accessed, the hardware must reset before the next access can occur. If two memories are available, a compiler (or a human writing code) may be able to arrange to access one while the other resets, increasing the overall performance. That is, a compiler may be able to divide variables into the two memories such that references to the variables alternate between the memories, allowing one memory to reset while the other one is being accessed.

---

†Engineers sometimes refer to the interface as a *Memory Management Unit* (*MMU*).

8.16 Memory Banks

One particular organization of multiple memories, known as a *memory bank organ-ization*, offers a special advantage: the ability to increase the total memory in a comput-er incrementally by adding memory modules. Each module is identical; the controller arranges the modules to form a single, large memory. Consider an example with two identical memory modules that each contain eight Gigabytes of memory (2^{33} bytes). Each module uses addresses 0 through $2^{33}-1$. The memory controller can be configured to treat the modules as two *banks* of memory that form a contiguous large memory with twice the addresses, as Figure 8.14 illustrates.

Figure 8.14 A single large memory formed from two memory banks, where each bank consists of a module that contains 8 Gigabytes of memory.

As the figure shows, the first bank is assigned addresses 0 through $2^{33}-1$, and the second bank is assigned addresses 2^{33} to $2^{34}-1$. Although the two banks have been configured to give the illusion of one large memory, the underlying hardware can fol-low the design in Figure 8.13. When it receives an address of 2^{33} or greater, the inter-face subtracts 2^{33} and sends the request to module 2. As a result, controllers for the two memory banks can operate in parallel. Thus, if instructions are placed in one bank and data in another, higher performance can result because instruction fetch will not inter-fere with data access and vice versa.

How do memory banks appear to a programmer? In most architectures, memory banks are transparent — software running on the processor views memory as a single array of bytes; if two successive accesses reference different banks, the hardware au-tomatically uses parallelism to improve performance. In embedded systems and other special-purpose architectures, a programmer may be responsible for placing items into separate memory banks to increase performance. For example, a programmer may need to place code at low memory addresses to ensure the code resides in one bank and data items at high memory addresses to ensure the data resides in another bank.

8.17 Interleaving

The term *interleaving* refers to an optimization used with physical memory systems that also exploits parallelism. The motivation for interleaving arises from the observation that many programs access data in sequential memory locations. For example, when copying a long text string from one place in memory to another or when iterating through elements of an array, a program references sequential memory locations. Memory banks do not help with sequential access because successive items reside in the same memory bank,

To optimize sequential access, interleaving places consecutive words of memory in separate physical memory modules. Interleaving achieves high performance during sequential memory accesses because a word can be fetched while the memory for the previous word resets. Like memory banks, interleaving is usually hidden from programmers — a programmer can write code without knowing that the underlying memory system has mapped successive words into separate memory modules. The memory hardware handles the details automatically.

The terminology *N-way interleaving* describes an interleaving scheme with N underlying memory modules (to make the hardware implementation efficient, N must be a power of two). For example, Figure 8.15 illustrates how words of memory are assigned to memory modules in a four-way interleaving scheme.

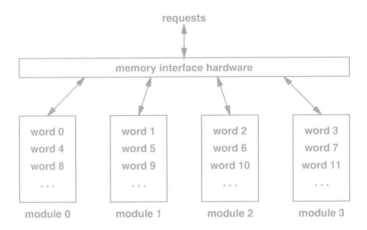

Figure 8.15 Illustration of 4-way interleaving in which successive words of a memory reside in successive modules to optimize performance.

The interface receives requests that each reference a word of memory. It computes the module that holds the word and a location in the module. How can the computation be performed efficiently? The answer lies in using the binary representation. In the figure, for example, module 0 stores words with addresses 0, 4, 8, and so on. What do the addresses have in common? When represented in binary, the addresses all have two low-order bits equal to 00. Similarly, the words stored by module 1 have low-order bits equal to 01, the words stored by module 2 have low-order bits equal to 10, and the words stored by module 3 have low-order bits equal to 11. Thus, when given a memory address, the interface hardware can extract the two low-order bits, and use them to select a module.

Bits from the address also allow the hardware to access the correct word within a module. The modules themselves are standard memory modules that provide an array of words addressed 0 through $MAX-1$, for some value of MAX. The interface hardware ignores the two low-order bits of an address and uses the rest of the bits as an index into the memory module. To see why it works, write 0, 4, 8, ... in binary, and remove the two low-order bits. The result is the sequence 0, 1, 2,... Similarly, removing the two low-order bits from 1, 5, 9... also results in the sequence 0, 1, 2,...

We can summarize:

If the number of modules is a power of two, the hardware for N-way interleaving is extremely efficient because low-order bits of an address are used to select a module and the remaining bits provide an address within the module.

8.18 Memory Sizes, Powers Of Two, And Prefixes

We said that the underlying memory hardware consists of M hardware units that each contain a word of N bytes. Furthermore, to make operations efficient, architects choose M and N to be powers of two. Using powers of two has an interesting consequence: we measure memory sizes in powers of two and adjust the meaning of metric prefixes accordingly. For example, instead of using powers of ten, industry defines a *Kilobyte (Kbyte)* of memory to consist of 2^{10} bytes, a *Megabyte (MB)* of memory to consist of 2^{20} bytes, and a *Gigabyte (GB)* to consist of 2^{30} bytes. The abnormal terminology can be confusing, even to experts. In computer networking, for example, a measure of *Megabits per second* refers to base ten, but data sizes typically use base two. Thus, one must be careful when comparing the size of data in memory with the speed at which data can be sent over a network. For example, although there are eight bits per byte, a network that sends eight Kilobits per second will not send a Kilobyte of data from memory in one second. We can summarize:

When used to refer to memory, the prefixes Kilo, Mega, and Giga are defined to be powers of 2; when used with other aspects of computing, such as computer networking, the prefixes are defined to be powers of 10.

8.19 Content Addressable Memory

An unusual form of memory exists that blends the two key aspects discussed above: technology and memory organization. Known as a *Content Addressable Memory (CAM)*, the technology does much more than merely store data items — it includes hardware that can search the stored data at high speed.

The easiest way to think about a CAM is to view it as memory that has been organized as a two-dimensional array (i.e., a table). Each row in the array, called a *slot*, stores one data item. A CAM contains a fixed number of slots, and an application using CAM can place one item in each slot. CAM includes an extra piece of hardware that stores a *search key*. The search key is exactly as large as a slot in the CAM. Once a program stores a value in the search key, the hardware performs a search of the array to determine whether any slot matches the search key. If any slot matches, the hardware identifies the slot. Figure 8.16 illustrates the organization of a CAM.

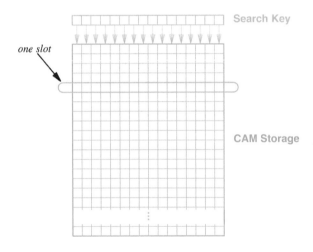

Figure 8.16 Illustration of a Content Addressable Memory (CAM), which stores values and also provides a search mechanism.

In the figure, each square represents a hardware unit that holds one byte. The number of columns in the array determines the number of bytes in each item stored in the CAM, and the number of rows determines the maximum number of items that can be stored.

Unlike an iterative search implemented in software, the search mechanism in CAM uses a parallel approach. In addition to storing a value, each hardware unit in a CAM includes digital logic that can perform a comparison. We can imagine that wires run from the search key hardware unit downward, connecting to the comparison hardware in each slot below. Once a value has been stored in the search key, the wires carry the values of the bits in the search down to every slot below. All slots perform comparison at the same time, with the hardware in each slot comparing the value stored in the slot to the value in the search key. For the most basic form of a CAM, the search mechanism performs an *exact match* search, and only reports success if all bits in the slot match the bits of the search key. Because the hardware for all slots operates in parallel, the time required to perform the search does not depend on the number of slots.

The parallel search in CAM does have two disadvantages. First, the specialized search hardware makes CAM much more expensive than DRAM. Second, because each bit in the CAM requires comparison circuitry as well as memory circuitry, Cam consumes much more power (and produces much more heat) than a conventional memory. Thus, an architect only uses CAM in specialized situations where a relatively small number of values must be stored and high-speed lookup is more important than cost and power consumption.

8.20 Ternary CAM

An alternative form of CAM, known as *Ternary CAM* (*TCAM*), extends the idea of CAM to provide *partial match searches*. In essence, each bit in a slot can have three values: zero, one, or "don't care." Like a standard CAM, a TCAM performs the search operation in parallel by comparing the search key to all slots simultaneously. Unlike a standard CAM, a TCAM only performs the match on bits that have the value zero or one. Partial matching allows a TCAM to be used in cases where two or more entries in the CAM overlap — a TCAM can find the best match (e.g., the *longest prefix* match used in network switches).

8.21 Summary

We examined two aspects of physical memory: the underlying technology and the memory organization. Many memory technologies exist. Differences among them include the speed, the access pattern, and power consumption. Synchronized DRAM has become popular for many computers.

To a processor, memory appears to be an array of bytes. Some architectures require instructions and integers to be aligned (e.g., on a 4-byte boundary); architectures that allow unaligned access often have better performance when values are aligned. A programmer can rearrange items in a struct to minimize wasted space of aligned items.

The reason for alignment arises from the underlying memory being organized as a set of words, with a controller that translates between word addresses and byte addresses. To avoid arithmetic computation, the word size and the total memory sizes are chosen to be powers of two.

Memory banks and interleaving use multiple, parallel controllers and multiple memory modules to improve performance. Banks can be used to build a large memory out of smaller modules. Interleaving places successive words of memory in separate modules to speed access to sequential bytes of memory.

Content Addressable Memory (CAM) combines memory technology and memory organization. A CAM organizes memory as an array of slots, and provides a high-speed search mechanism. A ternary CAM (TCAM) extends CAM technology to permit partial matches.

EXERCISES

8.1 Smart phones and other portable devices typically use DRAM rather than SRAM. Explain why.

8.2 Explain the purpose of a DRAM *refresh* mechanism.

8.3 Assume a computer has a physical memory organized into 64-bit words. Give the word address and offset within the word for each of the following byte addresses: 0, 9, 27, 31, 120, and 256.

8.4 Extend the above exercise by writing a computer program that computes the answer. Allow the program to take a series of inputs that each consist of two values: a word size specified as a number of bits in the word and a byte address. For each input, the program should generate a word address and offset within the word. Note: although it is specified in bits, the word size must be a power of two bytes.

8.5 On an ARM processor, attempting to load an integer from memory will result in an error if the address is not a multiple of 4 bytes. What term do we use to refer to such an error?

8.6 Write a hex dump function that takes two arguments: a starting address in memory and an ending address. Round the starting address down to a multiple of sixteen bytes, and round the ending address up to a multiple of sixteen bytes. Have the dump print sixteen bytes per line similar to Figure 8.6.

8.7 If a computer uses byte addressing and allows each address to occupy sixty-four bits, what is the maximum memory size the computer can have? How many times larger is the maximum memory size than the size of your laptop or smart phone?

8.8 Assume a computer requires 4-byte alignment, and a struct contains an int z, a char y, a short x, an int w, a char v, and an int u. How much space will be wasted?

8.9 Extend the previous exercise by rearranging the items in the struct to minimize wasted space. (a) As a percentage, how much was the wasted space reduced? (b) If the struct is used in an array, does the percentage of wasted space change? Explain.

8.10 Emulate a physical memory. Write a C function that declares a static array of 4-byte integers, *M*, and implements *fetch* and *store* operations on the array. Have the functions take a byte address within the array as an argument. Perform the computation to convert the byte address into an array index, and then use shift and Boolean operations to access individual bytes. Do not use byte pointers.

8.11 Redraw Figure 8.15 for an 8-way interleaved memory.

8.12 Simulate a TCAM. Write a program that matches an input string with a set of patterns. For the simulation, use printable characters instead of individual bits. Have each slot consist of 40 bytes, and have the search key use an asterisk as a "wild card" that matches any character (i.e., a value for "don't care"). Can you find a way to make the match proceed faster than iterating through all patterns?

Chapter Contents

9

Virtual Memory Technologies And Virtual Addressing

The previous chapter discusses main memory. It considers the hardware technologies used to create memory systems, the organization of physical memory into words, and the array-of-bytes view of memory presented to the processor. It also explains why some architectures require items to be aligned and why alignment can increase performance even if the architecture does not mandate alignment.

This chapter considers the important concept of virtual memory. It examines the motivation, the technologies used to create virtual address spaces, and the mapping between virtual and physical memory. Although the chapter focuses on the mechanisms, the chapter also explains how an operating system uses virtual memory facilities.

9.2 Definition Of Virtual Memory

We use the term *Virtual Memory* (*VM*) to refer to a system that hides the details of the underlying physical memory to provide a more convenient memory environment for running programs. In essence, a virtual memory system creates an illusion — an address space and a memory access scheme that overcome limitations of the physical memory and physical addressing scheme. The definition may seem vague, but we need to encompass a wide variety of technologies and uses. The next sections will define the concept more precisely by giving examples of virtual memory systems that have been created and the technologies used to implement each. We will learn that the variety in virtual memory schemes arises because no single scheme is optimal in all cases.

9.3 Memory Management Unit And A Virtual Address Space

We already saw an example of a memory system that fits our definition of virtual memory in Chapter 8: a memory controller that provides a byte-addressable interface on top of an underlying physical memory that uses word addressing. The controller hides the underlying memory architecture, and allows a processor to use byte addresses. Architects use the term *Memory Management Unit* (*MMU*) to describe hardware facilities that manage the underlying memory hardware and present a convenient interface. In essence, an MMU creates a new *address space* for the processor to use, and translates addresses from the new address space into operations on the underlying memory.

Chapter 8 introduces a second example that fits our definition of virtual memory system: memory banks. Interface hardware combines multiple memory modules in a way that gives the appearance of a single, large memory. For example, Figure 9.1 illustrates four 1-Gigabyte modules combined to form a memory of four Gigabytes.

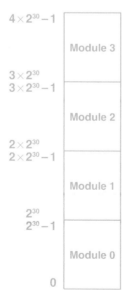

Figure 9.1 Four 1-Gigabyte memory modules arranged to form a single memory with addresses running from 0 through 4 Gigabytes $- 1$.

Recall from Chapter 8 that each module actually uses addresses 0 through 1 Gigabyte − 1, and the interface hardware hides the underlying addresses by translating each request before sending it to a specific module. When a mechanism hides the addresses used by the underlying hardware and provides a new set of addresses, we say that the mechanism provides a *virtual address space*. To distinguish them from the addresses used by the underlying hardware, we say that addresses in the virtual address space are *virtual addresses*.

9.4 Address Translation Using Powers Of Two

Understanding how hardware performs address translation will help us understand mechanisms covered later in the chapter. If a software engineer created an algorithm to handle address translation with a bank of four 1-Gigabyte modules, the algorithm might contain the series of tests that Algorithm 9.1 lists.

Algorithm 9.1

Given:
    Four 1-Gigabyte memory modules, a memory operation, and *V*,
    a virtual address from a 4-Gigabyte virtual address space

Carry out:
    Create a 4-Gigabyte virtual address space by translating the
    address, selecting the appropriate module, and performing the
    operation on the selected module.

Method:
    Let G be 2^{30}, the number of bytes in one Gigabyte of memory
    if (V >= 3×G) {
      perform the operation on module 3 using address V − 3×G;
    } else if (V >= 2×G) {
      perform the operation on module 2 using address V − 2×G;
    } else if (V >= 1×G) {
      perform the operation on module 1 using address V − 1×G;
    } else {
      perform the operation on module 0 using address V
    }

Algorithm 9.1 An algorithm a software engineer might use to create a 4-Gigabyte virtual address space from four 1-Gigabyte memory modules.

In essence, the algorithm divides the virtual address space into four equal-size pieces, and uses module 0 for the first piece, module 1 for the second, and so on. Before it can perform an operation on one of the modules, the algorithm must translate the virtual address to an address the module can handle (i.e., less than one Gigabyte). To do so, it subtracts the starting address for the piece of the address space the module handles.

Although it works correctly, Algorithm 9.1 would be far too slow to be practical because a comparison and subtraction must be performed for each memory reference. Fortunately, MMU hardware can avoid both the comparison and subtraction operations by making the size of each module and the number of modules powers of two and extracting bits from the virtual address. To understand how the hardware can use bit extraction, consider Figure 9.2, which shows binary values of address ranges for each module in Figure 9.1.

Module	Virtual Address Ranges In Binary (32 bits)
0	0 0 0 0 0 0 0 0 0 0 0 0 0 0 0 0 0 0 0 0 0 0 0 0 0 0 0 0 0 0 0 0 0 0 1 1 1 1 1 1 1 1 1 1 1 1 1 1 1 1 1 1 1 1 1 1 1 1 1 1 1 1 1 1
1	0 1 0 0 0 0 0 0 0 0 0 0 0 0 0 0 0 0 0 0 0 0 0 0 0 0 0 0 0 0 0 0 0 1 1 1 1 1 1 1 1 1 1 1 1 1 1 1 1 1 1 1 1 1 1 1 1 1 1 1 1 1 1 1
2	1 0 0 0 0 0 0 0 0 0 0 0 0 0 0 0 0 0 0 0 0 0 0 0 0 0 0 0 0 0 0 0 1 0 1 1 1 1 1 1 1 1 1 1 1 1 1 1 1 1 1 1 1 1 1 1 1 1 1 1 1 1 1 1
3	1 1 0 0 0 0 0 0 0 0 0 0 0 0 0 0 0 0 0 0 0 0 0 0 0 0 0 0 0 0 0 0 1 1 1 1 1 1 1 1 1 1 1 1 1 1 1 1 1 1 1 1 1 1 1 1 1 1 1 1 1 1 1 1

Figure 9.2 The binary values for the minimum and maximum address in each of four Gigabytes.

Notice that the two high-order bits of the virtual address tell which module to use. That is, all virtual addresses where the first two bits are 00 refer to module 0, all addresses where the first two bits are 01 refer to module 1, and so on. Furthermore, the remaining thirty bits of a virtual address span exactly 1 Gigabyte of the address space. The lowest virtual address assigned to a module has all zeros in the low-order bits, and the highest virtual address assigned to the module has all ones in the low-order bits.

To translate an address, an MMU merely extracts the two high-order bits and uses them to select one of the four modules. It then extracts the remaining thirty bits and uses them as an address within the module (zero to 1 Gigabyte − 1). Remember that hardware is iterated in space. The MMU has one hardware unit to hold each bit of a virtual address, which makes extracting bits trivial (just extend wires from the units that hold the bits).

To summarize:

> *Dividing a virtual address space on a boundary that corresponds to a power of two allows the MMU to choose a module and perform the necessary address translation without requiring arithmetic operations.*

9.5 Virtual Address Spaces For Concurrent Applications

The trivial examples above show that a memory system can present a processor with a virtual address space that differs from the underlying physical memory. Perhaps the most significant use of virtual memory arose when multi-user operating systems were invented. Such operating systems allow applications from multiple users to run at the same time. To make such an approach viable, an operating system must isolate each instance of a running application and protect it from others. Specifically, the system must prevent one application from examining or changing memory locations owned by another application. Virtual memory mechanisms provide the necessary isolation.

Conceptually, an operating system follows a straightforward approach: create virtual spaces and map them into memory. In the simplest case, assume memory is an array of bytes. When launching an application, create a new virtual address space for the application. When the application runs, translate each memory reference from the virtual address space to the appropriate location in memory allocated to the application. Figure 9.3 illustrates the concept by showing the virtual address spaces for two applications, each mapped to a region of the computer's memory.

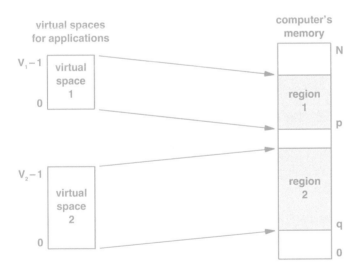

Figure 9.3 Illustration of two virtual address spaces for applications, each mapped onto a region of the computer's memory. The virtual addresses in each virtual space begin at zero.

Each application must be compiled and linked to use virtual addresses starting at zero. When an application runs, virtual memory hardware translates each virtual address into an address in the region assigned to the application. For example, if the application using virtual space 1 references byte 0, the reference will be translated to p, the lowest address in the region assigned to virtual space 1. Similarly, if the application using virtual space 2 references byte 0, the references will be translated to q.

9.6 Mechanisms Used To Create Virtual Address Spaces

How does an operating system create a virtual address space when one is needed, and how does it tell the processor to start using the virtual address space when it runs an application? The second question can be answered easily: the *processor mode* specifies which address space to use. When it boots, the processor executes in *kernel mode* (sometimes called *real mode*) where all addresses refer directly to bytes in memory without using any translation. The operating system can instruct the MMU to establish an address mapping to be used when it switches to *virtual mode*. Once a mapping has been specified, the processor can execute an instruction that changes the mode, enables the MMU, and branches to an application. The MMU translates each memory reference according to the mapping that was configured. When the application returns to the operating system, the mode switches back to kernel mode, and the translation stops.

Several mechanisms have been used to provide virtual address spaces; we will consider two:

- Base-Bound Registers
- Demand Paging

9.7 Base-Bound Registers

One of the oldest virtual memory mechanisms, *base-bound registers*, is also among the easiest to understand. The base-bound scheme requires the MMU to have two hardware registers: one holds the starting address of a region of memory and the other holds the integer size of the region. The operating system loads values into both registers before it changes mode and starts running an application. Figure 9.7 illustrates the mapping.

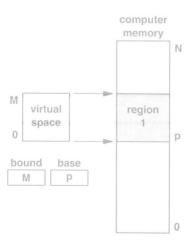

Figure 9.4 Illustration of base-bound registers mapping a virtual space onto a region of memory. The base register specifies the starting address and the bound register specifies the size.

Given a virtual address, the MMU first compares the address to the value in the bound register (M in the figure). If the address exceeds the bound, the MMU raises an exception and returns to the operating system. If the virtual address does not exceed the bound, the MMU adds the contents of the base register to the virtual address to obtain an address in the region of memory assigned to the virtual space, and accesses the memory.

To run multiple applications, the operating system stores a record of the size of the application's virtual space and the region of memory assigned to the application. When switching to one of the applications, the operating system only needs to load the base and bound registers with the appropriate values and change mode. The point is:

> An operating system can use a base-bound mechanism to allow each application to run in its own virtual address space. Changing to a given application only requires loading the base and bound registers and then changing the processor mode to start using them.

9.8 Virtual Memory Isolation And Protection

The base-bound approach provides *isolation* for each running application and *protection* of the memory they use. In addition, the scheme protects the memory used by the operating system. The bound register ensures that an application will not be able to access memory beyond its virtual space; the base register ensures that all references the application makes will translate to addresses in the region assigned to the application. Thus, an application cannot access memory regions assigned to other applications, and cannot access memory that the operating system uses. To be safe, all virtual memory systems for multiple applications must offer the same properties:

> To be safe, a virtual memory system that supports multiple applications running concurrently must provide isolation and protection that prevents one application from reading or altering memory that has been allocated to another application or to the operating system.

9.9 Loading Program Pieces And Demand Paging

Although it works correctly, the base-bound approach has a disadvantage: a region of memory must be reserved for each application program, and the region must hold the complete program (instructions and data). In most cases, when an application runs, the application does not execute all its instructions or access all its data items. For example, if an application includes a function that handles errors in the input, the function will not be called if no errors occur. Similarly, if an application includes an array large enough to hold 10,000 input values and the input only has 200 values, 9,800 locations in the array will not be used. Researchers proposed alternative virtual memory mechanisms that only load pieces of a program into memory when they are needed. All the proposals followed the same general approach: store an application on secondary storage (i.e., disk), load pieces of the application into memory only when they are needed, and extend the virtual memory hardware. In addition to providing isolation and protection, the extended hardware must be able to detect when a piece of a program is needed. We use the term *demand*, and say that the system loads pieces of the program *on demand* (i.e., when referenced).

Early proposals focused on choosing pieces that correspond to programming abstractions (i.e., each function or each module). From a software point of view, using such pieces makes sense. From a hardware point of view, however, variable-size pieces lead to inefficiency and memory fragmentation problems. Therefore, industry adopted an approach known as *demand paging* that divides a program into fixed-size pieces called *pages*. Initially, when memories and application programs were much smaller, architects chose a page size of 512 bytes or 1 Kbyte; current architectures use larger page sizes (e.g., many processors used in laptops and other consumer systems use 4-Kbyte pages).

9.10 Hardware And Software For Demand Paging

An effective demand paging system requires hardware and software mechanisms that work together. Figure 9.5 lists the responsibilities of each.

Demand Paging Hardware	Operating System Software
Translate addresses	Choose applications to run
Record when each page is used	Configure address translation
Check each memory reference and raise an exception when a page is not in memory	Move application pages between storage and memory as needed

Figure 9.5 Responsibilities of the hardware and operating system software when a system uses demand paging.

In essence, the virtual memory architecture uses hardware to handle the aspects that must be performed at high speed, and allows software to handle other aspects. Thus, the MMU hardware handles address translation and allows the operating system software to choose applications to run, create virtual spaces, and decide which pages from a given application to keep in memory and which to keep on secondary storage. The operating system software must configure the MMU to specify where each page from a virtual address space resides in memory and whether the page is currently *resident* in memory (initially, the pages are not). While the application runs, the MMU translates each memory address and also checks whether the referenced page is resident.

When it encounters a reference to a page that is not resident, the MMU does not fetch the page from secondary storage. Instead, it merely raises an exception called a *page fault* and allows the operating system to fetch the page. When a page fault occurs, the processor switches back to kernel mode and branches to a function in the operating system that handles page faults. Once the fault has been handled (i.e., the missing page has been loaded into memory), the operating system can instruct the processor to restart execution at the instruction that caused the fault.

The paging hardware and software must work together. For example, when a page fault occurs, the hardware saves the state of the computation in such a way that the values can be reloaded later when execution resumes. Similarly, the software must configure the MMU with the correct information about address translation before switching the processor to virtual mode to run the application. If it switches from running one application to running another, the operating system must reconfigure the MMU to use the correct address translation for the new application.

9.11 Page Replacement

Demand paging systems always know which page to load into memory next — a page fault occurs because a page was referenced and the page was not resident. After applications run a long time, however, all the free memory fills with pages. Before another page can be placed in memory, the operating system must make a difficult decision: to make space for a new page, select one of the existing pages, and write the selected page back to secondary storage. Overall performance will be optimized if the operating system chooses a page that will not be used in the near future. The process is known as *page replacement*.

Because operating system software handles page replacement, the algorithms and heuristics that an operating system uses fall beyond the scope of this text. We will see, however, that the hardware provides mechanisms that assist the operating system in making a decision.

9.12 Paging Terminology And Data Structures

The term *page* refers to a block of a program's address space, and the term *frame* refers to a slot in memory that can hold a page. Thus, we say that software *loads* a page into a frame of memory. When a page is in memory, we say that the page is *resident*; for a given application, zero or more pages of the application are resident at a given time.

We call the primary data structure used for demand paging a *page table*. Each running application has its own page table. The virtual memory system numbers all the pages that belong to the application, starting at 0, 1, 2, and so on. We can imagine that a page table for the application consists of a one-dimensional array indexed by a page number. We can also imagine that each entry in the page table array contains two fields: a pointer to the frame in memory that holds the page plus a *presence bit* that tells whether the pointer is valid (i.e., the bit is zero if the page is not resident in memory). Figure 9.6 illustrates a page table.

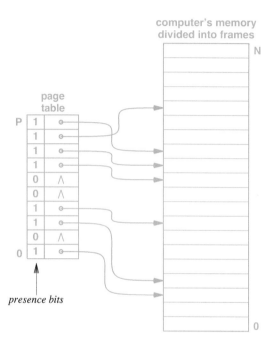

Figure 9.6 Illustration of a page table. An entry with the presence bit set to 1 contains a pointer to a frame in memory; if an entry has the presence bit set to 0, the page is not currently resident in memory.

9.13 Address Translation With A Demand Paging System

Conceptually, translation of a virtual byte address, V, to the address of a corresponding byte in memory, M, requires three steps:

1. Compute p, the number of the page on which address V lies.

2. Use p as an index into the page table to find the location of the frame in memory that holds the page.

3. Compute the *offset* in the page for address V, and make M *offset* bytes beyond the beginning of the frame in memory.

Mathematically, the page number, p, can be computed as the floor of the address divided by the page size:

$$pagenumber: \quad p = \left\lfloor \frac{V}{K} \right\rfloor \qquad (9.1)$$

The *offset* of address *V* within the page can be computed as the remainder of the division.

$$offset = V \bmod K \tag{9.2}$$

Given the page number, *p*, and *offset* computed as above, address *V* can be translated to a memory address, *M*, as follows:

$$memory address \ M = pagetable[p] + offset \tag{9.3}$$

9.14 Using Powers Of Two For Address Translation

As Chapter 8 points out, arithmetic operations, such as division or modulo, take far too much time to perform on each memory reference. Therefore, like other parts of a memory system, a demand paging system uses powers of two to avoid arithmetic computation. A designer always chooses the size of a page to be a power of two, 2^q. If all the frames in memory start on a multiple of the page size, the address of the first byte in each frame will have zeros in the q low-order bits. All pointers in a page table point to frames, and in each case the q low-order bits will be zero. To optimize space, a page table does not store full pointers, but instead omits the q low-order bits; the hardware automatically assumes the bits are zero.

Choosing the page size to be a power of two provides a more significant optimization: division and modulo operations specified in the equations 9.1 through 9.3 can be replaced by hardware that extracts bits, and the addition operation can be replaced by a *logical or*. As a result, an MMU performs the following to translate a virtual address, *V*, into a memory address, *M*:

$$M = pagetable[high\_order\_bits(V)] \quad or \quad low\_order\_bits(V) \tag{9.4}$$

Because hardware is iterated in space, extracting the high-order bits of an address becomes trivial: simply connect a wire to each of the small hardware units that holds one of the bits. The same approach allows hardware to extract low-order bits of the address. Finally, hardware exists to perform a *logical or* of two values. In this instance, the logical or combines a frame pointer that is guaranteed to have the q low-order bits set to zero with a value that is guaranteed to only have q bits. Thus, hardware can use the q wires from one value and the remainder from the other.

Figure 9.7 illustrates how MMU hardware uses bit extraction to perform a virtual address mapping. When considering the figure, remember that hardware can move bits in parallel. Thus, the arrow that points from the q low-order bits in the virtual address to the q low-order bits in the translated memory address represents a parallel data path with q wires — the hardware sends all q bits at the same time. Also, the arrow from the page table entry to the high-order bits in the physical address means that all bits from the page table entry can be transferred in parallel.

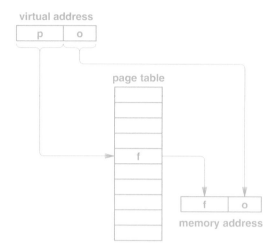

Figure 9.7 Illustration of how an MMU uses bit extraction to translate a virtual address to a memory address in a demand paging system.
Bit extraction requires the page size to be a power of two.

9.15 Presence, Use, And Modified Bits

The description above mentioned that each entry in a page table contains a bit that
specifies whether the pointer is valid. In fact, an entry contains three bits that the
demand paging hardware and operating system software use to coordinate. Figure 9.8
summarizes the control bits and how they are used.

Control Bit	Meaning
Presence bit	Tested by hardware to determine whether page is currently resident in memory
Use bit	Set by hardware whenever page is referenced
Modified bit	Set by hardware whenever page is changed

Figure 9.8 Control bits found in each page table entry and the actions
demand paging hardware takes with each. The bits assist the
page replacement software in the operating system.

Presence Bit. The *presence bit*, which is set by the operating system and tested by
the hardware, specifies whether the page is currently in memory. Once it has loaded a
page into a frame and stored the frame pointer in the page table entry, the operating system sets the presence bit to one. To remove a page from memory (e.g., when an application finishes), the operating system sets the presence bit to zero. The hardware exam-

ines the presence bit when it accesses a page table entry, and allows the translation to proceed if the page is present. Otherwise, the hardware raises a page fault exception.

Use Bit. When it loads a page into memory, the operating system initializes the use bit to zero. Whenever it accesses a page table entry, the MMU sets the use bit to one. A page that has not been used becomes a candidate for replacement.

Modified Bit. When it loads a page into memory, the operating system initializes the modified bit to zero. Whenever it accesses a page table entry for a store operation, the MMU sets the modified bit to one. Thus, the modified bit will be one if any byte on the page has been changed since the page was originally loaded into memory†.

9.16 Page Table Storage

Where do page tables reside? Some systems store page tables in a special MMU chip that is external from the processor. Of course, because memory references play an essential role in processing, the MMU must be designed to work efficiently. In particular, to ensure that memory references do not become a bottleneck, some processors use a special-purpose, high-speed hardware connection between the processor and MMU.

Surprisingly, many architectures store page tables in memory! That is, the processor (or the MMU) contains a special-purpose register that the operating system uses to specify the address of the page table being used at the present time. Recall that each running application needs its own page table. One advantage of placing page tables in memory arises from the ability to create page tables for several running applications and then switch among them quickly, simply by changing the register that points to the active page table. When a system stores page tables in memory, the memory consists of three regions as Figure 9.9 illustrates.

Figure 9.9 Illustration of the memory layout for a demand paging system that stores page tables in memory. The operating system reserves a large area of the computer's memory for frames.

According to our description above, a page table must be accessed frequently because address translation must be performed on *every* memory reference: each instruction fetch, each operand that references memory, and each store of a result. If the system stores page tables in memory, every memory access will cause an extra access to the page table, making the processor intolerably slow. The next section explains how demand paging systems avoid poor performance.

---

†A use bit is sometimes called a *dirty bit*, and a page that has been changed is said to be *dirty*.

9.17 Efficient Paging With A Translation Lookaside Buffer

Most modern computers employ demand paging, and most keep page tables in memory. They use a special mechanism to achieve high performance. Known as a *Translation Lookaside Buffer* (*TLB*), the mechanism uses special-purpose hardware to cache recent lookups. A TLB consists of a Content Addressable Memory as described in Chapter 8. When it first translates an address, the MMU places a copy of the virtual address and the corresponding memory address in the TLB. On successive lookups, the hardware performs two operations in parallel: the standard address translation steps that Figure 9.7 depicts and a high-speed search of the TLB. If the requested information is found in the TLB, the MMU aborts the standard translation and uses the information from the TLB. If the entry is not in the TLB, the standard translation proceeds.

To understand why a TLB makes a substantial improvement in performance, consider the fetch-execute cycle. A processor tends to fetch instructions from successive locations in memory. Furthermore, even if the program contains a branch, the probability is extremely high that the destination will be nearby, probably on the same page. Thus, rather than randomly accessing pages, a processor tends to fetch successive instructions from the same page. A TLB improves performance because it optimizes successive lookups by avoiding indexing into a page table. The difference in performance is especially dramatic for architectures that store page tables in memory. Without a TLB, such systems are too slow to be useful; a TLB makes them almost as fast as executing without variable address translation. We can summarize:

> *A special high-speed hardware device, called a Translation Lookaside Buffer (TLB), is used to optimize performance of a paging system. A virtual memory that does not have a TLB can be unacceptably slow.*

9.18 Consequences For Programmers

Experience has shown that demand paging works well for most computer programs. The code that programmers produce tends to be organized into functions that each fit onto a page. Similarly, data objects, such as character strings and structs, place data in consecutive memory locations, which means that once a page has been loaded, the page tends to remain resident for multiple references. Finally, some compilers understand paging, and optimize performance by placing data items onto pages.

One way that programmers can affect virtual memory performance arises from array access. Consider a two-dimensional array in memory. Most programming systems allocate an array in *row-major order*, which means that rows of an array are placed in memory as Figure 9.10 illustrates.

Figure 9.10 An illustration of a two-dimensional array stored in row-major order. Each row follows the previous row in memory.

As the figure shows, rows of the matrix occupy successive locations in memory. The chief alternative to row-major order, known as *column-major order*, arranges for columns to follow one another in memory, as Figure 9.11 illustrates.

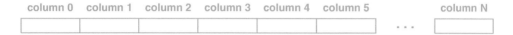

Figure 9.11 An illustration of a two-dimensional array stored in column-major order. Each column follows the previous column in memory.

Usually, a programmer cannot choose between row-major and column-major orders. Instead, the programming language and/or compiler make the choice. However, a programmer can control how software iterates through an array. When the array resides in a demand paged virtual memory, the difference in performance can be substantial. For example, suppose a system stores arrays in row-major order, and suppose an array, A[N,M], is sufficiently large so that one row occupies a page. In such a case, iterating across an entire row before moving to the next row will optimize performance because successive references refer to the same page.

/vs +2

```
for i = 1 to N {
    for j = 1 to M {
        A [ i, j ] = 0;
    }
}
```

By contrast, if an array is stored in row-major order, iterating through an entire column before moving to the next column will perform poorly because the paging system will jump to the next page on each reference. If the frames in memory are full of pages, each memory reference will cause a page fault.

```
for j = 1 to M {
    for i = 1 to N {
        A [ i, j ] = 0;
    }
}
```

Of course, the performance will be reversed if the system stores arrays in column-major order.

9.19 Single-Level Page Tables And Page Table Size

We use the term *single-level page table* to characterize the paging mechanism described above. In a single-level system, each virtual address space needs one page table. The operating system must maintain a page table for each running application, but at any time, the hardware only uses one page table.

How large is each page table in a single-level paging system? If an architecture uses 32-bit addresses and 4-Kbyte pages, a virtual address will be divided into a 20-bit page number and 12-bit offset. A 20-bit page number means each page table contains 2^{20} entries. If each page table entry occupies 4 bytes, the total size of one page table is:

$$32\text{-}bit\ page\ table\ size = 2^{10}\ entries \times 4\frac{bytes}{entry} = 4\ Megabytes \qquad (9.5)$$

In a memory that contains up to four Gigabytes, a 4-Megabyte page table occupies a reasonable amount of space. Consider what would happen, however, if we extend the single-level paging approach to a 64-bit architecture. Even if the system only uses 48 bits of each address, a page table for 4-Kbyte pages would have 2^{36} entries, making the size of the page table:

$$48\text{-}bit\ page\ table\ size = 2^{36}\ entries \times 4\frac{bytes}{entry} = 64\ Gigabytes \qquad (9.6)$$

Remember that an operating system must store one page table for each running application, and each page table would occupy 64 Gigabytes. Clearly, another approach must be used for demand paging with larger addresses.

9.20 The Advantage Of Multi-Level Page Tables

When 64-bit architectures appeared, industry moved to a *multi-level page table* mechanism. The multi-level approach arranges a set of tables in a hierarchy, divides a virtual address into multiple fields, and uses each field to navigate a table and move to the next level of the hierarchy. The final table follows the same approach as a page table in a single-level paging system, with pointers to frames in memory.

To understand the motivation for multiple levels, consider a *hello world* program running on a 32-bit paging system. Assume the code and the data fit into a single page and the program only uses one page for its stack. Also assume that the program starts at location zero in the virtual address space and the stack starts at the highest address (0xffffffff) and grows downward. Now consider what happens when the program runs. The operating system allocates a page table and starts the program. The program only references the lowest and highest pages, so the paging system will only fill in two entries in the page table. Unfortunately, even though the program only needs two entries and only uses 8 Kilobytes of memory, the operating system must allocate a 4-Megabyte page table, an order of magnitude more memory than the program uses.

Now consider how a two-level paging scheme can reduce the amount of memory needed. Instead of dividing a 32-bit virtual address into a 20-bit page number and a 12-bit offset, divide the address into three fields, as Figure 9.12 shows.

22 – 31	12 – 21	11 – 0
Level 2	Level 1	Offset

Figure 9.12 One possible division of a 32-bit virtual address to use two-level paging. Numbers above each field specify the bit in the field.

For our example, instruction and data references in the first page will be in the address range 0x00000000 through 0x00000fff and stack references in the last page will be in the address range 0xfffff000 through 0xffffffff. In terms of Figure 9.12, the first page will have zero bits in the Level 1 and Level 2 fields, and stack references will have one bits in the Level 1 and Level 2 fields. To implement the two-level paging scheme, the system uses the ten bits in the Level 2 field as an index into a top-level page table. Consequently, the top-level table will contain 1024 entries, and each entry will point to a second-level page table. The system uses the ten bits in the Level 1 field as an index into the second table. The second table contains a pointer to a frame in memory, exactly like a page table in a single-level paging system.

To see how the two-level approach reduces memory requirements, consider how it helps with the *hello world* example. Figure 9.13 shows that the program only needs three small page tables.

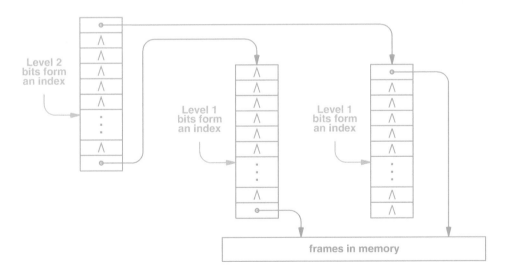

Figure 9.13 Page tables for the example 2-level paging scheme and a trivial *hello world* program.

As Figure 9.13 shows, for the *hello world* example, the two-level scheme only requires three page tables. The first, indexed by Level 2 bits in the virtual address only has two entries filled in: one for the highest part of the address space and one for the lowest. Each entry points to a page table that only needs one entry to be filled in to point to a frame in memory. The system extracts the Level 2 field from the virtual address and uses the value as an index into the top-level page table. It follows the pointer to a Level 1 page table, extracts the Level 1 field from the virtual address, and uses the value as an index into the page table.

Because the program only uses two pages of memory, most of the entries in the page tables go unused. In terms of memory use, the two-level approach only needs three tables of 1024 entries per table. If each entry is four bytes, the page tables occupy 12 Kbytes of memory, less than one-half percent of the 4 Megabytes taken by a single-level page table. The point is:

> *If an application only uses a small fraction of the possible addresses in a virtual address space, using multiple levels of page tables can substantially reduce the amount of memory needed for page tables.*

9.21 Multi-Level Page Tables For 64-Bit Architectures

We have seen that in a 64-bit architecture, a single-level paging scheme results in a huge page table size. More important, a typical program only occupies a tiny fraction of the address space, which means that using a single-level page table leaves most entries in the table unused. Therefore, to reduce page table sizes, a paging system must use multi-level page tables. The point is:

> *Because most programs only use a small fraction of a 64-bit address space, multi-level page tables must be used to reduce page table size enough to make a paging system practical.*

The example above uses two levels of page tables. Unfortunately, two levels do not suffice for a 64-bit architecture. In addition to the twelve low-order bits that specify an offset, fifty-two bits remain. Dividing them into two levels results in twenty-six bits per level, which produces 2^{26} entries per page table. If each entry occupies four bytes, each page table will require 256 Megabytes, far too large to be practical. Early 64-bit systems used forty-eight bits of the sixty-four. Even on such systems, a two-level paging scheme would result in each page table occupying a Megabyte. Therefore, 64-bit paging systems use more than two levels.

As an example, consider the x86-64 paging architecture. The initial version of the architecture limited addresses to forty-eight meaningful bits by ignoring the high-order sixteen bits of each address. The paging system used four levels of page tables to cover the forty-eight bits. Figure 9.14 shows how the system divided a virtual address into levels.

63 – 48	47 – 39	38 – 30	29 – 21	20 – 12	11 – 0
unused	Level 4	Level 3	Level 2	Level 1	Offset

Figure 9.14 The four-level paging scheme used in the initial paging system for the x86-64 architecture.

To accommodate specialized applications that store large amounts of data in memory, especially applications that run in cloud data centers, a later x86-64 paging design expanded the usable part of the address space to fifty-seven bits by adding another level of page tables. Figure 9.15 illustrates the change.

63 – 57	56 – 48	47 – 39	38 – 30	29 – 21	20 – 12	11 – 0
unused	Level 5	Level 4	Level 3	Level 2	Level 1	Offset

Figure 9.15 The five-level extended paging scheme for the x86-64 architecture.

9.22 Sparseness And Address Space Layout Randomization

To increase security, some operating systems use a technique known as *Address Space Layout Randomization* (*ASLR*). Although the details lie beyond the scope of this text, understanding the basic idea will help us understand why a larger address space can be useful, even if a program does not fill the space. Instead of locating a program at virtual address zero, ASLR places each of the code, data, bss, and stack segments at random locations, making it more difficult for malware to guess the run-time locations of objects.

From a paging point of view, ASLR means that the set of addresses a program uses will be positioned at random locations in the address space, even if the program is small. Thus, entries in the page tables will be *sparse* — for a typical program, only a few entries in each page table will be used. Furthermore, occupied entries will not always start at address zero and will not be contiguous. Having many levels of tables keeps the size of each table constrained.

The point is:

> *In addition to accommodating applications that use large amounts of memory, an expanded address space allows an operating system to improve security by using Address Space Layout Randomization.*

9.23 Page Table Walks And The Importance Of A TLB

We use the term *page table walk* to describe the steps taken to search the hierarchy of page tables. Using multiple levels of page tables increases the length of the page table walk. If every memory reference required walking through five page tables, the abysmal performance would make the paging system unusable.

What makes a five-level paging system so fast? We have already seen the answer: a TLB. If the TLB is sufficiently large, almost all address translation can be performed without walking through page tables.

9.24 Summary

Virtual memory systems present a convenient, abstract address space to the system using the virtual memory and implement the virtual space by using an underlying memory. Our definition of virtual memory covers basic mechanisms, such as a system that hides the details of word addressing and presents a uniform byte-addressable memory to a processor.

Operating systems use virtual memory to provide isolation and protection among multiple application programs that run concurrently on the same processor. Each application runs in an isolated address space that starts at virtual address zero.

An early virtual memory technology, known as base-bound, mapped each running application into a region of memory. Current systems use a technology known as demand paging. Instead of placing an entire application in an isolated region of memory, demand paging divides an application into fixed-size pieces called pages (typically 4 Kilobytes each), and only places a page in memory when the application references the page.

Mathematically, the steps demand paging systems take to translate an address require division and modulo computations. To avoid arithmetic computation, demand paging systems choose a page size that is a power of two. Doing so allows MMU hardware to avoid arithmetic operations and perform address translation by extracting bits from the virtual address.

Many demand paging systems store page tables in memory. A specialized, high-speed mechanism known as a Translation Lookaside Buffer (TLB) make demand paging perform well by caching recently used address translations. In typical programs, a TLB enables the MMU to translate addresses so fast that users do not notice any impact on performance.

Moving from 32-bit architectures to 64-bit architectures requires a significant change in paging because a single-level page table would occupy excessive space. The new designs use multiple levels of page tables because doing so can save substantial space when programs only occupy a small fraction of their address space. The use of multi-level page tables adds overhead by making a page table walk take more time; paging systems that employ multiple page tables rely on a TLB to make the system perform well.

EXERCISES

9.1   Consider the virtual address space in Figure 9.1, and suppose a program references location 1073741829. Which memory module will be referenced, and what byte address in the module will be referenced? In your answer, show the values in binary.

9.2   What two special-purpose registers did base-bound technology use, and when did an operating system change them?

9.3   In a demand paging system, what does the operating system need to configure before the hardware can translate addresses?

9.4   Conceptually, a page table is an array and each element contains a memory address as well as other items. On a 32-bit computer, is the stored memory address a full 32 bits long? Explain why or why not.

9.5   For the presence, use, and modified bits in a page table, tell when the bit changes and whether the hardware or software makes the change.

9.6   Assuming a page size of 4K bytes, compute the page number and the offset for addresses 100, 1500, 8800, and 10000.

9.7   Write a computer program that takes two input values, a page size, and an address, and computes the page number and offset for the address. If the page size is a power of two, compute the answer without using division or modulus operations.

9.8   Calculate the total amount of memory needed to hold a single-level page table for a 32-bit computer if each page table entry contains four bytes and the page size is 4K bytes, 8K bytes, and 16 Kbytes.

9.9   Write a computer program that takes as input a page size and an address space size, and performs the calculation in the previous exercise. (You may restrict sizes to powers of two.)

9.10 What is page replacement, and is it performed by hardware or software?

9.11 Consider a two-level paging scheme for a 32-bit architecture and a page size of 4k bytes. Assume the high-order four bits of an address are used as an index into a *directory page table* to select a page table. Assume the next 16 bits index a page table that points to a frame in memory. How much memory is required for the directory table and each page table?

9.12 What is a TLB, and why is it necessary?

9.13 Write a program that references all locations in a very large two-dimensional array stored in row-major order. Compare the execution times when the program iterates through rows and touches each column within a row to the time required when the program iterates through all columns and touches each row within a column. Look at the memory size on your computer and explain the performance results.

9.14 Assume a *hello world* program references page 0 and the top page in its address space. Draw a diagram of page tables similar to the diagram in Figure 9.13 for the five-level paging scheme in Figure 9.15.

9.15 Extend the previous exercise by calculating the size of each page table and the total size of all page tables.

Chapter Contents

10

Caches And Caching

10.1 Introduction

The previous chapters discuss main memory and virtual memory. They discuss the underlying technologies used to build memory systems, the organization of memory modules, and demand paging technologies used to create virtual address spaces.

This chapter focuses on a mechanism that can improve memory system performance. Instead of using faster DRAM technologies or new ways to organize underlying memories, the chapter presents the fundamental concept of caching. It covers the types of caching systems used with memory, explains why caching is essential, and describes why caching achieves high performance with low cost.

10.2 How Data Propagates Through A Storage Hierarchy

We think of data storage mechanisms as forming a conceptual hierarchy. Levels are arranged by access speed: an external disk takes the longest to access, main memory can be accessed faster, and general-purpose registers have the fastest access. Because high-speed mechanisms take more power and cost more, designers make fastest mechanisms store a small amount of data.

Data items migrate up and down the hierarchy, usually under control of software. In general, items move up the hierarchy when they are read, and down the hierarchy when they are written. For example, when a program starts to run and references a page in its address space, the demand paging system copies the page from external storage into a frame in memory. Similarly, to perform an arithmetic computation, a compiler arranges to move items from memory into registers. After the computation finishes, the result may be moved back to memory. If a data item must persist beyond the time a program runs, the programmer will copy the item from memory to secondary storage. We will see how caching fits into the storage hierarchy, and will learn that a memory cache uses hardware rather than software to move items up and down in its part of the hierarchy.

10.3 Definition of Caching

The term *caching* refers to an important optimization technique used to improve the performance of any hardware or software system that retrieves information. In memory systems, caching can reduce the Von Neumann bottleneck†. A *cache* acts as an intermediate storage mechanism. That is, a designer places a cache on the path between a mechanism that uses data and a mechanism that stores the data. The cache intercepts all requests and handles some requests quickly, without sending the requests to the storage mechanism.

A cache uses a small, temporary, high-speed mechanism to store a copy of selected data items, and answers requests from the local copy whenever possible. Performance improvements arise because a cache is designed to return answers faster than the mechanism that normally fulfills requests. Figure 10.1 illustrates a small cache positioned between a mechanism that makes requests and a large data storage mechanism that answers requests.

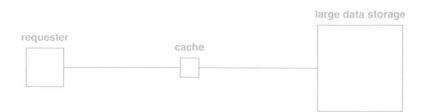

Figure 10.1 Conceptual organization of a cache positioned on the path between a mechanism that makes requests and a storage mechanism that answers requests.

10.4 Characteristics Of A Cache

The description may seem vague because computer and communication systems use caching in a variety of ways. This section clarifies the definition by giving more details; later sections explain how caching can be used.

Although many caching mechanisms exist, they share the following general characteristics:

---

†The Von Neumann bottleneck is defined on page 101.

- Small
- Active
- Transparent
- Automatic

Small. To keep economic cost low, designers keep the amount of storage associated with a cache much smaller than the amount of storage needed to hold the entire set of data items. In many cases, a cache holds less than one percent as much as the data store. Thus, a cache designer faces the question of which data items to keep in the cache.

Active. A cache contains an active mechanism that examines each request and decides how to respond. Activities include checking to see if a requested item is available in the local copies in the cache, retrieving a copy of an item from the data store if the item is not available locally, and deciding whether to keep a copy of a retrieved item in the cache. A cache may also have a policy that specifies discarding a copy after a specified time has elapsed.

Transparent. We use the term *transparent* to mean that a cache can be inserted without changing the requester or the data store. That is, the cache presents exactly the same interface to the requester as the data store presents, and the cache accesses the data store exactly the same way as a requester.

Automatic. A cache mechanism acts autonomously, and does not need extra input to decide which items to keep in its local storage. Instead, the cache contains a built-in algorithm and policy that determine how to manage the cached items.

10.5 Cache Terminology

Although caching is used in a variety of contexts, some of the terminology related to caching has achieved universal acceptance across all types of caching systems. We use the term *cache hit* (abbreviated *hit*) to refer to a situation where the cache satisfies a request from its local copies without accessing the underlying data store. Conversely, a *cache miss* (abbreviated *miss*) refers to a situation where a request cannot be satisfied from the local copies in the cache, which means the cache must send the request to the underlying data store.

Additional cache terminology focuses on the sequence of references presented to a cache. We say that a sequence of references exhibits *high locality of reference* if the sequence contains frequent repetitions of requests; otherwise, we say that the sequence has *low locality of reference*. We will see that high locality of reference leads to higher performance. Locality refers to items in the cache. Therefore, if a cache stores large data items (e.g., pages of memory) and requests reference parts of an item, repeated requests do not need to be absolutely identical provided they refer to the same item in the cache (e.g., a series of references to bytes that all lie on the same page).

10.6 Best-Case And Worst-Case Cache Performance

If the local storage on the cache contains an item, the cache mechanism can return the item faster than an access to the large data store. Figure 10.2 illustrates the cost to access an item as measured by the time it takes to satisfy a request.

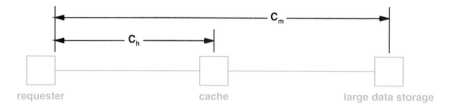

Figure 10.2 Illustration of access costs when using a cache. Costs are measured as the time taken from the requester's point of view.

In the figure, C_h represents the cost if an item is found in the cache (i.e., a hit), and C_m represents the cost if an item is not found in the cache (i.e., a miss). Interestingly, analysis of cache performance does not focus on individual access times. To see why, observe that because a cache keeps the answers to previous requests, performance depends on the order of requests. Thus, to understand caching, we must assess performance over a sequence of requests. For example, we can easily analyze the best and worst possible behavior for a sequence of N requests. At one extreme, if each request references a new item, caching does not improve performance at all — the cache must forward each request to the data store. Thus, in the worst case, the cost is:

$$C_{worst} = N \, C_m \tag{10.1}$$

It should be noted that our analysis ignores the administrative overhead required to maintain the cache. If we divide by N to compute the average cost per request, the result is C_m.

At the other extreme, if all requests in the sequence specify the same data item (i.e., the highest locality of reference), the cache can indeed improve performance. When it receives the first request, the cache fetches the item from the data store and saves a copy; the cache uses the saved copy to satisfy all successive requests. Thus, in the best case, the cost is:

$$C_{best} = C_m + (N - 1) \, C_h \tag{10.2}$$

Dividing by N produces the cost per request:

$$C_{per\_request} = \frac{C_m + (N - 1) \, C_h}{N} = \frac{C_m}{N} - \frac{C_h}{N} + C_h \tag{10.3}$$

As $N \to \infty$, the first two terms approach zero, which means that the cost per request in the best case becomes C_h. We can understand why caching is such a powerful tool:

> *If one ignores overhead, the worst-case performance of caching is no worse than if the cache were not present. In the best case, the cost per request is approximately equal to the cost of accessing the cache, which is lower than the cost of accessing the data store.*

10.7 Cache Performance On A Typical Sequence

To estimate performance of a cache on a typical sequence of requests, we need to examine how the cache handles a sequence that contains both hits and misses. Cache designers use the term *hit ratio* to refer to the percentage of requests in the sequence that are satisfied from the cache. Specifically, the hit ratio is defined to be:

$$hit\ ratio\ =\ \frac{number\ of\ requests\ that\ are\ hits}{total\ number\ of\ requests} \tag{10.4}$$

The hit ratio is a value between zero and one. We define a *miss ratio* to be one minus the hit ratio.

Of course, the actual hit ratio depends on the specific sequence of requests. Experience has shown that for many caches, the hit ratio tends to be nearly the same across the requests encountered in practice. In such cases, we can derive an equation for the cost of access in terms of the cost of a miss and the cost of a hit:

$$Cost\ =\ r\ C_h\ +\ (1-r)\ C_m \tag{10.5}$$

where r is the hit ratio defined in Equation 10.4 above.

The cost of accessing the data store, given by C_m in the equation, cannot be changed. Thus, a designer can improve performance of a cache in two ways: increase the hit ratio or decrease the cost of a hit.

10.8 Cache Replacement Policy

How can a cache designer increase the hit ratio? Two possibilities arise:

- Increase the cache size
- Improve the replacement policy

Increase the cache size. Recall that a cache is usually much smaller than a large data store. When it begins, a cache keeps a copy of each response. Once the local cache storage becomes full, an existing item must be removed before a new item can be added. A larger cache can store more items.

Improve the replacement policy. A cache uses a *replacement policy* to decide which item to remove when a new item is encountered and the cache is full. The replacement policy specifies whether to ignore the new item or how to choose an item to evict to make space for the new item. A replacement policy that chooses to keep those items that will be referenced again can increase the hit ratio.

10.9 LRU Replacement

What replacement policy works best? A designer considers two aspects. First, to increase the hit ratio, the replacement policy should retain those items that will be referenced again. Second, the replacement policy should operate quickly, especially for a memory cache. One replacement policy that satisfies both criteria has become extremely popular. Known as *Least Recently Used (LRU)*, the policy specifies replacing the item that was referenced the longest time in the past†.

To make LRU efficient, a cache mechanism keeps a list of data items that are currently in the cache. When a request refers to the item, the item moves to the front of the list; when evicting an item, the cache chooses the item at the back of the list.

LRU works well in many situations. If requests exhibit a high locality of reference, a few items will be referenced again and again, and those items will remain in the cache. Thus, the average cost of access remains low. We can summarize:

> *When its storage is full and a new item arrives, a cache must choose whether to retain the current set of items or replace one of the current items with the new item. The Least Recently Used (LRU) policy is a popular choice for replacement because it is efficient and tends to keep items that will be requested again.*

10.10 Multilevel Cache Hierarchy

One of the most unexpected and astonishing aspects of caching arises because an additional cache can improve the performance of an existing cache! To understand the optimization, recall that the insertion of a cache lowers the cost of retrieving items by placing some of the items closer to the requester. Now imagine an additional cache placed between the requester and the existing cache, as Figure 10.3 illustrates.

Figure 10.3 The organization of a system with an additional cache inserted.

---

†Note that "least recently" always refers to how long ago the item was last referenced, not how many times the item was referenced.

Will a second cache improve performance? Yes, provided the cost to access the new cache is lower than the cost to access the original cache (e.g., the new cache is closer to the requester). In essence, the cost equation becomes:

$$Cost \;=\; r_1\,C_{h1} \;+\; r_2\,C_{h2} \;+\; (1 - r_1 - r_2)\,C_m \qquad (10.6)$$

where r_1 denotes the fraction of hits for the new cache, r_2 denotes the fraction of hits for the original cache, C_{h1} denotes the cost of accessing the new cache, and C_{h2} denotes the cost of accessing the original cache.

When more than one cache occurs along the path from requester to data store, we say that the system implements a *multilevel cache hierarchy*. A set of Web caches provides an example of a multilevel hierarchy. The path between a browser running on a user's computer can pass through a cache at the user's ISP as well as the local cache mechanism used by the browser.

The point is:

> *Adding an additional cache can be used to improve the performance of a system that uses caching. Conceptually, the caches are arranged in a multilevel hierarchy.*

10.11 Preloading Caches

How can cache performance be improved further? Cache designers observe that although many cache systems perform well in the steady state (i.e., after the system has been running), the system exhibits higher cost during startup. That is, the initial hit ratio is extremely low because requests miss, causing the cache to fetch items from the data store. In some cases, the startup costs can be lowered by *preloading* the cache. That is, load selected items into the cache before execution begins.

Of course, preloading only works in cases where the cache can anticipate requests. For example, an ISP's Web cache can be preloaded with *hot* pages (i.e., pages that have been accessed frequently in the past day or pages for which the owner expects frequent access). As an alternative, some caches use an automated method of preloading. In one form, the cache periodically places a copy of its contents on nonvolatile storage, allowing recent values to be preloaded at startup. In another form, the cache uses a reference to *prefetch* related data. For example, if a processor accesses a byte of memory, the cache can fetch 128 bytes. Thus, if the processor accesses the next byte, which is likely, the value will come from the cache.

Prefetching is especially important for Web pages. A typical Web page contains references to multiple images, and before the page can be displayed, a browser must download a copy of each image and cache the copy on the user's computer. As a page is being downloaded, a browser can scan for references to images, and can begin to prefetch each of the images without waiting for the entire page to download.

10.12 Caches Used With Memory

Now that we understand the basic idea of caching, we can consider some of the ways caches are used in memory systems. In fact, the concept of caching originated with computer memory systems†. The original motivation for a memory cache was higher speed at low cost. Because memory was both expensive and slow, architects looked for ways to improve performance without incurring the cost of higher-speed memory. The architects discovered that a small amount of high-speed cache improved performance dramatically. The result was so impressive that by the 1980s, most computer systems had a cache located between the processor and memory. Physically, memory was on one circuit board and the cache occupied a separate circuit board, which allowed computer owners to upgrade the memory or the cache independently. As described above, a caching hierarchy can increase performance more than a single cache. Therefore, we will see that modern computers employ a hierarchy of memory caches and use caching in a variety of ways. The next sections present a few examples.

10.13 Main Memory Cache

Caching has become popular as a way to achieve higher memory performance without significantly higher cost. It may seem that designing a physical memory cache would be trivial. We can imagine the memory cache receiving a *fetch* request, checking to see if the request can be answered from the cache, and then, if the item is not present, passing the request to the underlying memory. Furthermore, we can imagine that once an item has been retrieved from the underlying memory, the cache saves a copy locally, and then returns the value to the processor.

In fact, our imagined scenario is misleading — a memory cache is much more complex than the above description. To understand why, remember that hardware achieves high speed through parallelism. For example, when it encounters a *fetch* request, a memory cache does not check the cache and then access the physical memory. Instead, the cache hardware performs two tasks in parallel: the cache simultaneously passes the request to the physical memory and searches for an answer locally. If it finds an answer locally, the cache must cancel the memory operation. If it does not find an answer locally, the cache must wait for the underlying memory operation to complete. Furthermore, when an answer does arrive from memory, the cache uses parallelism again by simultaneously saving a local copy of the answer and transferring the answer back to the processor. Parallel activities make the hardware complex. The point is:

> *To achieve high performance, a physical memory cache is designed to search the local cache and access the underlying memory simultaneously. Parallelism complicates the hardware.*

---

†In addition to introducing the use of microcode, Maurice Wilkes is credited with inventing the concept of a memory cache in 1965.

10.14 Write Through And Write Back

In addition to parallelism, memory caches must contend with *write* (i.e., *store*) operations. There are two issues: performance and coherence. Performance is easiest to understand: caching improves the performance for retrieval requests, but not for storage requests because a *write* operation must change the value in the underlying memory, not just in the cache. In addition to forwarding the request to the memory, a cache must check to see whether it has saved a local copy. If so, the cache must also update its copy. In fact, experience has shown that a memory cache should always keep a local copy of each value that is written because programs tend to access a value a short time after it has been stored.

Initial implementations of memory caches handled *write* operations as described above: the cache kept a copy and also forwarded the *write* operation to the underlying memory. We use the term *write-through cache* to describe the approach.

The alternative, known as *write-back* cache, arranges for the cache to keep a copy of a data value that is written and wait until later to update the underlying physical memory. To know whether the underlying physical memory must be updated, a write-back cache keeps an extra bit with each item that is known as the *dirty bit*. In a memory cache, a dirty bit is associated with each block in the cache. When an item is fetched and a copy is placed in the cache, the dirty bit is initialized to zero. When the processor modifies the item (i.e., performs a *write*), the cache sets the dirty bit to one. When it needs to eject a block from the cache, the hardware first examines the dirty bit associated with the block. If the dirty bit is one, a copy of the block is written to memory. If the dirty is zero, however, the block can simply be overwritten because data in the block is exactly the same as the copy in memory. The point is:

> A *write-back cache associates a dirty bit with each data item to record whether the item has been modified since it was fetched. When ejecting an item from the cache, the hardware writes a copy of a dirty item to memory, but does not need to write an item that is not dirty.*

To see why write-back improves performance, imagine a *for loop* in a program that increments a variable in memory on each iteration of the loop. A write-back cache places the variable in the cache when the loop initializes the variable. On each successive iteration when the loop changes the variable, only the local copy in the cache changes. Once the loop ends, the program stops referencing the variable. Eventually, the program generates enough other references so that the variable becomes the least recently used item in the cache. When it needs space for a new item, the cache will select the item for replacement, observe that it is dirty, and write the value to the underlying memory. Thus, although a variable can be referenced or changed many times, the cache only writes the value to the underlying memory once†.

---

†An optimizing compiler can further improve performance by using a general-purpose register to hold the variable until the loop finishes (another form of caching).

10.15 Cache Coherence

Memory caches are especially complex in a system with multiple processors (e.g., a multicore CPU). A write-back cache achieves higher performance than a write-through cache. A multiprocessor design can optimize cache performance by giving each core its own cache. Unfortunately, the two optimizations conflict. To understand why, look at Figure 10.4, which shows two cores that each have a private cache.

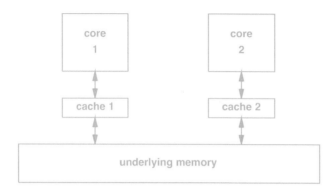

Figure 10.4 Illustration of two processors sharing an underlying memory. Because each processor has a separate cache, conflicts can occur if both processors reference the same memory address.

Now consider what happens if the two caches use a write-back approach and the two cores attempt to use the same variable X. When core 1 writes to the memory location for X, cache 1 holds the value. If core 1 updates the value, the new value will still be held in cache 1. If core 2 accesses the location for X, it will read the value from memory, and if core 2 changes X, the new value will be placed in cache 2. The problem should be obvious: using write-through and separate caches means the two cores can have different values for X.

To avoid such conflicts, all caches that access a given memory must follow a *cache coherence protocol* that coordinates the values. For example, when core 2 reads from an address, A, the coherence protocol requires cache 2 to inform cache 1. If it currently holds address A, cache 1 writes A to the memory so cache 2 can obtain the most recent value. Coherence requires a *read* of address A by any core to trigger a write-back of A in any cache that currently holds a cached copy of A. Similarly, if any core issues a *write* operation for an address, A, all other caches must be informed to discard cached values of A. Thus, in addition to requiring additional hardware and a mechanism that allows the caches to communicate, cache coherency introduces additional delay.

10.16 L1, L2, and L3 Caches

Recall that arranging multiple caches into a hierarchy can improve overall performance. Indeed, most computer memory systems have at least two levels in their memory cache hierarchy. To understand why computer architects added a second level of cache to the memory hierarchy, we must consider four facts:

- A traditional memory cache was separate from both the memory and the processor.

- To access a traditional memory cache, a processor used pins that connect the processor chip to the rest of the computer.

- Using pins to access external hardware takes much longer than accessing functional units that are internal to the processor chip.

- Advances in technology have made it possible to increase the number of transistors per chip, which means a processor chip can contain more hardware.

The conclusion should be clear. We know that adding a second cache can improve memory system performance, we further know that placing the second cache on the processor chip will make the cache access times much lower, and we know that technology now allows chip vendors to add more hardware to their chips. So, it makes sense to embed a second memory cache in the processor chip itself. If the hit ratio is high, most data references will never leave the processor chip — the effective cost of accessing memory will be approximately the same as the cost of accessing a register.

To describe the idea of multiple caches, computer manufacturers originally adopted the terms *Level 1 cache* (*L1 cache*) to refer to the cache onboard the processor chip, *Level 2 cache* (*L2 cache*) to refer to a cache outside the processor chip, and *Level 3 cache* (*L3 cache*) to refer to a cache built into the memory. That is, an L1 cache was originally *on-chip* and an L2 or L3 cache was *off-chip*.

In fact, chip sizes have become so large that a single chip can contain multiple cores and multiple caches. In such cases, manufacturers use the term *L1 cache* to describe a cache that is associated with one particular core, the term *L2 cache* to describe an on-chip cache that may be shared by a few cores, and the term *L3 cache* to describe an on-chip cache that is shared by many cores. Typically, all cores share an L3 cache. Thus, the distinction between on-chip and off-chip has faded.

We can summarize the terminology:

> *When using traditional terminology for a multilevel cache hierarchy, an L1 cache is embedded on the processor chip, an L2 cache is external to the processor, and an L3 cache is built into the memory hardware. More recent terminology defines an L1 cache to be associated with a single core, whereas L2 and L3 refer to on-chip caches that some or all cores share.*

10.17 Sizes Of L1, L2, And L3 Caches

Most computers employ a cache hierarchy. Of course, the cache at the top of the hierarchy is the fastest, but also the smallest. Figure 10.5 lists example cache memory sizes. The L1 cache may be divided into separate instruction and data caches, as described in the next section.

Cache	Size	Notes
L1	64 KB to 96 KB	Per core
L2	256 KB to 8 MB	May be per core
L3	8 MB to 24 MB	Shared among all cores

Figure 10.5 Example cache sizes. Cache size increases as the number of transistors on a chip increases and as memory sizes increase.

10.18 Instruction And Data Caches

Should all memory references pass through a single cache? To understand the question, imagine instructions being executed and data being accessed. Instruction fetch tends to behave with high locality — in many cases, the next instruction to be executed lies in an adjacent memory address. Furthermore, the most time-consuming loops in a program usually occupy only a few instructions, which means all the memory locations that contain code for the entire loop will fit into a cache. Although the data access in some programs exhibits high locality, the data access in others does not. For example, when a program accesses a hash table, the locations referenced appear to be random (i.e., the location referenced in one iteration will not necessarily lie close to the location referenced in the next).

Differences between instruction and data behavior raise the question of how inter-mixing the two types of references affects a cache. In essence, the more random the sequence of requests becomes, the worse a cache performs (because the cache will save each value, even though the value will not be needed again). We can state a general principle:

> *Inserting random references in the series of requests tends to worsen cache performance; reducing the number of random references that occurs tends to improve cache performance.*

10.19 Modified Harvard Architecture

Is performance optimized by having a separate cache for instructions and data? The simplistic answer is yes. When both data and instructions are placed in the same cache, data references tend to push instructions out of the cache, lowering performance. Adding a separate instruction cache will improve performance.

The simplistic answer does not address the main question of how to choose among tradeoffs. Because additional hardware will generate more heat, consume more power, and in portable devices, deplete the battery faster, an architect must weigh the costs of an additional cache with the benefits. If additional cache hardware will be added, the question is how best to use the hardware. We know, for example, that increasing the size of a single cache will increase performance by storing more items. If a cache becomes sufficiently large, intermixing instructions and data references will work fine. Would it be better to add a separate instruction cache or to increase the size of a single cache?

Many architects have decided that the optimal way to use a modest amount of additional hardware lies in introducing a new *I-cache* (*instruction cache*) and using the existing cache as a *D-cache* (*data cache*). Separating instruction and data caches is trivial in a Harvard Architecture because an I-cache is associated with the instruction memory and a D-cache is associated with the data memory. Should architects abandon the Von Neumann Architecture?

Many architects have adopted a compromise in which a computer has separate instruction and data caches, but the caches lead to a single memory. We use the term *Modified Harvard Architecture* to characterize the compromise. Figure 10.6 illustrates the modified architecture.

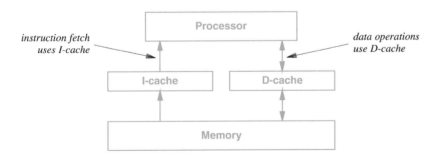

Figure 10.6 A Modified Harvard Architecture with separate instruction and data caches leading to the same underlying memory.

10.20 Implementation Of Memory Caching

Conceptually, each entry in a memory cache contains two values: a memory address and the value of the byte found at that address. In practice, storing a complete address with each entry is inefficient. Therefore, memory caches use clever techniques to reduce the amount of space needed. The two most important cache optimization techniques are known as:

- Direct mapped memory cache
- Set associative memory cache

We will see that, like virtual memory schemes, both cache implementations use powers of two to avoid arithmetic computation.

10.21 Direct Mapped Memory Cache

A *direct mapped memory cache* uses a mapping technique to avoid overhead. Although memory caches are used with byte-addressable memories, a cache does not store individual bytes. Instead, a cache divides both the memory and the cache into a set of fixed-size blocks, where the block size, B (measured in bytes), is chosen to be a power of two. The hardware places an entire block in the cache whenever a byte in the block is referenced. Using cache terminology, we refer to a block in the cache as a *cache line*; the size of a direct mapped memory cache is often specified by giving the number of cache lines times the size of a cache line. For example, the size might be specified as 8K lines with 8 bytes per line. To envision such a cache, think of bytes in memory being divided into 8-byte segments and assigned to lines of the cache. Figure 10.7 illustrates how bytes of memory would be assigned for a block size of eight in a cache that has four lines. (Note: a memory cache usually holds many more than four lines; a small cache size has been chosen as a simplified example for the figure.)

Observe that the blocks in memory are numbered modulo C, where C is the number of slots in the cache. That is, blocks are numbered from zero through $C-1$ (C is 4 in the figure). Interestingly, using powers of two means that no arithmetic is required to map a byte address to a block number. Instead, the block number can be found by extracting a set of bits. In the figure, the block number can be computed by extracting bits 3 and 4 from the address. For example, consider the byte with address 57 (1$\underline{11}$001 in binary, shown with bits 3 and 4 underlined). The bits 11 are 3 in decimal, which agrees with the block number in the figure. In address 44 (1$\underline{01}$100 in binary), bits 3 and 4 are 01 and the block number is 1. We can express the mapping in programming language terms as:

b = (byte_address >> 3) & 0x03;

In terms of a memory cache, no computation is needed — the hardware places the value in an internal register and extracts the appropriate bits to form a block number.

block   addresses of bytes in memory

3	56	57	58	59	60	61	62	63
2	48	49	50	51	52	53	54	55
1	40	41	42	43	44	45	46	47
0	32	33	34	35	36	37	38	39
3	24	25	26	27	28	29	30	31
2	16	17	18	19	20	21	22	23
1	8	9	10	11	12	13	14	15
0	0	1	2	3	4	5	6	7

Figure 10.7 An example assignment of block numbers to memory locations
for a cache of four blocks with eight bytes per block.

The key to understanding a direct mapped memory cache arises from the following
rule: only a memory block numbered i can be placed in cache slot i. For example, the
block with byte addresses 16 through 23 can be placed in slot 2, as can the block with
byte addresses 48 through 55.

If multiple memory blocks can be placed in a given slot, how does the cache know
which block is currently in a slot? The cache attaches a unique *tag* to each group of C
blocks. For example, Figure 10.8 illustrates how tag values are assigned to memory
blocks in our example cache that has four slots.

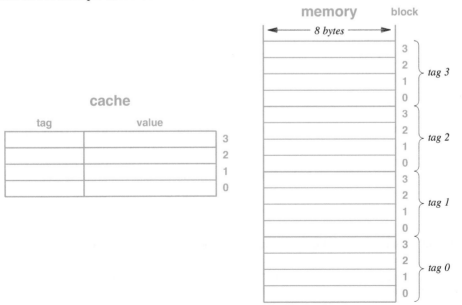

Figure 10.8 An example memory cache with space for four blocks and a
memory divided into conceptual blocks of 8 bytes. Each group
of four blocks in memory is assigned a unique tag.

To identify the block currently in a slot of the cache, each cache entry contains a tag value. Thus, if slot zero in the cache contains tag K, the value in slot zero corresponds to block zero from the area of memory that has tag K.

Why use tags? A cache must uniquely identify the entry in a slot. Because a tag identifies a large group of blocks rather than a single byte of memory, using a tag requires fewer bits to identify a section of memory than using a full memory address. Furthermore, as the next section explains, choosing the block size and the size of memory identified by a tag to be powers of two makes cache lookup extremely efficient.

10.22 Using Powers Of Two For Efficiency

Although the direct mapping described above may seem complex, using powers of two simplifies the hardware implementation. In fact, the hardware is elegant and extremely efficient. Instead of modulo arithmetic, both the tag and block number can be computed by extracting groups of bits from a memory address. The high-order bits of the address form the tag, the next set of bits forms a block number, and the final set of bits gives a byte offset within the block. Figure 10.9 illustrates the division.

Figure 10.9 Illustration of how using powers of two allows a cache to divide a memory address into three separate fields that correspond to a tag, a block number, and a byte offset within the block.

Once we know that all values can be obtained via bit extraction, the algorithm to look up an address in a direct-mapped memory cache becomes straightforward. Think of the cache as an array. The hardware extracts the block number from the address, and then uses the block number as an index into the array. Each entry in the array contains a tag and a value. If the tag in the address matches the tag in the cache slot, the cache returns the value. If the tag does not match, the cache hardware must fetch the block from memory, place a copy in the cache, and then return the value. Algorithm 10.1 summarizes the steps.

The algorithm omits an important detail. Each slot in the cache also contains a *valid bit* that specifies whether the slot has been used. Initially (i.e., when the computer boots), all valid bits are set to 0 (to indicate that none of the slots contain blocks from memory). When it stores a block in a slot, the cache hardware sets the valid bit to 1. When it examines the tag for a slot, the hardware reports a miss if the valid bit is not set, which forces a copy of the block to be loaded from memory.

Algorithm 10.1

Given:

A memory address

Find:

The data byte at that address

Method:

Extract the tag number, t, block number, b, and offset, o,
from the address by selecting the appropriate bit fields

Examine the tag in slot b of the cache

If the tag in slot b of the cache matches t   {

Use o to select the appropriate byte from the
block in slot b, and return the byte

} else {   /* Update the cache */

Fetch block b from the underlying memory

Place a copy in slot b

Set the tag on slot b to t

Use o to select the appropriate byte from the
block in slot b, and return the byte

}

Algorithm 10.1 Cache Lookup In A Direct Mapped Memory Cache

10.23 Hardware Implementation Of A Direct Mapped Cache

Algorithm 10.1 describes cache lookup as if the cache is an array and separate steps are taken to extract items and index the array. In fact, slots of a cache are not stored in an array in memory. Instead, they are implemented with hardware circuits, and the circuits work in parallel. For example, the first step that extracts items from the address can be implemented by placing the address in an internal register (a circuit that has a separate hardware unit for each bit), and arranging wires that extract bits. That is, once the address has been placed in the register, each bit of the address will be represented by a separate wire. The items t, b, and o in the address can be obtained merely by dividing the output wires into groups.

The second step in Algorithm 10.1 requires the cache hardware to examine one of the slots. The hardware uses a decoder to select exactly one of the slots. All slots are connected to common output wires; the hardware is arranged so that only a selected slot puts its output on the wires. A comparator circuit is used to compare the tag in the address with the tag in the selected slot. Figure 10.10 gives a simplified block diagram of the hardware to perform cache lookup.

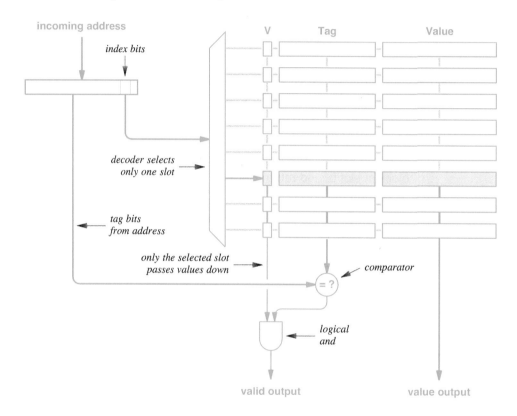

Figure 10.10 Block diagram of the hardware used to implement lookup in a memory cache.

The circuit takes a memory address as an input, and produces two outputs. The output labeled *valid* is 1 if and only if the specified address is found in the cache (i.e., the cache returns a value). The output labeled *value* is the contents of memory at the specified address.

In the figure, each slot has been divided into a valid bit, a tag, and a value to indicate that separate hardware circuits can be used for each field. Horizontal lines from the decoder to each slot indicate a connection that can be used to activate the circuits for the slot. At any time, the decoder only selects one slot (in the figure, the selected slot is shown shaded).

Vertical lines through the slots indicate parallel connections. Hardware in each slot connects to the wires, but only a selected slot places a value on the vertical wires. Thus, in the example, the input to the *logical and* circuit only comes from the *V* circuit of the selected slot, the input to the comparator only comes from the *Tag* circuit of the selected slot, and the output labeled *value output* only comes from the *Value* circuit of the selected slot. The key point is that cache lookup can be performed quickly by combinatorial circuits.

10.24 Set Associative Memory Cache

The chief alternative to a direct mapped memory cache is known as a *set associative memory cache*. In essence, a set associative memory cache uses hardware parallelism to provide more flexibility. Instead of maintaining a single cache, the set associative approach maintains multiple underlying caches, and provides hardware that can search all of them simultaneously. More important, because it provides multiple underlying caches, a set associative memory cache can store more than one block that has the same number.

As a trivial example, consider a set associative cache in which there are two copies of the underlying hardware. Figure 10.11 illustrates the architecture†.

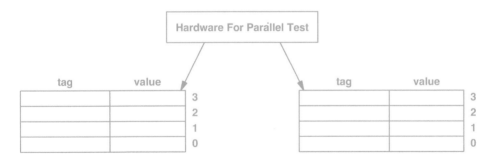

Figure 10.11 Illustration of a set associative memory cache with two copies of the underlying hardware. The cache includes hardware to search both copies in parallel.

To understand the advantages of the set associative approach, consider a reference string in which a program alternately references two addresses, A_1 and A_2, that have different tags, but both have block number zero. In a direct mapped memory cache, the two addresses contend for the same slot in the cache, which means that only one of them can be present in the cache at a given time. A reference to A_1 loads the value of A_1 into slot 0 of the cache, and a reference to A_2 overwrites the contents of slot 0 with the value of A_2. Thus, in an alternating sequence of references, every reference results in a cache miss. In a set associative memory cache, A_1 can be placed in one of the two

†In practice, a set associative cache usually has more than two parallel hardware units.

underlying caches, and A_2 can be placed in the other. Thus, every reference results in a cache hit.

A cache with more parallel units will perform better than a cache with fewer. In the extreme case, a cache is classified as *fully associative*, if each of the underlying caches contains only one slot, but the slot can hold an arbitrary value. Note that the amount of parallelism determines a point on a continuum: with no parallelism, we have a direct mapped memory cache, and with full parallelism, we have the equivalent of a *Content Addressable Memory* (*CAM*).

10.25 Consequences For Programmers

Experience has shown that caching works well for most computer programs. The code that programmers produce tends to contain loops, which means a processor will repeatedly execute a small set of instructions before moving on to another set. Similarly, programs tend to reference data items multiple times before moving on to a new data item. Furthermore, some compilers are aware of caching, and help optimize the generated code to take advantage of the cache.

Despite the overwhelming success of caching, programmers who understand how a cache works can write code that exploits a cache. For example, consider a program that must perform many operations on each element of a large array. It is possible to perform one operation at a time (in which case the program iterates through the array many times) or to perform all the operations on a single element of the array before moving to the next element (in which case the program iterates through the array once). From the point of view of caching, the latter is preferable because the element being used will remain in the cache.

10.26 The Relationship Between Virtual Memory And Caching

Two key technologies in virtual memory systems are related to caching: a TLB and demand page replacement. Recall that a TLB consists of a small, high-speed hardware mechanism that improves the performance of a demand paging system dramatically. In fact, a TLB is nothing more than a cache of address mappings: whenever it looks up a page table entry, the MMU stores the entry in the TLB. A successive lookup for the same page will receive an answer from the TLB.

Like many cache systems, a TLB usually uses the Least Recently Used replacement strategy. Conceptually, when an entry is referenced, the TLB moves the entry to the front of the list; when a new reference occurs and the cache is full, the TLB discards the page table entry on the back of the list to make space for the new entry. Of course, the TLB cannot afford to keep a linked list in memory. Instead, the TLB contains digital circuits that move values into a special-purpose *Content Addressable Memory* (*CAM*) at high speed.

Demand paging can also be viewed as a form of caching. The cache corresponds to main memory, and the data store corresponds to the external storage where pages are kept until needed. Furthermore, the page replacement policy serves as a cache replacement policy. In fact, paging borrows the phrase *replacement policy* from caching.

Interestingly, thinking of demand paging as a cache can help us understand an important concept: how a virtual address space can be much larger than physical memory. Like a cache, physical memory only holds a fraction of the total pages from a virtual address space. From our analysis of caching, we know that the performance of a demand-paged virtual memory can approach the performance of physical memory. In other words:

> *The analysis of caching shows that using demand paging on a computer system with a small physical memory can perform almost as well as if the computer had a large memory provided the references to pages exhibit high locality of reference.*

10.27 Virtual Memory Caching And Cache Flush

If caching is used with virtual memory, should the cache be placed between the processor and the MMU or between the MMU and the underlying memory? That is, should the memory cache store pairs of virtual address and contents or pairs of underlying memory address and contents? The answer is complex. On the one hand, using virtual addresses increases memory access speed because the cache can respond before the MMU translates the virtual address into a memory address. On the other hand, a cache that uses virtual addresses needs extra hardware that allows the cache to interact with the virtual memory system. To understand why, observe that a virtual memory system usually supplies the same address range to each running application (i.e., each process has an address space that starts at zero). Now consider what happens when the operating system switches from one application to another. Suppose the memory cache contains an entry for address 2000 before the switch occurs. If the cache remains unchanged during the switch and the new application reads location 2000, the cache will return the value from location 2000 in the old application. Therefore, when it changes from one process to another, the operating system must also change items in the cache.

How can a cache avoid the problem of ambiguity that occurs when multiple applications use the same range of addresses? Architects use two solutions:

- Cache flush
- Disambiguation

Cache Flush. One way to ensure that a cache does not report incorrect values consists of removing all existing entries from the cache. We say that the cache is *flushed*. In architectures that use flushing, the operating system must flush the cache whenever it switches from one application to another.

Disambiguation. The alternative to cache flushing involves the use of extra bits
that identify which application is running (or more precisely, which address space an
application is using). The processor may contain an extra hardware register that stores
an address space ID. Many operating systems create an address space for each application that runs, and use the integer *process ID* that identifies the application to identify
the address space the application uses. Whenever it switches to an application, the
operating system loads the application's process ID into the address space ID register.
As Figure 10.12 shows, a cache that uses disambiguation prepends the contents of the
address space ID register onto a virtual address when it stores the address in the cache.
Consequently, even if process 1 and process 2 both reference address 0, the two entries
in the cache will differ.

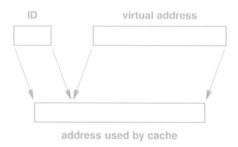

Figure 10.12 Illustration of an ID register used to disambiguate among a set
of virtual address spaces. Each address space is assigned a
unique number, which the operating system loads into the ID
register.

As the figure illustrates, the cache is designed to use a longer address than a virtual
memory system. Before passing a request to the cache, the processor creates an artifi-
cially long address by concatenating a virtual address onto the address space ID. The
processor then passes the longer address to the cache. From the cache's point of view,
there is no ambiguity: even if two applications reference the same virtual address, the
ID bits distinguish between the two addresses.

10.28 A Note About Cache Performance

While porting an operating system to new hardware, the author failed to enable the
L1 cache during system startup. The system ran, but was intolerably slow. When the
problem was corrected and the L1 cached enabled, the system performed more than fifteen times faster. The point is:

> *Using a memory cache can improve performance by an order of mag-
> nitude. In one case, performance improved by a factor of fifteen.*

10.29 Summary

Caching is a fundamental optimization technique that can be used in many contexts. A cache intercepts requests, automatically stores values, and answers requests quickly, whenever possible. Variations include a multilevel cache hierarchy and preloaded caches.

Caches provide an essential performance optimization for memory systems. Most computer systems employ a multilevel memory cache. Originally, an L1 cache resided on the same chip as the processor, an L2 cache was located external to the processor, and an L3 cache was associated with the memory. As integrated circuits became larger, manufacturers moved L2 and L3 caches onto the processor chip, using the distinction that an L1 cache is associated with a single core, whereas L2 and L3 caches are shared among several or all cores.

A technology known as a direct mapped memory cache handles lookup without keeping a list of cached items. Although we think of the lookup algorithm as performing multiple steps, a hardware implementation of a direct mapped memory cache can use combinatorial logic circuits to perform the lookup without needing a processor. A set associative memory cache extends the concept of a direct mapped memory cache to permit parallel access.

EXERCISES

10.1   What does the term *transparent* mean when applied to a memory cache?

10.2   If the hit ratio for a given piece of code is 0.2, the time required to access the cache is 20 nanoseconds, and the time to access the underlying physical memory is 1 microsecond, what is the effective memory access time for the piece of code?

10.3   Consider a computer where each memory address is thirty-two-bits long and the memory system has a cache that holds up to 4K entries. A naive cache implementation arranges each entry in the cache to store an address and a byte of data. How much total storage is needed for the cache?

10.4   Extend the previous exercise. Assume the total size of the cache is fixed, and find an alternative to the naive solution that allows the cache to store more data items. Hint: suppose the cache is used with a program that always writes and reads 4-byte integer values.

10.5   Instead of the implementation in Exercise 10.3, consider a direct mapped memory cache in which each entry stores a 2-byte tag and a block of data that consists of four bytes. How much total storage is needed to hold 4K entries?

10.6   Consult vendors' specifications and find the cost of memory access and the cost of a cache hit for a modern memory system (C_h and C_m in Section 10.6).

10.7   Use the values obtained in the previous exercise to plot the effective memory access cost as the hit ratio varies from zero to one.

10.8   Suppose the cache response time, C_h, is one-tenth of the time required to access memory, C_m. What value of the hit ratio, r, is needed to achieve an improvement of 30% in the mean access time using a cache as compared to using the memory system without a cache?

10.9   State two ways to improve the hit ratio of a cache.

10.10   What is cache coherence, and what type of system needs it?

10.11   Write a computer program to simulate a direct mapped memory cache using a cache of
             64 blocks and a block size of 128 bytes. To test the program, create a 1000 x 1000 ar-
             ray of integers. Simulate the address references if a program walks the array in row-
             major order and column-major order. What is the hit ratio of your cache in each case?

10.12   Draw a diagram that shows a 4-way set associative cache, and specify how the cache
             uses bits of an address.

Chapter Contents

11

Storage: File Systems, Blocks, And SSDs

11.1 Introduction

Previous chapters focus on main memory, the virtual address spaces that an operating system provides for applications, and memory caches. This chapter considers another primary component of a computer: storage. The chapter explains the ideal of long-term persistent data storage, the hardware mechanisms used for storage, and the operations that storage hardware offers. The chapter explains the most common use of storage facilities: storing data in the form of files. It examines the block-oriented interface the hardware uses, and briefly describes how file system software uses block storage to store files.

11.2 Persistent Storage Mechanisms And Files

Mechanisms that store data fall into two broad categories:

- Volatile — stored data disappears after power has been removed
- Persistent — stored values remain after power has been removed

We classify general-purpose registers and the DRAM technology used for main memory as *volatile* because they require constant power. Once a computer has been powered down, neither the registers nor the main memory retain data values; when the computer powers up again, new (perhaps random) values will appear. By contrast, the persistent storage mechanisms used with computers retain values even if a computer has been powered down for a long time (e.g., days or weeks).

Software engineers do not write code that interacts directly with persistent storage devices. Instead, an application creates named *files* and uses the files to hold persistent data. In addition, an application can create *folders*, also known as *directories*. Each folder holds one or more files; using folders helps organize files into meaningful groups.

To create and access files and folders, an application invokes *file system software* in the operating system. The file system uses *device driver software*, also in the operating system, to store and access data on the underlying persistent storage devices. Thus, all interaction with a persistent storage device goes through the operating system, as Figure 11.1 illustrates.

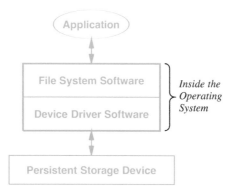

Figure 11.1 Illustration of an application using file system and device driver software to interact with a persistent storage device.

11.3 The History Of Persistent Storage

Early computer designers created a variety of persistent storage devices that used magnetism to record data. A computer-controlled electromagnet passed along a surface coated with a material, changed the magnetism in the surface material, and encoded ones and zeros. Later, to read the recorded data, a sensor passed over the surface and detected the magnetism.

By the 1960s, industry had settled on an electromechanical hardware device known as a *disk drive*. The abbreviation *disk* became popular, and arose because an electric motor turned a flat circular platter that was coated with magnetic material. An arm moved a *read/write head* across the platter, allowing data to be written at any place on the disk. Various forms of disk hardware were created, including hard drives and floppy disks. Over the decades, the physical size of disk drives shrunk from large cabinets several feet tall to a small box less than an inch tall and about five inches wide. Meanwhile, the data capacity of disks increased dramatically from Kilobytes to Megabytes, Gigabytes, and Terabytes.

11.4 Solid-State Drives (SSDs)

Instead of an electromechanical device, a modern computer uses a solid-state hardware device known as an *SSD* (*Solid-State Disk* or *Solid-State Drive*). An SSD has no moving parts, but instead uses *NAND flash memory* to hold data. Consequently, an SSD can access data faster than an old electromechanical disk. Physically, an SSD is small — the ones used in laptop computers are thin and approximately two inches wide. Despite the change in technology, many manufacturers still refer to their devices as disks. Thus, one might see a term such as *USB disk* as well as *flash disk* used with SSD hardware.

Flash technology has evolved since it first appeared, with increases in density allowing SSDs to store more data in the same physical space. At the lowest level, an SSD consists of individual *cells* that store data. Initially, flash technology used planer cells that each held one bit of data. *3D NAND* technology appeared that allows layers of NAND technology to be stacked vertically, which means a cell can hold more than one bit. Figure 11.2 summarizes four cell types.

Cell Type	Full Name	Bits Per Cell
SLC	Single-Level Cell	1
MLC	Multi-Level Cell	2
TLC	Triple-Level Cell	3
QLC	Quad-Level Cell	4

Figure 11.2 The types of cells used in NAND flash memory along with the number of bits per cell that each approaches.

11.5 The Block-Oriented Interface

Although the underlying technologies differ dramatically, both electromechanical and SSDs provide the same interface to a device driver. In fact, some early SSDs were created as exact replacements for electromechanical disks. The replacement had the same physical shape, same electrical connectors, and same capacity as the disk it replaced, allowing a computer owner to open the computer, unplug the existing disk, and plug in the replacement. More important, the replacement honored exactly the same commands and responded exactly the same way as the original disk.

How does an SSD appear to software? The interface between the device driver software in the operating system and the underlying device follows a *block-oriented* approach. Conceptually, an SSD holds a large, one-dimensional array of *blocks*, where each block is the same size. The SSD assigns each block a number: 0, 1, 2, and so on; one can think of the block numbers as providing an index into a giant array.

Traditionally, each block on an SSD contains 512 bytes. To achieve higher performance, some SSDs allow the operating system to format the drive, with a larger block size, but such optimizations do not change the basic concepts. Therefore, we will use a block size of 512 bytes in examples.

The term *block-oriented interface* arises because the hardware always transfers one block of data. Each time a device driver performs an operation on an SSD, the driver either writes a block to the SSD or reads a previously written block. A write operation copies 512 bytes from memory to a block on the SSD, and a read operation copies a block on the SSD to a 512-byte area in memory. The interface does not permit a device driver to read or write part of a block because the hardware can only transfer a full block. Figure 11.3 lists the two operations and the parameters they use.

Operation	Parameters	
Read a block	Block number	Address of buffer in memory
Write a block	Block number	Address of data in memory

Figure 11.3 The block-oriented operations that a storage device supports.

For each operation, the device driver must specify a block number. When it reads a block from the SSD, the driver passes the hardware a block number and a memory address of a buffer into which the incoming block should be placed; the buffer must have space to hold a complete 512-byte block. When it writes a block, the driver specifies the block number and the address of a buffer in memory that contains the data to be written. The memory buffer must contain 512 bytes of data (one complete block).

The point is:

> *The block-oriented interface used with an SSD device can only transfer a complete block at a time.*

11.6 DMA Hardware Used For Block Transfer

The description above states that the device driver passes the *address* of a buffer to the storage device. Why doesn't the driver pass the data to be written to a block or accept the data that has been read from a block? To understand, we need to know how an SSD device and a processor communicate. Chapter 13 explains DMA in more detail. For now, it is sufficient to understand that the processor, memory, and SSD device can all communicate over a hardware mechanism known as a *bus*, and that data can pass over the bus. Figure 11.4 illustrates the interconnection.

In addition to hardware that can communicate over a bus and hardware that stores and retrieves data, an SSD device contains a miniature embedded processor. The embedded processor accepts commands to read and write blocks of the SSD along with the parameters that Figure 11.3 lists. The embedded processor uses an approach known as *Direct Memory Access* (*DMA*) to transfer data directly over the bus to and from memory without using the computer's main processor. Thus, a device driver does not need to send a copy of the bytes to be written, and does not need to accept a copy of all the bytes being read. The driver passes a memory address, and the embedded processor in the SSD uses DMA to handle data transfer.

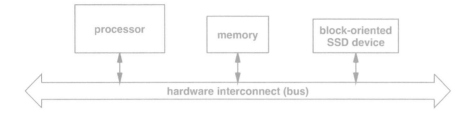

Figure 11.4 Illustration of a bus connecting a processor, memory and a block-oriented storage device.

To summarize:

> *To make block-oriented operations efficient, an SSD uses* Direct Memory Access *to transfer data directly between the device and memory; a device driver only sends a memory address to the device and does not pass data bytes*.

11.7 Storing Files In 512-Byte Blocks

An engineer designs applications that create files, write data to files, and read data from files without thinking about blocks or block storage. File system software in the operating system handles the task of storing variable-sized files on a block-oriented SSD. Although file system details lie beyond the scope of this text, understanding a few basics will help us understand the motivation for the unusual way SSDs work. In particular, two key file system concepts impact the design of SSDs:

- Storage of file data
- Storage of file metadata

Storage of file data. File systems use a straightforward method to store the actual data in a file: divide the file into 512-byte chunks, and place each chunk in a block on the SSD. Because a file may not contain an exact multiple of 512 bytes, the block that contains the last bytes of a file may not be full.

Storage of file metadata. We use the term *metadata* to refer to extra information the file system stores about a file, that may include:

- The name of the file and the owner
- The current size of the file
- Access permissions
- Time stamps
- Locations of data blocks

We will see that time stamps have special significance to an SSD because time stamps can change frequently. Each time stamp records a date and time, and a typical file system stores three time stamps for each file. The time stamps record: the time when the file was first created, the time when the file was last modified, and the time when the file was last accessed. The access time stamp must be changed whenever the file is read. Thus, when an application reads from a file, the file system does two things. First, the file system obtains the block that contains the data being read, and gives a copy to the application. Second, the file system updates the access time stamp in the metadata, and writes the metadata back to the SSD. The point is that the file system stores new metadata whenever an application writes a file.

Because it only stores individual blocks, an SSD does not know which blocks belong to which file. The file system must also store metadata that records the block numbers of the blocks that hold the data for a given file. We can imagine that the metadata for a file contains an array of block numbers. When an application accesses a file, the file system first reads the metadata for the file from the SSD, consults the array of block numbers to find the block that holds the bytes the application needs, and then reads the block of data from the SSD.

11.8 Blocks Of Cells, Logical Blocks, And Erase-Before-Write

Flash memory hardware does not provide access to individual bits or individual cells. Instead, the hardware groups cells into large *blocks*, and only allows an entire block to be accessed at any time. That is, the hardware only provides a way to read the values in an entire block of cells or to store values in an entire block of cells. For various reasons, SSDs do not use the same size blocks internally as they supply externally. For example, a block of cells may hold 128K bytes even though the external interface on the SSD transfers 512-byte blocks. Some SSDs use the term *logical block* to refer to a block that the SSD transfers to or from a computer. Later, we will see how an SSD stores multiple logical blocks (small blocks) in a single large block of cells.

The way flash technology works leads to an interesting and counterintuitive procedure for storing data. If a bit currently contains 1, storing a 0 to the bit changes the value to 0, as expected. However, if a bit currently contains 0, storing a 1 has no effect. So, to store data in a block of cells, flash memory systems use an approach known as *erase-before-write*. In the first step, the hardware *erases* a block of cells by setting all bits in the block to 1. In the second step, the hardware stores zeros and ones. Because all the bits have been initialized to 1 in the first step, the second step places an exact copy of data in the flash.

> *Writing a one to a bit in flash that already stores a zero has no effect.*
> *To store both zeros and ones, flash storage devices use an erase-*
> *before-write approach.*

11.9 Flash Lifetime

Flash storage has a limited lifetime. Each erase-write cycle wears it down. To understand why flash memory wears out, one needs to understand solid-state physics. The general idea is that an oxide layer traps electrons to hold a charge on a cell. Each erase-write cycle causes the oxide layer to deteriorate slightly. Eventually, the oxide becomes so thin that electrons can escape, which means the charge on a cell gradually leaks. When enough charge leaks, the value of a cell becomes ambiguous instead of clearly 0 or 1. Thus, the flash fails to retain values. For example, a typical USB flash drive has a lifetime of between 10,000 and 100,000 write-erase cycles.

To summarize:

> *After enough erase-write cycles, a storage device using flash technology begins to malfunction.*

11.10 The Internal Structure Of An SSD

We will see that an SSD uses an interesting storage system to help overcome the limited lifetime of flash. To understand the system, one must understand that an SSD contains an embedded processor that receives requests from a computer, controls the other hardware components in the SSD, and chooses how to implement the request.

Figure 11.5 contains a simplified diagram of the five major components in an SSD and their interconnection. In practice, SSD hardware contains additional components; the diagram gives a high-level view that explains basics.

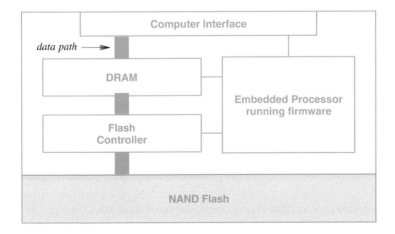

Figure 11.5 The conceptual organization of components in an SSD.

As Figure 11.5 shows, the embedded processor runs code found in firmware. The *flash controller* hardware unit controls the NAND flash by erasing, writing, and reading blocks of cells. We will imagine that the *DRAM* unit holds an array of bytes exactly the same size as a block of cells in the flash and contains DMA hardware that can send or receive data from the computer's memory. When the computer writes data to the SSD, the embedded processor instructs the DRAM to obtain a copy from the computer's memory, and then instructs the controller to write the data into the flash. When the computer reads data from the SSD, the embedded processor instructs the controller to transfer a copy of a block into DRAM, and then instructs the DRAM to transfer the data to the computer's memory.

11.11 Logical Block Storage And Update

Recall that the external interface allows a computer to read and write small blocks of data known as *logical blocks*. If a block of cells can hold 128K bytes, and the entire block of cells must be written at the same time, storing a small amount of data in each block would waste most of the space. To avoid waste, SSDs divide each block of cells into logical blocks and arrange to store individual logical blocks†. The idea is to write one logical block at a time. Before using any logical block in a block of cells, the processor erases the entire block, setting all bits to 1. Once the block has been erased, logical blocks in the block become available. To write one of the logical blocks, the embedded processor places the logical block to be written in the appropriate position in the DRAM buffer, and sets all other bits in the DRAM buffer to 1s. Then, the embedded processor tells the controller to copy the entire DRAM into one of the blocks of cells in the flash. Recall that writing 1 bits to flash has no effect. So, only the zero bits in the logical block being written will change. Figure 11.6 illustrates the idea:

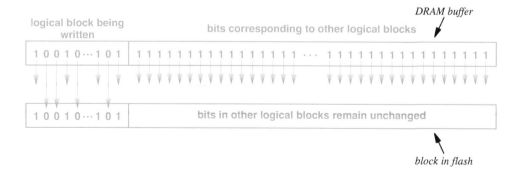

Figure 11.6 Illustration of an SSD writing one logical block from DRAM to a block of cells in flash. Because writing 1 bits has no effect, the only bits that change are the zero bits in the logical block being written.

---

†High-performance SSDs may use a larger logical block size, such as 4k bytes.

After a block of cells has been erased, each logical block in the block of cells can be written once. What happens if the contents of a given logical block change and the changes must be stored? Can the logical block be written again? No, not without erasing the entire block of cells first.

The embedded processor in an SSD can use the DRAM to update one of the logical blocks in a block without changing other logical blocks. Figure 11.7 lists the steps.

1. Copy the block that will be changed from flash to DRAM.
2. Replace the logical block that must be changed in the DRAM copy.
3. Erase the entire block in the flash.
4. Write the DRAM to the block in flash.

Figure 11.7 The steps needed to update part of a block of cells without changing other parts.

11.12 Repeated Wear, Location Mapping, And Wear Leveling

Although it works, the approach in Figure 11.7 to update an existing logical block has a severe downside: it requires a complete erase-write cycle for each change, even if only a few bits change. Repeated erase-write cycles eventually wear down an SSD. File systems that update metadata can make the wear problem especially severe for a block of cells that contains file metadata because the file system updates the access time stamp frequently, even if the application does not change data in the file. Furthermore, most file systems keep the time stamp information for a file in the same block for the lifetime of the file. Thus, each time an application reads or writes a file, the file system will write the updated metadata to the SSD, and the SSD will perform an erase-write cycle on the block of cells that holds the time stamp. As a result, a block of cells that holds a time stamp will be updated more frequently than others, resulting in more wear.

The point is:

> *Because file systems update time stamp metadata frequently, using a read-change-erase-write approach for changes causes some blocks of cells to wear faster than others.*

To avoid wearing one block of cells more than another, SSDs follow an unusual algorithm for storing and retrieving logical blocks. Industry uses the term *wear leveling* to characterize the way the approach spreads wear evenly across all blocks. To understand the algorithm, recall that an SSD contains an embedded processor. The embedded processor performs several tasks related to wear leveling. Most important, the processor maintains a *location map* that tells where to find a given block. When the SSD receives a request to read or write logical block i, the embedded processor consults its location map to find where logical block i has been stored (i.e., which block of cells and the offset within the block of cells). Using a location map allows the SSD to place a given logical block from the user at any valid offset in an arbitrary block of cells.

To ensure level wear, an SSD begins by erasing all blocks of cells in the SSD, making them available for use. As requests arrive to write logical blocks, the SSD places each in the next successive block of cells, spreading the used block across all blocks of cells. If a request arrives to write to a logical block that has already been written, the embedded processor does not use the copy-erase-update-write steps in Figure 11.7. Instead, the SSD leaves the old copy of the logical block unchanged, marks the old logical block location *garbage*, chooses a new, unused logical block, places the data in the new logical block, and updates the location map. Placing the new data in a new location avoids an erase cycle, and reduces wear.

To summarize:

> *Instead of updating an existing logical block, an SSD marks the old location for the logical block* garbage, *writes the changed version of the logical block to a new location, and then updates the location map to point to the new location.*

11.13 Overprovisioning And Bad Block Management

Each SSD has a capacity measured in Gigabytes; the hardware provides access to all the advertised capacity. Interestingly, an SSD has additional capacity used to handle problems. We say that an SSD is *overprovisioned*. The additional blocks of cells are classified as *reserve blocks*, and the embedded processor does not use them for normal allocation. As an SSD ages, blocks of cells eventually become worn. The SSD hardware monitors blocks and detects failing blocks. When it detects a problem, the hardware has two options:

- Replace the block.
- Skip the block.

Replacement occurs if an SSD still has unused reserved blocks. The processor removes the failing block from the set of blocks used for allocating, and substitutes one of the reserved blocks in its place. Once all the reserved blocks have been used, no more substitutions are possible. Therefore, the embedded processor marks the failing block *skip*, which means it will exclude the block from further allocations. We used the term *bad block management* to refer to the procedure of handling failing blocks.

11.14 Garbage Collection

Recall that every time it receives a *write* request for a logical block that has already been written, the SSD marks the current logical block *garbage*, finds an unused logical block, stores the logical block, and updates the location map. If the SSD continues to allocate new logical blocks, the set of available logical blocks will eventually run out (except the extra logical blocks reserved to handle bad blocks).

To prevent the SSD from running out of logical blocks, the embedded processor implements a procedure known as *garbage collection*. During garbage collection, the embedded processor searches through the flash memory to find blocks where every logical block in the block is garbage (i.e., all the logical blocks have been written again, leaving the old data invalid). Such blocks can be erased and made available for future allocations. If a block contains a few valid logical blocks, it may be possible to reclaim the block by copying the valid logical blocks to new locations, updating the location map, and then erasing the empty block. Figure 11.8 illustrates the idea.

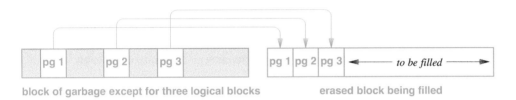

block of garbage except for three logical blocks   erased block being filled

Figure 11.8 Illustration of the SSD garbage collection procedure moving the remaining three logical blocks out of a block into a new block so the original block can be erased and made available.

In the figure, the block on the left only has three remaining logical blocks, and all the rest contain garbage. The block on the right has been erased and has many remaining logical blocks that can be filled. After copying the three remaining logical blocks from the left block, the embedded processor will update the location map so that future references to the logical blocks that have been moved will go to their new locations in the block on the right. Once the three logical blocks have been moved, the block on the left can be erased and made available again.

To summarize:

> *An SSD uses garbage collection to scan the flash memory and find blocks that can be erased to make them useful again. If only a few valid logical blocks remain in a block, the logical blocks can be moved, allowing the block to be erased.*

11.15 Assessment Of SSD Technology

Our introduction to SSDs provides a simplified view that only covers the basics. SSDs include additional hardware components and additional ways to handle the underlying flash memory. High-performance SSDs and SSDs engineered for specific purposes use more advanced algorithms for logical block allocation, garbage collection, and wear leveling. The point is that properties of NAND flash technology cause SSD designs to use complex procedures for wear leveling, overprovisioning, bad block management, and garbage collection.

11.16 Summary

When an application uses a file, file system software stores the file on persistent storage. Current persistent storage systems use Solid-State Drives (SSDs). Conceptually, an SSD allows a computer to *read* and *write* 512-byte blocks. Internally, an SSD contains an embedded processor running firmware that manages the underlying NAND flash memory and implements a location map.

Flash uses an erase-before-write approach in which an entire block of cells must be erased before they can be written. Partial writes are possible because writing 1 bits to flash has no effect.

An SSD uses overprovisioning to allow worn blocks to be replaced. In addition, complex procedures that place a new version of a logical block in a new location help an SSD avoid excessive erase cycles and achieve wear-leveling. As a consequence, an SSD must also handle garbage collection.

EXERCISES

11.1   A user creates a new file, writes exactly 512 bytes to the file, and closes the file. What will the file system store on SSD?

11.2   A user purchases a new computer with a 1TB SSD. Does the SSD contain exactly 1TB of flash or more? Explain.

11.3   Suppose that instead of the wear-leveling approach, an SSD implemented partial-block *write* operations by copying the old value of a block to DRAM, replacing the part that changed, erasing the block in flash, and writing the changed value. If an application changed an item once per second, how many erase-write cycles would the SSD use in a year? Five years?

11.4   You discover that it is possible to upgrade the SSD in your laptop, and start to shop for a replacement. The sales agent says that to get a model with the maximum read and write speed, you need a high-speed bus in your laptop. Explain why.

11.5   You have been called in to help investigate a crime, and have been given an SSD along with forensic systems that allow you to look at any part. You know the file system wrote 512-byte blocks, and you need to find the contents of blocks 0, 1, and 2. Can you ignore the embedded processor and read the blocks from the flash? Explain why or why not.

11.6   Why might a file system generate *write* operations on the underlying SSD when a user *reads* a file?

11.7   A vendor advertises an SSD with 10% overprovisioning. What does the vendor mean, and when would overprovisioning be used?

11.8   A high-performance SSD can be configured to use an internal logical block size of 4K bytes instead of 512 bytes. The vendor claims the SSD works well with a virtual memory system. What is the relationship between virtual memory (discussed in Chapter 9) and the claim above?

11.9   Would erasing a flash memory work if all bits were set to 0 instead of 1? Explain.

11.10   Suppose SSD hardware detects that a block of cells has failed completely. Is the entire SSD useless? Explain.

Chapter Contents

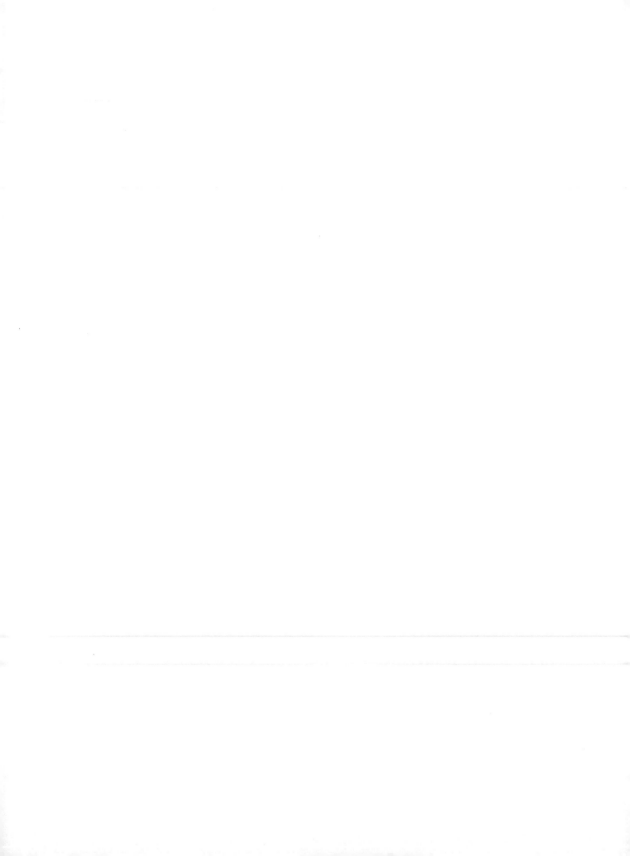

12

A Programmer's View Of
Devices, I/O, And Buffering

12.1 Introduction

Earlier chapters present a high-level view of processors and memory. The previous chapter focuses on persistent storage mechanisms, and explains SSDs used to store files.

This chapter begins a discussion of I/O. It looks at the topic from a programmer's perspective. The chapter describes the low-level device driver software needed to control a device as well as library and operating system software that applications use to interact with I/O facilities. Although few software engineers write device driver code, understanding how a device driver operates and how low-level I/O occurs can help a software engineer write more efficient applications. In addition to examining software components that implement I/O functionality, we will consider the concept of buffering, and see why it is essential for software engineers to use buffering.

12.2 Devices And Device Hardware

We use the term I/O device to describe a piece of hardware that allows a computer system to interact with the environment external to the computer. I/O devices span a broad range of interactions, ranging from devices that humans use directly (e.g., display screens, keyboards, mice, trackpads, and earphones) to devices that can monitor or control the environment without requiring direct human interaction (e.g., temperature sensors, surveillance cameras, building monitors, and network communication devices).

Recall that a device interacts with a processor over a *bus*. The next chapter explains a bus in detail, and describes how software running on a processor interacts with a device. For now, it is sufficient to know that a processor must send commands over the bus to control and operate the device, including commands to initialize the device hardware, obtain incoming data from the device, send outgoing data to the device, and perform other operations. Unfortunately, each hardware device defines a specific set of commands that a processor must use. A vendor defines a specific set of commands for each model of device the vendor manufactures. Thus, even if two devices perform the same basic function (e.g., Wi-Fi communication), the commands needed to operate the devices may differ significantly. The point is:

> *Each hardware device defines a set of commands that must be used to control and operate the device; the commands differ significantly across hardware vendors and their models.*

12.3 Device-Independent I/O And Encapsulation

In a modern computing system, applications can use a device without knowing which vendor manufactured the device and without knowing the commands used to operate the device. For example, an application can print a document merely by selecting a printer without knowing the hardware vendor that manufactured the printer, the model, or exact commands the hardware requires. Similarly, an application can read keystrokes from a keyboard without knowing any hardware details. How can an application perform I/O without knowing or using the commands the device expects? The answer lies in an operating system design that supports *device-independent I/O*.

To support device-independent I/O, an operating system contains two software components. First, the operating system defines a set of generic functions that applications use to communicate with devices. In most systems, the generic functions include *open* (initiate communication with a device), *read* (obtain incoming data from a device), *write* (send outgoing data to a device), and *close* (terminate use of the device). Second, the system contains *device driver* software for each hardware device. A device driver understands the hardware commands needed for one particular device, and uses the commands to perform each generic function. For example, when an application reads an incoming character from a keyboard, the device driver software issues the hardware commands needed to obtain the next keystroke from the particular brand and model of keyboard attached to the computer. Figure 12.1 illustrates the conceptual organization.

In essence, an operating system hides hardware details from applications. In particular, a device driver *encapsulates* information about the underlying hardware. The approach offers a significant advantage for software engineers. Before the advent of device-independent I/O, each application program included details about specific hardware devices, meaning that the application had to be changed before it could be run on a computer that had other hardware devices. The device-independent approach means an application can run unchanged and use any model of device from any vendor.

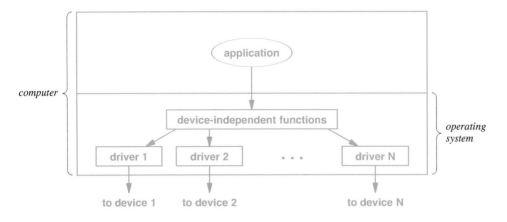

Figure 12.1 An application using device-independent I/O functions in an operating system and device driver software that performs each operation on a specific hardware device.

12.4 Conceptual Parts Of A Device Driver

A device driver contains multiple functions that all must work together, including code to accept requests from device-independent functions, code to communicate with the underlying device over a hardware bus, and code to issue the specific set of hardware commands for each request. Furthermore, a device driver must interact with the computer's operating system, blocking an application that needs to wait for input (e.g., to wait until a user enters a keystroke), and informing an application when output completes. To help manage complexity, we think of a device driver as partitioned into three parts:

- A *lower half* consisting of a handler function that the hardware invokes when a device completes an operation

- An *upper half* that consists of functions that each implement one of the device-independent functions (e.g., implement *read* or *write* operations)

- A set of *shared variables* that hold state information used to coordinate the two halves

The names *upper half* and *lower half* reflect the view that hardware is *low level* and application programs are *high level*. The lower-half of a device driver deals directly with low-level hardware. Figure 12.2 illustrates the organization of device driver software.

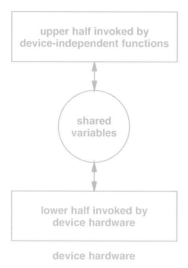

Figure 12.2 The conceptual division of a device driver into three parts. The upper-half accepts requests and the lower-half handles all hardware-specific details.

12.5 Two Main Categories Of Devices

Before we can understand more about device drivers, we need to know more about the underlying device hardware. The hardware can be divided into two broad categories, depending on the style of interface the device uses:

- Character-oriented devices
- Block-oriented devices

A *character-oriented* device transfers a single byte of data at a time. For example, the serial interface used to connect a keyboard to a computer transfers one character (i.e., byte) for each keystroke. From a device driver's point of view, a character-oriented device calls the lower-half of a device driver each time it has an incoming byte for the driver to read and each time the device is ready to accept an outgoing byte. To transfer N bytes, the lower half must be invoked N times.

A *block-oriented* device transfers an entire block of data at a time. In some cases, the underlying hardware specifies a block size, B, and all blocks must contain exactly B bytes. For example, an SSD may define a block size to be 512 bytes. In other cases, however, blocks are of variable size. For example, a network interface defines a block to be as large as a packet (although it places an upper-bound on packet size, packet switching hardware allows packet sizes to vary from one packet to the next). From a device driver's point of view, a block-oriented device only invokes the lower-half device driver function once for each block that it transfers.

12.6 Example Flow Through A Device Driver

The details of writing device drivers are beyond the scope of this text. However, to help us understand the concept, we will consider how a device driver might handle basic output. For our example, we will assume that an application sends data over the Internet. The application specifies data to be sent, and the protocol software takes two steps: it creates a network *packet* that is limited to 1500 bytes, and transfers the packet to the upper-half function in the device driver for the network device. Figure 12.3 illustrates the modules involved in a packet transfer, and lists the steps that are taken for output.

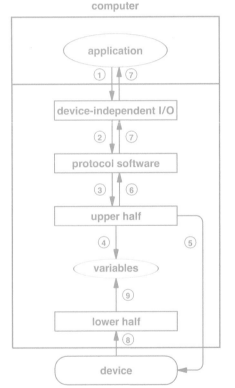

Steps Taken

1. The application uses a device-independent I/O function to send data over the Internet

2. The device-independent I/O function uses protocol software to form a packet

3. Protocol software passes the packet to the upper-half function of the device driver

4. The upper-half function stores the outgoing packet in the shared variables

5. The upper-half passes the address of the packet to the device and starts the device

6. The upper-half function returns to the protocol software

7. The protocol software returns to the device-independent function and the application

8. After sending the packet, the device invokes the lower half function of the device driver

9. The lower half function removes the copy of the packet from the shared variables

Figure 12.3 A simplified example of the steps that occur when an application sends data over the Internet. The device driver handles all communication with the device.

As the figure shows, even a straightforward operation requires a complex sequence of steps. To send data, an application calls a device-independent I/O function in the operating system, which uses protocol software to create a network packet and pass the packet to the upper-half output function of the appropriate device driver. The device driver places the packet in the shared variables section, and sends the address of the packet to the device, which causes the device to start transmission. The device accesses the packet in memory and begins to transmit the bits over the network. Meanwhile, the device driver returns to the protocol software, the device-independent I/O function, and the application. Later, once transmission completes, the device hardware invokes the lower half of the device driver, which can remove the packet from the shared variables.

12.7 An Input Queue In A Device Driver

The set of shared variables for a device driver often consists of a queue of incoming data items. To understand why, observe that data may arrive before an application is ready to read the data. For example, a user may type ahead on a keyboard, and packets may arrive over a network before the software is ready to handle them. In particular, network packets often arrive in *bursts*, with many packets arriving back-to-back followed by a period of no packets arriving. The software that processes incoming packets may not finish processing one packet before the next packet arrives.

Arranging a queue in the device driver solves the problem of bursty network traffic. During a burst, the hardware keeps delivering incoming packets, and the device driver arranges for each packet to be inserted into the queue. Meanwhile, software continues to extract the next packet from the queue and process the packet. Once a burst ends, the packet processing software continues to extract and process packets, which leaves the queue empty and ready for the next burst. The point is:

> *An input queue in a device driver allows the driver to accept and store data that arrives without waiting for software to handle each incoming data item before accepting the next item from the device.*

12.8 An Output Queue In A Device Driver

A device driver may also use a queue for outgoing data. To understand why, observe that a device often operates much slower than a processor. For example, an application can fill outgoing blocks with data much faster than SSD hardware can accept and store blocks. Fortunately, applications do not write blocks continuously. Instead, applications tend to write small files. For example, when a user saves work, a word processing application will store the data in a file. Typical documents only occupy a few blocks on an SSD†.

If a device driver always waited for the underlying SSD to store a block before the driver returned, an application would spend much of its time waiting for SSD hardware. An SSD device driver that has a queue of outgoing blocks avoids delays by allowing the file system to write a block of data without waiting for the SSD to complete writing of the previous block. The driver places each outgoing block in its output queue. Pro-

---

†As an example, the file that holds the text for this chapter occupies 84 blocks on an SSD.

vided the queue is large enough, it can hold enough blocks for an entire file, meaning the file can be written without any delay. The driver keeps writing blocks as long as blocks remain in the queue. Once an application finishes writing to a file, the device driver will continue to write blocks to the SSD until the queue is empty, leaving it ready for the next time an application writes a file. Figure 12.4 illustrates a device driver using an output queue.

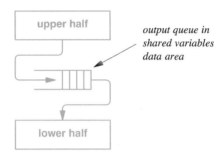

Figure 12.4 The conceptual organization of a device driver that uses an output queue. The upper half deposits outgoing items in the queue, and the lower half repeatedly extracts an item from the queue and sends the item to the device.

Once the last item has been written and the output queue is empty, the device driver issues commands that move the device hardware to an idle state. Later, when a new item is added to the queue, the driver restarts the device. Thus, output proceeds as long as the queue contains at least one item.

To summarize:

> *An output queue in a device driver allows the driver to accept and store a sequence of outgoing data items without forcing software to wait until the underlying device handles one data item before accepting the next.*

12.9 Isolating I/O Devices From Applications

As we have seen, a modern operating system contains a set of device-independent I/O functions and device drivers that translate operations into commands for the underlying device hardware. The design isolates applications from the low-level details of the underlying hardware. In practice, additional layers of software help increase the isolation because applications do not use I/O operations directly. Instead, programming systems offer a set of high-level *abstractions*. For example, instead of interacting directly with a printer, an application can create a document and then invoke a printing abstraction that prints a document. Similarly, instead of using display hardware directly, an application invokes *window* abstractions that allow the application to create and manipulate windows on the screen. Instead of interacting with an SSD, an application uses a file abstraction and the file system handles the details of storing the file in blocks on an SSD.

Surprisingly, most embedded systems software now uses higher-level abstractions. Until recently, embedded systems remained the last vestige of low-level programming — code running on an embedded system controlled I/O devices directly. The availability of more powerful processors, larger memories, and the *Internet of Things* (*IoT*) has motivated the use of device-independent I/O and higher-level abstractions in embedded systems.

The point is:

> *On a modern computing system, I/O remains hidden from most applications. Instead of interacting with devices, such as SSDs, display screens, and printers, application software uses high-level abstractions, such as files and windows.*

12.10 The Motivation For A Standard I/O Library

Early in the history of computing, programmers recognized the importance of sharing code. In particular, a programmer would write a function to handle a common task, place the function in a *library*, and allow other programmers to include the function in their programs. The Unix operating system introduced the concept of a *standard I/O library* that contained functions used for I/O.

Before the standard I/O library existed, the underlying operating system offered device-independent I/O functions that allowed an application to transfer outgoing data to a device, receive incoming data from a device, and issue commands to otherwise control the device. In fact, standard I/O functions did not add new capabilities. Why was a library of standard I/O functions created, and what possible advantage did the library functions offer?

The motivation for an I/O library arises from two basic ideas. First, a device driver always transfers data between memory owned by the operating system and a hardware device. For output, a driver accepts outgoing data from an application, places the data in the shared variables area, and then transfers the data to the device. For input, a driver arranges for the device to transfer incoming data to the shared variables area, and then transfers the data to the application. Second, a processor includes a special *system call instruction*† that an application uses to call an operating system function. It takes more time to make a system call than to call a function. That is, each call of an operating system function incurs extra overhead.

---

†Some architectures use alternative names for a system call instruction, such as *trap*.

12.11 Reducing System Call Overhead

To understand how we can reduce the overhead of system calls, consider a worst-case example. Suppose an application needs to send a total of N bytes of data to a device. The number of system calls the application will make depends on the amount of data written during each call. At one extreme, the highest overhead occurs if the application makes a separate system call to transfer each byte of data because the application will make a total of N system calls. Writing one byte of data at a time will require N system calls. At the other extreme, writing all N bytes at the same time means the application will only need to make one system call. Even if an application does not write all N bytes at one time, writing more than one byte during each call improves performance. Writing K bytes at a time results in one system call instead of K system calls.

We can state a general principle:

To reduce overhead and optimize I/O performance, a software engineer must reduce the number of system calls that an application makes. Transferring K bytes of data per system call instead of one byte of data reduces the number of system calls by a factor of K.

12.12 Standard I/O Functions

Although it can reduce overhead and improve performance, transferring a large number of bytes per system call may not work well for all applications. For example, an application that reads or writes a text file may be designed to examine one character at a time. Similarly, an image processing application may examine each individual pixel. Standard I/O functions solve the problem by allowing applications to transfer a small number of bytes per function call, while ensuring that each system call transfers a large number of bytes. The standard I/O functions handle both input and output, and are commonly used for file I/O†. Figure 12.5 illustrates the conceptual organization of application code, standard I/O library functions, and device-independent I/O functions in the operating system.

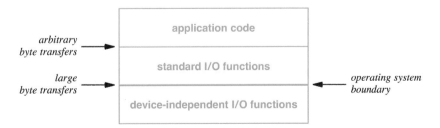

Figure 12.5 The conceptual organization of application code, standard I/O functions, and device-independent I/O functions in the operating system.

_____

†A later section discusses using standard I/O functions with devices instead of files.

correspondence.

Standard I/O Function	Purpose Of The Function	Corresponding OS Function
fopen	Open a file and create a buffer	open
fread	Obtain buffered input	read
fwrite	Send buffered output	write
fclose	Close a buffered file	close

Figure 12.6 The names of functions in the Unix standard I/O library, the purpose of each function and the name of the corresponding device-independent I/O function in the operating system.

12.13 Buffered Input

To understand how standard I/O functions work, consider reading from a file. To open a file for input, the application code calls *fopen*, which allocates an input *buffer* for the file, and calls the operating system function *open* to open the file. A buffer is an array of bytes that will hold data from the file. The size of a buffer varies among versions of the operating system, but we will use a buffer size of 8192 bytes (8K bytes) as an example. Once a file has been opened, the application code can call *fread* to read bytes from the file. When the application code calls *fread* for the first time, *fread* calls the operating system function *read* to read 8192 bytes from the file into the buffer. It then returns however many bytes the application code requested. On subsequent calls, *fread* extracts bytes from the buffer without calling an operating system function. Once all the bytes have been extracted from the buffer, *fread* calls *read* to read another 8192 bytes from the file into the buffer. Thus, even if the application only extracts one byte on each call of *fread*, each call of system function *read* will transfer 8192 bytes.

12.14 Buffered Output

Standard I/O functions also use buffering for output. When the application code calls *fopen* to open a file for output, *fopen* allocates an output buffer for the file. The application code calls the standard I/O function *fwrite* to store data in the file. On each call, *fwrite* adds outgoing data to the buffer without making a system call. Once the buffer is full, *fwrite* uses the system call *write* to write 8192 bytes of data from the buffer. It then marks the buffer empty and continues to place data in the buffer. Thus,

Of course, standard I/O functions must handle a few additional details. For example, *fread* must handle the case where the application code has read all the data from the file and reached end-of-file. On output, *fclose* must handle the condition where calls of *fwrite* have placed data in the buffer without filling the buffer completely. That is, the application has specified closing the file even though the buffer remains partially filled. Before calling *close* to close the file, *fwrite* must call *write* to transfer the remaining data from the buffer to the file.

Interestingly, buffered I/O does not require much code. In the C language, a function that performs I/O can be implemented with a few lines of code. Even the standard I/O library functions, which contain additional code to handle special cases and check for errors, do not require much code. The point is:

> *Although buffering can provide a significant increase in performance, each buffered I/O function only requires a few lines of code.*

12.15 Flushing A Buffer

It may seem that buffered output will not work for all applications. For example, consider an application that allows two users to communicate over a computer network. When it emits a message, an application assumes the message will be transmitted immediately and delivered to the other end without delay. Unfortunately, the buffered approach means an outgoing message may be placed in a buffer and left unsent.

To handle interactive applications, buffered I/O systems provide an additional function that the application can call to force a partially filled buffer to be written. We use the term *buffer flushing* to describe the process, and say the application flushes the buffer. For example, in the Unix standard I/O system, function *fflush* flushes the buffer by calling *write* if any data remains in the buffer.

> *To accommodate applications that need to force data to be written to a device, buffered output systems include a function to flush a buffer.*

12.16 Using Buffered I/O With Devices

The description above explains how buffering can be used for I/O to files. The question arises: does it make sense to use buffered I/O with other devices? In general, the answer is no. Input buffering poses a special case because most devices only deliver incoming data when an external event occurs. For example, a keyboard delivers a character whenever the user presses a key. An application that reads from a keyboard (e.g., a text editor or a word processor) must respond to each keystroke. Thus, it makes no sense to buffer incoming characters before processing them.

Although buffered output does not work well with many devices, the presence of a *flush* function means buffering can be used in some cases. For example, consider an application displaying an animation. The application can generate bytes of the next animation frame by calling a buffered output function to place successive bytes in the buffer. Once it has generated a complete frame, the application can flush the buffer, causing the entire frame to be sent to the display device.

12.17 The Relationship Between Buffering And Caching

Buffering is closely related to the concept of caching that is described in Chapter 10. The chief difference arises from the data access patterns: a cache system accommodates random access to data items, and a buffering system works best with sequential access.

In essence, a cache stores items that *have been* referenced, and a buffer stores items that *will be* referenced (assuming sequential references). Thus, in a virtual memory system, a cache stores entire pages of memory — when any byte on the page is referenced, the entire page is placed in the cache. In contrast, a buffer stores sequential bytes. When a byte is referenced, a buffering system preloads the buffer with the following bytes — if the referenced byte lies at the end of a page, the buffering system preloads bytes from the next page.

12.18 Summary

Each device defines a set of commands that must be used to operate the device. A modern operating system isolates applications from device details. The system provides a set of device-independent I/O functions that applications use and a set of device drivers that each translate requests into the commands needed for one of the underlying devices.

A device driver contains an upper half called by the device-independent I/O functions, a lower half invoked by the device hardware, and a set of shared variables. The shared variables contain queues for incoming or outgoing data items. An input queue allows a driver to absorb a burst of incoming data that arrives faster than an application can process the data. An output queue allows an application to generate successive outgoing data items without waiting for the device hardware to finish handling a current item.

A fundamental technique known as *buffering* can improve sequential I/O performance dramatically by reducing the number of system calls an application makes. The Unix standard I/O library provides buffered I/O functions commonly used for file I/O. Buffering reduces system call overhead by transferring more data per system call; a buffer of N bytes can reduce the number of system calls by a factor of N.

EXERCISES

12.1   What does a device driver provide, and how do device drivers make it easier for software engineers to write applications?

12.2   Name the three conceptual parts of a device driver, and state the role of each.

12.3   Explain the use of an output queue in a device driver by describing how and when items are inserted in the queue, as well as how and when they are removed.

12.4   A user invokes an application that writes a small file. The application displays a progress bar that shows how much of the file the application has written. Just as the progress bar reaches 50%, the battery fails and the device crashes. When the user reboots the device, he or she discovers that less than 20% of the file has actually been written. Explain why the progress bar reported that half the file had been written.

12.5   When a program calls *fwrite*, is the program making a system call? Explain.

12.6   What does the *flush* function do, and why is it needed?

12.7   To increase the performance of an application, a programmer rewrites the application so that instead of calling *read* to read one byte at a time, the application reads two thousand bytes of data into an array, and then processes the bytes. What technique is the programmer using?

12.8   In the previous question, suppose the application reads a file of 60,000 bytes. How many system calls will the original version of the program make to read the file, and how many system calls will the optimized version of the program make?

12.9   Implement two programs and compare the time needed to read a large file using *write* and *fwrite*.

12.10   Compare the running times of the two programs in the previous exercise when reading a file of 10 bytes, and explain the results.

12.11   The standard I/O function *fseek* allows random access. Use *fopen* to open a file, and then repeat using *fseek* and *fread* to read one byte at positions 100, 200, 300, and so on to 8000. Change the program to read bytes at positions 0, 8000, 16000, 24000, and so on. Explain the difference in the running times of the two programs.

12.12   Build an output buffering routine, *bufputc*, that accepts as an argument a character to be printed. On each call to *bufputc*, store the character in a buffer, and call *write* when the buffer is entirely full. Implement another function *bufflush* to flush the buffer when finished using it. Compare the performance of your buffered routine to a program that uses *write* for each character.

Chapter Contents

13

Buses And Bus Architectures

13.1 Introduction

Previous chapters described the connections among a processor, memory, and I/O devices. This chapter extends the ideas by explaining a fundamental architectural feature present in all computer systems, a bus. It describes the motivation for using a bus, explains the basic operation, and shows how both memory and I/O devices can share a common bus. We will learn that a bus defines an address space and understand the relationship between a bus address space and a memory address space.

13.2 Definition Of A Bus

A *bus* is a digital communication mechanism that allows two or more functional units to transfer data and pass control signals. Most buses are designed for use inside a single computer system; some are used within a single integrated circuit. Many bus designs exist because a bus can be optimized for a specific purpose. For example, a *memory bus* connects a processor with the memory system, and an *I/O bus* connects a processor with a set of I/O devices. A more general-purpose design allows a processor, memory system, and I/O devices to communicate over a single bus.

13.3 Processors, I/O Devices, And Buses

The notion of a bus is broad enough to encompass most external connections (e.g., a connection between a processor and a coprocessor). Thus, instead of viewing the connection between a processor and another unit as a set of wires, we can be more precise: a bus connects a processor to other units, including I/O devices. Figure 13.1 uses a graphic that is common in engineering diagrams to illustrate the concept.

Figure 13.1 Illustration of a bus used to connect a processor, memory, and I/O devices. Buses are used for most external connections.

We can summarize:

A bus is a digital communication mechanism that interconnects functional units of a computer system. A computer contains one or more buses that interconnect the processors, memories, and I/O devices.

13.3.1 Proprietary And Standardized Buses

A bus design is said to be *proprietary* if the design is owned by a private company and not available for use by other companies (i.e., covered by a patent). The alternative to a proprietary bus is known as a *standardized bus*, which means the specifications are available. Because they permit equipment from two or more vendors to communicate and interoperate, standardized buses allow a computer system to contain devices from multiple vendors. Of course, a bus standard must specify all the details needed to construct hardware, including the exact electrical specifications (e.g., voltages), timing of signals, and the encoding used for data. Furthermore, to ensure correctness, each device that attaches to the bus must implement the bus standard precisely.

13.3.2 Shared Buses And An Access Protocol

As Figure 13.1 illustrates, most buses are *shared*, which means that multiple hardware units connect to a single bus. To permit sharing, an architect must define an *access protocol* to be used on the bus. The access protocol specifies how an attached unit can determine whether the bus is available or is in use, and how attached units take turns using the bus.

13.3.3 Multiple Buses

A typical computer system contains multiple buses. For example, in addition to a central bus that connects the processor, I/O devices, and memory, some computers have a special-purpose bus used to access coprocessors. Other computers have multiple buses to permit the computer to accept devices that connect to a variety of buses.

Interestingly, most computers also contain buses that are *internal* (i.e., not visible to the computer's owner). For example, a multicore processor may have one or more internal buses on the processor chip that allow the cores on the chip to communicate with one another or with an onboard memory cache.

13.3.4 A Parallel Vs. Serial Bus

We use the terms *parallel* and *serial* to characterize the hardware used for data transfers. A *parallel bus* has hardware for each bit of data, and the units operate simultaneously, transferring multiple bits at the same time. In contrast, a *serial bus* can only transfer one bit at a time.

To understand parallel transfer, imagine that a bus consists of thirty-two wires, and each component that attaches to the bus has an interface that contains thirty-two small hardware units that can each send or receive one bit. To send data to a device, a processor tells each of its small units whether to send a 0 or 1, and the device tells each of its hardware units to read the value coming over the wire. Figure 13.2 illustrates the arrangement.

Figure 13.2 A simplified view of a processor and a device using a parallel bus. The processor sends 32 bits at the same time, and each wire transfers one bit.

We use the term *passive* to describe a bus that consists only of wires and does not contain any electronic components. For a passive bus, each component that attaches to the bus must contain the electronic circuits needed to communicate over the bus. In practice, some buses contain a digital circuit known as a *bus arbiter* that coordinates devices attached to the bus. However, such details are beyond the scope of this text.

13.4 Physical Bus Connections And Sockets

Physically, a parallel bus can consist of tiny wires etched in silicon on a single chip, a cable that contains multiple wires, or a set of parallel metal wires on a printed circuit board. Many computers provide an easy way to change an I/O device: arrange for I/O devices to plug into sockets. That is, instead of attaching parallel wires from the bus to the device, install a set of *sockets* on the bus, and attach a connector to each device that matches the sockets. Figure 13.3 illustrates sockets connected to a bus.

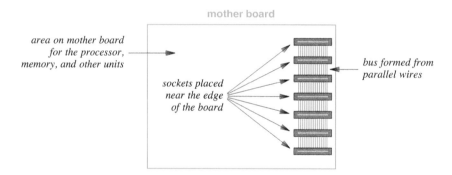

Figure 13.3 Illustration of sockets connected to a bus. Sockets make it easy to upgrade or replace a device by unplugging the old device and plugging in a new device.

13.5 Control, Address, And Data Lines In A Bus

To operate correctly, a device must adhere to the bus standard. Recall, for example, that a bus is shared and that the bus specifies an *access protocol* that determines when a given device can use the bus. To implement the access protocol, each device must have a digital circuit that connects to the bus and follows the bus standard. Known as a *bus interface* or a *bus controller*, the circuit implements the bus access protocol and controls exactly when and how a device uses the bus. The size and complexity of interface hardware depends on the bus protocol, and may require multiple chips.

Although the physical structure of a bus provides interesting engineering challenges, we are more concerned with the conceptual structure. We will examine how communication over a bus uses the wires, the operations the bus supports, and the consequences for programmers.

Informally, engineers call each of the wires in a parallel bus a *line*. The lines of a bus handle three functions:

- Control use of the bus
- Specify address information
- Transfer data from one unit to another

To help us understand how a bus operates, we will assume that the bus contains three separate sets of lines that correspond to the three functions†. Figure 13.4 illustrates the concept.

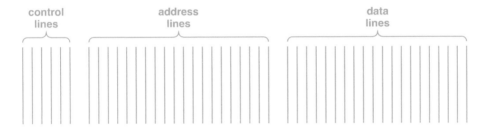

Figure 13.4 Conceptual division of wires in a bus into lines for control, address specification, and data transfer.

As the figure implies, bus lines need not be divided equally among the three uses. In particular, control functions usually require fewer lines than other functions.

13.6 The Fetch-Store Paradigm

Recall that memory systems use the *fetch-store* paradigm in which a processor can either *fetch* (i.e., *read*) a value from memory or *store* (i.e., *write*) a value to memory. A bus uses the same basic paradigm. That is, a bus only supports *fetch* and *store* operations. As unlikely as it seems, we will learn that when a processor communicates with a device or transfers data across a bus, the communication always uses *fetch* or *store* operations. Interestingly, the fetch-store paradigm is used with all devices, including microphones, video cameras, sensors, and displays, as well as with storage devices, such as SSDs. Later, we will see how a device driver uses the fetch-store approach to interact with devices. For now, it is sufficient to understand the following:

> *Like a memory system, a bus that connects I/O devices employs the fetch-store paradigm; all control or data transfer operations either use a* fetch *or a* store *operation.*

---

†The description here simplifies details; a later section explains how the functionality can be achieved without physically separate groups of wires.

13.7 Fetch-Store Operations On A Parallel Bus

Knowing that a bus uses the fetch-store paradigm helps us understand the three conceptual categories of lines in Figure 13.4. All three categories must be used during a *fetch* or *store* operation. Control lines ensure that only one pair of entities attempts to communicate over the bus at any time and that the communicating entities interact meaningfully. Address lines specify the address of the device being accessed, and data lines handle transfer of data values.

Figure 13.5 explains how a processor uses the three categories of lines during a *fetch* or *store* operation. For each operation, the figure lists the steps taken.

Fetch

1. Use the control lines to obtain access to the bus
2. Place an address on the address lines
3. Use the control lines to request a *fetch* operation
4. Test the control lines to wait for the operation to complete
5. Read the value from the data lines
6. Set the control lines to allow another device to use the bus

Store

1. Use control lines to obtain access to the bus
2. Place an address on the address lines
3. Place a value on the data lines
4. Use the control lines to specify a *store* operation
5. Test the control lines to wait for the operation to complete
6. Set the control lines to allow another device to use the bus

Figure 13.5 The steps taken to perform a *fetch* or *store* operation over a bus, and the group of lines used in each step.

13.8 Data Transfer Rate, Bus Width, And Serial Buses

How fast can data be sent over a bus? The answer depends on two things: the rate at which bits can be sent over one wire and the number of wires that can be used to send bits simultaneously. The hardware standards for the bus specify all the details about the bus, including the steps a processor or device takes to use the bus, the signals sent across the bus, and the rate at which data can be sent. The standards also specify the number of parallel wires that can be used simultaneously for data transfer. We define the *width* of a bus to be the number of data bits that can be transferred at the same time.

Bus performance can be enhanced by increasing the width of a bus because a wider bus will transfer more bits in the same amount of time. For many years, computer vendors worked to increase the width of their buses. The original bus in an IBM PC was only sixteen bits wide. The computer industry then moved to wider buses. For example, a *PCI* (*Peripheral Component Interconnect*) bus used in personal computers started at thirty-two bits wide, and later changed to a version that is sixty-four bits wide.

Surprisingly, more modern bus designs take the opposite approach by using a narrower bus. In the extreme case, a bus that has one wire can only transfer one bit at a time. Engineers do not usually talk about a bus having a width of one bit. Instead, they use the term *serial bus*. For example, the PCIe (Peripheral Component Interconnect Express), designed as a successor to the PCI bus, is serial, as is the widely used *USB* (*Universal Serial Bus*) technology.

Why did computer architects abandon the idea of making buses wider and wider? The answer comes from physics. As computer clocks became faster and faster, the time to send a bit over a wire grew shorter. Interestingly, when the electrical signals on a wire change back and forth between 0 and 1 at high speed, the wire acts like a miniature radio transmitter by emitting electromagnetic energy. Whenever it encounters a metal object, electromagnetic energy induces an electrical current. Although the energy generated by a wire in a bus seems insignificant, miniaturization led designers to use smaller and smaller wires and to place the wires of a bus closer and closer together. Consequently, the energy emitted by a wire could generate unwanted current in adjacent wires, causing the electrical signal on those wires to become incorrect. The problem became worse as data rates increased because changing rapidly between 1s and 0s acts like a high-frequency signal, and higher-frequency signals emit more energy. Using a serial bus solves the problem because the bus does not have adjacent wires to pick up the generated energy. Thus, a serial bus can send data at a much higher bit rate.

Although a serial bus can transfer at many bits per second, the rate cannot be arbitrarily high. For various reasons, hardware faces limits on the speed at which it can change signals. How can a serial bus achieve higher throughput? In fact, serial technologies have adopted the parallel approach — have multiple serial connections operating in parallel. To avoid the problem of electromagnetic interference, they do not have parallel wires close together. Instead, serial bus technologies use multiple *lanes*, each of which operates like a serial bus. Physical space separates lanes (e.g., a separate cable for each lane). Thus, the lanes can operate in parallel without interference between the signals on one lane and the signals on another. For example, with enough lanes, version 4 of the PCIe bus can transfer eight Gigabytes per second.

> *Although adding more parallel wires to a bus can increase the data transfer rate, electromagnetic interference means that a serial bus with multiple lanes can perform better.*

13.9 Large Data Transfers And Direct Memory Access

Whether a bus uses parallel or serial technology, the bus hardware defines a maximum amount of data the bus can transfer in a single *fetch* or *store* operation. Typically, a bus defines a small transfer size, such as thirty-two bits. An application may need to transfer more data than a single bus transfer permits. For example, consider a network interface device that must send or receive a packet of 1500 bytes (12000 bits). How can a computer transfer a network packet to a network device, a document to a printer, or a block of data to an SSD? To use a bus directly, the device driver must iterate. That is, the driver divides the data object into pieces such that each piece is exactly the amount the bus will accept and transfer at one time. The device driver then uses the bus repeatedly, sending one piece of the object per bus operation. Of course, the device must be designed to accept and collect successive pieces.

Is there a better way to perform a large data transfer? Chapter 11 describes the solution: device hardware that can perform *Direct Memory Access* (*DMA*). A DMA mechanism works as follows:

- The device driver places a large object in memory
- The driver sends the memory address and size to the device
- The device repeatedly uses the bus to transfer and collect pieces of the object
- The device performs the operation (e.g., sends a packet)
- The device invokes the lower half when the operation completes

If a device must use repeated bus transfer to obtain an object, what advantage does DMA offer? DMA offloads computation from the processor. Instead of requiring the processor to run device driver code that transfers each piece of a large object to a device, DMA arranges for device hardware to perform the transfer without using the processor. The point is:

> *The DMA approach increases the performance of a computing system by arranging for device hardware to perform large data transfers, thereby leaving the processor free to run other applications.*

13.10 Bus Transfer Size And The Size Of Data Items

In many computer systems, a single bus connects the processor, memory, and I/O devices. In such systems, a computer architect chooses a bus transfer size and the sizes of common data items to match. For example, an architecture may choose thirty-two bits as the size for signed and unsigned integers, floating point values, general-purpose registers, the size of data values that the ALU and other functional units use, and bus transfers. When the size of a data item exactly matches the bus transfer size, the item can be transferred in one bus operation. The point is:

In many computers, all data transfers among the processor, memory, and I/O devices occur over a bus. To optimize performance of the hardware, an architect chooses a single size for bus transfers and data items, such as general-purpose registers, integers, and floating point numbers.

13.11 Bus Address Space

The addresses used on a bus define the *bus address space*. To understand the idea, start by thinking of a *memory bus* that connects a processor to memory modules. Each unit connected to the bus contains an interface circuit. Figure 13.6 illustrates a bus that connects a processor and two memory modules that each have an interface circuit.

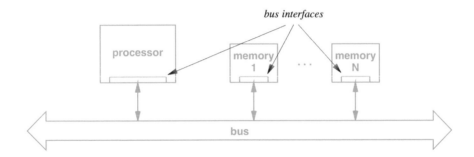

Figure 13.6 Illustration of a memory bus interconnecting a processor and two memory modules. Each unit attached to the bus contains an interface circuit that handles the details of bus access.

The interface has two sides. The side that connects to the bus implements the bus protocol and handles bus communication. Therefore, the side that connects to the bus must understand all the hardware details, such as the voltage to use and the timing of signals sent over the bus. The other side implements fetch and store operations. For example, when the processor loads a value from memory into a general-purpose register, the processor instructs the bus interface to *fetch* the value over the bus.

The interface in each memory module performs another important function: *address recognition*. To implement address recognition, the interface in a memory module must be configured to respond to a unique range of addresses. The range of addresses that a memory module recognizes must not overlap with the range of addresses that another memory module recognizes. When the processor issues a *fetch* or *store* request for an address, X, only the memory module configured to have X in its range will handle the request; all other modules will ignore the request. Figure 13.7 lists the steps a module takes when deciding whether to respond to a request†.

---

†Although the figure captures the general approach, a bus interface consists of hardware which does not actually execute a loop.

```
Let R be the range of addresses assigned to this module
Repeat forever {
        Monitor the bus until a request appears;
        if (the request specifies an address in R) {
                respond to the request
        } else {
                ignore the request
        }
}
```

Figure 13.7 The steps a memory module follows to decide whether to
respond to a given request.

To summarize:

*When a request passes across a bus, all attached memory modules re-
ceive the request. A memory module only responds if the address in
the request lies in the range that has been assigned to the module.*

13.12 Invalid Addresses And Bus Errors

We use the term *bus error* to refer to errors that the bus hardware reports. Allowing each memory module to act independently means that two types of bus errors can
occur; a typical bus includes mechanisms that detect and report each of the two errors.

- Address conflict
- Unassigned address

Address Conflict. An *address conflict* occurs when two or more interfaces are misconfigured so that multiple interfaces respond to a given address. In any case, most bus
protocols include a test for address conflicts — if two or more interfaces attempt to
respond to a given request, the bus hardware detects the problem.

Unassigned Address. An *unassigned address* error occurs if a processor attempts
to access an address that has not been assigned to any interface. To detect such errors,
most bus protocols rely on a *timeout* mechanism — after sending a request over the bus,
the processor starts a timer. If no interface responds, the timer expires, which causes
the processor hardware to report the error. The same timeout mechanism used to detect
unassigned addresses also detects malfunctioning hardware (e.g., a memory module that
stops responding to requests).

When it detects an address conflict or a reference to an unassigned address, bus hardware raises a *bus error exception*. The processor receives the exception and passes it to the operating system. Typically, an operating system terminates the application that caused the bus error, and possibly saves a core dump.

13.13 Memory Addresses And Sockets

Early computers required humans to configure the addresses for each memory module and each device that connected to a bus. Manual configuration caused many errors, and the question arose of how to prevent the errors that occur from misconfigured hardware. Fortunately, architects invented several approaches that help eliminate bus errors. Some bus hardware allows the operating system to detect and report address conflicts when the system boots. More advanced bus systems provide a mechanism that an operating system can use to assign addresses to each memory module and each device when the system boots.

The problem of configuring addresses for each memory module poses a significant challenge because each module responds to a range of addresses, and preventing conflicts means checking that none of the ranges overlap. Fortunately, architects have devised a clever scheme to solve the problem: *preconfigured sockets*. The idea is straightforward: manufacture computer memory as a set of small physical modules that each plug into a socket on the bus. Make each module respond to addresses that start at zero. That is, a user may purchase four modules that each respond to 0 through $K-1$ for some K. Instead of requiring the interface in each module to be configured, add circuitry to the sockets on the bus so that each socket responds to a range of addresses. For example, have the first socket handle addresses 0 through $K-1$, the second socket handle addresses K through $2K-1$, and so on. Make K a power of two, which means a socket can test the high-order bits when deciding whether to handle an address, and can pass the low-order bits to the module. The point is:

> *To avoid memory configuration problems, architects use small memory modules that each plug into a socket on the bus. A computer owner can install additional memory without configuring the hardware because each socket is configured with the range of addresses to which the memory module should respond.*

13.14 The Question Of Multiple Buses

Should a computer system contain multiple buses? If so, how many? Computers designed for high performance (e.g., mainframe computers) often contain several buses. Each bus is optimized for a specific purpose. For example, a mainframe computer might have one bus for memory, another for high-speed I/O devices, and another for slow-speed I/O devices. As an alternative, less powerful computers (e.g., personal computers) often use a single bus for all connections. A single bus offers the advantages of lower cost and complete generality. With a single bus, a processor does not need multiple bus interfaces, and a device that supports DMA can access memory easily.

Of course, designing a single bus for all connections means choosing a compromise. That is, the bus may not be optimal for any given purpose. In particular, if the processor uses a single bus to access instructions and data in memory as well as perform I/O, the bus can easily become a bottleneck. Thus, a system that uses a single bus often needs a large memory cache that can answer most memory requests without using the bus.

13.15 Using Fetch-Store With Devices

Recall that a bus provides communication between a processor and an I/O device, and all bus communication uses the fetch-store paradigm. The two ideas may seem contradictory — although it works well for data transfer, fetch-store does not appear to handle device control. For example, consider an operation like testing whether a Wi-Fi radio has connected to a wireless access point or an operation that starts moving a sheet of paper through a printer. How can *fetch* and *store* operations handle such cases?

To understand how software uses a bus to control devices, remember that a bus provides a way to transfer a set of bits from one unit to another without specifying what each bit means. The names *fetch* and *store* mislead us into thinking about values in memory. On a bus, however, the interface hardware of each device provides a unique interpretation of the bits. Thus, a device can interpret certain bits as a control operation rather than as a request to transfer data.

An example will clarify the relationship between the fetch-store paradigm and device control. Because real hardware devices have complex interfaces, our example will use an imaginary hardware device. Our imaginary device is quite simplistic: it displays sixteen status lights and allows software to control the lights by turning individual lights on or off and controlling the brightness of the display. The device will attach to a bus that only offers *fetch* and *store* operations. Therefore, we need to design interface hardware that uses the fetch-store paradigm for all control operations. To begin, we list the operations to be performed. Figure 13.8 lists the five functions for our imaginary device.

- Turn the display on
- Turn the display off
- Set the display brightness
- Turn the ith status light on
- Turn the ith status light off

Figure 13.8 A list of the functions our imaginary status light display must provide. Each function must be implemented using the fetch-store paradigm.

Once a set of operations has been selected, a designer casts each operation into the fetch-store paradigm. The device must use bus addresses that are not used by other devices, and the designer must assign a meaning to *fetch* and *store* for each address. For example, if our imaginary status light device is attached to a bus that has a width of thirty-two bits, a designer might choose bus addresses 10000 through 10011, and might assign meanings according to Figure 13.9.

Address	Operation	Meaning
10000 – 10003	store	Nonzero data value turns the display on, and a zero data value turns the display off
10000 – 10003	fetch	Returns zero if display is currently off, and nonzero if display is currently on
10004 – 10007	store	Change brightness. Low-order four bits of the data value specify brightness value from zero (dim) through fifteen (bright)
10008 – 10011	store	The low-order sixteen bits each control a status light; a zero bit sets the corresponding light off and a one bit sets the light on

Figure 13.9 Example assignment of addresses, operations, and meanings for the device control functions listed in Figure 13.8.

13.16 Operation Of An Interface

Although we use the names *fetch* and *store* for bus operations, a device interface does not act like a memory — data is not stored for later recall. Instead, a device treats the address, operation, and data in a bus request merely as a set of bits that cause an action. The interface contains logic circuits that compare the address in each request to the addresses assigned to the device. If a match occurs, the interface examines the operation and data bits to choose an action. For example, hardware for the first item in Figure 13.9 tests for address 10000 and a *store* request. It then uses the data bits to choose an action:

```
if ( address == 10000 && op == store) {
    if ( data != 0 )
        turn_on_display;
    else
        turn_off_display; }
```

Although we have used programming language notation to express the operations, interface hardware does not perform the tests sequentially. Instead, an interface is constructed from Boolean circuits that test the address, operation, and data values in parallel and take the appropriate action.

13.17 Asymmetric Specifications And Bus Errors

The example in Figure 13.9 does not define the effect of *fetch* and *store* operations on all the addresses. For example, the specification does not define a *fetch* operation for address 10004. To capture the idea that *fetch* and *store* operations do not need to be defined for each address, we say that the assignment is *asymmetric*. For example, the asymmetric specification in Figure 13.9 allows a *store* operation to the four bytes starting at 10004, but a bus error will result if the processor attempts to *fetch* from those four bytes. A programmer who writes a device driver must read the hardware specification carefully to learn exactly what fetch and store operations the hardware accepts and what they mean.

13.18 An Example Bus Address Space And Address Map

The bus address space defines the processor's view of memory and devices. To understand how, imagine a computer with a single bus that connects multiple memory modules and multiple I/O devices. Figure 13.10 illustrates the arrangement.

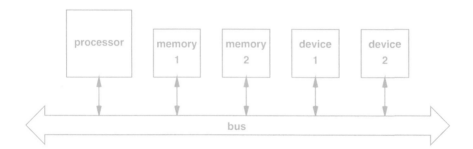

Figure 13.10 Illustration of an example computer with a single bus connecting memory modules as well as I/O devices.

In the figure, the processor will send *fetch* and *store* requests over the bus to load and store items in memory and to interact with I/O devices. Each memory module and each device must be assigned a unique address range of bus addresses. To keep the example easy to understand, we will assume the bus uses 32-bit addresses (addresses 0 through 0xffffffff), each memory module contains 1 Gigabyte of memory (0x4fffffff bytes), each device uses 128 addresses, and the top Gigabyte of the addresses is used for devices. Each memory module and device on the bus must be assigned an address range. Figure 13.11 lists one possible assignment.

Figure 13.12 shows a graphical representation of the assignments in Figure 13.11 called an *address map*. Each device occupies such a small amount of the address space that an individual device does not show on the overall map.

Device	Address Range		
memory 1	0x00000000	through	0x4fffffff
memory 2	0x10000000	through	0x8fffffff
device 1	0xfffffe80	through	0xffffff7f
device 2	0xffffff80	through	0xffffffff

Figure 13.11 One possible assignment of bus addresses for the set of devices shown in Figure 13.11.

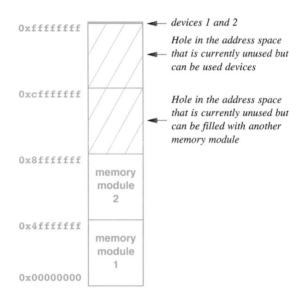

Figure 13.12 Illustration of the address space that results from the address assignments in Figure 13.11.

13.19 Holes In A Bus Address Space And Utilization

As Figure 13.12 shows, the assignment of addresses fills the lower half of the address space with memory. Because the example computer only has two memory modules installed, the third Gigabyte of the space remains unfilled. It will be used if the owner installs a third memory module. Similarly, at present most of the fourth Gigabyte of the addresses space remains unfilled because only the top 256 bytes correspond to devices. Informally, engineers say that the address space contains *holes* that correspond to the unused blocks. As we have seen, if a processor accidentally accesses an address that has not been assigned, the bus hardware detects the problem and reports a bus error.

The assignment in Figure 13.12 illustrates an important idea. The example reserves one quarter of the address space for devices. Even if the owner of the system installs a third memory module, nearly twenty-five percent of address space will remain unused. The situation comes up in many systems.

> *Because each device only requires a few addresses, the part of the bus address space devoted to devices will be sparsely populated.*

The question arises: how can a system be designed that achieves higher potential utilization of the bus address space? The answer lies in devoting a smaller part of the space to devices. One technique uses smaller memory modules. For example, if each memory module occupies one-half Gigabyte, only one-eighth of the address space needs to be dedicated to devices, leaving up to three and one-half Gigabytes for memory. Figure 13.13 illustrates the idea.

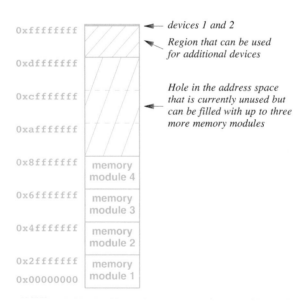

Figure 13.13 The address map that results if each memory module holds one-half Gigabyte of memory.

13.20 The Program Interface To A Bus

Except for some embedded systems, the only software that accesses a bus directly resides in the operating system. Specifically, device drivers and bus initialization functions send *fetch* and *store* commands to the bus. Early architectures provided special instructions to control I/O devices. However, most modern architectures use an approach known as *memory mapped I/O*.

To understand memory-mapped I/O, consider the address assignment of the imaginary light display in Figure 13.9†. To turn the device on, the program must store a nonzero value in bytes 10000 through 100003. When using memory-mapped I/O, a device driver writes to the device registers as if they are memory locations. To see how memory-mapped code works, we will consider a computer where an integer consists of four bytes. To turn on the device, a program needs to store a nonzero value into the integer that starts at location 10000. The following C code performs the operation:

```
int     *ptr;           /* declare ptr to be a pointer to an integer */
ptr = (*int)10000;      /* set pointer to address 10000 */
*ptr = 1;               /* store nonzero value in addresses 10000 - 10003 */
```

Although the code appears to be storing a value into memory, address 10000 on the bus corresponds to the display device. Thus, when the program stores 1 to address 10000, the device will recognize the address and accept the data value; no memory module will respond to the address. We can summarize:

> *Early processors used special instructions to communicate with I/O devices; most modern processors use a memory-mapped approach in which a device driver uses normal memory operations to communicate with a device.*

13.21 Bridging Between Two Buses

Suppose a laptop that has a PCI-e bus also has a USB port. If a user plugs a thumb drive into the USB port, software on the computer will be able to access files on the thumb drive as easily as files on the computer's main SSD. How can a processor access devices on two buses? One approach uses a hardware mechanism, known as a *bridge*, to interconnect the two buses in a way that allows requests and responses to pass across the bridge. Figure 13.14 illustrates a bridge interconnecting two buses.

In essence, a bridge maps a set of addresses from one bus onto another. That is, the bridge is configured to use a set of K addresses. Each bus chooses an address range of size K and assigns it to the bridge. The two assignments are not usually the same; the bridge is designed to perform translation. Whenever an operation on one bus involves the addresses assigned to the bridge, circuits in the bridge translate the address and perform the operation on the other bus. Thus, if a processor on bus 1 performs a *store* operation to one of the bridged addresses, the bridge hardware accepts the request on bus 1 and performs an equivalent *store* operation on bus 2. We say that a bridge offers *transparent* interconnection because processors and devices attached to the two buses remain unaware that a bridge translates some addresses.

---

†Figure 13.9 appears on page 251.

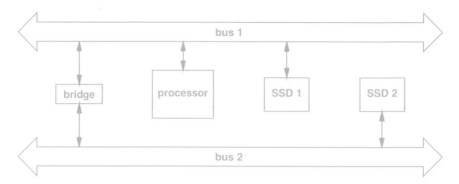

Figure 13.14 Illustration of a bridge interconnecting two buses. The bridge
honors the standards for each bus.

13.22 An Example Bridge Mapping

Logically, a bridge performs a one-to-one mapping from the address space of one
bus to the address space of another. That is, the bridge maps a set of addresses on one
bus into the address space of the other. Figure 13.15 illustrates how a bridge can map
one-half of a Gigabyte of address space between two buses.

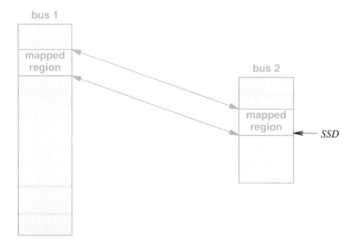

Figure 13.15 Example of a bridge mapping a region of addresses between
two buses.

As the figure illustrates, one bus may be smaller than the other (i.e., does not have
as many total addresses). Furthermore, the region being mapped can appear at different
locations on the two buses. For example, suppose that on bus 1, the lowest address in

the mapped region is *0xc0000000*, and on bus 2 the lowest address in the mapped region is *0x20000000*. Also suppose the processor attaches to bus 1 and an SSD attaches to bus 2. Assume the SSD recognizes addresses starting at *0x20000000* (i.e., the SSD uses the lowest address in the mapped region). When the processor stores to address *0xc0000000* on bus 1, the bridge will change the address to *0x20000000* and issue the *store* request on bus 2. The SSD will receive the request and respond. The bridge will send the response back to the processor on bus 1. Thus, the processor will be able to communicate with the SSD as if the SSD attaches directly to bus 1.

To summarize:

> *The term* bridge *refers to a hardware mechanism that interconnects two buses and maps a region of addresses between them. A bridge allows a processor connected to one bus to communicate with a device connected to the other bus.*

13.23 Consequences For Device Driver Programmers

In most cases, a bridge remains *transparent*, meaning that a processor connected to one bus can communicate directly with a device on the other bus without either of them knowing that a bridge performs address mapping. A problem arises, however, with devices that perform DMA. For such devices, a processor must pass a memory address to the device so the device can access data items in memory. Because a bridge only translates addresses used in *fetch* and *store* instructions, any data passed to the device will not be translated. Thus, to specify a DMA address, a device driver may need to know how the bridge maps addresses so it can send a mapped address to the device.

13.24 Switching Fabrics As An Alternative To Buses

Although a bus forms the fundamental interconnection in most computer systems, bus technology has a disadvantage: bus hardware can only perform one transfer at a time. That is, although multiple hardware units can attach to a given bus, at most one pair of attached units can communicate at any time. Using a bus always entails three steps: wait for exclusive use of the bus, perform a transfer, and release the bus to allow another transfer to occur.

Some buses extend the paradigm by permitting multiple attached units to transfer N bytes of data each time they obtain the bus. For situations that require multiple simultaneous transfers, architects have invented alternative technologies. Known as *switching fabrics*, the technologies use a variety of forms. Some fabrics handle a few attached units, and other fabrics can handle hundreds or thousands. Similarly, some fabrics restrict transfers so only a few attached units can initiate transfers at the same time, and other fabrics permit many simultaneous transfers. One of the reasons for the variety of architectures arises from economics: higher performance (i.e., more simultaneous exchanges) cost much more, and the higher cost may not be justified.

Perhaps the easiest switching fabric to understand consists of a *crossbar switch*. We can imagine a crossbar to be a matrix with N inputs and M outputs. The crossbar contains $N \times M$ electronic switches that each connect an input to an output. At any time, the crossbar can turn on switches to connect pairs of inputs and outputs as Figure 13.16 illustrates.

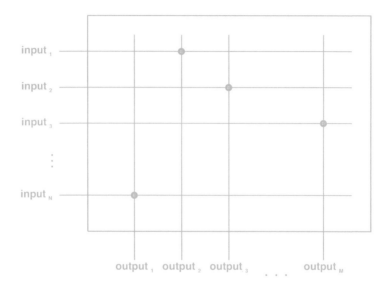

Figure 13.16 A conceptual view of a crossbar switch with N inputs and M outputs with a dot showing an active connection. The crossbar mechanism ensures that at any time, only one connection is active for a given row or a given column.

The figure helps us understand the high cost of switching fabrics. First, each line in the diagram represents a parallel data path composed of multiple wires. Second, each potential intersection between an input and output requires an electronic switch that can connect the input to the output at that point. Thus, a crossbar requires $N \times M$ switching components, each of which must be able to switch a parallel connection. By comparison, a bus requires at most $N + M$ electronic components (one to connect each input and each output to the bus). Despite the expense, switching fabrics have become popular for high-performance systems.

13.25 Summary

A bus is the fundamental hardware mechanism used to interconnect memory, I/O devices, and processors within a computer system. Early buses used a parallel approach, meaning that the bus consists of parallel wires that permit multiple bits to be transferred simultaneously. Modern buses use a serial approach to prevent the signals on a wire from interfering with signals on other wires.

Each bus defines a protocol that attached devices use to access the bus. Bus protocols follow the fetch-store paradigm; an I/O device connected to a bus is designed to receive *fetch* or *store* operations and interpret them as control operations on the device.

A bus defines an address space that may contain holes (i.e., unassigned addresses). A computer system can have a single bus to which memory and I/O devices attach, or can have multiple buses that each attach to specific types of devices. A hardware mechanism called a *bridge* can be used to connect two buses by mapping a region of the address space from one bus onto the address space of the other bus.

The term *switching fabric* refers to an alternative to a bus that achieves higher throughput by using parallelism. Because of their high cost, switching fabrics are restricted to high-end systems.

EXERCISES

13.1   In a computer, what is a bus, and what does it connect?

13.2   Your friend claims that their computer has a special bus that is patented by the vendor. What term do we use to characterize a bus design that is owned by one company?

13.3   What is the fetch-store paradigm?

13.4   What is the advantage of having a separate socket for each memory chip?

13.5   Suppose a device has been assigned bus addresses 0x4000000 through 0x4000003. Write C code that stores the value 0xffff01A4 into the addresses.

13.6   If a bus can transfer 64 bits in each cycle and runs at a rate of 66 million cycles per second, what is the bus throughput of the bus measured in Megabytes per second?

13.7   What is a switching fabric, and what is its chief advantage over a bus?

13.8   How many simultaneous transfers can occur over a crossbar switching fabric of N inputs and M outputs?

13.9   Search the Internet, and make a list of switching fabric designs.

13.10   Look on the Internet for an explanation of a *CLOS network*, which is used in switching fabrics, and write a short description.

13.11   What does a bridge connect?

Chapter Contents

14

Programming Devices And Interrupt-Driven I/O

14.1 Introduction

Earlier chapters introduce I/O. The previous chapter explains how a bus provides the connection between a processor and a set of I/O devices. The chapter discusses the bus address space, and shows how an address space can hold a combination of both memory and I/O devices. Finally, the chapter explains that a bus uses the fetch-store paradigm, and shows how *fetch* and *store* operations can be used to interrogate or control an external device.

This chapter continues the discussion. The chapter describes and compares the two basic styles of interaction between a processor and an I/O device. It focuses on interrupt-driven I/O, and explains how device driver software in the operating system interacts with an external device.

14.2 The Two I/O Paradigms

Recall from the previous chapter that I/O devices connect to a bus, and that a processor interacts with a device by issuing *fetch* and *store* operations to bus addresses that have been assigned to the device. Although the basic mechanics of I/O are easy to specify, several questions remain unanswered. What control operations should each device support? How can a device operate independently from the processor? How does the interaction between a processor and I/O devices affect overall system performance?

The interactions between a processor and a device can be divided into two basic paradigms:

- Programmed I/O
- Interrupt-driven I/O

The next sections explain the two approaches and the advantages of each, as well as how they work.

14.3 Programmed I/O

The earliest computers took a straightforward approach to I/O: an external device consisted of basic digital circuits that controlled the hardware in response to *fetch* and *store* operations. Even a straightforward task often required the CPU to issue a series of several commands. For example, obtaining the next input item sometimes required the CPU to issue three commands to make the device hardware ready to perform an input operation, obtain the item from the device, and reset the device hardware for the next item.

Using the CPU to issue detailed commands has an advantage: less complex device hardware. A device only needs small circuits to perform basic steps plus a circuit that receives commands from the CPU and activates the circuit that performs the command. That is, with programmed I/O, a device does not need hardware to execute a complex sequence of steps on its own. Informally, engineers call the devices *dumb*. Formally, architects characterize the form of interaction by saying that the I/O is *programmed*.

Over the years, the use of programmed I/O has faded. However, two special cases still remain:

- Embedded systems
- System startup

Embedded Systems. The smallest embedded systems use special processors known as *microcontrollers*. Although it cannot run a general-purpose operating system, a microcontroller has the advantages of lower cost and low power consumption, which can be important for systems powered by batteries.

System Startup. When it first powers on, a computer runs bootstrap code to find and load an operating system. Because the computer does not yet have an operating system running, bootstrap code must use the programmed I/O approach to interact with devices. In addition, once it starts, the operating system must initialize each device, and device initialization code uses the programmed I/O.

14.4 Synchronization

It may seem that writing software to perform programmed I/O is trivial: a program merely assigns a value to an address on the bus. To understand I/O programming, however, we need to remember two things. First, a nonintelligent device cannot remember a list of commands. Instead, circuits in the device perform each command precisely when the processor sends the command. Second, a processor operates much faster than an I/O device — even a slow processor can execute dozens of instructions in the time it takes for the circuits in a device to respond.

As an example, consider starting a Wi-Fi network device. Among other things, the hardware includes a radio transmitter and a receiver. At startup, initialization code must reset the hardware and then power up the two radio devices. Interestingly, resetting the hardware and powering up a radio may take a millisecond or more. Even a slow processor can execute hundreds of instructions during a millisecond. If the processor issues a command to power up the receiver immediately after issuing a command to power up the transmitter, hardware in the device might not finish powering up the transmitter.

To prevent such problems, programmed I/O requires the processor to *synchronize* with the device. That is, once it issues a command, the processor must wait until the device is ready for another command. We can summarize:

> *Because a processor can operate orders of magnitude faster than an I/O device, programmed I/O requires the processor to synchronize with the device that is being controlled.*

14.5 Synchronization Using Polling

Programmed I/O employs a basic form of synchronization known as *polling*. In essence, before it starts the next operation, the processor must ask the device whether the previous operation has completed. A processor cannot merely ask once. Instead, the processor must ask repeatedly until the device declares that it is ready. Thus, when powering up a Wi-Fi device, the processor must use polling at each step, as Figure 14.1 explains.

- Issue a command to reset the device
- Poll to determine when the hardware finishes the reset
- Issue a command to power up the transmitter
- Poll to determine when the hardware finishes
- Issue a command to power up the receiver
- Poll to determine when the hardware finishes

Figure 14.1 Steps taken to initialize a Wi-Fi device. The processor must wait for the hardware to finish one step before starting the next.

14.6 Code For Polling

Looking at code for polling will help us understand how polling uses a bus. To poll a device, the processor performs a *fetch* operation. That is, one or more of the addresses assigned to the device correspond to status information — when the processor fetches a value from the address, the device responds by giving its current status (busy or not busy).

To examine code for polling, we need to know the exact details of a hardware device. Unfortunately, most devices are incredibly complex. To keep an example simple, we will use an imaginary device with a straightforward programming interface. Although our imaginary device seems simplistic compared to commercial devices, the polling interface remains the same.

Recall that a device must be assigned a set of addresses in the bus address space, and the device responds to *fetch* and *store* instructions to those addresses. Because a designer does not know the actual bus addresses that a device will use, the designer creates a specification that uses *relative* addresses, 0 though $N-1$. Later, when the device is installed in a computer, actual bus addresses will be assigned. The use of relative addresses in the specification means a programmer can write software that specifies *offsets* beyond a starting address rather than actual bus addresses. Once the device has been installed, the software can obtain the starting address for the device, and then use the offsets in *fetch* and *store* instructions.

An example of relative offsets will clarify the concept. Our imaginary Wi-Fi device defines twenty contiguous bytes of addresses. Furthermore, the design has grouped the addresses into five 32-bit words. Many device interfaces define control and status values on word boundaries rather than on individual byte boundaries. The specification in Figure 14.2 shows how the device interprets *fetch* and *store* operations for each of the addresses.

Addresses	Operation	Meaning
0 – 3	fetch	Nonzero if the device is connected to Wi-Fi
4 – 7	store	Nonzero causes device to reset
8 – 11	store	Nonzero causes transmitter to power up
12 – 15	store	Nonzero causes receiver to power up
16 – 19	fetch	Nonzero if the device is busy

Figure 14.2 A bus interface specification for an imaginary Wi-Fi device. A processor issues *fetch* and *store* to control the device and determine its status.

The figure lists the meaning of *fetch* and *store* operations on addresses assigned to our imaginary I/O device. Any operation not listed must be considered an error because the device will not respond. Thus, a *store* operation on addresses 0 through 3 will result in a bus error.

As described above, the specification lists relative addresses that start at zero. When the device is connected to a bus, the device will be assigned in the bus address space, and software will use the actual addresses when communicating with the device. For example, suppose the device is assigned bus addresses starting at *0x110000*. A *fetch* operation for addresses *0x110000 + 16* through *0x110000 + 19* will return an integer that tells whether the device is currently busy fulfilling the previous command.

Given a hardware specification similar to the one in Figure 14.2, writing code that controls a device is straightforward. For example, assume our Wi-Fi device has been assigned the starting bus address 0x110000. Addresses 0 through 3 in the figure will correspond to actual addresses 0x110000 through 0x110003. To determine whether the device is connected, the processor merely needs to access the value in addresses 0x110000 through 0x110003. In C, the code to access the device status appears to be a memory reference:

```
int     *p = (int *)0x110000;
if (*p != 0) {                  /* Test whether Wi-Fi device is connected */
        /* printer is on */
} else {
        /* printer is off */
}
```

The example assumes an integer size of four bytes. The code declares *p* to be a pointer to an integer, initializes *p* to 0x110000, and then uses **p* to obtain the value at address 0x110000.

Now that we understand how software communicates with a device, we can consider a sequence of steps and synchronization. Figure 14.3 shows C code that performs the steps in Figure 14.1.

```
int     *p;               /* Pointer to the device address area      */

p = (int *)0x110000;      /* Initialize pointer to device address     */
*(p+1) = 1;               /* Reset the device                        */
while (*(p+4) != 0) ;     /* Poll to wait for the device to finish    */
*(p+2) = 1;               /* Power up the transmitter                 */
while (*(p+4) != 0) ;     /* Poll to wait for the device to finish    */
*(p+3) = 1;               /* Power up the receiver                    */
while (*(p+4) != 0) ;     /* Poll to wait for the device to finish    */
```

Figure 14.3 C code that uses polling to carry out the steps from Figure 14.1 on the imaginary printing device specified in Figure 14.2.

To understand the code, remember that the C programming language uses *pointer arithmetic*. With an integer size of four bytes, the expression *p+1* refers to address *0x110004*, four bytes beyond *p*. Storing to that address causes the Wi-Fi device to reset. Similarly, the expression *p + 4* refers to *0x110014*, the address that must be tested to determine whether the device has finished the previous operation.

Programmers who have not written a program to control a device may find the code shocking because it contains three occurrences of while statements that each appear to be an infinite loop (notice the semicolon). If such statements appeared in a conventional application program, the program would incorrectly loop continually, testing the value at a memory location repeatedly, without making any changes to the location. In the example, however, the code references a device instead of a memory location. Thus, when the processor fetches a value from location *p+4*, the request passes to a device, which interprets it as a request for status information. So, unlike a value in memory, the value returned by the device will eventually change — if the processor polls enough times, the device will complete its current operation and return zero as the status value. The point is:

> Although polling code appears to contain infinite loops, the code can
> be correct because the value returned by a device will change over
> time.

14.7 Control And Status Registers

We use the term *Control and Status Registers* (*CSRs*) to refer to the set of addresses that a device uses. More specifically, a *control register* corresponds to a contiguous set of addresses (usually the size of an integer) that respond to a *store* operation, and a *status register* corresponds to a contiguous set of addresses that respond to a *fetch* operation.

In practice, CSRs are usually more complicated than the simplified version listed in Figure 14.2. For example, a status register may assign meanings to individual bits (e.g., the low-order bit of the status word specifies whether the device is active, the next bit specifies whether an error has occurred, and so on). More important, to conserve addresses, many devices combine control and status functions into a single set of addresses. That is, a single address can serve both functions — a *store* operation to the address controls the device, and a *fetch* operation to the same address reports the device status.

As a final detail, some devices interpret a *fetch* operation as both a request for status information and a *control* operation. For example, a trackpad delivers bytes to indicate motion of a user's fingers. The processor uses a *fetch* operation to obtain data from the trackpad. Surprisingly, each *fetch* has a side effect: it automatically resets the hardware to measure the next motion.

14.8 Using A Struct To Define CSRs

The example code in Figure 14.3 uses a pointer and pointer arithmetic to reference individual addresses the device uses. In practice, programmers usually create a C struct that defines the CSRs, and then use named members of the struct to reference items in the CSRs. For example, Figure 14.4 shows how the code from Figure 14.3 appears when a struct is used to define the CSRs.

```
struct    csr {              /* Template for printer CSRs              */
    int    csr_connected;    /* Nonzero if the device is connected     */
    csr_reset;               /* Nonzero to reset the device            */
    int    csr_transmitter;  /* Nonzero to power up the transmitter    */
    int    csr_receiver;     /* Nonzero to power up the receiver       */
    int    csr_busy          /* Is the device busy? (nonzero = 'yes')  */
};


struct    csr    *p;              /* Pointer to the device CSRs             */
p = (struct csr *)0x110000;       /* Set p to the device address            */
p->csr_reset = 1;                 /* Reset the device                       */
while (p->csr_busy) ;             /* Poll to wait for the device to finish  */
p->csr_transmitter = 1;           /* Power up the transmitter               */
while (p->csr_busy) ;             /* Poll to wait for the device to finish  */
p->csr_receiver = 1;              /* Power up the receiver                  */
while (p->csr_busy) ;             /* Poll to wait for the device to finish  */
```

Figure 14.4 The code from Figure 14.3 rewritten to use a C struct.

As the example shows, code that uses a struct avoids pointer arithmetic. In addition, each CSR register can have a meaningful name, making it much easier to read and debug the code. A programmer reading the code can guess the purpose of each item, even if the programmer is not intimately familiar with the underlying device. In addition, using a struct improves program organization because all the offsets of individual CSRs are specified in one place instead of being distributed throughout the code. To summarize:

> *Instead of distributing CSR references throughout the code, a programmer can improve readability by declaring a structure that defines all the CSRs for a device and then referencing fields in the structure.*

14.9 Processor Use And Polling

The chief advantage of a programmed I/O architecture arises from the economic benefit: because they do not contain sophisticated digital circuits, devices that rely on programmed I/O are inexpensive. The chief disadvantage of programmed I/O arises from the computational overhead: each step requires the processor to interact with the I/O device.

To understand why polling is especially undesirable, we must recall the fundamental mismatch between I/O devices and computation: I/O devices operate several orders of magnitude slower than a processor. Furthermore, if a processor uses polling to control an I/O device, the amount of time the processor waits depends on the device, not on the processor.

> *When using programmed I/O, the amount of time a processor waits for an I/O device to finish a task depends only on the device; purchasing a faster processor will not result in faster I/O.*

Turning the statement around produces a corollary: if a processor uses polling to wait for an I/O device, replacing the processor with a faster model merely means that the new processor will waste more clock cycles waiting for the device. The next section discusses an alternative to programmed I/O that allows a processor and I/O devices to operate independently.

14.10 Interrupt-Driven I/O

In the 1950s and 1960s, computer architects became aware of the mismatch between the speed of processors and I/O devices. The difference was particularly important when the first generation of computers, which used vacuum tubes, was replaced by a second generation that used solid-state technology. Although the use of solid-state technology (i.e., transistors) increased the speed of processors, the speed of I/O devices remained approximately the same. Thus, architects explored ways to overcome the mismatch between I/O and processor speeds. One approach emerged as superior, and led to a revolution in computer architecture that produced the third generation of computers. Known as an *interrupt* mechanism, the facility is now standard in processor designs.

The central premise of interrupt-driven I/O is straightforward: instead of wasting time polling, allow a processor to continue to perform other computations while an I/O device operates. When the device finishes, arrange for the device to inform the processor so that the processor can handle the device. As the name implies, the device hardware temporarily interrupts the computation in progress to allow the operating system to handle I/O. Once the device has been serviced, the processor resumes the computation exactly where it was interrupted.

In practice, interrupt-driven I/O requires that all aspects of a computer system be designed to support interrupts, including:

- I/O device hardware
- Bus architecture and functionality
- Processor architecture
- Programming paradigm

I/O Device Hardware. Instead of merely operating under control of a processor, an interrupt-driven I/O device must operate independently once it has started. Later, when it finishes, a device must be able to interrupt the processor.

Bus Architecture And Functionality. A bus must support two-way communication that allows a processor to start an operation on a device and allows the device to interrupt the processor when the operation completes.

Processor Architecture. A processor needs a mechanism that can cause the processor to suspend normal computation temporarily, handle a device that has interrupted, and then resume the computation that was interrupted.

Programming Paradigm. Perhaps the most significant change involves a shift in the programming paradigm. Polling uses a sequential, *synchronous* style of programming in which the programmer specifies each step of the operation an I/O device performs. As we will see in the next chapter, interrupt-driven programming uses an *asynchronous* style of programming in which the programmer writes code to handle events.

14.11 An Interrupt Mechanism And Fetch-Execute

As the term *interrupt* implies, device interrupt events are temporary. When a device needs service (e.g., when an operation completes), hardware in the device sends an interrupt signal over the bus to the processor. The processor temporarily stops executing instructions, saves the state information needed to resume execution later, and handles the device. When it finishes handling an interrupt, the processor reloads the saved state and resumes executing exactly at the point the interrupt occurred. That is:

> *An interrupt mechanism temporarily borrows the processor to handle an I/O device. Hardware automatically saves the state of the computation when an interrupt occurs and restores the state of the computation, allowing the processor to continue once interrupt processing finishes.*

From an application programmer's point of view, an interrupt is *transparent*, which means a programmer writes application code as if interrupts do not exist. The hardware is designed so that the result of computation is the same if no interrupts occur, one interrupt occurs, or many interrupts occur during the execution of the instructions.

How does I/O hardware interrupt a processor? In fact, a device can only request service — the processor must allow the interrupt to proceed. We can think of interrupts being implemented by a modified fetch-execute cycle that allows a processor to respond to a request. As Algorithm 14.1 explains, an interrupt occurs *between* the execution of two instructions.

Algorithm 14.1

Repeat forever {

    Test: if any device has requested interrupt, handle the interrupt, and then continue with the next iteration of the loop.

    Fetch: access the next instruction of the program from memory.

    Execute: Perform the instruction.

}

Algorithm 14.1 A Fetch-Execute Cycle That Handles Interrupts.

14.12 Handling An Interrupt

Recall that the lower-half of a device driver consists of code invoked by the device. We can now be more precise: when it installs a device driver for a given device, the operating system arranges for the lower-half function of the device driver to be invoked when the device requests an interrupt. When an interrupt occurs, the processor hardware takes the five steps that Figure 14.5 lists.

- Save the current execution state

- Use the bus to determine which device interrupted

- Call the lower-half device driver for the device

- Clear the interrupt signal on the bus

- Restore the current execution state and resume execution

Figure 14.5 Five steps that processor hardware performs to handle an interrupt. The steps are hidden from a programmer.

Saving and restoring state is easiest to understand: the hardware saves information when an interrupt occurs (usually on the stack memory), and a special *return from interrupt* instruction reloads the saved state. In some architectures, the hardware saves complete state information, including the contents of all general-purpose registers. In other architectures, the hardware saves basic information, such as the instruction counter, and requires software to save and restore additional values, such as the general-purpose registers. In any case, saving and restoring state are symmetric operations — hardware is designed so the instruction that returns from an interrupt reloads exactly the same state information that the hardware saves when an interrupt occurs. We say that the processor temporarily *switches the execution context* when it handles an interrupt.

14.13 Interrupt Vectors

How does the processor know which device is interrupting? Several mechanisms have been used. For example, some architectures use a special-purpose coprocessor to handle all I/O. To start a device, the processor sends requests to the coprocessor. When a device needs service, the coprocessor detects the situation and interrupts the processor.

Most architectures use control signals on a bus to inform the processor when an interrupt is needed. The processor checks the bus on each iteration of the fetch-execute cycle. When it detects an interrupt request, interrupt hardware in the processor sends a special command over the bus to determine which device needs service. The bus hardware is arranged so that exactly one device can respond at a time. Typically, each device is assigned a unique number, and the device responds by giving its number.

Interrupt numbers assigned to devices are not random. Instead, numbers are configured in a way that allows the processor hardware to interpret the number as an index into an array of pointers at a reserved location in memory. An item in the array, which is known as an *interrupt vector*, contains a pointer to the lower-half device driver software that handles interrupts for the device; we say that the interrupts are *vectored*. The software is known as an *interrupt handler*. Figure 14.6 illustrates the data structure.

The figure shows a basic interrupt vector arrangement in which each physical device is assigned a unique interrupt vector. In practice, computer systems designed to accommodate many devices often use a variation in which multiple devices share a common interrupt vector. After the interrupt occurs, code in the interrupt handler uses the bus a second time to determine which physical device interrupted. Once it determines the physical device, the handler chooses an interaction that is appropriate for the device. The chief advantage of sharing an interrupt vector among multiple devices arises from scale — a processor with a fixed set of interrupt vectors can accommodate an arbitrary number of devices.

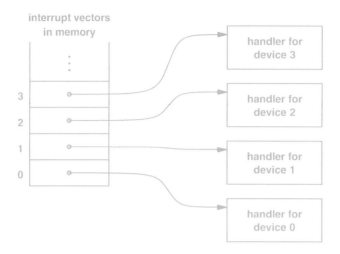

Figure 14.6 Illustration of interrupt vectors in memory. Each vector points to an interrupt handler for the device.

14.14 Interrupt Initialization And Disabled Interrupts

How are values installed in an interrupt vector table? Operating system software must initialize interrupt vectors because neither the processor nor the device hardware enters or modifies the table. Instead, the hardware blindly assumes that the interrupt vector table has been initialized — when an interrupt occurs, the processor saves state, uses the bus to request a vector number, uses the value as an index into the table of vectors, and then branches to the code at that address. No matter what address is found in a vector, the processor will jump to the address and attempt to execute the instruction.

To ensure that no interrupts occur before the table has been initialized, most processors start in a mode that has interrupts *disabled*. That is, the processor continues to run the fetch-execute cycle without checking for interrupts. Later, once it has initialized the interrupt vectors, the operating system must execute a special instruction that explicitly *enables* interrupts. In many processors, the interrupt status is controlled by the *mode* of the processor; interrupts are automatically enabled when the processor changes from the initial startup mode to a mode suitable for executing programs.

14.15 Interrupting An Interrupt Handler

Once an interrupt occurs and an interrupt handler is running, what happens if another device becomes ready and requests an interrupt? The simplest hardware follows a straightforward policy: once an interrupt occurs, further interrupts are automatically disabled until the current interrupt completes and returns. Thus, no confusion can occur.

The most sophisticated processors offer a *multiple level interrupt mechanism* which is also known as *multiple interrupt priorities*. Each device is assigned an interrupt priority level, typically in the range 1 through 7. At any given time, the processor is said to be operating at one of the priority levels. Priority zero means the processor is not currently handling an interrupt (i.e., is running an application); a priority K greater than zero means the processor is currently handling an interrupt from a device that has been assigned to level K. The interrupt levels determine whether an interrupt handler can be interrupted according to the following rule:

> *When operating at interrupt priority level K, a processor can only be interrupted by a device that has been assigned to level $K+1$ or higher.*

Note that when an interrupt happens at priority K, no more interrupts can occur at priority K or lower. The consequence is that at most one interrupt can be in progress at each interrupt priority level.

14.16 Configuration Of Interrupts

We said that each device must be assigned an interrupt vector and (possibly) an interrupt priority. Both the hardware in the device and the software running on the processor must agree on the assignments — when a device returns an interrupt vector number, the corresponding interrupt vector must point to the handler for the device.

How are interrupt assignments made? Two approaches have been used:

- Manual assignment only used for small, embedded systems
- Automated assignment used on most computer systems

Manual Assignment. Some small embedded systems still use the method that was used on early computers: a manual approach in which computer owners configure both the hardware and software. For example, some devices are manufactured with physical switches on the circuit board, and the switches are used to enter an interrupt vector address. Of course, the operating system must be configured to match the values chosen for the device hardware because the operating system must initialize the interrupt vector table to the correct values.

Automated Assignment. Automated interrupt vector assignment is the most widely used approach because it eliminates manual configuration and allows devices to be installed without requiring the hardware to be modified. When the computer boots, the processor uses the bus to determine which devices are attached. The processor assigns a unique interrupt vector number to each device, places a copy of the appropriate device handler software in memory, and builds the interrupt vector in memory. Automated assignment increases the delay that occurs when booting the computer.

14.17 Dynamic Bus Connections And Pluggable Devices

Our description of buses and interrupt configuration has assumed that devices are attached to a bus while a computer is powered down, that interrupt vectors are assigned at startup, and that all devices remain in place as the computer operates. Early buses were indeed designed as we have described. However, more recent buses have been invented that permit devices to be connected and disconnected while the computer is running. We say that such buses support *pluggable* devices. For example, a *Universal Serial Bus* (*USB*) permits a user to plug in a device at any time.

How does a USB operate? In essence, a USB appears as a single device on the computer's main bus. When the computer boots, the USB is assigned an interrupt vector as usual, and a handler is placed in memory. Later, when a user plugs in a new device, the USB hardware generates an interrupt, and the processor executes the handler. The handler, in turn, sends a request over the USB bus to interrogate devices and determine which device has been attached. Once it identifies the device, the USB handler loads a secondary device-specific handler. When a device needs service, the device requests an interrupt. The USB handler receives the interrupt, determines which device interrupted, and passes control to the device-specific handler.

14.18 Interrupts, Performance, And Smart Devices

Why did the interrupt mechanism cause a revolution in computer architecture? The answer is easy. First, I/O is an important aspect of computing that must be optimized. Second, interrupt-driven I/O automatically overlaps computation and I/O without requiring a programmer to take any special action. That is, interrupts adapt to any speed processor and I/O devices automatically. A programmer does not need to estimate how many instructions can be performed during an I/O operation because an interrupt always occurs exactly when the device finishes processing. We can summarize:

> *An architecture that uses interrupts makes programming easier and offers better overall performance than an architecture that uses programmed I/O and polling. In addition, interrupts allow any speed processor to adapt to any speed I/O devices automatically.*

Interestingly, once the basic interrupt mechanism had been invented, architects realized that further improvements were possible. To understand the improvements, consider a Wi-Fi network interface device. The underlying hardware requires several steps to read an incoming packet from the network and place it in memory. Figure 14.7 summarizes the steps.

- If the receiver is not on, power it up
- If the Wi-Fi is not connected, have it connect
- Wait for a packet to arrive
- Read bytes of the packet from the network and place them in a hardware FIFO
- Transfer bytes of data from the FIFO into memory

Figure 14.7 Example of the steps required to read an incoming packet from a network.

Early hardware required the processor to handle each step by starting the operation and waiting for an interrupt. In our example, if the radio is not on, the processor would issue a command to power up the radio, and then wait for an interrupt to indicate that the radio is on.

A key insight emerged: adding more digital logic to an I/O device can reduce how much the device relies on the processor. Informally, architects use the term *smart device* to characterize a device that can perform a series of steps on its own. A smart version of a Wi-Fi device contains sufficient logic (perhaps even an embedded processor) to handle all the steps involved in reading an incoming packet. Thus, a smart device does not interrupt as often, and does not require the processor to issue a command for each step. Figure 14.8 lists an example interaction between a processor and a smart Wi-Fi device.

- The processor uses the bus to send the Wi-Fi device the address of an empty buffer in memory and request a *read* operation
- The Wi-Fi device performs all steps required, including powering up the receiver, capturing an incoming packet, and placing the bytes in the buffer in memory
- The Wi-Fi device only interrupts one time after the operation completes

Figure 14.8 The interaction between a processor and a smart disk device when reading a disk block.

Our discussion of device interaction has omitted many details. For example, most I/O devices detect and report errors (e.g., an incoming packet is malformed). Thus, interrupt processing can be more complex than described: when an interrupt occurs, the processor must interrogate the CSRs associated with the device to determine whether the operation was successful or an error occurred. Furthermore, for devices that report *soft errors* (i.e., temporary errors), the processor can retry the operation.

14.19 Smart Devices, DMA, And Offloading

Recall that a device can use DMA (*Direct Memory Access*) technology to transfer data between the device and memory. Most Wi-Fi devices use DMA — once it receives an incoming packet, the Wi-Fi device transfers the packet to the specified buffer in memory. Of course, DMA requires a smart device because the device must be able to transfer many bytes of data across the bus without using the processor.

In addition to DMA, smart devices can *offload* other functions from the processor, leaving the processor free to perform other computations. For example, each network contains a checksum used to detect network errors. A sender uses the bytes in a packet to compute a checksum for the packet. When the packet arrives, the receiver recomputes the checksum to see if any of the bits in the packet were damaged during transmission. A smart Wi-Fi interface can offload checksum processing, which increases overall system performance because it allows the processor to perform other computations.

To summarize:

> *A smart device can use* Direct Memory Access (DMA) *to move data objects into and out of memory without using the processor; a smart device can also offload other processing, such as computing the checksum on a network packet.*

14.20 Extending DMA With Buffer Chaining

It may seem that a smart device using DMA is sufficient to guarantee high performance: data can be transferred between the device and memory without using the processor, and the device does not interrupt for each step of the operation. However, an optimization has been discovered that further improves performance.

To understand how DMA can be improved, consider a high-speed network. Packets tend to arrive from the network in *bursts*, which means a set of packets arrives back-to-back with minimum time between successive packets. If the network interface device uses DMA, the device will interrupt the processor after accepting an incoming packet and placing the packet in memory. The processor then specifies the location of a buffer for the next packet and restarts the device. The sequence of events must occur quickly (i.e., before the next packet arrives). Unfortunately, other devices on the system may also be generating interrupts, which means the processor may be delayed slightly. For the highest-speed networks, a processor may not be able to service an interrupt in time to capture the next packet.

To solve the problem of back-to-back arrivals, some smart I/O devices use a technique known as *buffer chaining*. The processor allocates multiple buffers, and creates a linked list in memory. The processor then passes the list to the I/O device, and allows the device to fill each buffer. Because a smart device can use the bus to read values from memory, the device can follow the linked list and place incoming packets in successive buffers. Figure 14.9 illustrates the concept†.

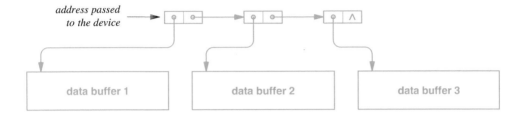

Figure 14.9 Illustration of buffer chaining. A processor passes a list of
buffers to a smart I/O device, and the device fills each buffer on
the list without waiting for the processor.

The network example given above describes the use of buffer chaining for high-speed input. A buffer chain can also be used with output: a processor places data in a set of buffers, links the buffers on a list, passes the address of the linked list to a smart I/O device, and starts the device. The device moves through the list, taking the data from each buffer in memory and sending the data to the device. Using a buffer chain for output allows a processor to keep the device busy sending packets with no delay between them. Instead of waiting for the device to interrupt before it starts the device sending the next packet, the processor can continue to create new outgoing packets and link them onto the buffer chain while the device sends previously created packets.

14.21 Scatter Read And Gather Write Operations

Buffer chaining is especially helpful for computer systems in which the buffer size used by software is smaller than the size of a data block used by an I/O device. On input, chained buffers allow a device to divide a large data transfer into a set of smaller buffers. On output, chained buffers allow a device to extract data from a set of small buffers and combine the data into a single block. For example, some operating systems create a network packet by placing the packet header in one buffer and the packet payload in another buffer. Buffer chaining allows the operating system to send the packet without the overhead of copying all the bytes into a single, large buffer.

We use the term *scatter read* to capture the idea of dividing a large block of incoming data into multiple small buffers, and the term *gather write* to capture the idea of combining data from multiple small buffers into a single output block. Of course, to make buffer chaining useful, a linked list of output buffers must specify the size of each buffer (i.e., the number of bytes to write). Similarly, a linked list of input buffers must include a length field that the device can set to specify how many bytes were deposited in the buffer.

---

†Although the figure shows three buffers, network devices typically use a chain of 32 or 64 buffers.

14.22 Operation Chaining

Although buffer chaining handles situations in which the same operation repeats for many buffers, further optimization is possible in cases where a device can perform multiple operations. To understand, consider a network interface that offers *read* and *write* operations on individual packets. To optimize performance, we need to start another operation as soon as the current operation completes. Unfortunately, the operations are a mixture of reads and writes.

The technology used to start a new operation without delay is known as *operation chaining*. Like buffer chaining, a processor that uses operation chaining must create a linked list in memory, and must pass the list to a smart device. Unlike buffer chaining, however, nodes on the linked list specify a complete operation: in addition to a buffer pointer, the node contains an operation and necessary parameters. For example, a node on the list used with a network might specify a *read* or *write* operation and a pointer to a packet buffer. Figure 14.10 illustrates operation chaining.

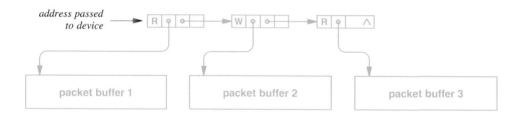

Figure 14.10 Illustration of operation chaining for a smart disk device. Each node specifies an operation (*R* or *W*), a disk block number, and a buffer in memory.

14.23 Summary

Two paradigms can be used to handle I/O devices: programmed I/O and interrupt-driven I/O. Programmed I/O requires a processor to handle each step of an operation by polling the device. Because a processor is much faster than an I/O device, the processor spends many cycles waiting for the device.

Third-generation computers introduced interrupt-driven I/O, which allows a device to perform a complete operation before informing the processor. A processor that uses interrupts includes extra hardware that tests once during each execution of a fetch-execute cycle to see whether any device has requested an interrupt.

Interrupts are vectored, which means the interrupting device supplies a unique integer that the processor uses as an index into an interrupt vector table (i.e., an array of pointers to handlers). To guarantee that interrupts do not affect a running program, the hardware saves and restores state information during an interrupt. Multilevel interrupts are used to give some devices priority over others.

Smart I/O devices contain additional logic that allows them to perform a series of steps without assistance from the processor. Smart devices use DMA along with the techniques of buffer chaining and operation chaining to further optimize performance. Smart devices can further enhance performance by offloading processing, such as checksum computation for incoming or outgoing packets.

EXERCISES

14.1 Assume a RISC processor takes two microseconds to execute each instruction and an I/O device can wait at most 1 millisecond before its interrupt is serviced. What is the maximum number of instructions that can be executed with interrupts disabled?

14.2 List and explain the two I/O paradigms.

14.3 Expand the acronym CSR and explain what it means.

14.4 A software engineer is trying to debug a device driver, and discovers what appears to be an infinite loop:

```
while (*csrptr->tstbusy != 0)
        ;   /* do nothing*/
```

When the software engineer shows you the code, how do you respond?

14.5 Read about devices on a bus and the interrupt priorities assigned to each. Does an SSD or mouse have higher priority? Why?

14.6 In most systems, part or all of the device driver code must be written in assembly language. Why?

14.7 Conceptually, what data structure is an interrupt vector, and what does one find in each entry of the data structure?

14.8 What is the most significant advantage of a device that uses chained operations?

14.9 What is the chief advantage of interrupts over polling?

14.10 Suppose a user installs ten devices in their laptop, and all perform DMA. Suppose all ten devices attempt to operate at the same time. What component(s) in the computer might become a bottleneck?

14.11 If a smart network device uses DMA and packets sent on the network each contain 1500 bytes, how many times will the network device interrupt each time the user sends a packet? Explain.

14.12 When a device uses chaining, what is the type of the data structure that a device driver places in memory to give a set of commands to the device?

Chapter Contents

15

Data Paths And Instruction Execution

15.1 Introduction

Previous chapters describe processors, instructions, and the concept of a fetch-execute cycle. They also describe memory as an array of bytes.

This chapter continues the discussion by explaining how a processor works. It describes some of the hardware components found in a processor, such as an arithmetic-logic unit, memories, and registers. It goes on to explain how the units are interconnected and how data items travel from one unit to another as the processor executes an instruction and then moves on to another instruction. We will learn that the steps hardware takes to interpret instructions differs completely from the way one writes software to perform the operations.

15.2 Data Paths

The topic of how hardware can be organized to create a programmable computer is complex. Rather than look at all the details of a large design, architects begin by describing the major hardware components and their interconnection. At a high level, an architect is only interested in how hardware extracts the next instruction from memory and how the hardware executes the instruction. Therefore, the high-level description ignores many details and only shows the interconnections across which data values must move as the processor executes instructions. For example, when we consider the addition operation, we will see the paths across which two operands travel to reach an *Arithmetic Logic Unit* (*ALU*) and to carry the result to another unit. Our diagrams will not show other details, such as wires that carry power to hardware units and the wires that carry control signals. Computer architects use the terms *data paths* to describe the concept and *data path diagram* to describe a figure that depicts the data paths.

To make the discussion of data paths clear, we will examine a simplified computer. The key factors include:

- Our instruction set contains four instructions
- We assume a program has already been loaded into memory
- We ignore startup and assume the processor is running
- We assume each data item and each instruction occupies exactly 32 bits
- We only consider integer arithmetic
- We completely ignore error conditions, such as arithmetic overflow

Although the example computer is extremely simple, the basic hardware units we will examine are exactly the same as a conventional computer. Thus, the example is sufficient to illustrate the main hardware components, and the example interconnections are sufficient to illustrate how data paths are designed.

15.3 An Example Instruction Set

A computer design must begin with the design of an *instruction set*. Once the details of instructions have been specified, a computer architect can design hardware that performs each of the instructions. To illustrate how hardware is organized, we will consider an imaginary computer that has the following properties:

- A set of sixteen *general-purpose registers*†
- A memory that holds instructions (i.e., a program)
- A separate memory that holds data items

Each register can hold a thirty-two-bit integer value. The *instruction memory* contains a sequence of instructions to be executed. As described above, we ignore startup, and assume a program has already been placed in the instruction memory. The *data memory* holds data values. We will also assume that both memories on the computer are byte-addressable, which means that each byte of memory is assigned an address.

Figure 15.1 lists the four basic instructions that our imaginary computer implements.

---

†Hardware engineers often use the term *register file* to refer to the hardware unit that implements a set of registers; we will simply refer to them as *registers*.

Instruction	Meaning
add	Add the integers in two registers and place the result in a third register
load	Load an integer from the data memory into a register
store	Store the integer in a register into the data memory
jump	Jump to a new location in the instruction memory

Figure 15.1 Four example instructions and the meaning of each instruction.

The *add* instruction obtains integer values from two registers, adds the values together, and places the result in a third register. For example, consider an *add* instruction that specifies adding the contents of registers 2 and 3 and placing the result in register 4. If register 2 contains 50 and register 3 contains 60, the *add* instruction will place 110 in register 4 (i.e., the sum of the integers in registers 2 and 3).

In assembly language, such an instruction is specified by giving the instruction name followed by operands. For example, a programmer might code the *add* instruction described in the previous paragraph by writing:

```
add     r4, r2, r3
```

where the notation *rX* is used to specify register X. The first operand specifies the *destination register* (where the result should be placed), and the other two specify *source registers* (where the instruction obtains the values to sum).

The *load* and *store* instructions move values between the data memory and a register. Like many commercial processors, our imaginary processor requires both operands of an *add* instruction to be in registers. Also like commercial computers, our imaginary processor has a large data memory, but only a few registers. Consequently, to add two integers that are in memory, the two values must be loaded into registers. The *load* instruction makes a copy of an integer in memory and places the copy in a register. The *store* instruction moves data in the opposite direction: it makes a copy of the value currently in a register and places the copy in an integer in memory.

One of the operands for a *load* or *store* specifies the register to be loaded or stored. The other operand is more interesting because it illustrates a feature found on many commercial processors: a single operand that combines two values. Instead of using a single constant to specify a memory address, memory operands contain two parts. One part specifies a register, and the other part specifies a constant that is often called an *offset*. When the instruction is executed, the processor reads the current value from the specified register, adds the offset, and uses the result as a memory address.

An example will clarify the idea. Consider a *load* instruction that loads register 1 from a value in memory. Such an instruction might be written as:

```
load    r1, 20(r3)
```

where the first operand specifies that the value should be loaded into register 1. The second operand specifies that the memory address is computed by adding the offset 20 to the current contents of register 3.

Why are processors designed with operands that specify a register plus an offset? Using such a form makes it easy and efficient to iterate through an array. The address of the first element is placed in a register, and bytes of the element can be accessed by using the offset part of the operand. To move to the next element of the array, the register must be incremented by the element size. For now, we only need to understand that such operands are used, and consider how to design hardware that implements them.

As an example, suppose register 3 contains the value 10000, and the *load* instruction shown above specifies an offset of 20. When the instruction is executed, the hardware adds 10000 and 20, treats the result as a memory address, and loads the integer from location 10020 into register 1.

The fourth instruction, a *jump*, controls the flow of execution by giving the processor an address in the instruction memory. Normally, our imaginary processor works like an ordinary processor by executing an instruction and then automatically moving to the next instruction in memory. When it encounters a *jump* instruction, however, the processor does not move to the next instruction. Instead, the processor uses the operand in the *jump* instruction to compute a memory address, and then starts executing at that address.

Like the *load* and *store* instructions, our *jump* instruction allows both a register and offset to be specified in its operand. For example, the instruction

```
            jump     60(r11)
```

specifies that the processor should obtain the contents of register 11, add 60, treat the result as an address in the instruction memory, and make the address the next location where an instruction is executed. It is not important now to understand why processors contain a *jump* instruction — you only need to understand how the hardware handles the move to a new location in a program.

15.4 Instructions In Memory

We said that the instruction memory on our imaginary computer contains a set of instructions for the processor to execute, and that each instruction occupies thirty-two bits. A computer designer specifies the exact format of each instruction by specifying what each bit means. Figure 15.2 shows the instruction format for our imaginary computer.

	operation	reg A	reg B	dst reg	unused
add	0 0 0 0 1				

	operation	reg A	unused	dst reg	offset
load	0 0 0 1 0				

	operation	reg A	reg B	unused	offset
store	0 0 0 1 1				

	operation	reg A	unused	unused	offset
jump	0 0 1 0 0				

Figure 15.2 The binary representation for each of the four instructions listed in Figure 15.1. Each instruction is thirty-two bits long.

Look carefully at the fields used in each instruction. Each instruction has exactly the same format, even if some of the fields are not used. A uniform format makes it easy to design hardware that extracts the fields from an instruction.

The *operation* field in an instruction (sometimes called an *opcode* field) contains a value that specifies the operation. For our example, an *add* instruction has the operation field set to 1, a *load* instruction has the operation field set to 2, and so on. Thus, when it picks up an instruction, the hardware can use the operation field to decide which operation to perform.

The three fields with the term *reg* in their name specify three registers. Only the *add* instruction needs all three registers; in other instructions, one or two of the register fields are not used. The hardware ignores the unused fields when executing an instruction other than *add*.

The order of operands in Figure 15.2 may seem unexpected and inconsistent with the code above. For example, the code for an *add* instruction has the destination (the register to contain the result) on the left, and the two registers to be added on the right. In the binary representation of the instruction, fields that specify the two registers to be added precede the field that specifies the destination. Figure 15.3 shows a statement written by a programmer and the instruction when it has been converted to bits in memory. We can summarize the point:

The order of operands in an assembly language program is chosen to be convenient to a programmer; the order of operands in an instruction in memory is chosen to make the hardware efficient.

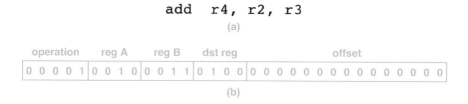

Figure 15.3 (a) An example *add* instruction as it appears to a programmer, and (b) the instruction stored in memory.

In the figure, the field labeled *reg A* contains 2 to specify register 2, the field labeled *reg B* contains 3 to specify register 3, and the field labeled *dst reg* contains 4 to specify that the result should be placed in register 4.

When we examine the hardware, we will see that the binary representation used for instructions is not capricious — the format simplifies the hardware design. For example, if an instruction has an operand that specifies a memory address, the register in the operand is always assigned to the field labeled *reg A*. Thus, if the hardware must add the offset to a register, the register is always found in field *reg A*. Similarly, if a value must be stored in a register, the register is always found in field *dst reg*.

15.5 Moving To The Next Instruction

Before computers, various mechanical and electrical machines had been built that could carry out a sequence of steps to perform a useful task. Computers differ from previous machines in a significant way: instead of performing a fixed sequence of steps, a computer is *programmable*, which means that although the computer has hardware to perform every possible instruction in its instruction set, the designer does not specify the exact sequence of instructions that must be performed. Instead, a programmer stores a program in memory and the processor moves through the memory, extracting and executing successive instructions one at a time. How can hardware be arranged to enable programmability? What pieces of hardware are needed to execute instructions from memory? The next sections provide the answers.

A key element needed for programmability, the *program counter*, which is also called an *instruction pointer*, allows a computer to access instructions in memory. A program counter consists of a register (i.e., a piece of hardware in the processor that holds a memory address). The program counter holds the address of the next instruction to execute. For example, if we imagine a computer with thirty-two-bit memory addresses, a program counter will hold a thirty-two-bit value. To execute instructions, the hardware repeats the following three steps.

- Use the program counter as a memory address and fetch an instruction
- Use bits in the instruction to control hardware that performs the operation
- Move the program counter to the next instruction

The processor must include hardware that can move the program counter to the next instruction after it finishes executing the current instruction. That is, the program counter must move to the next sequential instruction in memory,

In our example computer, each instruction occupies thirty-two bits. Recall, however, that memory is byte-addressable, which means the program counter contains the address of the first byte of the instruction. To move to the next instruction, hardware must increment the program counter by four because each thirty-two-bit instruction occupies four bytes. In essence, the processor must perform arithmetic: add four to the program counter and place the result back in the program counter. To perform the computation, the constant 4 and the current program counter value are passed to a thirty-two-bit adder. Figure 15.4 illustrates the basic components used to increment the program counter and how the components are interconnected.

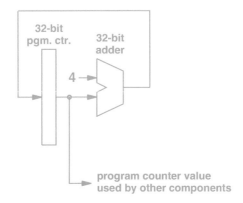

Figure 15.4 Hardware that increments a program counter.

The circuit in the figure appears to be an infinite loop that will simply run wild incrementing the program counter continuously. To understand why the circuit works, recall that a clock controls and synchronizes all the circuits in a processor. In the case of the program counter, the hardware uses the clock to control how frequently the addition occurs. As a consequence, the incremented value will only be placed in the program counter after the current instruction finishes executing. Although no clock is shown, we will assume that each component of the circuit is connected to the clock, and the component only acts according to the clock. Thus, the adder will compute a new value immediately, but the program counter will not be updated until the clock pulses. Throughout our discussion, we will assume that the clock pulses once per instruction.

Each line in the figure represents a *data path* that consists of multiple parallel wires. In the figure, each data path is thirty-two bits wide. That is, the adder takes two inputs, both of which are thirty-two bits. The value coming from the program counter is obvious because the program counter has thirty-two bits. The other input, marked with label *4* represents a thirty-two-bit constant with the numeric value 4. The adder produces a thirty-two-bit result by computing the sum of its two inputs.

15.6 Fetching An Instruction

The next step in constructing a computer consists of fetching an instruction from memory. For our simplistic example, we will assume that a dedicated *instruction memory* holds the program to be executed, and that a memory hardware unit takes an address as input and extracts a thirty-two-bit data value from the specified location in memory. That is, wires that contain an address form the input to the memory unit. When the address on the input wires changes to a new address, the memory hardware looks up the value at that address and places the value on the output wires. Figure 15.5 illustrates how the current value in the program counter forms an input to the instruction memory.

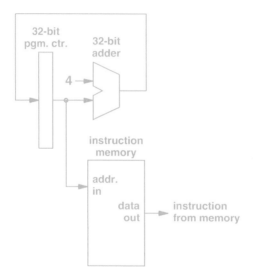

Figure 15.5 The data path used during *instruction fetch* in which the value in a program counter is used as a memory address.

15.7 Decoding An Instruction

When the hardware fetches an instruction from memory, the resulting value contains thirty-two bits. The next conceptual step in execution consists of *instruction decoding*. That is, the hardware separates fields of the instruction: the operation, registers, and offset. Recall from Figure 15.2 how the bits of an instruction are organized. Because our example uses separate bit fields for each item, instruction decoding is trivial — the hardware simply separates the wires that carry bits for the operation field, each of the three register fields, and the offset field. Figure 15.6 illustrates how the output from the instruction memory feeds into an instruction decoder that separates fields of the instruction.

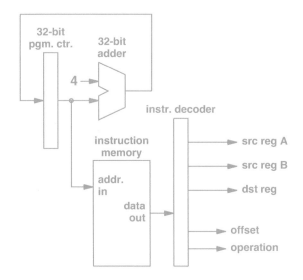

Figure 15.6 Illustration of an instruction decoder connected to the output of the instruction memory.

In the figure, individual outputs from the instruction decoder do not each have thirty-two bits. The operation consists of five bits, the outputs that correspond to registers consist of four bits each, the output labeled *offset* consists of fifteen bits. Thus, we can think of a line in the data path diagram as indicating one or more bits of data.

It is important to understand that the output from the decoder consists of fields from the instruction. For example, the path labeled *offset* contains the fifteen offset bits from the instruction. Similarly, the data path labeled *src reg A* contains the four bits from the *reg A* field in the instruction. The point is that the data for *reg A* only specifies which register to use, and does not carry the value that is currently in the register. We can summarize:

> *Our example instruction decoder merely extracts bit fields from an instruction without interpreting the fields.*

Unlike our imaginary computer, a real processor may have multiple instruction formats (e.g., the fields in an arithmetic instruction may be in different locations than the fields in a memory access instruction). Furthermore, a real processor may have variable-length instructions. As a result, an instruction decoder may need to examine the operation to decide the location of fields. Nevertheless, the principle remains the same: a decoder extracts fields from an instruction and passes each field along a data path.

15.8 Connections To A Register Unit

The register fields of an instruction are used to select registers that the instruction accesses. In our example, a *jump* instruction uses one register, a *load* or *store* instruction uses two registers, and an *add* instruction uses three. Therefore, each of the three possible register fields must connect to a register storage unit as Figure 15.7 illustrates.

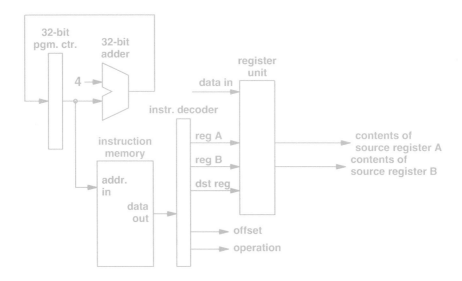

Figure 15.7 Illustration of a register unit attached to an instruction decoder.

15.9 Control And Coordination

Although all three register fields connect to the register unit, the unit does not always use all three. Instead, the hardware contains logic that determines whether a given instruction reads existing values from registers or writes data into one of the registers. In particular, the *load* and *add* instructions each write a result to a register, but the *jump* and *store* instructions do not.

It may seem that the operation portion of the instruction should be passed to the register unit to allow the unit to know how to act. To understand why the figure does not show a connection between remaining fields of the instruction and the register unit, remember that we are only examining data paths (i.e., the hardware paths along which data can flow). In an actual computer, each of the units illustrated in the figure will have additional connections that carry control signals. For example, each unit must receive a clock signal to ensure that it coordinates to take action at the correct time (e.g., to ensure that the data memory does not store a value until the correct address has been computed).

In practice, most computers use an additional hardware unit, known as a *controller*, to coordinate overall data movement and each of the functional units. A controller must have one or more connections to each of the other units, and must use the *operation* field of an instruction to determine how each unit should operate to perform the instruction. In the diagram, for example, a connection between the controller and register unit would be used to specify whether the register unit should fetch the values of one or two registers, and whether the unit should accept data to be placed in a register. For now, we will assume that a controller exists to coordinate the operation of all units.

15.10 Arithmetic Operations And Multiplexing

Our example set of instructions illustrates an important principle: hardware is designed to reuse functional units. Consider arithmetic. Only the *add* instruction performs arithmetic explicitly. A real processor will have several arithmetic and logical instructions (e.g., *subtract, shift, logical and*), and will use the *operation* field in the instruction to decide which operation the ALU should perform.

Our instruction set also has an implicit arithmetic operation associated with the *load*, *store*, and *jump* instructions. Each of those instructions requires an addition operation to be performed when the instruction is executed. Namely, the processor must add the offset value, which is found in the instruction itself, to the contents of a register. The resulting sum is then treated as a memory address.

The question arises: should a processor have a separate hardware unit to compute the sum needed for an address, or should a single ALU be used for both general arithmetic and address arithmetic? Such questions form the basis for key decisions in processor design. Separate functional units have the advantage of speed and ease of design. Reusing a functional unit for multiple purposes has the advantage of taking less power.

Our design illustrates reuse. Like many processors, our design contains a single *Arithmetic Logic Unit (ALU)* that performs all arithmetic operations†. For our sample instruction set, inputs to the ALU can come from two sources: either a pair of registers or a register and the offset field in an instruction. How can a hardware unit choose among multiple sources of input? The mechanism that accommodates two possible inputs is known as a *multiplexor*. The basic idea is that a multiplexor has K data inputs, one data output, and a set of control lines used to specify which input is sent to the output. To understand how a multiplexor is used, consider Figure 15.8, which shows a multiplexor between the register unit and ALU. When viewing the figure, remember that each line in our diagram represents a data path with thirty-two bits. Thus, each input to the multiplexor contains thirty-two bits as does the output. The multiplexor selects all thirty-two bits from one of the two inputs and sends them to the output.

---

†Incrementing the program counter is a special case.

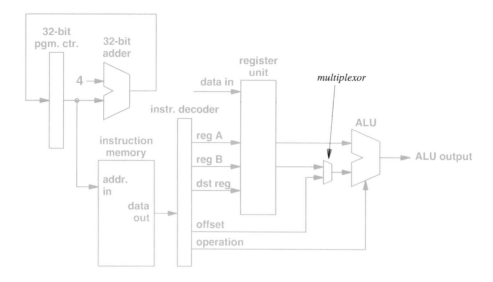

Figure 15.8 Illustration of a multiplexor used to select an input for the ALU.

In the figure, inputs to the multiplexor come from the register unit and the offset field in the instruction. How does the multiplexor decide which input to pass along? Recall that our diagram only shows the data path. In addition, the processor contains a controller, and all units are connected to the controller. When the processor executes an *add* instruction, the controller signals the multiplexor to select the input coming from the register unit. When the processor executes other instructions, the controller specifies that the multiplexor should select the input that comes from the offset field in the instruction.

Observe that the *operation* field of the instruction is passed to the ALU. Doing so permits the ALU to decide which operation to perform. In the case of an arithmetic or logical instruction (e.g., *add*, *subtract*, *right shift*, *logical and*), the ALU uses the operation to select the appropriate action. In the case of other instructions, the ALU performs addition.

15.11 Operations Involving Data In Memory

When it executes a *load* or *store* operation, the computer must reference an item in the data memory. For such operations, the ALU is used to add the offset in the instruction to the contents of a register, and the result is used as a memory address. In our simplified design, the memory used to store data is separate from the memory used to store instructions. Figure 15.9 illustrates the data paths used to connect a data memory.

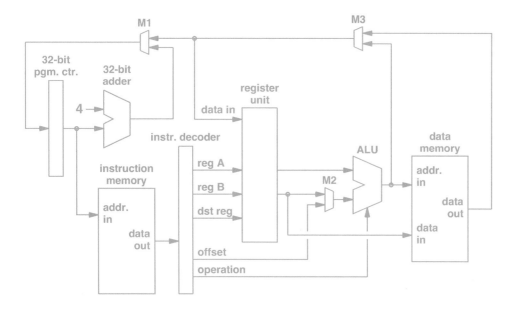

Figure 15.9 Illustration of data paths including data memory.

15.12 Example Execution Sequences

To understand how computation proceeds, consider the data paths that are used for each instruction. The following paragraphs explain the sequence. In each case, the program counter gives the address of an instruction, which is passed to the instruction memory. The instruction memory fetches the value from memory, and passes bits of the value to the instruction decoder. The decoder separates fields of the instruction and passes them to other units. The remainder of the operation depends on the instruction.

Add. For an *add* instruction, the register unit is given three register numbers, which are passed along paths labeled *reg A*, *reg B*, and *dst reg*. The register unit fetches the values in the first two registers, and passes them to the ALU. The register unit also prepares to write to the third register. The ALU uses the operation code to determine that addition is required. To allow the *reg B* output from the register unit to reach the ALU, the controller (not shown) must set multiplexor M2 to accept the value from the *B* register data path and ignore the *offset* value from the decoder. The controller sets multiplexor M3 to pass the output from the ALU to the register unit's *data input*, and sets multiplexor M1 to ignore the output from the ALU. Once the output from the ALU reaches the input connection on the register unit, the register unit stores the value in the register specified by the path labeled *dst reg*, and the operation completes.

Store. After a *store* instruction has been fetched from memory and decoded, the register unit fetches the values for registers *A* and *B*, and places them on its output lines. The controller set multiplexor M2 to pass the *offset* to the ALU and ignore the value of register *B*. The controller instructs the ALU to perform addition, which adds the offset and contents of register *A*. The resulting sum passes to the data memory as an address. Meanwhile, the register *B* value (the second output of the register unit) passes to the *data in* connection on the data memory. The controller instructs the data memory to perform a *write* operation, which writes the value of register *B* into the location specified by the value on the address lines, and the operation completes.

Load. After a *load* instruction has been fetched and decoded, the controller sets multiplexor M2 so the ALU receives the contents of register *A* and the *offset* field from the instruction. As with a *store*, the controller instructs the ALU to perform the addition, and the result passes to the data memory as an address. The controller signals the data memory to perform a *fetch* operation, and the output of the data memory is the value at the location given by the address input. The controller sets multiplexor M3 to ignore the output from the ALU and pass the output of the data memory to the *data in* path of the register unit. The controller signals the register unit to store its input value in the register specified by register *dst reg*. Once the register unit stores the value, execution of the instruction completes.

Jump. After a *jump* instruction has been fetched and decoded, the controller sets multiplexor M2 to pass the *offset* field from the instruction, and instructs the ALU to perform the addition. The ALU adds the offset to the contents of register *A*. To use the result as an address, the controller sets multiplexor M3 to pass the output from the ALU and ignore the output from the data memory. Finally, the controller sets multiplexor M1 to pass the value from the ALU to the program counter. Thus, the result from the ALU passes to the 32-bit program counter. The program counter receives and stores the new value, and the instruction completes. Recall that the program counter always specifies the address in memory from which to fetch the next instruction. Therefore, when the next instruction executes, the instruction will be extracted from the address that was computed in the previous instruction (i.e., the program will jump to the new location).

15.13 Summary

Unlike earlier machines that had the sequence of steps hardwired into the machine, a computer uses programmability in which the steps to be taken come from instructions from memory; the functionality of a computer can be changed by loading a new program into memory. Although the overall design of a processor that executes instructions involves complex subsystems and details, the basics can be understood easily.

A processor contains multiple hardware components, such as a program counter, memories, register units, and an ALU. Connections among components form the computer's *data paths*. We examined a set of components sufficient to execute basic instructions, and reviewed hardware for the steps of instruction fetch, decode, and execute, including register and data access. Using fixed fields in instructions makes hardware design easier — fields from the instruction can be extracted by selecting sets of wires that carry the bits of the instruction.

In addition to the data paths, a processor contains a controller that connects to each of the hardware units and tells the units how to act on a given instruction. A *multiplex-*

or allows the controller to choose among two data inputs, depending on the instruction. In essence, each multiplexor allows data from one of several sources to be sent to a given output. When an instruction executes, a controller uses fields of the instruction to determine how to set the multiplexors and other units to execute the instruction. Multiplexors permit hardware reuse (e.g., a single ALU can either add an offset to an address or perform arithmetic operations).

We reviewed execution of basic instructions and saw how multiplexors along the data path in a computer can control which values pass to a given hardware unit. We saw, for example, that a multiplexor selects whether the program counter increments by four to move to the next instruction in memory or has the previous value replaced by the output of the ALU to perform a *jump*.

EXERCISES

15.1   Does the example system follow the Von Neumann Architecture? Why or why not?

15.2   Consult Figure 15.3, and show each individual bit when the following instruction is stored in memory:

```
add  r1, r14, r9
```

15.3   Consult Figure 15.3, and show each individual bit when the following instruction is stored in memory:

```
load  r7, 43(r15)
```

15.4   Why is the following instruction invalid?

```
jump  40000(r15)
```

Hint: consider storing the instruction in memory.

15.5   The example presented in this chapter uses four instructions. Given the binary representation in Figure 15.2, how many possible instructions (opcodes) can be created?

15.6   Explain why the circuit in Figure 15.5 is not merely an infinite loop that runs wildly.

15.7   When a *jump* instruction is executed, what operation does the ALU perform?

15.8   A data path diagram, such as the diagram in Figure 15.9, hides many details. If the example is changed so that every instruction is sixty-four bits long, what trivial change must be made to the figure?

15.9   Make a table of all instructions from the example system, and show how each of the multiplexors is set when an instruction is executed.

15.10   Modify the example system to include additional operations *right shift* and *subtract*.

15.11   In Figure 15.9, which input does multiplexor M1 forward during an *add* instruction?

15.12   In Figure 15.9, for what instructions does multiplexor M3 select the input from the ALU?

15.13   Redesign the computer system in Figure 15.9 to include a *relative branch* instruction. Assume the offset field contains a signed value, and add the value to the current program counter to produce the next value for the program counter.

15.14   Can the system in Figure 15.9 handle multiplication? Why or why not?

Chapter Contents

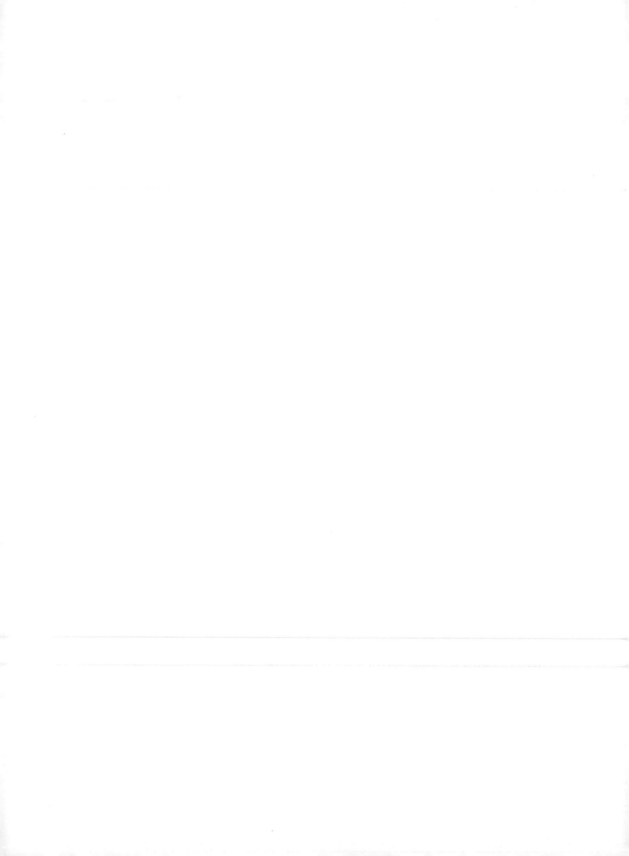

16

CPUs: Microcode, Protection, And Processor Modes

16.1 Introduction

Previous chapters consider key aspects of processors: instruction sets, operands, and the data paths that connect hardware units inside a processor. This chapter considers a broad class of general-purpose processors, and extends our description of processor hardware by examining hardware modes, the use of microcode, and techniques that achieve high-performance processing.

16.2 A Central Processor

Early in the history of computers, centralization emerged as an important architectural approach — as much functionality as possible was collected into a single processor. The processor, which became known as a *Central Processing Unit* (*CPU*), controlled the entire computer, including both calculations and I/O.

In contrast to early designs, a modern computer system follows a decentralized approach. The system contains multiple processors, many of which are dedicated to a specific function or a hardware subsystem. For example, a smart I/O device, such as a network interface, can include a processor that handles packet transfers.

Despite the shift in paradigm, the term CPU has survived because one chip contains the hardware used to perform most computations and coordinate and control other processors. In essence, the CPU manages the entire computer system by telling other processors when to start, when to stop, and what to do.

16.3 CPU Complexity

Because it must handle a wide variety of control and processing tasks, modern CPU hardware is extremely complex. Some CPU chips contain several billion transistors. Why is a CPU so complex? Why are so many transistors needed?

Multiple Cores. In fact, a modern CPU chip does not contain just one processor. Instead, the chip contains multiple processors called *cores*. The cores all function in parallel, permitting multiple computations to proceed at the same time. Multicore designs are required for high performance because a single core cannot be clocked at arbitrarily high speeds.

Multiple Roles. One aspect of CPU complexity arises because a CPU must fill several major roles: running application programs, running an operating system, handling external I/O devices, starting or stopping the computer, and managing memory. No single instruction set is optimal for all roles, so a CPU often includes many instructions.

Protection And Privilege. Most computer systems incorporate a system of protection that gives some subsystems higher privilege than others. For example, the hardware prevents an application program from directly interacting with I/O devices, and the operating system code is protected from inadvertent or deliberate change.

Hardware Priorities. A CPU uses a priority scheme in which some actions are assigned higher priority than others. For example, the interrupt mechanism means that I/O devices operate at higher priority than application programs — if the CPU is running an application program when an I/O device needs service, an interrupt causes the CPU to stop running the application and handle the device.

Generality. A CPU is designed to support a wide variety of applications. Consequently, the CPU instruction set often contains instructions that are used for each type of application.

Data Size. To speed processing, a CPU often includes facilities to handle large data values (e.g., 64-bit arithmetic). Recall that hardware is iterated in space, which requires sixty-four copies of the hardware to operate on integers of sixty-four bits. Thus, the data paths and other units in the CPU must all have sixty-four copies of the underlying hardware.

High Speed. The final, and perhaps most significant, source of CPU complexity arises from the desire for speed. To achieve highest performance, the functional units in a CPU must be replicated, and the design must permit the replicated units to operate in parallel. Of course, parallelism implies more transistors.

16.4 Modes Of Execution

The features listed above can be combined or implemented separately. For example, a given core can be granted access to other parts of memory with or without higher priority. How can a CPU accommodate all the features in a way that allows programmers to understand and use them without becoming confused?

In most CPUs, the hardware uses a set of parameters to handle the complexity and control operation. We say that the hardware has multiple *modes of execution*. At any given time, the current execution mode determines how the CPU operates. Figure 16.1 lists items usually associated with a CPU mode of execution.

- The subset of instructions that are valid
- The type and size of data items
- The region(s) of memory that can be accessed
- The functional units that are available
- The amount of privilege available

Figure 16.1 Items typically controlled by a CPU mode of execution. The characteristics of a CPU can change dramatically when the mode changes.

16.5 Backward Compatibility

How much variation can execution modes introduce? In principle, the modes available on a CPU do not need to share much in common. As one extreme case, some CPUs have a mode that provides *backward compatibility* with a previous model. Backward compatibility allows a vendor to sell a CPU with new features, but also permits customers to use the CPU to run old software.

Intel's line of processors (i.e., 8086, 186, 286,...) exemplifies how backward compatibility can be used. When Intel first introduced a CPU that operated on thirty-two-bit integers, the CPU included a *compatibility mode* that implemented the sixteen-bit instruction set from Intel's previous CPU. In addition to using different sizes of integers, the two architectures have different numbers of registers and different instructions. The two architectures differ so significantly that it is easiest to think of the design as two separate pieces of hardware with the execution mode determining which of the two is used at any time.

We can summarize:

A CPU uses an execution mode to determine the current operational characteristics. In some CPUs, the characteristics of modes differ so widely that we think of the CPU as having separate hardware subsystems and the mode as determining which piece of hardware is used at the current time.

16.6 Changing Modes

How does a CPU change execution modes? Mode changes arise from two sources:

- Hardware-initiated (the hardware forces a mode change)
- Software-initiated (a program requests a mode change)

Hardware-initiated mode change. Hardware can force the mode of a CPU to change. For example, when an I/O device issues an interrupt to request service, the hardware informs the CPU. Hardware in the CPU changes mode, and then uses the interrupt vector table to jump to the operating system code that handles the device.

Software-initiated mode change. When a program executes a *system call* instruction, the hardware changes the CPU to a highly privileged mode before it jumps to the operating system code. Some CPUs provide a mode with an additional level of privilege to allow the CPU to run a hypervisor with multiple operating systems.

To accommodate major changes in mode, additional facilities may be needed to prepare for the new mode. For example, consider a case in which two modes of execution do not share general-purpose registers (e.g., in one mode the registers have sixteen bits and in another mode the registers contain thirty-two bits). It may be necessary to place values in alternate registers before changing mode and using the registers. In such cases, a CPU provides special instructions that allow software to create or modify values before changing the mode.

16.7 Privilege And Protection

The mode of execution usually includes CPU facilities that control privilege and protection, and the mode must be appropriate for the computation being performed. On the one hand, when it services an I/O interrupt, the CPU must run in a mode that allows device driver software to use the bus to interact directly with device hardware. On the other hand, when it runs an arbitrary application program, the CPU must run in a mode that prevents the application from accidentally or maliciously issuing commands directly to I/O devices. Thus, before it executes an application program, an operating system changes to a mode that has reduced privileges. When running in a less privileged mode, the CPU does not permit direct control of I/O devices (i.e., the CPU treats a privileged operation as an error).

16.8 Multiple Levels Of Protection

How many levels of privilege are needed, and what operations should be allowed at each level? The subject has been discussed by hardware architects and operating system designers for many years. CPUs have been invented that offer no protection, and CPUs have been invented that offer eight levels, each with more privilege than the previous level. The idea of protection is to prevent problems by using the minimum amount of privilege necessary at any time. We can summarize:

> *By using a protection scheme to limit the operations that are allowed, a CPU can detect attempts to perform unauthorized operations.*

Although no protection scheme suffices for all cases, a CPU that runs an operating system needs at least two levels of privilege: *kernel mode* for the operating system and *user mode* for applications, as Figure 16.2 illustrates.

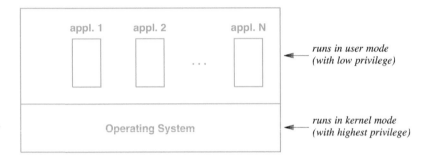

Figure 16.2 Illustration of a CPU that offers two levels of protection, one for the operating system and the other for application programs.

We can summarize:

> *When a CPU runs an operating system, the CPU needs at least two levels of privilege: the operating system runs with highest privilege and an application runs with minimal privilege.*

When we discuss memory, we will see that the issues of protection and memory access are intertwined. More important, we will see how memory access mechanisms, which are part of the CPU mode, provide additional forms of protection.

16.9 Microcoded Instructions

How should a complex CPU be implemented? Interestingly, one of the key abstractions used to build a complex instruction set comes from software: complex instructions are programmed! That is, instead of implementing the instruction set directly with digital circuits, a CPU is built in two pieces. First, a hardware architect builds a fast, but small processor known as a *microcontroller*†. Second, to implement the CPU

---

†The small processor is also called a *microprocessor*, but the term is somewhat misleading.

instruction set that programmers will use (called a *macro instruction set*), the architect writes software for the microcontroller. The software that runs on the microcontroller is known as *microcode*. Figure 16.3 illustrates the two-level organization, and shows how each level is implemented.

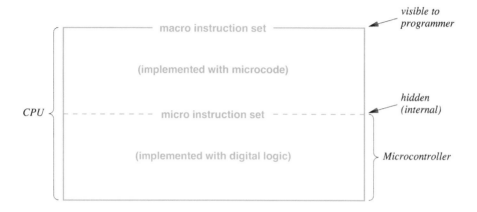

Figure 16.3 Illustration of a CPU implemented with a microcontroller. The macro instruction set that the CPU provides is implemented with microcode.

The easiest way to think about microcode is to imagine writing a set of functions, where each function implements one of the CPU macro instructions. The CPU invokes the microcode during instruction execution. That is, once it has obtained and decoded a macro instruction, the CPU invokes the microcode function that corresponds to the macro operation.

The macro architecture and micro architecture may differ dramatically. As an example, suppose that the integer size for the macro instruction set is thirty-two bits. Further suppose the macro instruction set includes an *add32* instruction for integer addition. The microcontroller may only offer sixteen-bit arithmetic. To implement a thirty-two-bit addition, the microcode must add sixteen bits at a time, and must add the carry from the low-order bits into the high-order bits. Figure 16.4 lists the microcode steps that are required.

The exact details are unimportant; the figure illustrates how the architecture of the microcontroller and the macro instruction set can differ dramatically. Also note that because each macro instruction is implemented by a microcode program, a macro instruction can perform arbitrary processing. For example, it is possible for a single macro instruction to implement a trigonometric function, such as *sine* or *cosine*, or to move large blocks of data in memory. Of course, to achieve higher performance, an architect can choose to limit the amount of microcode that corresponds to a given instruction.

```
/* The steps below assume that two 32-bit operands are
   located in registers labeled R5 and R6, and that the
   microcode must use 16-bit registers labeled r0 through
   r3 to compute the results.
*/
add32:
       move low-order 16 bits from R5 into r2
       move low-order 16 bits from R6 into r3
       add r2 and r3, placing result in r1
       save value of the carry indicator
       move high-order 16 bits from R5 into r2
       move high-order 16 bits from R6 into r3
       add r2 and r3, placing result in r0
       copy the value in r0 to r2
       add r2 and the carry bit, placing the result in r0
       check for overflow and set the condition code
       move the thirty-two bit result from r0 and r1 to
           the desired destination
```

Figure 16.4 An example of the steps required to implement a thirty-two-bit macro addition instruction with a microcontroller that only supports sixteen-bit arithmetic.

16.10 Microcode Variations

The description above implies that a CPU uses microcode for each macro instruction. In fact, computer designers have invented many variations. For example, on some CPUs, a hardware circuit implements the fetch-execute cycle and only invokes a microcode function once an instruction has been decoded. On other CPUs, microcode implements the entire fetch-execute cycle. As another variation, a CPU can be designed that only uses microcode for complex instructions. That is, the CPU implements most of the macro instruction set with digital circuits, and then uses microcode to implement complex instructions. For example, a CPU may have hardware to perform integer and floating point arithmetic operations, but relies on microcode to compute the sine function. Using microcode for extensions allows a vendor to create minor variations of a basic CPU easily and quickly because micro code can be changed easily and quickly.

16.11 The Advantage Of Microcode

Why use microcode? There are three motivations. First, microcode raises the level of abstraction — engineers who write microcode make fewer mistakes than engineers who design circuits. Second, writing microcode takes less time, so new versions of a

CPU can be created quickly. Third, basing a CPU on microcode makes it much easier to produce the next generation of the CPU. To summarize:

> *A design that uses microcode is less prone to errors and can be up-dated faster than a design that does not use microcode.*

Of course, microcode does have some disadvantages that balance the advantages:

- Microcode has more overhead than a hardware implementation.
- Because it executes multiple micro instructions for each macro instruction, the microcontroller must run at much higher speed than the CPU.
- The cost of a macro instruction depends on the microcode used.

16.12 FPGAs And Changes To An Instruction Set

Because a microcontroller is an internal mechanism intended to help designers, the micro instruction set is usually hidden in the final design. The microcontroller and microcode typically reside on the integrated circuit along with the rest of the CPU, and are only used internally. Only the macro instruction set is available to programmers. Interestingly, some CPUs have been designed that make the microcode dynamic and accessible to customers who purchase the CPU. That is, the CPU contains facilities that allow the underlying hardware to be changed after the chip has been manufactured.

Why would a customer change a CPU? The motivations are flexibility and performance: allowing a customer to make some changes to CPU instructions defers the decision about a macro instruction set, and allows a CPU's owner to tailor instructions to a specific use. For example, a company that sells video games might add macro instructions to manipulate graphics images, and a company that makes networking equipment might create macro instructions to process packet headers. Using the underlying hardware directly (e.g., with microcode) can result in higher performance.

One technology that allows modification has become especially popular. Known as *Field Programmable Gate Array* (*FPGA*), the technology permits gates to be altered after a chip has been manufactured. Reconfiguring an FPGA is a time-consuming process. Thus, the general idea is to reconfigure the FPGA once, and then use the resulting chip. An FPGA can be used to hold an entire CPU, or an FPGA can be used as a supplement that holds a few extra instructions.

We can summarize:

> *Technologies like dynamic microcode and FPGAs allow a CPU instruction set to be modified or extended after the CPU has been purchased. The motivations are flexibility and higher performance.*

16.13 Vertical Microcode

The question arises: what architecture should be used for a microcontroller? From the point of view of someone who writes microcode, the question becomes: what instructions should the microcontroller provide? We discussed the notion of microcode as if a microcontroller consists of a conventional processor (i.e., a processor that follows a conventional architecture). We will see shortly that other designs are possible.

In fact, a microcontroller cannot be exactly the same as a standard processor. Because it must interact with hardware units in the CPU, a microcontroller needs a few special hardware facilities. For example, a microcontroller must either have an ALU of its own or be able to access the main ALU, and must be able to store results in the general-purpose registers that the macro instruction set uses. Similarly, a microcontroller must be able to decode operand references and fetch values. Finally, the microcontroller must have access to other hardware components, including memory.

Despite the requirements for special features, microcontrollers have been created that follow the same general approach used for conventional processors. That is, the microcontroller's instruction set contains conventional instructions such as *load*, *store*, *add*, *subtract*, *branch*, and so on. For example, the microcontroller used in a CISC processor can consist of a small, fast RISC processor. We say that such a microcontroller has a *vertical* architecture, and use the term *vertical microcode* to characterize the software that runs on the microcontroller.

Programmers find vertical microcode convenient because the programming interface is familiar. Most important, the semantics of vertical microcode are exactly what a programmer expects: one micro instruction is executed at a time. The next section discusses an alternative to vertical microcode.

16.14 Horizontal Microcode

From a hardware perspective, vertical microcode is unattractive. One of the primary disadvantages arises from the performance requirements. Most macro instructions require multiple micro instructions, which means that executing macro instructions at a rate of K per second requires a microcontroller to execute micro instructions at a rate of $N \times K$ per second, where N is the average number of micro instructions per macro instruction. Therefore, all hardware associated with the microcontroller must operate at an extremely high speed (e.g., the memory used to hold microcode must be able to deliver micro instructions at a high rate).

A second disadvantage of vertical microcode arises because a vertical technology cannot exploit the parallelism of the underlying hardware. Computer engineers have invented an alternative form known as *horizontal microcode* that overcomes some limitations of vertical microcode. Horizontal microcode has the advantage of working well with the underlying hardware because it has the ability to operate multiple hardware units simultaneously. Unfortunately, programmers often find horizontal microcode difficult to understand and master because the programming interface seems unfamiliar.

The point is:

Horizontal microcode allows the hardware to run faster, but is more difficult to program.

To understand horizontal microcode, recall the data path description from the previous chapter: a CPU consists of multiple functional units, with data paths connecting them. Operation of the units must be controlled, and each unit is controlled independently. Furthermore, moving data from one functional unit to another requires explicit control of the two units: one unit must be instructed to send an item across a data path, and the other unit must be instructed to receive the item.

An example will clarify the concept. To keep the example easy to understand, we will make a few simplifying assumptions and restrict the discussion to six functional units. Figure 16.5 shows interconnection among the six functional units.

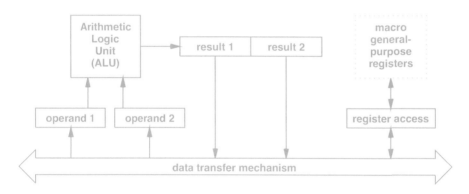

Figure 16.5 An illustration of the internal structure within a CPU. Solid arrows indicate a hardware path along which data can move.

The figure shows an *Arithmetic Logic Unit* (*ALU*) that performs arithmetic and logical operations, such as addition, subtraction, and bit shifting. The remaining functional units provide mechanisms that connect the ALU to the rest of the system. For example, the hardware units labeled *operand 1* and *operand 2* denote operand storage units (i.e., internal hardware registers). The ALU expects operands to be placed in the storage units before an operation is performed, and places the result of an operation in the two hardware units labeled *result 1* and *result 2†*. Finally, the *register access* unit provides a hardware interface to the general-purpose registers.

In the figure, arrows indicate paths along which data can pass as it moves from one functional unit to another; each arrow is a data path that handles multiple bits in parallel (e.g., 32 bits). Most of the arrows connect to the *data transfer mechanism*, which serves as a conduit between functional units. We can think of the data transfer unit as a specialized type of bus.

---

†Recall that an arithmetic operation, such as multiplication, can produce a result that is twice as large as

16.15 Example Horizontal Microcode

Each functional unit is controlled by a set of wires that carry commands (i.e., binary values that the hardware interprets as a command). Although Figure 16.5 does not show command wires, we can imagine that the number of command wires connected to a functional unit depends on the type of unit. For example, the unit labeled *result 1* only needs a single command wire because the unit can be controlled by a single binary value: zero causes the unit to stop interacting with other units, and one causes the unit to send the current contents of the result unit to the data transfer mechanism. Figure 16.6 summarizes the binary control values that can be passed to each functional unit in our example, and gives the meaning of each.

Unit	Command	Meaning
ALU	0 0 0 0 0 1 0 1 0 0 1 1 1 0 0 1 0 1 1 1 0 1 1 1	No operation Add Subtract Multiply Divide Left shift Right shift Continue previous operation
operand 1	0 1	No operation Load value from data transfer mechanism
operand 2	0 1	No operation Load value from data transfer mechanism
result 1	0 1	No operation Send value to data transfer mechanism
result 2	0 1	No operation Send value to data transfer mechanism
register access	0 0 x x x x 0 1 x x x x 1 0 x x x x 1 1 x x x x	No operation Move register xxxx to data transfer Move data transfer to register xxxx No operation

Figure 16.6 Possible command values and the meaning of each for the example functional units in Figure 16.5. Commands are carried on parallel wires.

As Figure 16.6 shows, the register access unit forms a special case because each command has two parts: the first two bits specify an operation, and the last four bits specify a register to be used in the operation. Thus, the command 0 1 0 0 1 1 means that the value in register 3 should be moved to the data transfer mechanism.

Now that we understand how the hardware is organized, we can see how horizontal microcode works. Imagine that each microcode instruction consists of commands to functional units — when it executes an instruction, the hardware sends bits from the instruction to functional units. Figure 16.7 illustrates how bits of a microcode instruction correspond to commands in our example.

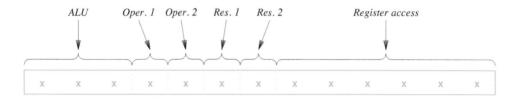

Figure 16.7 Illustration of thirteen bits in a horizontal microcode instruction that correspond to commands for the six functional units.

16.16 A Horizontal Microcode Example

How can horizontal microcode be used to perform a sequence of operations? In essence, a programmer chooses which functional units should be active during a given instruction, and encodes the information in bits of the microcode. For example, suppose a programmer needs to write horizontal microcode that adds the value in general-purpose register 4 to the value in general-purpose register 13 and places the result in general-purpose register 4. Figure 16.8 lists the operations that must be performed.

- Move the value from register 4 to the hardware unit for operand 1

- Move the value from register 13 to the hardware unit for operand 2

- Arrange for the ALU to perform addition

- Move the value from the hardware unit for result 2 (the low-order bits of the result) to register 4

Figure 16.8 An example sequence of steps that the functional units must execute to add values from general-purpose registers 4 and 13, and place the result in general-purpose register 4.

Each of the steps can be expressed as a single micro instruction in our example system. The instruction has bits set to specify which functional unit(s) operate when the instruction is executed. For example, Figure 16.9 shows a microcode program that corresponds to the four steps.

In the figure, each row corresponds to one instruction, which is divided into fields that each correspond to a functional unit. A field contains a command to be sent to the functional unit when the instruction is executed. Thus, commands determine which functional units operate at each step.

Instr.	ALU			OP$_1$	OP$_2$	RES$_1$	RES$_2$		REG. INTERFACE				
1	0	0	0	1	0	0	0	0	1	0	1	0	0
2	0	0	0	0	1	0	0	0	1	1	1	0	1
3	0	0	1	0	0	0	0	0	0	0	0	0	0
4	0	0	0	0	0	0	1	1	0	0	1	0	0

Figure 16.9 An example horizontal microcode program that consists of four instructions with thirteen bits per instruction. Each instruction corresponds to a step listed in Figure 16.8.

Consider the code in the figure carefully. The first instruction specifies that only two hardware units will operate: the unit for operand 1 and the register access unit. The fields that correspond to the other four units contain zero bits, which means that those units will not operate when the first instruction is executed. The first instruction also uses the data transfer mechanism — data is sent across the transfer mechanism from the register access unit to the unit for operand 1†. That is, fields in the instruction cause the register access unit to send a value across the transfer mechanism, and cause the operand 1 unit to receive the value.

16.17 Operations That Require Multiple Cycles

Timing is among the most important aspects of horizontal microcode. Some hardware units take longer to operate than others. For example, multiplication can take longer than addition. That is, when a functional unit is given a command, the results do not appear immediately. Instead, the program must delay before accessing the output from the functional unit.

---

†For purposes of this simplified example, we assume the data transfer mechanism always operates and does not require any control.

A programmer who writes horizontal microcode must ensure that each hardware unit is given the correct amount of time to complete its task. The code in Figure 16.9 assumes that each step can be accomplished in one micro instruction cycle. However, a micro cycle may be too short for some hardware units to complete a task. For example, an ALU may require two micro instruction cycles to complete an addition. To accommodate longer computation, an extra instruction can be inserted following the third instruction. The extra instruction merely specifies that the ALU should continue the previous operation; no other units are affected. Figure 16.10 illustrates an extra microcode instruction that can be inserted to create the necessary delay.

| ALU | | | OP₁ | OP₂ | RES₁ | RES₂ | | REG. INTERFACE | | | | |

ALU			OP$_1$	OP$_2$	RES$_1$	RES$_2$			REG. INTERFACE			
1	1	1	0	0	0	0	0	0	0	0	0	0

Figure 16.10 An instruction that can be inserted to delay processing until the ALU can complete the previous operation. Timing and delay are crucial aspects of horizontal microcode.

16.18 Horizontal Microcode And Parallel Execution

Now that we have a basic understanding of how hardware operates and a general idea about horizontal microcode, we can appreciate an important property: the use of parallelism. Parallelism is possible because the underlying hardware units operate independently. A programmer can specify parallel operations because an instruction contains separate fields that each control one of the hardware units.

As an example, consider an architecture that has an ALU plus separate hardware units to hold operands. Assume the ALU requires multiple instruction cycles to complete an operation. Because the ALU accesses the operands during the first cycle, the hardware units used to hold operands remain unused during successive cycles. Thus, if an operand will be needed later, a programmer can insert an instruction that simultaneously moves a new value into an operand unit while allowing the ALU to continue the previous operation. Figure 16.11 illustrates such an instruction.

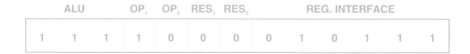

ALU			OP$_1$	OP$_2$	RES$_1$	RES$_2$		REG. INTERFACE			
1	1	1	1	0	0	0	0	1	0	1	1	1

Figure 16.11 An example instruction that simultaneously continues an ALU operation and loads the value from register 7 into operand 1. Horizontal microcode makes parallelism easy to specify.

The point is:

> *Because horizontal microcode instructions contain separate fields that each control one hardware unit, horizontal microcode makes it easy to specify simultaneous, parallel operation of the hardware units.*

16.19 Look-Ahead And High-Performance Execution

In practice, the microcode used in CPUs is much more complex than the simplistic examples in this chapter. One of the most important sources of complexity arises from the desire to achieve high performance. Because silicon technology allows manufacturers to place billions of transistors on a single chip, it is possible for a CPU to include many functional units that all operate simultaneously.

A later chapter considers architectures that make parallel hardware visible to a programmer. For now, we will consider an architectural question: can multiple functional units be used to improve performance without changing the macro instruction set? In particular, can the internal organization of a CPU be arranged to detect and exploit situations in which parallel execution will produce higher performance?

We have already seen a trivial example of an optimization: Figure 16.11 shows that horizontal microcode can allow an ALU operation to continue at the same time a data value is transferred to a hardware unit that holds an operand. However, our example requires a programmer to code the parallel behavior explicitly when creating the microcode.

To understand how a CPU exploits parallelism automatically, imagine a system that includes an intelligent microcontroller and multiple functional units. Instead of working on one macro instruction at a time, the intelligent controller is given access to many macro instructions. The controller looks ahead at the instructions, finds values that will be needed, and directs functional units to start fetching or computing the values. For example, suppose the intelligent controller finds the following four instructions on a 3-address architecture:

```
add     R1, R3, R7
sub     R4, R4, R6
add     R9, R5, R2
shift   R8, 5
```

We say that an intelligent controller *schedules* the instructions by assigning the necessary work to functional units. For example, the controller can assign each operand to a functional unit that fetches and prepares operand values. Once the operand values are available for an instruction, the controller assigns the instruction to a functional unit that performs the operation. The instructions listed above can each be assigned to an ALU. Finally, when the operation completes, the controller can assign a functional unit the task of moving the result to the appropriate destination register. The point is: if the

CPU contains enough functional units, an intelligent controller can schedule all four macro instructions to be executed at the same time.

16.20 Parallelism And Execution Order

Our above description of an intelligent microcontroller overlooks an important detail: the semantics of the macro instruction set. In essence, the controller must ensure that computing values in parallel does not change the meaning of the program. For example, consider the following sequence of instructions:

```
add       R1, R3, R7
sub       R4, R4, R6
add       R9, R1, R2
shift     R8, 5
```

Unlike the previous example, the operands overlap. In particular, the first instruction specifies register 1 as a destination, and the third instruction specifies register 1 as an operand. The macro instruction set semantics dictate sequential processing of instructions, which means that the first instruction will place a value in register 1 *before* the third instruction references the value. To preserve sequential semantics, an intelligent controller must understand and accommodate such overlap. In essence, the controller must balance between two goals: maximize the amount of parallel execution, while preserving the original (i.e., sequential) semantics.

16.21 Out-Of-Order Instruction Execution

How can a controller that schedules parallel activities handle the case where an operand in one instruction depends on the results of a previous instruction? The controller uses a mechanism known as a *scoreboard* that tracks the status of each instruction being executed. In particular, a scoreboard maintains information about dependencies among instructions and the original macro instruction sequence execution. Thus, the controller can use the scoreboard to decide when to fetch operands, when execution can proceed, and when an instruction is finished. In short, the scoreboard approach allows the controller to execute instructions out of order, but then reorders the results to reflect the order specified by the code.

To achieve highest speed, a modern CPU contains multiple copies of functional units that permit multiple instructions to be executed simultaneously. An intelligent controller uses a scoreboard *mechanism to schedule execution in an order that preserves the appearance of sequential processing.*

16.22 Conditional Branches And Branch Prediction

Conditional branches pose another problem for parallel execution. For example, consider the following computation:

$$Y \leftarrow f(X)$$
$$if \ (Y > Z) \{$$
$$Q$$
$$\} \ else \ \{$$
$$R$$
$$\}$$

When translated into machine instructions, the computation contains a conditional branch that directs execution either to the code for Q or the code for R. The condition depends on the value of Y, which is computed in the first step. Now consider running the code on a CPU that uses parallel execution of instructions. In theory, once it reaches the conditional branch, the CPU must wait for the results of the comparison — the CPU cannot start to schedule code for R or Q until it knows which one will be selected.

In practice, there are two approaches used to handle conditional branches. The first, which is known as *branch prediction*, is based on measurements which show that in most code, the branch is taken approximately sixty percent of the time. Thus, building hardware that schedules instructions along the branch path provides more optimization than hardware that schedules instructions along the non-branch path. Of course, assuming the branch will occur may be incorrect — if the CPU eventually determines that the branch should not be taken, the results from the branch path must be discarded and the CPU must follow the other path. The second approach simply follows both paths in parallel. That is, the CPU schedules instructions for both outcomes of the conditional branch. As with branch prediction, the CPU must eventually decide which result is valid. That is, the CPU continues to execute instructions, but holds the results internally. Once the value of the condition is known, the CPU discards the results from the path that is not valid, and proceeds to move the correct results into the appropriate destinations. Of course, a second conditional branch can occur in either Q or R; the scoreboard mechanism handles all the details.

The point is:

A CPU that offers parallel instruction execution can handle conditional branches by precomputing values on one or both branches, and choosing which values to use at a later time when the computation of the branch condition completes.

It may seem wasteful for a CPU to compute values that will be discarded later. However, the goal is higher performance, not elegance. We can also observe that if a CPU is designed to wait until a conditional branch value is known, the hardware will merely sit idle. Therefore, high-speed CPUs, such as those manufactured by Intel and AMD, are designed with parallel functional units and sophisticated scoreboard mechanisms.

16.23 Consequences For Programmers

Can understanding how a CPU is structured help programmers write faster code? In some cases, yes. Suppose a CPU is designed to use branch prediction and that the CPU assumes the branch is taken. A programmer can optimize performance by arranging code so that the most common cases take the branch. For example, if a programmer knows that it will be more common for Y to be less than Z, instead of testing $Y > Z$, a programmer can rewrite the code to test whether $Y \leq Z$, thereby reversing the cases of the branch being taken vs. not taken.

16.24 Summary

A modern CPU is a complex processor that uses multiple modes of execution to handle some of the complexity. An execution mode determines operational parameters such as the operations that are allowed and the current privilege level. Most CPUs offer at least two levels of privilege and protection: one for the operating system and one for application programs.

To reduce the internal complexity, a CPU is often built with two levels of abstraction: a microcontroller is implemented with digital circuits, and a macro instruction set is created by adding microcode.

There are two broad classes of microcode. A microcontroller that uses vertical microcode resembles a conventional RISC processor. Typically, vertical microcode consists of a set of functions that each correspond to one macro instruction; the CPU runs the appropriate microcode function during the fetch-execute cycle. Horizontal microcode, which allows a programmer to schedule functional units to operate on each cycle, consists of instructions in which each bit field corresponds to a functional unit. A third alternative uses *Field Programmable Gate Array* (*FPGA*) technology to create the underlying system.

Advanced CPUs extend parallel execution by scheduling a set of instructions across multiple functional units. The CPU uses a scoreboard mechanism to handle cases where the results of one instruction are used by a successive instruction. The idea can be extended to conditional branches by allowing parallel evaluation of each path to proceed, and then, once the condition is known, discarding the values along the path that is not taken.

EXERCISES

16.1 If a quad-core CPU chip contains 2 billion transistors, approximately how many transistors are needed for a single core?

16.2 List seven reasons a modern CPU is complex.

16.3 The text says that some CPU chips include a *backward compatibility* mode. Does such a mode offer any advantage to a user?

16.4 Suppose that in addition to other hardware, the CPU used in a smart phone contains additional hardware for three previous versions of the chip (i.e., three backward compatibility modes). What is the disadvantage from a user's point of view?

16.5 Virtualized software systems used in cloud data centers often include a *hypervisor* that runs and controls multiple *operating systems*, and *applications* that each run on one of the operating systems. How do the levels of protection used with such systems differ from conventional levels of protection?

16.6 Some manufacturers offer a chip that contains a processor with a basic set of instructions plus an attached FPGA. An owner can configure the FPGA with additional instructions. What does such a chip provide that conventional software cannot?

16.7 Read about FPGAs, and find out how they are programmed. What languages are used to program an FPGA?

16.8 Create a microcode algorithm that performs 32-bit multiplication on a microcontroller that only offers 16-bit arithmetic, and implement your algorithm in C using *short* variables.

16.9 You are offered two jobs for the same salary, one programming vertical microcode and the other programming horizontal microcode. Which do you choose? Why?

16.10 Find an example of a commercial processor that uses horizontal microcode, and document the meaning of bits for an instruction similar to the diagram in Figure 16.7.

16.11 What is the motivation for a *scoreboard* mechanism in a CPU chip, and what functionality does it provide?

16.12 If Las Vegas casinos computed the odds on program execution, what odds would they give that a branch is taken? Explain your answer.

Chapter Contents

17

Parallelism

17.1 Introduction

Previous chapters cover three key components of computer architecture: processors, memory systems, and I/O. This chapter begins a discussion of fundamental concepts that cross the boundaries among architectural components.

The chapter focuses on the use of parallel hardware, and shows that parallelism can be used throughout computer systems to increase speed. The chapter introduces terminology and concepts, presents a taxonomy of parallel architectures, and examines computer systems in which parallelism is the fundamental paradigm around which the entire system is designed. The chapter also discusses limitations and problems with parallel architectures.

The next chapter extends the discussion by examining a second fundamental technique: pipelining. We will see that both parallelism and pipelining are important in high-speed designs.

17.2 Parallel And Pipelined Architectures

Some computer architects assert that there are only two fundamental techniques used to increase hardware speed: *parallelism* and *pipelining*. Other architects take a broader view of parallelism and pipelining, using the techniques as the fundamental basis around which a system is designed. When an architecture becomes so completely dominated by one of the two techniques, users often refer to the system as a *parallel computer* or a *pipelined computer*.

17.3 Characterizations Of Parallelism

Rather than classify an architecture as *parallel* or *nonparallel*, computer architects use a variety of terms to characterize the type and amount of parallelism that is present in a given design. In many cases, the terminology describes the possible extremes for a type of parallelism. We can classify an architecture by stating where the architecture lies between the two extremes. Figure 17.1 lists the key characterizations using nomenclature proposed by Michael J. Flynn in a classic paper†. Later sections explain each of the terms and give examples.

- Microscopic vs. macroscopic
- Symmetric vs. asymmetric
- Fine-grain vs. coarse-grain
- Explicit vs. implicit

Figure 17.1 Terminology used to characterize the amount and type of parallelism present in a computer architecture.

17.4 Microscopic Vs. Macroscopic

Parallelism is fundamental; an architect cannot design a computer without thinking about parallel hardware. Interestingly, the pervasiveness of parallelism means that unless a computer uses an unusual amount of parallel hardware, we typically do not discuss the parallel aspects. To capture the idea that much of the parallelism in a computer remains hidden inside subcomponents, we use the term *microscopic parallelism*. Like microbes in the world around us, microscopic parallelism is present, but does not stand out without closer inspection.

The point is:

> *Parallelism is so fundamental that virtually all computer systems contain some form of parallel hardware. We use the term* microscopic *parallelism to characterize parallel facilities that are present, but not especially visible.*

To be more precise, we say that *microscopic parallelism* refers to the use of parallel hardware within a specific component (e.g., inside a processor or inside an ALU), whereas *macroscopic parallelism* refers to the use of parallelism as a basic premise around which a system is designed.

†M. J. Flynn, "Some Computer Organizations and Their Effectiveness," *IEEE Transactions on Computers*, C-21(9):948–960, September 1972.

17.5 Examples Of Microscopic Parallelism

In earlier chapters, we have seen examples of using *microscopic parallelism* within processors, memory systems, and I/O subsystems. The following paragraphs highlight a few examples.

ALU. An Arithmetic Logic Unit handles logical and arithmetic operations. Most ALUs perform integer arithmetic by processing multiple bits in parallel. Thus, an ALU that is designed to operate on integers contains parallel hardware that allows the ALU to compute a Boolean function on a pair of thirty-two-bit values in a single operation. The alternative consists of an ALU that processes one bit at a time, an approach that is known as *bit serial processing*. It should be easy to see that bit serial processing takes much longer than computing bits in parallel. Therefore, bit serial arithmetic is reserved for special cases.

Registers. The general-purpose registers in a CPU make heavy use of microscopic parallelism. Each bit in a register is implemented by a separate digital circuit (specifically, a latch). Furthermore, to guarantee the highest-speed computation, parallel data paths are used to move data between general-purpose registers and the ALU.

Physical Memory. As another example of microscopic parallelism, recall that a physical memory system uses parallel hardware to implement *fetch* and *store* operations — the hardware is designed to transfer an entire word on each operation. As in an ALU, microscopic parallelism increases memory speed dramatically. For example, a memory system that implements sixty-four-bit words can access or store approximately sixty-four times as much data in the same time as a memory system that accesses a single bit at a time.

Parallel Bus Architecture. As we have seen, a bus connects processor, memory, and I/O devices. Each interface connected to a parallel bus contains a set of N hardware units that each transfer one bit. The units work together to send N bits over N parallel wires at the same time. A typical parallel bus has thirty-two or sixty-four parallel wires.

17.6 Examples Of Macroscopic Parallelism

As the examples in the previous section demonstrate, microscopic parallelism is essential for high-speed performance — without parallel hardware, various components of a computer system cannot operate at high speed. Computer architects are aware that the global architecture often has a greater impact on overall system performance than the performance of any single subsystem. That is, adding more parallelism to a single subsystem may not improve the overall system performance†.

To achieve the greatest impact, parallelism must span multiple components of a system — instead of merely using parallelism to improve the performance of a single component, the system must allow multiple components to work together. We use the

---

†Chapter 19 discusses performance in more detail.

term *macroscopic parallelism* to characterize the use of parallelism across multiple, large-scale components of a computer system. A few examples will clarify the concept.

Multiple, Identical Processors. Systems that employ macroscopic parallelism usually employ multiple processors in one form or another. For example, some laptops are advertised as *dual core* or *quad core* computers, meaning that the PC contains two or four copies of the processor on a single chip. The chip is arranged to allow both processors to operate at the same time†. The hardware does not control exactly how the cores are used. Instead, the operating system assigns code to each core. For example, the operating system can assign one core the task of handling I/O (i.e., running device drivers), and assign other cores application programs to run.

Multiple, Dissimilar Processors. Another example of macroscopic parallelism arises in systems that make extensive use of special-purpose coprocessors. For example, a computer optimized for high-speed graphics might have four displays attached, with a special graphics processor running each display. A graphics processor, typically found on an interface card, does not use the same architecture as a CPU because the graphics processor needs instructions optimized for graphics operations.

17.7 Symmetric Vs. Asymmetric

We use the term *symmetric parallelism* to characterize a design that uses replications of identical elements, usually processors or cores, that can operate simultaneously. For example, the multicore processors mentioned above are said to be symmetric because all cores are identical.

The alternative to a symmetric parallel design is a parallel design that is *asymmetric*. As the name implies, an asymmetric design contains multiple elements that function at the same time, but differ from one another. For example, a laptop with a CPU, a GPU, a math coprocessor, and an I/O coprocessor is classified as using asymmetric parallelism because the four processors can operate simultaneously, but differ from one another internally‡.

17.8 Fine-Grain Vs. Coarse-Grain Parallelism

We use the term *fine-grain parallelism* to refer to computers that provide parallelism on the level of individual instructions or individual data elements, and the term *coarse-grain parallelism* to refer to computers that provide parallelism on the level of programs or large blocks of data. For example, a graphics processor that uses sixteen parallel hardware units to update sixteen bytes of an image at the same time is said to use fine-grain parallelism. In contrast, a dual core laptop that uses one core to print a document while another core composes an email message is described as using coarse-grain parallelism.

---

†Chapter 20 discusses multicore architectures in more detail.

‡Some architects also apply the term *asymmetric* to a multicore design if the cores do not have the same access to memory and I/O devices.

17.9 Explicit Vs. Implicit Parallelism

An architecture in which the hardware handles parallelism automatically without requiring a programmer to initiate or control parallel execution is said to offer *implicit parallelism*, and an architecture in which a programmer must control each parallel unit is said to offer *explicit parallelism*. We will consider the advantages and disadvantages of explicit and implicit parallelism later.

17.10 Types Of Parallel Architectures (Flynn Classification)

Although many systems contain multiple processors of one type or another, the term *parallel architecture* is usually reserved for designs that permit arbitrary *scaling*. That is, when they refer to a parallel architecture, architects usually mean a design in which the number of processors can be arbitrarily large (or at least reasonably large). As an example, consider a computer that can have either one or two processors. Although adding a second processor increases parallelism, such an architecture is usually classified as a *dual-processor computer* rather than a parallel architecture. Similarly, a laptop with four cores is classified as a *quad-core computer*. However, a cluster of thirty-two interconnected PCs that can scale to one thousand twenty-four PCs is classified as a parallel architecture.

The easiest way to understand parallel architectures is to divide the architectures into broad groups, where each group represents a type of parallelism. Of course, no division is absolute — most practical computer systems are hybrids that contain facilities from more than one group. Nevertheless, we use the classification to define basic concepts and nomenclature that allow us to discuss and characterize the systems.

A popular way to describe parallelism considers whether processing or data is replicated. Known as the *Flynn classification*, the system focuses on whether the computer has multiple, independent processors each running a separate program or a single program being applied to multiple data items. Figure 17.2 lists terms used by the Flynn classification to define types of parallelism; the next sections explain the terminology and give examples.

Name	Meaning
SISD	Single Instruction stream Single Data stream
SIMD	Single Instruction stream Multiple Data streams
MISD	Multiple Instruction streams Single Data stream†
MIMD	Multiple Instruction streams Multiple Data streams

Figure 17.2 Terminology used by the Flynn classification to characterize parallel computers†.

---

†MISD is a specialized category that is reserved for unusual hardware, such as the pipeline architecture shown in Figure 18.5 on page 351 that executes multiple instructions on a single piece of data or a redundant processor used to increase reliability.

17.11 Single Instruction Single Data (SISD)

The phrase *Single Instruction Single Data (SISD)* stream is used to describe an architecture that does not support macroscopic parallelism. The term *sequential architecture* or *uniprocessor architecture* is often used in place of SISD to emphasize that the architecture is not parallel. In essence, SISD refers to a conventional (i.e., Von Neumann) architecture — the processor runs a standard fetch-execute cycle and performs one operation at a time. The term refers to the idea that a single, conventional processor is executing instructions that each operate on a single data item. That is, unlike a parallel architecture, a conventional processor can only execute one instruction at any time, and each instruction refers to a single computation.

Of course, we have seen that an SISD computer can use parallelism internally. For example, the ALU may be able to perform operations on multiple bits in parallel, the CPU may invoke a coprocessor, or the CPU may have mechanisms that allow it to fetch operands from two banks of memory at the same time. However, the overall effect of an SISD architecture is sequential execution of instructions that each operate on one data item.

17.12 Single Instruction Multiple Data (SIMD)

The phrase *Single Instruction Multiple Data (SIMD)* streams describes a parallel architecture in which each instruction specifies a single operation (e.g., integer addition), but the instruction is applied to many data items at the same time. Typically, an SIMD computer has sufficient hardware to handle sixty-four simultaneous operations (e.g., sixty-four simultaneous additions).

Vector Processors. An SIMD architecture does not offer advantages for applications such as word processing or email. Instead, SIMD only works for applications that apply the same operation to a set of values. For example, graphics applications and some scientific applications work well on an SIMD architecture that can apply an operation to a large set of values. Some designers adopt the mathematical term *vector* or the computing term *arrays* and call an SIMD machine a *vector processor* or an *array processor*.

As an example of how an SIMD machine works, consider normalizing the values in a vector, V, that contains N elements. Normalization requires that each item in the vector be multiplied by a floating point number, Q. On a sequential architecture (i.e., an SISD architecture), the algorithm required to normalize the vector consists of a loop as Figure 17.3 shows.

```
for i from 1 to N {
    V[i] ← V[i] × Q;
}
```

Figure 17.3 A sequential algorithm for vector normalization.

On an SIMD architecture, the underlying hardware can apply an arithmetic operation to all the values in an array simultaneously (assuming the size of the array does not exceed the parallelism in the hardware). For example, in a single step, hardware that has sixty-four parallel units can multiply each value in an array of sixty-four elements by a constant. Thus, the algorithm to perform normalization of an array on an SIMD computer takes one step:

$$V \leftarrow V \times Q;$$

Of course, if vector V is larger than the hardware capacity, multiple steps will be required. The important point is that a vector instruction on an SIMD architecture is not merely a shorthand for a loop. Instead, the underlying system contains multiple hardware units that operate in parallel to provide substantial speedup; the performance improvement can be significant, especially for computations that use large matrices.

Not all instructions in an SIMD architecture can be applied to an array of values. Instead, an architect identifies a subset of operations to be used with vectors, and defines a special *vector instruction* for each. For example, normalization of an entire array is only possible if the architect chooses to include a vector multiplication instruction that multiplies each value in the vector by a constant.

In addition to operations that use a constant and a vector, SIMD computers usually provide instructions that use two vectors. That is, a vector instruction takes one or more operands that each specify a vector. For example, SIMD architectures are used for problems involving matrix multiplication. On most SIMD machines, an operand that specifies a vector gives two pieces of information: the location of the vector in memory and an integer that specifies the size of the vector (i.e., number of items in the vector). On some machines, vector instructions are controlled by special-purpose registers — the address and size of each vector are loaded into registers before a vector instruction is invoked. In any case, software determines the number of items in a vector up to the maximum size supported by the hardware†.

Graphics Processors. SIMD architectures are also popular for use with graphics. To understand why, it is important to know that typical graphics hardware uses sequential bytes in memory to store values for pixels on a screen. For example, consider a video game in which foreground figures move while a background scene stays in place. Game software must copy the bytes that correspond to the foreground figure from one location in memory to another. A sequential architecture requires a programmer to specify a loop that copies one byte at a time. On an SIMD architecture, however, a programmer can specify a vector size, and then issue a single *copy* command. The underlying SIMD hardware then copies multiple bytes simultaneously.

---

†An exercise considers speedup in cases where vectors exceed the capacity of the hardware; a definition of *speedup* can be found in Section 17.15.

17.13 Multiple Instructions Multiple Data (MIMD)

The phrase *Multiple Instructions Multiple Data streams* (*MIMD*) is used to describe a parallel architecture in which each of the processors performs independent computations at the same time. Although many computers contain multiple internal processing units, the MIMD designation is reserved for computers in which the processors are visible to a programmer. That is, an MIMD computer can run multiple, independent programs at the same time.

Symmetric Multiprocessor (SMP). The most well-known example of an MIMD architecture consists of a computer known as a *Symmetric Multiprocessor* (*SMP*). An SMP contains a set of *N* processors (or *N* cores) that can each be used to run programs. In a typical SMP design, the processors are identical: they each have the same instruction set, operate at the same clock rate, have access to the same memory modules, and have access to the same external devices. Thus, any processor can perform exactly the same computation as any other processor. Figure 17.4 illustrates the concept.

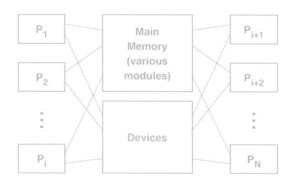

Figure 17.4 The conceptual organization of a symmetric multiprocessor with N identical processors that each have access to memory and I/O devices.

While some researchers explored ways to increase the speed and power of silicon chips, other researchers investigated the symmetric multiprocessor form of MIMD as an alternate way to provide more powerful computers. One of the most well-known projects, which was conducted at Carnegie Mellon University, produced a prototype known as the *Carnegie multiminiprocessor* (*C.mmp*). During the 1980s, vendors first created commercial products, informally called *multiprocessors*, that used the SMP approach. Sequent Corporation (currently owned by IBM) created a symmetric multiprocessor that runs the Unix operating system, and Encore Corporation created a symmetric multiprocessor named *Multimax*.

Asymmetric Multiprocessor (AMP). Although SMPs are popular, other forms of MIMD architectures are possible. The chief alternative to an SMP design is an *Asymmetric Multiprocessor* (*AMP*). An AMP contains a set of *N* programmable processors that can operate at the same time, but does not require all processors to have identical capabilities. For example, an AMP design can choose a processor that is appropriate to a given task (i.e., one processor can be optimized for management of high-speed disk storage devices and another processor can be optimized for graphics display).

In most cases, AMP architectures follow a *master-worker* approach in which one processor (or in some cases a set of processors) controls the overall execution and invokes other processors as needed. The processor that controls execution is known as the *master*, and other processors are known as *workers*.

In theory, an AMP architecture that has N processors can have many distinct types of processors. In practice, however, most AMP designs have between two and four types of processors. Typically, a general-purpose AMP architecture includes at least one processor optimized for overall control (the master), and others optimized for subsidiary functions such as arithmetic computation or I/O.

Math And Graphics Coprocessors. Commercial computer systems have been created that use an asymmetric architecture. One of the most widely known AMP designs became popular in the late 1980s and early 1990s when PC manufacturers began selling *math coprocessors*. The idea of a math coprocessor is straightforward: the coprocessor is a special-purpose chip that the CPU can invoke to perform floating point computation. Because it is optimized for one task, a coprocessor can perform the task faster than the CPU.

CDC Peripheral Processors. Control Data Corporation helped pioneer the idea of using an AMP architecture in mainframes when they created the 6000 series of mainframe computers. The CDC architecture used ten *peripheral processors* to handle I/O. Figure 17.5 illustrates the conceptual organization with peripheral processors between the CPU and I/O devices. Interestingly, CDC's peripheral processors were not limited to I/O — a peripheral processor resembled a minicomputer with a general-purpose instruction set that could be used however a programmer chose. The peripheral processors had access to memory, which meant a peripheral processor could read or store values in any location. Although they were much slower than the CPU, all ten peripheral processors on the CDC could execute simultaneously. Thus, it was possible to optimize program performance by dividing tasks among the peripheral processors as well as the CPU.

Although CDC computers are no longer manufactured, the basic idea of programmable I/O processors continues to be used. Surprisingly, multicore chips have made the general approach feasible again because many cores make it possible to dedicate one or more cores to I/O.

I/O Processors. Most mainframe computers use an AMP architecture to handle I/O at high speed without slowing down the CPU. Each external I/O connection is equipped with a dedicated, programmable processor. Instead of manipulating a bus or handling interrupts, the CPU merely downloads a program into the programmable processor. The processor then handles all the details of I/O. For example, the mainframe computers sold by IBM Corporation use programmable I/O processors called *channels*.

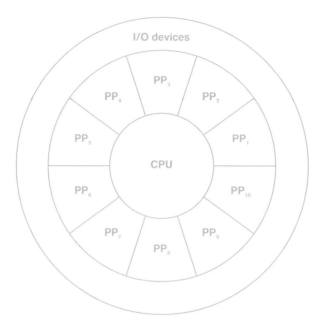

Figure 17.5 Illustration of the asymmetric architecture used in the CDC 6000 mainframe computers.

17.14 Communication, Coordination, And Contention

It may seem obvious that a multiprocessor architecture will always have better performance than a uniprocessor architecture. Consider, for example, a symmetric multiprocessor, M. Intuitively, computer M can outperform a uniprocessor because M can perform N times as many operations at any time. Moreover, if a chip vendor finds a way to make a single processor run faster than M, the vendor who sells M merely replaces each of the processors in M with the new chip to have a faster multiprocessor. Indeed, many companies that created multiprocessors made these claims to attract customers.

Unfortunately, our intuition about computer performance can be misleading. Architects have found three main challenges in designing a high-performance parallel architecture:

- Communication
- Coordination
- Contention

Communication. Although it may seem trivial to envision a computer that has dozens of independent processors, the computer must also provide a mechanism that allows the processors to communicate with each other, with memory, and with I/O devices. More important, the communication mechanism must be able to scale to handle a large number of processors. An architect must spend a significant amount of effort to create a parallel computer system that does not have severe communication bottlenecks.

Coordination. In a parallel architecture, processors must work together to perform computation. Therefore, a coordination mechanism is needed that allows processing to be controlled. We said that asymmetric designs usually designate one of the processors to act as a master that controls and coordinates all processing; some symmetric designs also use the master-worker approach. Other architectures use a distributed coordination mechanism in which the processors must be programmed to coordinate among themselves without a master.

Contention. When two or more processors attempt to access a resource at the same time, we say that the processors *contend* for the resource. Resource *contention* creates one of the greatest challenges in designing a parallel architecture because contention increases as the number of processors increases.

To understand why contention is a problem, consider memory. If a set of N processors all have access to a given memory, a mechanism is needed that only permits one processor to access the memory at any time. When multiple processors attempt to use the memory simultaneously, the hardware contention mechanism blocks all except one of them. That is, $N-1$ of the processors are idle during the memory access. In the next round, $N-2$ processors remain idle. It should be obvious that:

> *In a parallel architecture, contention for shared resources lowers performance dramatically because only one processor can use a given resource at any time; the hardware contention mechanism forces other processors to remain idle while they wait for access.*

17.15 Performance Of Multiprocessors

Multiprocessor architectures have not fulfilled the promise of scalable, high-performance computing. There are several reasons: operating system bottlenecks, contention for memory, and I/O. In a modern computer system, the operating system controls all processing, including allocating tasks to processors and handling I/O. Only one copy of an operating system can run because a device cannot take orders from multiple processors simultaneously. Thus, in a multiprocessor, at most one processor can run operating system software at any time, which means the operating system is a shared resource for which processors must contend. As a consequence, the operating system quickly becomes a bottleneck that processors access serially — if K processors need access, $K-1$ of them must wait.

Contention for memory has proven to be an especially difficult problem. First, hardware for a multiported memory is extremely expensive. Second, one of the more important optimizations used in memory systems, caching, causes problems when used with a multiprocessor. If the cache is shared, processors contend for access. If each processor has a private cache, all caches must be coordinated so that any update is propagated to all caches. Unfortunately, such coordination introduces overhead.

Many multiprocessor architectures suffer from another weakness: the architecture only outperforms a uniprocessor when performing intensive computation. Surprisingly, most applications are not limited by the amount of computation they perform. Instead, most applications are *I/O bound*, which means the application spends more time waiting for I/O than performing computation. For example, most of the delay in common applications, such as word spreadsheets, video games, and Web browsing, arises when the application waits for I/O from a file or the network. Therefore, adding additional computational power to the underlying computer does not lower the time required to perform the computation — the extra processors sit idle waiting for I/O.

To assess the performance of an N-processor system, we define the notion of *speedup* to be the ratio of the performance of a single processor to the performance of a multiprocessor. Specifically, we define speedup as:

$$Speedup = \frac{\tau_1}{\tau_N}$$

where τ_1 denotes the execution time taken on a single processor, and τ_N denotes the execution time taken on a multiprocessor†. In each case, we assume performance is measured using the best algorithm available (i.e., we allow the program to be rewritten to take advantage of parallel hardware).

When multiprocessors are measured performing general-purpose computing tasks, an interesting result emerges. In an ideal situation, we would expect performance to increase linearly as more processors are added to a multiprocessor system. Experience has shown, however, that problems like memory contention, interprocessor communication, and operating system bottlenecks mean that multiprocessors do not achieve linear speedup. Instead, performance often reaches a limit as Figure 17.6 illustrates.

Surprisingly, the performance illustrated in the figure may not be achievable in practice. In some multiprocessor designs, communication overhead and memory contention dominate the running time: as more and more processors are added, the performance starts to decrease. For example, a particular symmetric multiprocessor design exhibited a small speedup with a few processors. However, when sixty-four processors were used, communication overhead made the performance worse than a single processor system. We can summarize:

> When used for general-purpose computing, a multiprocessor may not perform well. In some cases, added overhead means performance decreases as more processors are added.

---

†Because we expect the processing time on a single processor to be greater than the processing time on a multiprocessor, we expect the speedup to be greater than one.

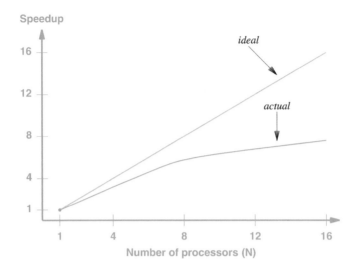

Figure 17.6 Illustration of the ideal and typical performance of a multiprocessor as the number of processors is increased. Values on the
y-axis list the relative speedup compared to a single processor.

17.16 Consequences For Programmers

Parallelism usually makes programming more complex. A programmer must be
aware of parallel execution, and must prevent one parallel activity from interfering with
another. The following sections describe some of the mechanisms and facilities that
programmers use.

17.16.1 Locks And Mutual Exclusion

Writing code that uses multiple processors is inherently more complex than writing
code for a single processor. To understand the complexity, consider using a shared
variable. For example, suppose two processors use a variable x to store a count. A programmer writes a statement such as:

```
x = x + 1;
```

A compiler translates the statement into a sequence of machine instructions, such
as the sequence in Figure 17.7.

```
load    x, R5      # Load variable x into R5
incr    R5         # Increment the value in R5
store   R5, x      # Store R5 back into x
```

Figure 17.7 An example sequence of machine instructions used to increment a variable in memory. In most architectures, increment entails a *load* and a *store* operation.

Unfortunately, if two processors attempt to increment x at nearly the same time, the value of x might be incremented once instead of twice. The error arises because each of the two processors operates independently and competes for access to memory. Thus, the operations might be performed in the order given in Figure 17.8.

- Processor 1 loads x into its register 5

- Processor 1 increments its register 5

- Processor 2 loads x into its register 5

- Processor 1 stores its register 5 into x

- Processor 2 increments its register 5

- Processor 2 stores its register 5 into x

Figure 17.8 A sequence of steps that can occur when two independent processors or cores access variable x in shared memory.

To prevent problems like the one illustrated in Figure 17.8, multiprocessor hardware provides *hardware locks*. A programmer must associate a lock with each shared item, and use the lock to ensure that no other processors can change the item while an update is in progress. For example, if lock 17 is associated with variable x, a programmer must obtain lock 17 before updating x. The idea is called *mutual exclusion*, and we say that a processor must gain *exclusive use* of a variable before updating the value. Figure 17.9 illustrates the sequence of instructions.

```
lock    17         # wait for lock 17
load    x, R5      # Load variable x into R5
incr    R5         # Increment the value in R5
store   R5, x      # Store R5 back into x
release 17         # release lock 17
```

Figure 17.9 Illustration of the instructions used to guarantee exclusive access to a variable. A separate lock is assigned to each shared item.

The underlying hardware guarantees that only one processor will be granted a lock at any time. Thus, if two or more processors both attempt to obtain a given lock at the same time, one obtains access (i.e., continues to execute) and the other is blocked. In fact, an arbitrary number of processors can be blocked while one processor holds the lock. Once the processor that holds the lock releases it, the hardware selects a blocked processor, grants the processor the lock, and allows the processor to proceed. Thus, the hardware ensures that at most one processor can hold a given lock at any time.

Locking adds a nontrivial amount of complexity to programs for several reasons. First, because locking is unusual, a programmer not accustomed to programming multiprocessors can easily forget to lock a shared variable, and because unprotected access may not always result in an error, the problem can be difficult to detect. Second, locking can severely reduce performance — if K processors attempt to access a shared variable at the same time, the hardware will keep $K-1$ of them idle while they wait for access. Third, because separate instructions are used to obtain and release a lock, locking adds overhead. Thus, a programmer must decide whether to obtain a lock for each individual operation or whether to obtain a lock, hold the lock while performing a series of operations on the variable, and then release the lock.

17.16.2 Programming Explicit And Implicit Parallel Computers

The most important aspect of parallelism for a programmer concerns whether software or hardware is responsible for managing parallelism: a system that uses implicit parallelism is significantly easier to program than a system that uses explicit parallelism. For example, consider a processor designed to handle packets arriving from a computer network. In an implicit design, a programmer writes code to handle a single packet, and the hardware automatically applies the same program to N packets in parallel. In an explicit design, the programmer must plan to read N packets, send each to a different core, wait for the cores to complete processing, and extract the resulting packets. In many cases, the code required to control parallel cores and determine when they each finish is more complex than the code to perform the desired computation. More important, code to control parallel hardware units must allow hardware to operate in arbitrary order. For example, because the time required to process a packet depends on the packet's contents, a controller must be ready for the hardware units to complete processing in arbitrary order. The point is:

> *From a programmer's point of view, a system that uses explicit parallelism is significantly more complex to program than a system that uses implicit parallelism.*

17.16.3 Programming Symmetric Vs. Asymmetric Multiprocessors

One of the most important advantages of symmetry arises from the positive consequences it has for programmers: a symmetric multiprocessor can be substantially easier
to program than an asymmetric multiprocessor. First, if all processors are identical, a
programmer only needs one compiler and one language. Second, symmetry means a
programmer does not need to consider which tasks are best suited for which type of
processor. Third, because identical processors usually operate at the same speed, a programmer does not need to worry about the time required to perform a task on a given
processor. Fourth, because all processors use the same encoding for instructions and
data, a binary program or a data value can be moved from one processor to another.

An asymmetric design does offer some advantages. First, a programmer can use
specialized hardware that may perform a specific task faster than a general-purpose
symmetric processor. For example, a specialized processor can perform Machine
Learning computations much faster than a general-purpose processor. Second, asymmetry may allow an architect to replicate special-purpose processors independent of
general-purpose processors (e.g., an eight-core machine with one specialized graphics
processor).

Of course, any form of multiprocessor introduces a complication: in addition to
everything else, a programmer must consider how coding decisions will influence performance. For example, consider a computation that processes packets arriving over a
network. A conventional program keeps a global counter in memory, and updates the
counter when a packet arrives. On a shared memory architecture, however, updating a
value in memory is more expensive because a processor must obtain a lock before updating a shared value in memory. Thus, a programmer needs to consider the effect of
minor details, such as updating a shared counter in memory.

17.17 Redundant Parallel Architectures

Our discussion has focused on the use of parallel hardware to improve performance
or increase functionality. However, it is also possible to use parallel hardware to improve reliability and prevent failure. That is, multiple copies of hardware can be used
to verify each computation.

The term *redundant hardware* usually refers to multiple copies of a hardware unit
that operate in parallel to perform an operation. The basic difference between redundant
hardware and the parallel architectures described above arises from the data items being
used: a parallel architecture arranges for each copy of the hardware to operate on a
separate data item; a redundant architecture arranges for all copies to perform exactly
the same operation.

The point of using redundant hardware is verification that a computation is correct.
What happens when redundant copies of the hardware disagree? The answer depends

on the details and purpose of the underlying system. One possibility uses votes: K copies of a hardware unit each perform the computation and produce a value. A special hardware unit then compares the output, and selects the value that appears most often. Another possibility uses redundant hardware to detect hardware failures: if two copies of the hardware disagree, the system displays an error message, and then halts until the defective unit can be repaired or replaced.

17.18 Distributed And Cluster Computers

The parallel architectures discussed in this chapter are called *tightly coupled* because the parallel hardware units are located inside the same computer system. The alternative, which is known as a *loosely coupled* architecture uses multiple computer systems that are interconnected by a communication mechanism that spans longer distances. For example, we use the term *distributed architecture* to refer to a set of computers that are connected by a computer network or the Internet. In a distributed architecture, each computer operates independently, but the computers can communicate by sending messages across a network.

A special form of distributed computing system is known as a *network cluster* or a *cluster computer*. In essence, a cluster computer consists of a set of independent computers, such as commodity PCs, connected by a high-speed computer network. Scientists use cluster computers to run computations on extremely large sets of data, Internet search companies use clusters to respond to users' search terms, and cloud providers use the cluster approach to build cloud data centers. The general idea is that for a cluster of N computers, computation can be divided many ways. The computers in a cluster are flexible — they can be dedicated to solving a single problem or separate problems. Computers in the cluster run independently. If they are working on a single problem, the results may be collected to produce the final output.

A special case of cluster computing is used to construct a high-capacity Web site that handles many small requests. Each computer in the cluster runs a copy of the same Web server. A special-purpose system known as a *Web load balancer* disperses incoming requests among computers in the cluster. Each time a request arrives, the load balancer chooses the least-loaded computer in the cluster and forwards the request. Thus, a Web site with N computers in a cluster can respond to approximately N times as many requests per second as a single computer.

Another form of loosely coupled distributed computing is known as *grid computing*. Grid computing uses the global Internet as a communication mechanism among a large set of computers. The computers (typically personal computers owned by individuals) agree to provide spare CPU cycles for the grid. Each computer runs software that repeatedly accepts a request, performs the requested computation, and returns the result. To use the grid, a problem must be divided into many small pieces. Each piece of the problem is sent to a computer, and all computers can execute simultaneously.

17.19 A Modern Supercomputer

Informally, the term *supercomputer* is used to denote an advanced computing system that has significantly more processing power than mainframe computers. Because they are often used for scientific calculations, supercomputers are typically assessed by the number of floating point operations per second the computer can perform.

Parallelism has always played an important role in supercomputers. Early supercomputers had 16 or 64 processors. A modern supercomputer consists of a cluster of many PCs that are interconnected by a high-speed Local Area Network. Furthermore, the processor in each PC has multiple cores. Modern supercomputers carry parallelism to a surprising extreme. For example, the Frontier supercomputer, which was built in 2022 by HP Enterprise and its subsidiary Cray, became the first exascale supercomputer because it can perform one quintillion (10^{18}) calculations per second. The computer has a total of 8,730,112 cores!

17.20 Summary

Parallelism is a fundamental optimization technique used to increase hardware performance. Most components of a computer system contain parallel hardware; an architecture is only classified as parallel if the architecture includes parallel processors. Explicit parallelism gives a programmer control over the use of parallel facilities; implicit parallelism handles parallelism automatically.

A uniprocessor computer is classified as a Single Instruction Single Data (SISD) architecture because a single instruction operates on a single data item at any given time. A Single Instruction Multiple Data (SIMD) architecture allows an instruction to operate on an array of values. Typical SIMD machines include vector processors and graphics processors. A Multiple Instructions Multiple Data (MIMD) architecture employs multiple, independent processors that operate simultaneously and can each execute a separate program. Typical MIMD machines include symmetric and asymmetric multiprocessors. Alternatives to SIMD and MIMD architectures include redundant, distributed, cluster, and grid architectures as well as Multiple Instruction Single Data (MISD) architectures discussed in the next chapter.

In theory, a general-purpose multiprocessor with N processors should perform N times faster than a single processor. In practice, however, memory contention, communication overhead, and coordination mean that the performance of a multiprocessor does not increase linearly as the number of processors increases. In the extreme case, overhead means that performance can decrease as additional processors are added.

Programming a computer with multiple processors can be a challenge. In addition to other considerations, a programmer must use locks to guarantee exclusive access to shared items.

A modern supercomputer consists of a large cluster of processors. If a problem can be partitioned into subparts, the processors in a supercomputer cluster can work on subparts in parallel.

EXERCISES

17.1   Define macroscopic parallelism and give an example.

17.2   If a computer has four cores plus two GPU cores, does the system have symmetric parallelism, asymmetric parallelism, or some of both? Explain?

17.3   Use the Flynn classification scheme to classify a dual-core smart phone.

17.4   What is contention, and how does it affect performance?

17.5   A C programmer is writing code that will run on multiple cores, and must increment a shared variable x. Instead of writing:

```
x = x + 1;
```

the C programmer writes:

```
x++;
```

Does the second form guarantee that two cores can execute the increment without interfering with one another? Explain.

17.6   You receive two job offers for the same salary, one writing code for a system that uses explicit parallelism and another writing code for a system that uses implicit parallelism. Which do you choose, and why?

17.7   Consider multiplying two 10 x 20 matrices on a computer that has vector capability but limits each vector to sixteen items. How is matrix multiplication handled on such a computer, and how many vector multiplications are required?

17.8   In the previous exercise, how many scalar multiplications are needed on a uniprocessor (i.e., an SISD architecture)? If we ignore addition and only measure multiplication, what is the speedup? Does the speedup change when multiplying 100 x 100 matrices?

17.9   If you have access to single-processor and dual-processor computers that run at approximately the same clock rate, write a program that consumes large amounts of CPU time, run multiple copies on both computers, and record the running times. What is the effective speedup?

17.10 In the previous question, change the program to reference large amounts of memory (e.g., repeatedly set a large array to a value x, then set the array to value y, and so on). How do memory references affect the speedup?

17.11 Can a multiprocessor ever achieve speedup that is *better* than linear? To find out, consider an encryption-breaking algorithm that must try twenty-four (four factorial) possible encryption keys and must perform up to 1024 operations to test each key (stopping early only if an answer is found). If we assume a multiprocessor requires K milliseconds to perform 1024 operations, on average how much time will the processor spend solving the entire problem? How much time will a 32-processor MIMD machine spend solving the problem? What is the resulting speedup?

17.12 Search the Web to find a list of the top 10 supercomputers and the performance of each.

Chapter Contents

18

Data Pipelining

18.1 Introduction

Earlier chapters present processors, memory systems, and I/O as the fundamental aspects of computer architecture. The previous chapter shows how parallelism can be used to increase performance, and explains a variety of parallel architectures.

This chapter focuses on the second major technique hardware engineers use to increase performance: pipelining. The chapter discusses the motivation for pipelining, and explains how a pipeline can increase hardware performance.

18.2 The Concept Of Pipelining

The term *pipelining* refers broadly to any architecture in which digital information flows through a series of stations (e.g., processing components) that each inspect, interpret, or modify the information as Figure 18.1 illustrates.

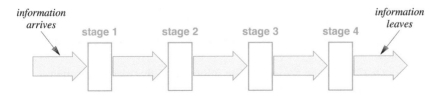

Figure 18.1 Illustration of the pipeline concept. The example pipeline has four stages, and information flows through each stage.

Although we are primarily interested in hardware architectures and the use of pipe-lining within a single computer system, the concept itself is not limited to hardware. Pipelining is not restricted to a single computer, a particular type or size of digital infor-mation, or a specific length of pipeline (i.e., a particular number of stages). Instead, pipelining is a fundamental concept in computing that is used in a variety of situations.

To help us understand the concept, we will consider a set of characteristics. Figure 18.2 lists ways to characterize pipelines, and succeeding paragraphs explain each of the characteristics.

- Hardware or software implementation
- Large or small scale
- Synchronous or asynchronous flow
- Buffered or unbuffered flow
- Small data items or continuous streams
- Serial or parallel path
- Homogeneous or heterogeneous stages

Figure 18.2 The variety of ways a pipeline can be used in digital systems.

Hardware Or Software Implementation. Pipelining can be implemented with ei-ther software or hardware. Although the general concept remains the same, software pipelines help programmers grapple with complex programs and hardware pipelines focus on improving performance.

Large Or Small Scale. Stages in a pipeline can range from simplistic to powerful, and a pipeline can range in length from short to long. At one extreme, a small hardware pipeline can be contained entirely within a small functional unit on a chip. At the other extreme, the pipeline in a specialized processor may contain more than one hundred stages.

Synchronous Or Asynchronous Flow. A *synchronous pipeline* behaves like an as-sembly line, which means that all stages forward an output item to the next stage simul-taneously. In an *asynchronous pipeline*, a station forwards its output when processing completes.

Buffered Or Unbuffered Flow. A *buffered* pipeline places a fixed-size *buffer* between each pair of stages, and allows a given stage to fill the buffer before the stage needs to wait. Buffering works well in situations where the time a stage spends pro-cessing an item varies.

Small Data Items Or Continuous Streams. The information that passes through a pipeline can consist of a sequence of small data items (e.g., network packets) or a con-tinuous stream (e.g., a video).

Serial Or Parallel Path. The path used to carry information from one stage to another may consist of parallel wires or a serial communication technology.

Homogeneous Or Heterogeneous Stages. Although Figure 18.1 uses the same size and shape for each stage of a pipeline, homogeneity is not required. Some implementations of pipelines choose a type of hardware that is appropriate for each stage.

18.3 Software Pipelining

From a programmer's point of view, software pipelining offers an attractive way to structure programs for two reasons. First, a software pipeline provides a way to handle complexity. Second, a software pipeline allows programs to be reused. In essence, both goals are achieved because a software pipeline allows a programmer to divide a large, complex task into smaller, reusable pieces.

Consider the software pipeline facilities provided by the Unix shell (i.e., the command interpreter). To create a software pipeline, a user enters a list of command names separated by the vertical bar character to specify that the programs should be run as a pipeline. The shell arranges the programs so the output from one program becomes the input of the next. Each program can have zero or more arguments that control processing. For example, the following input to the shell specifies that three programs, *cat*, *sed*, and *more* are to be connected in a pipeline:

```
cat x | sed 's/stranger/friend/g' | more
```

In the example, the *cat* program writes a copy of file *x* (presumably a text file) to a *pipe*, which becomes the input of the *sed* program, and the *sed* program writes output to a pipe that becomes the input of the *more* program. *Sed* has an argument that specifies translating every occurrence of the word *stranger* to *friend*. The *more* program displays the output in the user's window.

18.4 Hardware Pipelining

Architects use hardware pipelining as a fundamental performance optimization technique. Two forms of hardware pipelining exist:

- Instruction pipeline
- Data pipeline

Instruction Pipeline. Chapter 5 describes how a processor uses a hardware pipeline to decode and execute instructions during the fetch-execute cycle. To be precise, we use the term *instruction pipeline* to describe a pipeline in which machine instructions pass through the stages of the pipeline. Because the instruction set and operand types vary among processors, the number of stages in an instruction pipeline and the exact operations performed by each stage depend on the processor. The description below explains how an instruction pipeline increases processing speed.

Data Pipeline. We use the term *data pipeline* to describe a hardware pipeline in which the items flowing through the pipeline consist of arbitrary data values rather than instructions. For example, one type of data pipeline handles packets that arrive over a computer network. Each incoming packet passes sequentially through the stages of the pipeline, and each stage examines and modifies the packet (e.g., to verify a checksum or decrypt an encrypted message). Data pipelining offers some unusual and interesting ways to use pipelining. In addition, data pipelining has the potential for especially large performance improvements.

18.5 How Hardware Pipelining Increases Performance

Consider a data processing task that has multiple steps, and compare the performance of a pipeline to a monolithic design. For purposes of this example, we will consider the steps that an Internet router takes when a packet arrives. Figure 18.3 lists six basic operations the router performs. Readers do not need to understand the details, but should appreciate that some router hardware does indeed use pipelining.

1. Receive: accept an incoming packet
2. Verify integrity: to ensure that the packet was not damaged, verify the checksum or CRC.
3. Prevent forwarding loops: decrement a TTL value in the packet, and discard the packet if the value reaches zero.
4. Select an output path: use the destination address field in the packet to choose an output over which to send the packet.
5. Prepare for transmission: compute a new checksum or CRC for the outgoing packet so the next router along the path can verify integrity.
6. Transmit the packet: send the packet along the path to the destination.

Figure 18.3 An example series of steps that hardware in an Internet router performs to forward a packet.

Consider the design of hardware that implements the steps in the figure. Because the steps involve complex computation, it may seem that software running on a processor should receive an incoming packet, perform all the steps, and send the packet to its next destination. Figure 18.4 illustrates a software-based router and shows the algorithm the software runs.

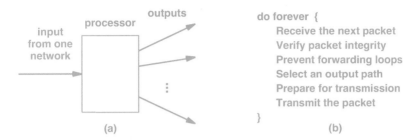

do forever {
    Receive the next packet
    Verify packet integrity
    Prevent forwarding loops
    Select an output path
    Prepare for transmission
    Transmit the packet
}

(a)   (b)

Figure 18.4 (a) Illustration of the connections on a processor used in a parallel implementation of an Internet router, and (b) the algorithm
the processor executes. Each processor handles input from one
network.

Software running cannot perform fast enough to keep up with packets arriving over
high-speed networks. One way to build a high-speed router uses a parallel architecture
that has N processors instead of one processor — each incoming packet goes to one of
the N processors. A second form of parallelism uses a special-purpose data pipeline of
multiple processors arranged as Figure 18.5 illustrates†.

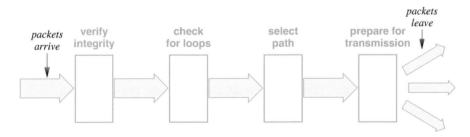

Figure 18.5 Illustration of a pipeline used in place of a single processor in an
Internet router.

It may seem that the pipeline in the figure is no faster than the single processor in
Figure 18.4. Suppose, for example, that each processor in the pipeline runs at the same
speed as the single processor in Figure 18.4. The pipeline will still perform exactly the
same operations on each packet as the single processor, and will still take the same
amount of time. For example, the step labeled *verify integrity* will take the same
amount of time on both architectures, the step labeled *check for loops* will take the
same amount of time on both architectures, and so on. Thus, if we ignore the delay introduced by passing packets among stages of the pipeline, the processors in the pipeline
will take exactly the same total time to process a packet as a single processor takes.
The point is:

---

†A pipeline provides an example of the Flynn MISD type of parallel architecture mentioned in the previous chapter.

*A data pipeline passes a data item through a series of stages that
each examine or modify the item. If it uses the same speed processors
as a non-pipeline architecture, a data pipeline will not improve the
overall time needed to process a given data item.*

If the total processing time required for an item is the same in the pipelined and
non-pipelined architectures, what advantage does a data pipeline offer? Surprisingly,
even if the individual processors in Figure 18.5 each run at exactly the same speed as
the processor in Figure 18.4, the pipeline architecture can handle more packets per
second. To see why, observe that an individual processor executes fewer instructions
per packet and all processors in the pipeline work in parallel. After operating on one
data item, a processor moves on to the next data item. Thus, a data pipeline architecture allows a given processor to move on to the next data item more quickly than a non-
pipeline architecture. As a result, data can enter (and leave) a pipeline at a higher rate.

We can summarize:

*Even if a data pipeline uses the same speed processors as a non-
pipeline architecture, a data pipeline has higher overall throughput
(i.e., number of data items processed per second) because the processors operate in parallel.*

18.6 When Pipelining Can Be Used

A pipeline will not yield higher performance in all cases. Figure 18.6 lists conditions that must be met for a pipeline to perform faster than a single processor.

- Partitionable problem
- Equivalent processor speed
- Low overhead data movement

Figure 18.6 The three key conditions that must be met for a data pipeline to
perform better than the same computation on a single processor.

Partitionable Problem. It must be possible to partition processing into stages that
can be computed independent of one another. Computations that employ a sequence of
steps work well in a pipeline, but computations that involve iteration often do not.

Equivalent Processor Speed. It should be obvious that if the processors used in a
data pipeline operate slowly, the overall time required to perform a computation will be
much higher than on a single processor. To achieve higher performance than a single
processor, the processors used in the pipeline must run at least as fast as the single processor.

Low Overhead Data Movement. In addition to the time required to perform computation, a data pipeline has additional overhead: the time required to move a data item from one stage of the pipeline to the next. If moving the data incurs extremely high latency, pipelining will not increase performance.

The requirements arise because of an important principle:

> *The throughput of a pipeline is limited by the stage that takes the most time.*

As an example, consider the data pipeline in Figure 18.5. Suppose that all processors in the pipeline are identical, and assume that a pipeline processor takes exactly the same time to execute an instruction as the single processor. To make the example concrete, assume that a processor can execute ten instructions each microsecond. Further suppose the four stages in the figure take fifty, one hundred, two hundred, and one hundred fifty instructions, respectively, to process a packet. The slowest stage requires two hundred instructions, which means the total time the slowest stage takes to process a packet is:

$$total\ time\ =\ \frac{200\ inst}{10\ inst\ /\ \mu sec}\ =\ 20\ \mu sec \tag{18.1}$$

Looking at this another way, we can see that the maximum number of packets that can be processed per second is the inverse of the time per packet of the slowest stage. Thus, the overall throughput of the example pipeline, T_p, is given by:

$$T_p\ =\ \frac{1\ packet}{20\ \mu sec}\ =\ \frac{1\ packet \times 10^6}{20\ sec}\ =\ 50,000\ packets\ per\ second \tag{18.2}$$

In contrast, a non-pipelined architecture must execute all 500 instructions for each packet, which means that the total time required for a packet is 50 μsec. Thus, the throughput of the non-pipelined architecture is limited to:

$$T_{np}\ =\ \frac{1\ packet}{50\ \mu sec}\ =\ \frac{1\ packet \times 10^6}{50\ sec}\ =\ 20,000\ packets\ per\ second \tag{18.3}$$

18.7 The Conceptual Division Of Processing

Data pipelining improves performance because pipelining uses a special form of parallelism. By dividing a series of sequential operations into groups and using a separate stage of the pipeline to handle each group, pipelining allows stages to operate in parallel. Of course, a pipeline architecture differs from a conventional parallel architecture in a significant way: although the stages operate in parallel, a given data item must pass through all stages. Figure 18.7 illustrates the concept.

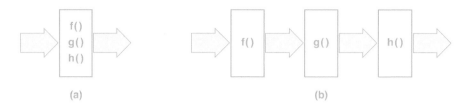

Figure 18.7 (a) Processing on a conventional processor, and (b) equivalent processing in a data pipeline. The functions performed in sequence are divided among stages of the pipeline.

The point of the figure is that the three stages operate in parallel. Stage three performs function h on one data item at the same time that stage two performs function g on a second data item and stage one performs function f on a third data item. As long as the pipeline is full (i.e., there are no delays between items), the overall system benefits from N stages all running in parallel, processing N data items at the same time.

18.8 Pipeline Architectures

Recall from the previous chapter that we distinguish between hardware architectures that merely use parallelism and architectures in which parallelism forms the central paradigm around which the entire architecture is designed. We make an analogous distinction between hardware architectures that use pipelining and architectures in which pipelining forms the central paradigm around which the entire system is designed. We reserve the name *pipeline architectures* for the latter. Thus, one might hear an architect say that the processor in a given system uses instruction pipelining, but the architect will not characterize the system as a pipeline architecture unless the overall design centers around a pipeline.

Most hardware systems that follow a pipeline architecture are dedicated to special-purpose functions. For instance, the example above describes how pipelining can be used to improve performance of a packet processing system. Network equipment often uses hardware pipelines to increase processing speed because the high data rates used with optical fibers exceed the capacity of single-processor systems.

General-purpose computers rely less on data pipelines for two reasons. First, few applications can be partitioned into a set of independent operations that can be applied sequentially. Instead, a typical application uses iteration, accesses items randomly, and keeps large volumes of state information during processing. Second, even in situations where program functions can be partitioned into a pipeline, the number of stages in the pipeline and the hardware needed to implement each stage varies from one application to the next. As a result, general-purpose computers usually restrict pipeline hardware to an instruction pipeline in the processor or a special-purpose pipeline in an I/O device.

18.9 Pipeline Setup, Stall, And Flush Times

Our description of pipelines overlooks several details. For example, many pipeline implementations incur overhead associated with starting and stopping the pipeline. We use the term *setup time* to describe the amount of time required to start a pipeline after it has been idle. Setup may involve synchronizing processing among stages or passing a special control token through the pipeline to restart each stage. More important, setup may operate sequentially, finishing the initialization of the hardware in one stage before starting to initialize the hardware in the next stage.

In addition, a pipeline can require significant time to terminate processing because the pipeline must finish processing any data items already in progress before the pipeline shuts down. We use the term *flush time* to refer to the amount of time that elapses between stopping the input to the pipeline and the time the pipeline finishes the items already in progress. We say that items currently in the pipeline must be *flushed* before the pipeline can be shut down.

The need to flush items through a pipeline can arise in two cases. First, once all data items have entered the pipeline, the pipeline must be shut down. Second, as we have seen in Chapter 5, a pipeline can *stall* if a stage cannot complete processing fast enough to pass a data item on to the next stage. In a high-speed hardware pipeline, even mundane operations such as a memory reference or an I/O operation can cause a stage to stall. Thus, high flush (or setup) times can reduce pipeline performance significantly.

The point is:

> *Although a pipeline offers higher performance when processing data items continuously, the times required to flush a pipeline and start an idle pipeline can lower performance.*

18.10 Definition Of Superpipeline Architecture

A final concept completes our description of pipelines. Architects use the term *superpipeline* to describe an extension of the pipeline approach in which a given stage of the pipeline is subdivided into a set of partial stages. Superpipelining is most often used with an instruction pipeline, but the concept applies to data pipelines as well. The general idea is: if dividing processing into N stages can increase overall throughput, adding more stages can increase throughput further.

A traditional instruction pipeline might have five stages that correspond to instruction fetch, instruction decode, operand fetch, ALU operation, and memory write. A superpipeline architecture subdivides one or more stages into multiple pieces. For example, a superpipeline might subdivide the operand fetch stage into four steps: decode an operand, fetch immediate values or values from registers, fetch values from memory, and fetch indirect operand values. As with standard pipelining, the subdivision provides higher throughput — because each substage takes less time, a superpipeline has higher throughput than a standard pipeline.

18.11 Summary

Many computer systems employ a special form of parallelism known as pipelining. A data pipeline passes each data item through a series of stages. When compared to performing processing on a single processor, dividing the processing among K processors that run at the same speed as the original processor does not reduce the total processing time taken for a given data item. However, the pipeline increases the overall throughput (i.e., the number of items that can be processed per unit of time).

A data pipeline works best when processing data items continuously. Starting an idle pipeline can incur a setup delay because hardware in each stage must be initialized. A delay can also occur when shutting down a pipeline because the pipeline must flush all data items currently being processed.

Some instruction pipelines use a superpipeline approach that subdivides one or more stages of the instruction pipeline into multiple substages that each handle one part of the processing. Subdividing a stage can further increase overall throughput.

A data pipeline does not decrease the overall time required to process a single data item. However, using a pipeline does increase the overall throughput (items processed per second). The stage of a pipeline that requires the most time to process an item limits the throughput of the pipeline.

EXERCISES

18.1   A scientist uses a cluster of PCs and arranges to have software on each processor perform one step of a computation. The processor reads up to 1 MB of data (whatever is available), processes the data, and then passes its output to the next processor over a 32-bit bus. What characteristics from Figure 18.2 does the arrangement have?

18.2   Your team has been given the task of moving a video processing program from an old single-core processor to a new quad-core processor that has a high-speed interconnect among cores. Conventional parallel approaches will not work because the frames of video must be processed in order. What technique can you suggest that offers a possible way to use the new hardware to improve performance?

18.3   A computer system has a single processor, and to speed up processing, an engineer builds a data pipeline with eight processors. To measure the performance of the pipeline, the engineer measures the time it takes to process a data item on a single processor and compares the time it takes to send the same data item through the pipeline. What performance do you expect the measurements to show? Explain.

18.4   Most data pipeline hardware performs specialized tasks (e.g., graphics processing). Would installing a data pipeline in all computers increase the performance of all programs? Why or why not?

18.5   A manager notices that the company has a few idle computers in each of ten data centers. The data centers are spread across the country, with low-speed Internet connections used to communicate among the data centers. The manager proposes that rather than using a computer in the local data center, performance could be increased by building a "giant data pipeline" across all ten data centers. What do you tell the manager about the idea?

18.6   You are given a program that runs on one processor, and are asked to divide the program into pieces that will run on a data pipeline that has eight processors. You can divide the program two ways. In one, the pipeline processors perform 680, 2000, 1300, 1400, 800, 1900, 1200, and 200 instructions, respectively. In the other, the processors perform 680, 1400, 1300, 1400, 1400, 1000, 1200, and 1100 instructions, respectively. Which division do you choose, and why?

18.7   What is the maximum throughput of a homogeneous pipeline in which four processors each handle one million instructions per second and processing a data item requires 50, 60, 40, and 30 instructions, respectively? Assume a constant execution time for all types of instructions and no delay passing data items among pipeline stages.

18.8   In the previous exercise, what is the relative gain in throughput compared to an architecture without pipelining? What limits the maximum speedup?

18.9   Extend the previous exercise by considering heterogeneous processors that have speeds of 1.0, 1.2, 0.9, and 1.0 million instructions per second, respectively.

18.10   If you are asked to apply superpipelining to subdivide one of the stages of an existing pipeline, which stage should you choose? Why?

Chapter Contents

19

Assessing Performance

19.1 Introduction

Earlier chapters cover three fundamental aspects of computer architecture: processors, memories, and I/O devices. They characterize each mechanism, and explain the salient features. Previous chapters consider two techniques used to increase computational performance: parallelism and pipelining.

This chapter takes a broader view of performance. It examines how performance can be measured, and discusses how an architect evaluates an instruction set. More important, the chapter presents Amdahl's law, and explains consequences for computer architecture.

19.2 Measuring Computational Power And Performance

How can we measure computational power? What makes one computer system perform better than another? These questions have engendered research in the scientific community, caused heated debate among representatives from the sales and marketing departments of commercial computer vendors, and resulted in a variety of answers.

The chief problem that underlies performance assessment arises from the flexibility of a general-purpose computer system: a general-purpose computer can perform a variety of tasks. More important, because optimization involves choosing among alternatives, optimizing an architecture for a given task means that the architecture will be less than optimal for other tasks. Consequently, the performance of a computer system depends on the task the system performs.

We can summarize:

> *Because a computer system can perform a wide variety of tasks and no architecture is optimal for all tasks, the performance of a system depends on the task being performed.*

The dependency between performance and the task being performed has two important consequences. First, it means that many computer vendors can each claim that their computer performs well. For example, a vendor whose computer performs matrix multiplication at high speed uses matrix multiplication examples to measure performance, while a vendor whose computer performs integer operations at especially high speed uses integer examples to measure performance. Both vendors can claim that their computer performs better than others. Second, from a scientific point of view, we can see that no single measure of computer system performance suffices for all cases. The point is fundamental to understanding performance assessment:

> *A variety of performance measures exist because no single measure suffices for all situations.*

19.3 Measures Of Computational Power

Recall that early computer systems consisted of a central processor with little or no I/O capability. As a consequence, early measures of computer performance focused on the execution speed of the CPU. Even when performance measures are restricted to a CPU, however, multiple measures apply. The most important distinction arises in the performance of:

- Integer computation
- Floating point computation

Because scientific and engineering calculations rely heavily on floating point, applications that focus on floating point have become known as *scientific applications*, and we call the resulting computation *scientific computation*. When assessing how a computer performs on scientific applications, engineers focus entirely on the performance of floating point operations. That is, they ignore the speed of integer operations, and only measure the speed of floating point operations (specifically, floating point addition, subtraction, multiplication, and division). Of course, addition and subtraction are generally faster than multiplication and division, and a program contains other instructions (e.g., instructions to call functions and control iteration). On many computers, however, a floating point operation takes so much longer than a typical integer instruction that floating point computation dominates the overall performance of a scientific program.

Rather than reporting the time required to perform a floating point operation, engineers report the number of floating point operations that can be performed per unit time. In particular, the primary measure reports the average number of floating point operations the hardware can execute per second (*FLOPS*).

Of course, floating point speed only matters for scientific computation; the speed of floating point hardware becomes irrelevant for programs that only use integer arithmetic. More important, a measure of FLOPS does not make sense for a processor that does not provide floating point hardware. Thus, as an alternative to measuring floating point performance, a vendor may choose to exclude floating point and report the average number of other instructions that a processor can execute per unit time. Typically, such vendors measure *millions of instructions per second (MIPS)*.

Simplistic measures of performance such as MIPS or FLOPS only provide a rough estimate of performance. To see why, consider the time required to execute an instruction. For example, consider a processor on which floating point multiplication or division takes twice as long as floating point addition or subtraction. If we assume that an addition or subtraction instruction takes Q nanoseconds and weight each of the four instruction types equally, the average time the computer takes to perform a floating point instruction, T_{avg} is:

$$T_{avg} = \frac{Q + Q + 2 \times Q + 2 \times Q}{4} = 1.5 \ Q \quad ns \ per \ instr. \qquad (19.1)$$

However, when the computer performs addition and subtraction, the time required is only Q nanoseconds per instruction (i.e., 33% less than the average). Similarly, when performing multiplication or division, the computer requires $2 \times Q$ nanoseconds per instruction (i.e., 33% more than the average). In practice, the times required for addition and division can differ by more than a factor of two, which means that actual performance can vary by more than 33%. An exercise considers one possible ratio.

The point is:

> *Because some instructions take substantially longer to execute than others, the average time required to execute an instruction only provides a crude approximation of performance. The actual time required depends on which instructions are executed.*

19.4 Application-Specific Instruction Counts

How can we produce a more accurate assessment of performance? One answer lies in assessing performance for a specific application. For example, suppose we need to know how a floating point hardware unit will perform when multiplying two $N \times N$ matrices. By examining the program, it is possible to derive a set of expressions that give the number of floating point additions, subtractions, multiplications, and divisions that will be performed as a function of N. For example, assume that multiplying a pair of

$N \times N$ matrices requires N^3 floating point multiplications and $N^3 - N^2$ floating point additions. If each addition requires Q nanoseconds and each multiplication requires $2 \times Q$ nanoseconds, multiplying two matrices will require a total of:

$$T_{total} = 2 \times Q \times N^3 + Q \times (N^3 - N^2) \qquad (19.2)$$

As an alternative to precise analysis, engineers use a weighted average. That is, instead of calculating the exact number of times each instruction is executed, an approximate percentage is used. For example, suppose a graphics program is run on many input data sets, the number of floating point operations is counted to obtain the list in Figure 19.1.

Instruction Type	Count	Percentage
Add	8513508	72
Subtract	1537162	13
Multiply	1064188	9
Divide	709458	6

Figure 19.1 Example of instruction counts for a graphics application run on many input values. The third column shows the relative percentage of each instruction type.

Once a set of instruction counts has been obtained, the performance of hardware can be assessed by using a weighted average. When the graphics application is run on the hardware described above, we expect the average time for each floating point instruction to be:

$$T_{avg} = .72\,Q + .13\,Q + .09 \times 2\,Q + .06 \times 2\,Q = 1.16\,Q \ \ ns \ per \ instr. \quad (19.3)$$

As the example shows, a weighted average can differ significantly from a uniform average. In this case, the weighted average is 23% less than the average in Equation 19.1 that was obtained using uniform instruction weights†.

19.5 Instruction Mix

Although it provides a more accurate measurement of performance, the weighted average example above only applies to one specific application and only assesses floating point performance. Can we give a more general assessment? One approach has become popular: use a large set of programs to obtain relative weights for each type of instruction, and then use the relative weights to assess the performance of a given architecture. That is, instead of focusing on floating point, keep a counter for each instruction type (e.g., integer arithmetic instructions, bit shift instructions, subroutine calls,

---

†Equation 19.1 can be found on page 363.

conditional branches), and use the counts and relative weights to compute a weighted average performance.

Of course, the weights depend on the specific programs chosen. Therefore, to be as accurate as possible, we must choose programs that represent a typical workload. Architects choose an *instruction mix* that represents typical programs.

In addition to helping assess performance of a computer, an instruction mix helps an architect design an efficient instruction set. The architect drafts a tentative instruction set, assigns an expected cost to each instruction, and uses weights from the instruction mix to see how the proposed instruction set will perform. In essence, the architect uses the instruction mix to evaluate how the proposed architecture will perform on typical programs. If the performance is unsatisfactory, the architect can change the design.

We can summarize:

> *An instruction mix consists of a set of instructions along with relative weights that have been obtained by counting instruction execution in a set of example programs. An architect can use an instruction mix to assess how a proposed architecture will perform.*

19.6 Standardized Benchmarks

What instruction mix should be used to compare the performance of two architectures? To answer the question, we need to know how the computers will be used: the programs the computers are intended to run, and the type of input the programs will receive. In essence, we need to find a set of applications that are typical. Engineers and architects use the term *benchmark* to refer to such programs — a benchmark provides a standard workload against which a computer can be measured.

Of course, devising a benchmark is difficult, and the community does not benefit if each vendor creates a separate benchmark. To solve the problem, an independent not-for-profit corporation was formed in the 1980s. Named *Standard Performance Evaluation Corporation (SPEC)*, the corporation was created to "establish, maintain and endorse a standardized set of relevant benchmarks that can be applied to the newest generation of high-performance computers"†. SPEC has devised a series of standard benchmarks that are used to compare performance. For example, the *SPEC cint2006* benchmark is used to evaluate integer performance, and the *SPEC cfp2006* benchmark is used to evaluate floating point performance.

The benchmarks produced by SPEC are primarily used for measurement, not design. That is, each benchmark consists of a set of programs that are run and measured. The score that results from running a SPEC benchmark, known as a *SPECmark*, is often quoted in the industry as a vendor-independent measure of computer performance.

Interestingly, SPEC has produced many benchmarks that each test one aspect of performance. For example, SPEC offers six separate benchmarks that focus on integer

---

†The description is taken from the SPEC bylaws (see http://www.spec.org).

arithmetic and another fourteen benchmarks that focus on various aspects of floating point performance. In addition, SPEC provides benchmarks to assess the power computers consume, performance of a Java environment, and performance of Unix systems running the *Network File System* (*NFS*) for remote file access during software development tasks.

19.7 I/O And Memory Bottlenecks

CPU performance only accounts for part of the overall performance of a computer system. As users of personal computers have realized, a faster CPU or more cores does not guarantee faster response for all computing tasks. A colleague of the author complains that although CPU power increases by an order of magnitude every ten years, the time required to launch an application also seems to increase.

What prevents a faster CPU from increasing the overall speed? We have already seen one answer: the Von Neumann bottleneck (i.e., memory access). Recall that the speed of memory can affect the rate at which instructions can be fetched as well as the rate at which data can be accessed. Thus, rather than merely measuring CPU performance, some benchmarks are designed to measure memory performance. The memory benchmark consists of a program that repeatedly accesses memory. Some memory benchmarks are designed to test sequential access (i.e., access to contiguous bytes), while others are designed to test random access. More important, memory benchmarks also make repeated references to a memory location to test memory caching.

As the chapters on I/O point out, peripheral devices and the buses over which peripheral devices communicate can also form a bottleneck. Thus, some benchmarks are designed to test the performance of I/O devices. For example, a benchmark to test a disk will repeatedly execute *write* and *read* operations that each transfer a block of data to the disk and then read the data back. As with memory, some disk benchmarks focus on measuring performance when accessing sequential data blocks, and other benchmarks focus on measuring performance when accessing random blocks.

19.8 Moving The Boundary Between Hardware And Software

One of the fundamental principles that underlies computer performance arises from the relative speed of hardware and software: hardware (especially hardware designed for a special purpose) operates faster than software. As a consequence, moving a given function to hardware will result in higher performance than executing the function in software. In other words, an architect can increase overall performance by adding special-purpose hardware units.

A corollary arises from an equally important principle: software provides much more flexibility than hardware. The consequence is that functionality implemented with hardware cannot be changed. Therefore, an architect can increase overall flexibility and generality by allowing software to handle more functions. The recent use of FPGAs provides an example of hardware functions moving to software — instead of building a chip with fixed gates, an FPGA allows functions in the design to be programmed.

The point is that hardware and software represent a tradeoff:

Performance can be increased by moving functionality from software to hardware; flexibility can be increased by moving functionality from hardware to software.

19.9 Choosing Items To Optimize, Amdahl's Law

When an architect needs to increase performance, the architect must choose which items to optimize. Adding hardware to a design increases cost; special-purpose, high-speed hardware is especially expensive. Therefore, an architect cannot merely specify that arbitrary amounts of high-speed hardware be used. Instead, a careful choice must be made to select functions that will be optimized with high-speed hardware and functions that will be handled with conventional hardware.

How should the choice be made? A computer architect, Gene Amdahl, observed that it is a waste of resources to optimize functions that are seldom used. For example, consider the hardware used to handle division by zero errors or the circuitry used to power down a computer system. There is little point in optimizing such hardware because it is seldom used.

Amdahl suggested that the greatest gains in performance are made by optimizing functions that account for the most time. His principle, which is known as *Amdahl's law*, focuses on operations that each require extensive computation or operations that are performed most frequently. Usually, the principle is stated in a form that refers to the potential for speedup:

Amdahl's Law: *the performance improvement that can be realized from faster hardware technology is limited to the fraction of time the faster technology can be used.*

Amdahl's law can be expressed quantitatively by giving the overall speedup in terms of the fraction of time enhanced hardware is used and the speedup that the enhancement delivers. Equation 19.4 gives the overall speedup:

$$Speedup_{overall} = \frac{1}{1 - Fraction_{enhanced} + \dfrac{Fraction_{enhanced}}{Speedup_{enhanced}}} \qquad (19.4)$$

The equation works for two extremes. If the enhanced hardware is never used (i.e., the fraction is 0), there is no speedup, and Equation 19.4 results in a ratio of 1. If the enhanced hardware is used 100% of the time (i.e., the fraction is 1), the overall speedup equals the speedup of the enhanced hardware. At fractional values between 0 and 1, the overall speedup is weighted according to how much the enhanced hardware is used.

19.10 Amdahl's Law And Parallel Systems

Chapter 17 discusses parallel architectures, and explains that performance has been disappointing. In particular, overhead from communication among processors and contention for shared resources such as memory and I/O buses limit the effective speed of the system. As a result, parallel systems that contain N processors do not achieve N times the performance of a single processor.

Interestingly, Amdahl's Law applies directly to parallel systems and explains why adding more processors does not help. The speedup that can be achieved by optimizing the processing power (i.e., adding additional processors) is limited to the amount of time the processors are being used. Because a parallel system spends most of the time waiting for communication or bus access rather than using the processors, adding additional processors does not produce a significant increase in performance.

19.11 Summary

A variety of performance measures exist. Simplistic measures of processor performance include the average number of floating point operations a computer can perform per second (FLOPS) or the average number of instructions the computer can execute per second (MIPS). More sophisticated measures use a weighted average in which an instruction that is used more often is weighted more heavily. Weights can be derived by counting the instructions in a program or a set of programs; such weights are specific to the application(s) used. We say that weights, which are useful in assessing an instruction set, correspond to an instruction mix.

A benchmark refers to a standardized program or set of programs used to assess performance; each benchmark is chosen to represent a typical computation. Some of the best-known benchmarks have been produced by the SPEC Corporation, and are known as SPECmarks. In addition to measuring performance of various aspects of integer and floating point performance, SPEC benchmarks are available to measure such mechanisms as remote file access.

Amdahl's Law helps architects select functions to be optimized (e.g., moved from software to hardware or moved from conventional hardware to high-speed hardware). The law states that functions to be optimized should account for the most time. Amdahl's Law explains why parallel computer systems do not always benefit from a large number of processors.

EXERCISES

19.1   Write a C program that measures the performance of integer addition and subtraction operators. Perform at least 10,000 operations and calculate the average time per operation.

19.2   Write a computer program that measures the difference in execution times between integer addition and integer division. Execute each operation 10,000 times, and compare the difference in running times. Repeat the experiment, and verify that no other activities on the computer interfere with the measurement.

19.3   Extend the measurement in the previous exercise to compare the performance of sixteen-bit, thirty-two-bit, and (if your computer supports it) sixty-four-bit integer addition. That is, use *short, int, long,* or *long long* variables as needed. Explain the results.

19.4   Computer professionals commonly use addition, subtraction, multiplication, and division as ways to measure performance of a processor. However, many programs also use logical operations, such as *logical and, logical or, bit complement, right shift, left shift,* and so on. Measure such operations, and compare the performance to integer addition.

19.5   If floating point addition and subtraction each take Q microseconds and floating point multiplication and division each take 3Q microseconds, what is the average time required for all four operations?

19.6   Extend the previous exercise and compute the percentage difference between the time for addition and the average time, and the percentage difference between the time for multiplication and the average time.

19.7   In the previous problem, repeat the measurement with compiler optimization enabled and determine the relative speedup.

19.8   Write a program that compares the average time required to perform integer arithmetic operations and the average time required to reference memory. Calculate the ratio of memory cost to integer arithmetic cost.

19.9   Write a program that compares the average times required to perform floating point operations and integer operations. For example, compare the average time required to perform 10,000 floating point additions and the average time required to perform 10,000 integer additions.

19.10 A programmer decides to measure the performance of a memory system. The programmer finds that according to the DRAM chip manufacturer, the time needed to access an integer in the physical memory is 80 nanoseconds. The programmer writes an assembly language program that stores a value into a memory location four billion times, measures the time taken, and computes the average performance. Surprisingly, it only takes an average of 52 nanoseconds per store operation. How is such a result possible?

19.11 Turn the previous exercise around, and state why accurate measurement of a physical memory is difficult.

19.12 A hashing function places values in random locations in an array called a *hash table*. A programmer finds that even when memory caching is turned off, storing and then looking up 50,000 values in an extremely large hash table (16 megabytes) has worse performance than using the same data in a smaller hash table (16 kilobytes). Explain why.

Chapter Contents

20

Multicore Processors

20.1 Introduction

Earlier chapters describe processors, the fetch-execute cycle, and the internal data paths within a processor. Chapter 17 covers parallelism as a fundamental technique used to enhance performance. Chapter 10 explains memory caches and their importance, and Chapter 13 introduces buses and their use.

This chapter examines multicore processors. We will see that multicore designs combine aspects from previous topics to form a general-purpose, high-speed, parallel processing system.

20.2 The Move To Multicore Processor Chips

In the twentieth century, most processor chips contained a single CPU. Vendors advertised the clock speed of their processor chips, and clock speeds rose for decades. By the early 2000s, a new type of chip appeared with multiple *cores*. Vendors began advertising *dual-core processors* and *quad-core processors*. Consumers became confused, and asked basic questions. What is a core, and what, exactly does a core do? How many cores will I need in my new computer? What will happen if I do not have enough cores?

The motivation for multicore chips arose from the convergence of two conflicting goals: a need for additional computational power and physical limits on the clock rate at which a processor runs. As we will learn in the next chapter, processor chips generate heat proportional to the square of the rate at which the clock runs. In the 1990s, clock speeds reached a rate so high that processor chips needed special heat sinks and fans for cooling; further increases in clock rates produced so much heat that chips would overheat and fail.

Multicore architectures offered a solution to the conflict. Instead of trying to increase the clock rate further, vendors could keep the clock running at a rate that does not overheat the processor. Instead of building a single CPU that computed faster, vendors could place multiple CPUs on a chip, arrange for the CPUs to run autonomously, and allow programmers to use the CPUs simultaneously. Industry uses the term *core* to refer to one of the CPUs, and *multicore chip* to refer to a chip that contains multiple CPUs.

20.3 The Multicore Concept: Parallelism And Shared Memory

Multicore architectures adopted two characteristics used in earlier MIMD† computers:

- Parallelism
- Shared Memory

Parallelism. A multicore processor consists of a single computer chip that contains multiple processors that can each operate autonomously. We will see that placing processors on the same chip has advantages over earlier parallel multiprocessor designs.

Shared Memory. All cores on a multicore chip share the same memory. If one core stores a value into location X, and another core later fetches a value from location X, the second core will retrieve the value that the first core deposited.

Figure 20.1 illustrates the conceptual view of a multicore processor with a set of N cores that have access to a common shared memory.

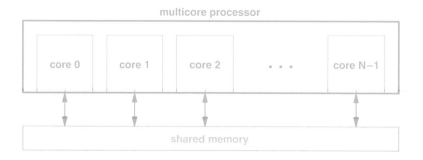

Figure 20.1 The conceptual view of a multicore processor with a set of cores that all access a single shared memory.

Although the basic concept seems straightforward, many details complicate multicore designs. The next sections consider several aspects.

---

†Recall that Multiple Instruction Multiple Data (MIMD) parallelism means that each processor has its own program code and the code may operate on data items specific to the processor.

20.4 Multicore Processor Vs. Multiprocessor

By the 1980s, the computer industry produced several commercial multiprocessor computer systems. Although some multiprocessor designs arranged for each processor to have its own memory, several designs arranged for all the processors to share a single memory, which means the systems followed the same overall organization as a multicore processor. The question arises: what distinguishes a multicore processor from the earlier multiprocessors that used shared memory?

In general, a multiprocessor consists of completely independent computer systems connected by a communication mechanism (e.g., a network, switching fabric, or bus). The systems each operate independently. Software running on the systems can send messages to the software on another processor, but the hardware remains relatively independent. In contrast, a multicore chip design integrates all cores into a single, cohesive system, and the hardware permits cores to coordinate.

The next sections explain the following features of multicore processors that distinguish them from traditional multiprocessors:

- Asymmetry
- Direct communication among cores
- Tight coupling and extremely low latency
- Shared access to all I/O devices
- The ability to associate interrupts with cores
- The ability to start and stop cores
- Coordinated memory caches

20.5 Asymmetry

Parallel computer designs use the term *symmetric* (or *homogeneous*) to characterize a computer built from a set of identical processors, and the term *asymmetric* (or *heterogeneous*) to characterize a computer built from a set of processors that do not all have the same type. Early commercial multiprocessors typically followed a symmetric approach, leading to the term *Symmetric Multi-Processor* (*SMP*). In terms of a multicore chip, the first multicore designs also followed a symmetric approach with each core identical to the other cores. With the rising popularity of GPUs, some multicore designs have adopted the heterogeneous approach by including a set of GPU cores in addition to a set of conventional CPU cores.

A symmetric multicore chip has two advantages. First, the vendor does not need to choose a mix of processor types when designing a chip. Thus, the vendor does not risk having too many or too few of a given type of processor. Second, homogeneity makes operating system software easier to write because the operating system can schedule a computational task on any idle core.

20.6 Direct Communication Among Cores

A multicore chip contains a hardware mechanism that cores use to communicate with one another. Although details vary among vendors and models, the general idea remains the same: a given core can use the mechanism to contact another core. Software running on one core can initiate contact with another core.

As Chapter 13 discusses, most computer systems use bus hardware to interconnect the functional units of a computer. We can imagine that the interconnect among cores consists of a special-purpose bus. Unlike an external bus that connects a processor to I/O devices, the bus that interconnects cores resides entirely on the processor chip. We say that the bus is *on-board* the chip.

Some multiprocessors have a dedicated on-board bus that only provides communication among cores. In other multiprocessors, the on-board bus also has a connection to an external bus that connects the processor to memory and I/O devices. Figure 20.2 illustrates how an on-board bus might connect to an external bus.

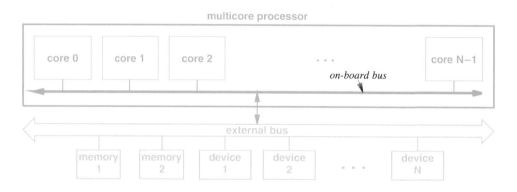

Figure 20.2 Illustration of an internal bus that connects cores to one another and to an external bus.

20.7 Tight Coupling And Extremely Low Latency

In a traditional multiprocessor system, an external bus, switching fabric, or computer network interconnects the processors. Such interconnections span a chassis with multiple boards. As a result, the latency required for communication between two processors includes the time required to pass an item from a processor chip though interface hardware to an external bus or network controller, across the interconnect mechanism to another system, and then through the interface on that system to the processor.

In contrast to a traditional multiprocessor, the internal bus connecting cores only spans the multicore chip (i.e., at most a few centimeters instead of multiple meters). Thus, in terms of latency, inter-core communication occurs orders of magnitude faster than inter-processor communication on a traditional multiprocessor. We use the term *coupling* to refer to processor interconnection, and say that the on-board bus makes the cores in a multicore chip more *tightly coupled* than the *loosely coupled* interconnection in a traditional multiprocessor.

A tightly coupled architecture permits software to treat the cores as a single set of resources. That is, an operating system can assign the cores to computational tasks as needed, and can move a core from one task to another quickly. In particular, we will see that an operating system can assign a core to an application program, allow the core to run the application, and then move the core to another application.

20.8 Shared Access To All I/O Devices

As Figure 20.2 illustrates, each core can use the on-board bus to access the external bus. Thus, each core can access I/O devices as well as memory. Because any core can run code that initiates data transfer or control operations on a device, any core can interact directly with any device.

The idea of arranging the hardware to allow any core to access any device may seem unimportant. However, the alternative — arranging for one core to perform all I/O — imposes overhead that slows I/O operations. In essence, one core "owns" all the I/O devices and only that core can communicate with them directly. All other cores must perform I/O indirectly by passing requests to the core that handles I/O.

20.9 The Ability To Associate Interrupts With Specific Cores

The tightly coupled approach means architects anticipate that software running on a multicore chip will coordinate and use all cores. In particular, they assume that an operating system will manage the assignment of cores to computational tasks. For example, if a user runs three applications concurrently, the operating system may assign core 0 to the first application, core 1 to the second application, and core 2 to the third application.

An operating system must also arrange how to handle device interrupts. To optimize interrupt handling, a multicore processor allows the operating system to configure the hardware with a specific core for each device. That is, instead of merely posting an interrupt on the bus and allowing the hardware to pass the interrupt to the first core that responds, the operating system can *pin* each device to a specific core. When the device interrupts, the interrupt only affects the core to which the device has been pinned; other cores continue processing without being interrupted.

To which core should a given device be pinned? Operating systems have used two approaches:

- Pin all interrupts to the same core
- Pin interrupts to multiple cores

Pin all interrupts to the same core. Using one core (e.g., core 0) separates interrupt processing from other processing, and leaves all other cores free to run applications. However, pinning all interrupts to the same core means that the system can only handle one interrupt at a time, even if other cores remain idle. Thus, restricting interrupts to a single core can lower overall I/O performance.

Pin interrupts to multiple cores. To maximize performance, use all cores to handle interrupts. That is, configure the hardware so that interrupts from the first device go to core 0, interrupts from the second device go to core 1, and so on. If a system contains more devices than cores, at least one of the cores must handle interrupts from more than one device. To keep the performance high, balance the interrupt processing load as evenly as possible. For example, if a core has already been assigned a high-speed device, assign the core a low-speed device rather than another high-speed device.

To summarize:

> *Multicore hardware allows the operating system to pin the interrupts from a given device to a specified core. Balancing the interrupt load across cores can maximize I/O performance.*

20.10 The Ability To Start And Stop Cores

In a traditional multiprocessor, booting a processor incurs significant overhead. The hardware, including the bus, memory, and I/O devices, must power up. Then the processor must run the initial bootstrap that loads the operating system into memory, and the operating system must configure interrupt vectors and device drivers.

Because it follows a tightly coupled approach and uses shared memory, booting an additional core on a multicore processor takes much less time than booting an independent processor. When it first powers up, a multicore chip starts core 0, which performs the same startup steps as a single-core processor. When it boots an additional core, however, the hardware has already been initialized, the memory has already been configured, the operating system has been already been loaded, and the devices have already been initialized. Thus, the operating system only needs to make a few minor changes before the new core can begin processing. For example, the operating system may choose to change interrupts to associate one or more devices with the new core.

Multicore systems also include a mechanism that can be used to stop a core. Of course, cores must be stopped when a system shuts down. However, the ability to stop and restart cores quickly offers an important advantage for a tightly coupled system: power savings. As the next chapter explains, power management has become an important aspect of computer systems. When a user runs multiple applications, the operating system can assign one core to each application. Without the ability to stop cores, once a user terminates an application, the core that was running the application will sit idle until the user runs a new application. Stopping an idle core reduces power consumption, which can extend the battery life for a battery-powered device or reduce energy cost for a system that does not use battery power.

To summarize:

> *Multicore architectures include mechanisms to stop and restart extra
> cores quickly. Instead of leaving idle cores running, an operating sys-
> tem uses the mechanisms to stop idle cores and thereby reduce power
> consumption.*

20.11 Shared Memory And Multicore Caching

Chapter 10 describes memory caching and explains that caching serves as a fundamental optimization required for high-speed memory access. The chapter defines the
three levels of memory caches: L1, L2, and L3. Like conventional processors, a multicore processor relies on caching to improve the speed of memory access. A question
arises: where should the L1, L2, and L3 caches be placed in a multicore processor?

In a conventional processor, a single L1 cache resides on the processor chip. The
design makes sense because the processor is likely to reference the same cache line repeatedly (e.g., to fetch instructions from successive memory locations). In a multicore
processor, however, each core typically runs a different application than other cores.
Consequently, the set of memory addresses that a core references will differ from the
set of memory addresses another core references. If all cores share a single L1 cache,
cores would compete for cache lines. When a core references memory, the value for the
referenced address moves into one of the lines in the cache. Then, when another core
references memory, the address it references moves into a cache line. Once the cache
become full, each memory reference will displace an item cached by another core. As a
result, the cache will not perform well because the probability of a cache hit becomes
low.

To avoid competition for L1 cache lines, a multicore design provides each core
with its own L1 cache. Thus, other cores cannot affect values that a core places in its
L1 cache — a value can only be replaced when the core that owns the cache needs
space for a new value. We say that the L1 cache is *private* to the core.

What about an L2 cache? Some multicore architectures give each core a private
L2 cache as well as a private L1 cache. Other multicore architectures use a shared L2
cache. The choice between private and shared L2 caches represents a tradeoff: having a
private L2 cache for each core increases performance, but also increases the power consumed.

20.12 Cache Inconsistency

Although the design increases performance, having a shared memory and a
separate L1 cache for each core introduces a potential problem: cache inconsistency†.
To understand the problem, consider what might happen if two cores access and update
the same variable in memory. Figure 20.3 illustrates one possible error.

---

†The inconsistency problem occurs in any multiprocessor in which each processor has a separate cache

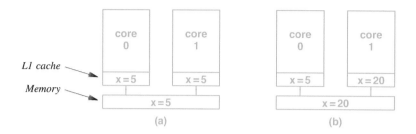

Figure 20.3 (a) Cores 0 and 1 access variable x in memory and cache the value, which is 5. (b) Later, core 1 stores 20 into x, which makes the value in core 0's cache invalid.

We use the term *stale* to refer to an outdated value left in a cache after another core has changed the value. In the figure, when core 1 changed the value of variable x, the change made the value 5 in core 0's cache stale.

20.13 Preventing Inconsistency: Cache Coherence

To avoid inconsistencies and stale cached values, a multicore processor includes an extra hardware mechanism in each cache that coordinates all caches and keeps the values consistent. The caches communicate over the on-board bus. We use the informal term *snooping* to describe a cache watching the on-board bus, and the term *cache coherence* to describe the effect of preventing any core from using a stale value.

Multicore caches have used two approaches to provide cache coherence.

- Snooping
- Invalidation

Snooping. To implement snooping, the hardware in each cache watches the on-board bus. When another core stores value V to memory address A, the hardware checks the local cache for address A. If the local cache contains address A, the coherence hardware extracts V from the bus and replaces the cached value with V. If the local cache does not already contain address A, the coherence hardware for that cache ignores the new store operation (i.e., does not create a new cache entry for address A).

Invalidation. As with snooping, the hardware in each cache uses the on-board bus for invalidation. When another core stores a value V to memory address A, the hardware sends a signal over the bus to indicate that previously cached values of address A should be invalidated. When the bus contains an invalidation signal for address A, the coherence hardware on each cache checks the local cache for address A. If an entry exists, instead of updating the value, the coherence hardware invalidates the entry†.

---

†Our description of invalidation only covers the basic approach; more sophisticated invalidation mechanisms exist that permit variables to be shared.

Both snooping and invalidation guarantee that all cores see consistent values for all memory addresses. In the case of snooping, if a cache contains an entry for address A, the cache will contain the latest value that has been stored into A. In the case of invalidation, when another core stores to address A, the coherence hardware will invalidate the entry for A in the cache, forcing the processor to obtain the new value from memory.

Interestingly, systems that use invalidation tend to perform better than systems that use snooping. To understand why, consider what happens every time a *store* operation occurs. Snooping requires the cache coherence hardware to extract both an address and a value from the bus, and then must locate and update the cached entry. Invalidation does not require the hardware to extract the value. Furthermore, after one core issues a *store* operation, the address will be effectively removed from all other caches. Thus, if a core issues successive *store* operations to the same address (typical behavior), other caches will only need to change the cached value on the first *store* operation.

To summarize:

> *Cache coherence hardware can use snooping or invalidation. Although both approaches work correctly, invalidation performs better in most cases.*

20.14 Programming Multicore: Threads And Scheduling

How should cores be allocated to computational tasks? In general, spreading tasks across cores maximizes parallelism, two approaches have been used:

- Build a parallel program that manages cores
- Use threads and allow the operating system to manage cores

Build a parallel program that manages cores. The approach requires a programmer to design an application that chooses how to use multiple cores (i.e., when to start them, when to stop them, and exactly what computation each core will handle). The scientific computing community often uses the approach by creating an application that divides input data into K subsets and uses K cores to process the subsets simultaneously. Unfortunately, conventional applications cannot be divided among cores easily, and the resulting performance has been disappointing.

Use threads and allow the operating system to manage cores. The chief alternative to building a special-purpose parallel program consists of writing programs that use an operating system abstraction known as a *thread of control*† to exploit multicore parallelism. When a user runs a sequential application, the operating system creates a new thread of control to run the program. A concurrent application may choose to create additional threads (e.g., a concurrent web server creates a new thread for each incoming request).

---

†Some operating systems use the term process.

An operating system chooses how to assign threads onto cores. If a multicore processor has N cores and the applications currently running on the system have a total of $T<N$ threads, the operating system can assign one thread to each core so that all threads run simultaneously. For example, if a user simultaneously plays music and sends a text, the operating system might assign the music application to core 0 and the text application to core 1.

If a user starts more applications than cores (i.e., $T>N$), the operating system must use a timesharing approach by assigning a thread to each core and then later moving core(s) to other threads. Some operating systems divide threads into N groups and assign each group to one of the cores. A core runs one of its assigned threads for a while, then runs another for a while, and so on.

20.15 Thread Scheduling And Affinity

The exact details of which threads a core runs and how long the core spends running one thread before moving to another depend on the operating system. Some operating systems schedule processing so that over a period of time, all threads receive approximately the same amount of processor time. Although it seems fair, such a policy can lead to unfairness because an application that creates more threads will receive more processor time.

To avoid having one application receive significantly more processor time than another, some operating systems assign a core (or set of cores) to each application. Each time the application creates an additional thread, the new thread inherits the assignment from the original application. Consider what happens when a user launches an application. The operating system creates a thread for the application and must assign a core to run the thread. Suppose the operating system assigns core 2. If the application creates nine additional threads, each of the nine will inherit the assignment, so all ten of the threads for the application will execute on core 2. The core can only run one of the ten threads at a given time, which means that even though the application has created many threads, the application will only receive a total of one full-time core.

To implement the assignment of cores to applications, an operating system may use an *affinity mask*. The mask consists of a bit string with one bit for each core. If the ith bit has the value 1, the application is permitted to use core i. A newly created thread inherits a copy of the affinity mask from the thread that creates it (i.e., from the *parent* thread). Consequently, all threads from a given application run on the set of cores assigned when the application is launched.

To summarize:

> *An operating system must choose how to schedule threads on cores. The system can use an affinity mask to help guarantee fairness and prevent an application that creates many threads from receiving more processor time than other applications.*

20.16 Simultaneous Multi-Threading (SMT)

Allowing an operating system to schedule processing among threads works well for most applications. However, a question arises: can a system achieve higher parallelism among threads? To understand increased parallelism, consider two threads that have been assigned to a given core. Suppose one of the two is about to execute a floating point multiplication and the other is about to execute an integer addition. The floating point multiplication uses a floating point unit and the integer addition uses an ALU. In theory, the thread performing integer calculations could run at the same time as the thread performing a floating point calculation because a floating point hardware unit and an ALU can operate simultaneously. Of course, if the two threads both attempted to execute instructions that use the same hardware unit, only one of them could proceed.

Multicore vendors have created a technology known as *Simultaneous Multi-Threading (SMT)*, which Intel calls *hyperthreading*. The technology requires advanced hardware that has:

- Knowledge of available threads
- Knowledge of the internal hardware units each instruction uses
- A thread scheduler

Knowledge of available threads. To use an SMT system, the operating system must configure the hardware for a core with information about a set of threads to run on the core at a given time. The hardware must know the contents of general-purpose and special-purpose registers that each thread is using, including a program counter that specifies the next instruction to execute.

Knowledge of the internal hardware units each instruction uses. An SMT system must know which internal hardware units each instruction uses when it executes and which hardware units the instruction does not use. For example, SMT hardware must know that a floating point multiplication uses the floating point registers and the floating point multiplication unit, and must know that a floating point instruction does not use the ALU.

A thread scheduler. Unlike a conventional multicore processor that requires an operating system to schedule one thread at a given time on each core, an SMT system has a small scheduler built into the hardware. The operating system configures the SMT hardware with information about the set of threads to run, and the SMT scheduler examines the next instruction that each thread will execute, and allows threads to proceed simultaneously as long as the instruction in each thread only uses internal hardware units that none of the instructions in other threads use. To support SMT, the hardware contains K parallel copies of registers, with one copy for each thread. We can imagine that instead of a sequential scheduler examining the K possible threads one-at-a-time, parallel hardware checks all K threads simultaneously, and allows threads to proceed when they are ready.

In practice, some SMT hardware offers more sophisticated capabilities that help guarantee fairness among cores. For example, suppose three threads have been assigned to a core and all three execute a series of instructions that use the ALU, the SMT scheduler chooses threads round-robin to prevent one thread from running continuously and denying processing to the other two threads.

To summarize:

> *An SMT system uses special parallel hardware that allows multiple threads to run simultaneously on a given core as long as the internal hardware unit that a thread uses does not overlap with hardware units used by other threads. The operating system configures the SMT hardware in a core with a set of threads, and the SMT scheduling system handles the task of choosing thread(s) to run at a given time.*

20.17 Inter-core Communication Via Messages And Software Interrupts

Many multicore processors run a single operating system that manages all cores by assigning processing tasks and coordinating use of shared devices. In such systems, inter-core communication occurs frequently. For example, a core running the operating system scheduler may need to tell another core when to start running a thread. Similarly, if core X receives a device interrupt and the thread waiting for the I/O happens to be assigned to core Y, core X must tell core Y that the I/O has completed. To handle such cases, multicore processors provide mechanisms for inter-core communication. Possible mechanisms include:

- Inter-core message passing
- Inter-core software interrupts

Inter-core message passing. Recall that a multicore processor contains an internal bus that interconnects cores. An inter-core message-passing facility allows a core to use the bus to send a (small) message to another core. In general, inter-core messages provide *control signals* instead of data. Thus, a core that runs an operating system scheduler may send a message that tells another core to start, switch to a new thread, or stop running the current thread.

Inter-core software interrupts. A software interrupt mechanism allows a core to cause a low-priority interrupt on another core. The interrupt itself does not pass a data item. However, because all cores share memory, an operating system can place a message in the shared memory and then use the software interrupt mechanism to force another core to handle the message.

20.18 Mutual Exclusion Among Cores

In any system where computer programs executing concurrently share memory, interference can occur, resulting in incorrect values. To understand the problem, consider two cores running programs that update a global variable in memory. For example, suppose both cores run software that increments a global integer named *cntr*. A programmer writes:

cntr++

On most architectures, a compiler chooses a register to use and generates a sequence of instructions to perform the increment. If the compiler chooses register 5, the sequence might be:

load the contents of variable cntr into register 5
add 1 to register 5
store the value from register 5 into variable cntr

When it runs on a single core, the code will correctly increment the value of *cntr*. When multiple cores run the code simultaneously, however, the results may be incorrect. Although both cores use register 5, no interference occurs because each core has its own hardware for register 5. Because the cores operate independently, individual operations may occur in any order. Suppose the variable *cntr* currently contains the value 210 when core 2 and core 3 execute code that contains *cntr++*. If the two cores run the code simultaneously, the operations may intermix steps. Figure 20.4 illustrates an order of steps that produces an incorrect value.

Time	Core 2	Core 3
t	load *cntr* into reg 5	
t + 1	increment reg 5	load *cntr* into reg 5
t + 2	store reg 5 into *cntr*	increment reg 5
t + 3		store reg5 into *cntr*

Figure 20.4 An execution sequence on two cores as they each increment variable *cntr*. Core 3 overwrites the value that core 2 has stored.

Two cores execute code to increment *cntr*, which means that the final value should be 212. In fact, at time *t* core 2 fetches the value of *cntr*, and at time *t + 1* core 3 fetches the value. Both cores obtain the value 210. At the time *t + 1*, core 2 increments its copy to 211, and at time *t + 2*, core 2 stores its copy (value 211) into *cntr*. At time *t + 2*, while core 2 is storing its copy, core 3 is incrementing its copy. Finally, at time *t + 3*, core 3 stores its copy, which means *cntr* has a final value of 211 instead of the intended value of 212.

How can software running on multiple cores access shared variables without such errors? The answer lies in hardware mechanisms that guarantee *mutual exclusion*. Mutual exclusion means that only one core accesses a given variable at a given time, even if multiple cores share the variable. To be precise, we say that the mechanisms provide *cooperative mutual exclusion* because exclusion is not automatic. Instead, as we will see, a programmer must insert code that invokes the mutual exclusion mechanism before accessing a shared variable.

20.19 Locks, And Busy Waiting

Several mechanisms have been used for mutual exclusion. Some early multiprocessor systems had a separate hardware unit that provided a set of *locks*, along with special *lock* and *unlock* hardware instructions. The locking system was built so that if multiple processors attempted to lock a given lock simultaneously, one of the processors would succeed and all others would fail.

To use the locking system, software employed a technique known as *busy waiting*. Busy waiting means a program contains a loop that repeatedly attempts to lock one of the locks. If the attempt fails, the loop continues, and the program tries again. If the attempt succeeds, the program exits the loop, uses the shared variable, and then unlocks the lock.

20.20 Using A Memory Location As A Lock (Test-And-Set)

Modern multicore processors do not use a separate hardware unit to provide mutual exclusion locks. Instead, processors integrate locking with memory. Using memory offers a significant advantage: unlike hardware units that have a fixed number of locks, using memory allows software to allocate an arbitrary number of locks. The size of an individual lock depends on the memory architecture, but typically consists of one word. Thus, an operating system might declare each lock to be a global integer, or the system might declare an array of integers to hold all the locks the system uses.

To allow a memory location to serve as a lock, a processor must provide a way to lock the memory location and a way to unlock it. When a memory location contains zero, the location is unlocked; a non-zero value (typically 1) means the location is locked. Unlocking a memory location does not require a special instruction — software stores a zero in the location. Locking a location requires a special instruction that guarantees only one core will succeed when multiple cores attempt to lock the location simultaneously. We use the term *test-and-set* to refer to an instruction used for locking†. Conceptually, a test-and-set instruction performs two steps. First, the instruction tests the memory location to see whether it has already been locked by another core (i.e., contains a non-zero value). Second, the instruction stores a non-zero value in the location. The instruction sets the condition codes to indicate whether the location was already locked before the test-and-set executed.

---

†Intel multicore processors use a variant of test-and-set known as *compare-and-swap*. Although the details differ, compare-and-swap performs the same function of locking a memory location.

To make test-and-set work correctly, a core must perform the two steps *atomically*, which means the hardware prevents other cores from changing the value of the memory location between the two steps. If a memory location contains zero and multiple cores execute test-and-set on the location simultaneously, the hardware allows one of them to set the location and tells the others that the location was already set when they executed the test-and-set instruction.

To summarize:

> *Because it atomically examines a memory location and sets it to a new value, a test-and-set instruction allows software on multiple cores to implement mutual exclusion in which only one core modifies a global variable at any time.*

20.21 An Example Of Test-And-Set

To use test-and-set, software must declare a memory location to serve as a lock, and must follow the busy-waiting approach to access the lock. For example, consider multiple cores incrementing a global variable as shown in Figure 20.4. To prevent multiple cores from accessing and changing the value simultaneously, software must declare a memory location to serve as a lock, use test-and-set to lock the location before incrementing the counter, and unlock the location after incrementing the counter. Figure 20.5 lists the steps.

```
int     cntr = 210;     /* Counter to be updated by multiple cores  */
int     lock1;          /* Memory location to use as a lock          */

/* Try locking until test-and-set succeeds (busy waiting) */
while( test-and-set(lock1) == FAILURE )
        ;  /* continue the loop */

/* Increment the counter (no other cores will interfere */
cntr++;

/* Unlock memory location lock1 */
lock1 = 0;
```

Figure 20.5 The steps software takes when using a mutual exclusion lock to prevent other cores from interfering during update of a shared variable.

Cooperative mutual exclusion places all responsibility on the programmer. The programmer must define a lock variable, and must use test-and-set on the lock before every piece of code that modifies the variable. The point is:

If a programmer accidentally forgets to use test-and-set before modifying a global variable, the resulting value may be incorrect.

20.22 Atomic Update And Cache Coherence

Consider coordinating multiple cores to guarantee that when they execute test-and-set instructions for a given memory location simultaneously exactly one of them succeeds. It may appear that such coordination requires special-purpose hardware units. Interestingly, instead of special-purpose hardware, the coordination can be integrated into the memory cache. Specifically, a small modification to the cache coherence system provides the necessary functionality.

To understand how cache coherence relates to test-and-set, recall that when a core stores a value in a memory location, the entries for the location in each of the other caches must be invalidated. The cache coherence hardware handles the invalidation by sending a message over the internal bus. Thus, each store operation causes a message to propagate across the bus to the caches on other cores. An extension to the coherence mechanism makes it possible for the hardware to detect whether the memory location currently contains a zero or non-zero value. In the case that multiple cores attempt to lock the location simultaneously, the hardware can detect which core succeeded.

20.23 Summary

A multicore processor contains multiple, autonomous processors interconnected by an internal bus, with shared access to memory and I/O devices. An operating system can manage all cores, assigning each device interrupt to a specific core, stopping and starting individual cores as needed, and scheduling threads on the cores. Each core has an independent memory cache, and a cache coherence system keeps the cached data consistent. Cores communicate over the internal bus by using message passing and/or software interrupts.

To prevent interference when cores modify shared variables in memory, a programmer must use mutual exclusion. The hardware offers a special test-and-set instruction that makes mutual exclusion possible by guaranteeing that only one core can lock a given location at a time, even if multiple cores execute test-and-set on the location simultaneously. Instead of adding a separate hardware unit, vendors integrate the hardware that guarantees atomicity of test-and-set with the cache coherence hardware.

Chapter Contents

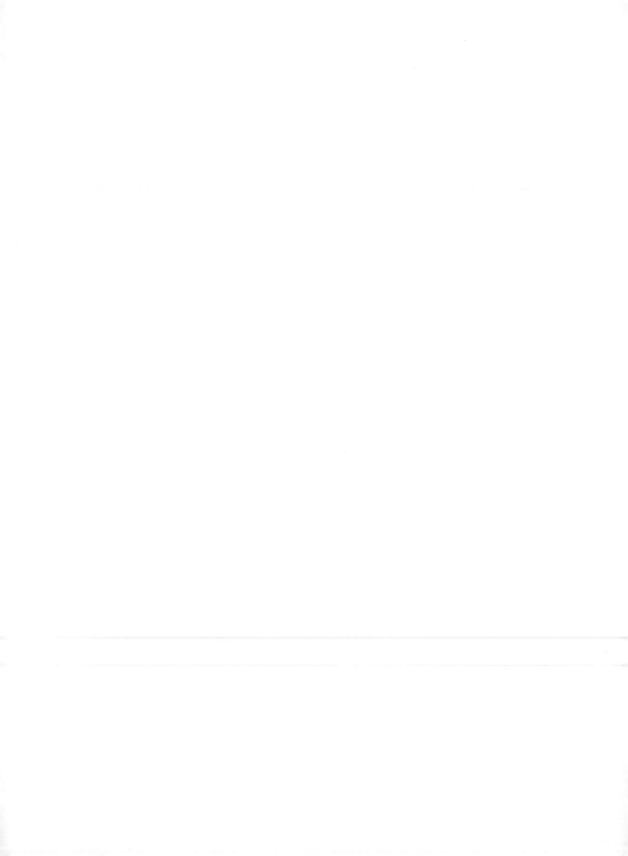

21

Power And Energy

21.1 Introduction

The related topics of power consumption and total energy consumption have become increasingly important in the design of computing systems. For portable devices, designs strive for a balance between maximizing battery life and maximizing features that users desire. For large data centers, the power consumed and the consequent cooling required have become critical factors in the design and scale of the data center.

This brief chapter introduces the topic without going into much detail. It defines terminology, explains the types of power that digital circuits consume, and describes the relationship between power and energy. Most important, the chapter describes how software systems can be used to shut down parts of a system to reduce power consumption.

21.2 Definition Of Power

We define *power* to be the rate at which energy is consumed (e.g., transferred or transformed). For an electronic circuit, power is the product of voltage and current. Taking the definitions from physics, power is measured in units of *watts*, where a watt is defined as one joule per second (J/s). The higher the wattage of an electronic device, the more power it consumes; some devices use *kilowatts* (10^3 watts) of power. For a large data center cluster, the aggregate power consumed by all the computers in the cluster is so large that it is measured in *megawatts* (10^6 watts). For small hand-held devices, such as cell phones, the power requirements are so minimal that they are measured in *milliwatts* (10^{-3} watts).

It is important to note that the amount of power a system uses can vary over time. For example a smart phone uses less power when the display is turned off than when the screen is on. Therefore, to be precise, we define the *instantaneous power* at time t, *P(t)*, to be the product of the voltage at time t, *V(t)*, and the current at time t, *I(t)*:

$$P(t) \; = \; V(t) \times I(t) \tag{21.1}$$

We will see that the ability of a system to vary its power usage over time can be important for both extremely large and extremely small computing systems (e.g., powerful computers in a data center and small battery-powered devices).

The maximum power that a system uses is especially important for large systems, such as a cluster of computers in a data center. We use the term *peak instantaneous power* to specify the maximum power a system will need. Peak power is especially important when constructing a large computing system because the designer must arrange to meet the peak power requirements. For example, when planning a data center, a designer must guarantee that an electric utility can supply sufficient power to meet the peak instantaneous power demand.

21.3 Definition Of Energy

From the above, the total *energy* that a system uses is computed as the power consumed over a given time, measured in joules. Electrical energy is usually reported in multiples of watts multiplied by a unit of time. Typically, the time unit is an hour, and the multiples of watts are kilowatts, megawatts, or milliwatts. Thus, the energy consumed by a data center during a week might be reported in *kilowatt hours (kWh)* or *megawatt hours (MWh)*, and the energy consumed by a battery during a week might be reported in *milliwatt hours (mWh)*.

If power utilization is constant, the energy consumed can be computed easily by multiplying power utilization, *P*, by the time the power is used. For example, during the time period from t_0 to t_1, the energy used is given by:

$$E \; = \; P \times (t_1 - t_0) \tag{21.2}$$

A system that uses exactly 6 kilowatts during an hour has an energy consumption of 6 kWh as does a system that has an energy consumption of 3 kilowatts for a period of two hours.

As we described above, most systems do not consume power at a constant rate. Instead, the power consumption varies over time. To capture the idea that power varies continuously, we define energy to be the integral of instantaneous power over time:

$$E \; = \; \int_{t=t_0}^{t_1} P(t) \, dt \tag{21.3}$$

Although power is defined to be an instantaneous measure that can change over time, some electronic systems specify a value known as the *average power*. Recall that power is the rate at which energy is used, which means the average power over a time interval can be computed by taking the amount of energy used during the interval and dividing by the time:

$$P_{avg} = \frac{E}{(t_1 - t_0)} \qquad (21.4)$$

21.4 Power Consumption By A Digital Circuit

We will learn that a digital circuit is created from logic gates. At the lowest level, each logic gate uses transistors which consume power in two ways†:

- Switching or dynamic power (denoted P_s or P_d)
- Leakage power (denoted P_{leak})

Switching Power. The term *switching* refers to a change in the output in response to an input. When one or more inputs of a gate change, the output may change. A change in output can only occur because electrons flow through transistors. Individual transistors consume more power during switching, which means that the total power for the system increases.

Leakage Power. Although we think of a digital circuit as having a binary value (on or off), solid-state physicists realize that transistors are imperfect switches. That is, even when a transistor is off, a few electrons can penetrate the semiconductor boundary. Therefore, whenever power is supplied to a digital circuit, some amount of current will always flow, even if the outputs are not switching. We use the term *leakage* to refer to current that flows when a circuit is not operating.

For a given transistor, the amount of leakage current is insignificant. However, a single processor can have a billion transistors, meaning that the aggregate leakage current can be quite high. In fact, for some digital systems, the leakage current accounts for more than half of the power utilization. The point can be summarized:

> *In a typical computing system, leakage power accounts for 40 to 60 percent of the power the system consumes.*

A further fact about leakage concerns how it can be managed. A basic principle asserts that leakage always occurs when power is present:

> *Leakage current can only be eliminated by removing power from a circuit.*

---

†In addition to the two major sources, a transistor consumes a minor amount of *short-circuit power* when it switches between logical 1 and 0 because electrical current powering the transistor temporarily flows to the

21.5 Switching Power Consumed By A CMOS Digital Circuit

Modern systems often use software to manage power consumption. To understand power management techniques, we need a few basic concepts. First, we will consider the total energy consumed by switching. The energy, required for a single change of a gate is denoted E_d, and is given by:

$$E_d = \frac{1}{2} C V_{dd}^2 \tag{21.5}$$

where C is a value of capacitance that depends on the underlying CMOS technology, and V_{dd} is the voltage at which the circuit operates†.

To understand the power consequences of Equation 21.5, consider a clock. The clock generates a square wave at a fixed frequency. Suppose the clock signal is connected to an inverter. The inverter output will change twice during a clock cycle, once when the clock goes from zero to one and once when the clock goes from one back to zero. Therefore, if the clock has period T_{clock}, the average power used is:

$$P_{avg} = \frac{C V_{dd}^2}{T_{clock}} \tag{21.6}$$

The frequency of the clock is the inverse of the period:

$$F_{clock} = \frac{1}{T_{clock}} \tag{21.7}$$

which means we can rewrite Equation 21.6 in terms of clock frequency:

$$P_{avg} = C V_{dd}^2 F_{clock} \tag{21.8}$$

One additional term is used to compute the average power: a fraction of the circuit whose outputs are switching. We use α to denote the fraction, $0 \leq \alpha \leq 1$, which makes the final form of Equation 21.8 for average power:

$$P_{avg} = \alpha C V_{dd}^2 F_{clock} \tag{21.9}$$

Equation 21.9 captures the three main components of power that are pertinent to the following discussion. Constant C is a property of the underlying technology and cannot be changed easily. Thus, the three components that can be controlled are:

- The fraction of the circuit that is active, α

- The clock frequency, F_{clock}

- The voltage in the circuit, V_{dd}

---

†The notation V_{dd} is used to specify the voltage used to operate a CMOS circuit; the notation V (voltage) can be used if the context is understood.

21.6 Cooling, Power Density, And The Power Wall

Recall that instantaneous power use is often associated with data centers or other large installations where a key aspect is peak power utilization. In addition to the question of whether an electric utility is able to deliver the megawatts needed during peak use, designers focus on two other aspects of power use: cooling and power density.

Cooling. When a digital device operates, it generates heat. A huge power load means many devices are operating, and each device is generating heat. Consequently, the heat being produced is related to the power being consumed. All electronic circuits must be cooled or circuits will overheat and burn out. For the smallest devices, enough heat escapes to the surrounding air that no further cooling is needed. For medium-size devices, cooling requires a fan that blows cold air across the circuits constantly; the air must be brought in through a *Heating, Ventilation, and Air Conditioning (HVAC)* system. In the most extreme cases, air cooling is insufficient, and a form of liquid cooling is required.

Power Density. Although the total amount of heat a circuit produces dictates the total cooling capacity required, another aspect of heat is important: the concentration of heat in a small area. In a data center, for example, if many computers are placed adjacent to one another, they can overheat. Thus, spacing is added between computers and between racks of computers to permit cool air to flow through the racks and remove heat.

Power density is also important on an individual integrated circuit, where power density refers to the amount of power that is dissipated per a given area of silicon. For many years, the semiconductor industry followed Moore's Law. The size of an individual transistor continued to shrink, and every eighteen months, the number of transistors that fit on a single chip doubled. However, following Moore's Law had a negative aspect: power density also increased. As power density increases, the amount of heat generated per unit area increases, which means that a modern processor produces much more heat per square centimeter than earlier processors.

Consequently, packing transistors closer together has led to a major problem: we are reaching the limits of the rate at which heat can be removed from a chip. Engineers refer to the limit as the *power wall* because it means power cannot be increased. With current cooling technologies, the limit can be approximated:

$$PowerWall \quad \approx \quad 100 \ \frac{watts}{cm^2} \qquad\qquad (21.10)$$

21.7 Energy Use

Unlike power, which measures instantaneous flow of current, energy measures the total power consumed over a given time interval. A focus on energy is especially pertinent to portable devices that use batteries. We can think of a battery as a bucket of energy, and imagine the device extracting energy as needed. The total time a battery can power a device (measured in milliwatt hours) is derived from the amount of energy in the battery.

Modeling a battery as a bucket of energy (analogous to a bucket of water) is overly simplistic. However, three aspects of water buckets apply to batteries. First, like water in a bucket, the energy stored in a battery can evaporate. In the case of a battery, chemical and physical processes are imperfect — internal resistance allows a trivial amount of current to flow inside the battery. Although the flow is almost imperceptible, allowing a battery to sit for a long time (e.g., a year) will result in loss of charge. Second, just as some of the water poured from a bucket is likely to spill when extracting energy from a battery, some of the energy is lost. Third, energy can be removed from a battery at various rates, just as water can be extracted from a bucket at various rates. The important idea behind the third property is a battery becomes more efficient at lower current levels (i.e., lower power levels). Thus, designers look for ways to minimize power that a battery-operated device consumes.

21.8 Power Management

The above discussion shows that reducing power consumption is desirable in all cases. In a large data center, reducing power consumption reduces the heat generated. For a small portable device, reducing power consumption extends the battery life. Two questions arise: what methods can be used to reduce power consumption, and which of the power reduction techniques can be controlled by software?

Recall from Equation 21.9†, three primary factors contribute to power consumption: α, the fraction of a circuit that is active, F_{clock}, the clock frequency, and V_{dd}, the voltage used to operate a circuit. The next sections describe how voltage and frequency can be used to reduce power consumption; a later section considers the fraction of a circuit that is active.

21.8.1 Voltage And Delay

Because power utilization depends on the square of the voltage, lowering voltage will produce the largest reduction in power. However, voltage is not an independent variable. First, decreasing voltage increases *gate delay*, the time a gate takes to change its outputs after inputs change. A processor is designed carefully so that all hardware units operate according to the clock. If the delay for a single gate becomes sufficiently large, the delay across an entire hardware unit (many gates) will exceed the design specification.

For current technology, the delay can be estimated by:

$$Delay \quad = \quad \beta \quad \frac{K \; V_{dd}}{(\, V_{dd} - V_{TH} \,)} \tag{21.11}$$

---

†Equation 21.9 can be found on page 394.

where V_{dd} is the voltage used, V_{TH} is a *threshold voltage* determined by the underlying CMOS technology, K is a constant that depends on the technology, and β is a constant (approximately 1.3 for current technology).

A second aspect of power is related to voltage: leakage current. The leakage current depends on the temperature of a circuit and the threshold voltage of the CMOS technology. Lowering voltage decreases leakage current, but has an interesting consequence: lower voltage means increased delay, which results in more total energy being consumed. To understand why decreasing leakage can be significant, recall that leakage can account for 40% to 60% of the power a circuit uses. The point is:

> *Although power depends on the square of voltage, reducing voltage increases delay which increases total energy usage.*

Despite the problems, voltage is the most significant factor in power reduction. Therefore, researchers who work on solid-state physics and silicon technologies have devised transistors that operate correctly at much lower voltages. For example, although early digital circuits operated at 5 volts, current technologies used in cell phones operate at lower voltages. A fully charged cell phone battery provides about 4 volts, and the circuits continue to operate as the battery discharges. In fact, some cell phones that use NiMH battery technology can still receive calls with a battery that provides only 1.2 volts, and the phone only declares a battery dead when the voltage falls below 0.8 volts. (Lithium-based batteries tend to die at approximately 3.65 volts.)

21.8.2 Decreasing Clock Frequency

Clock frequency forms a second factor in power utilization. In theory, power is proportional to clock frequency, so slowing the clock will save power. In practice, reducing the clock frequency lowers performance, which may be critical in systems that have real-time requirements (e.g., a system that displays video or plays music).

Interestingly, adjusting the clock frequency can be used in conjunction with a reduction in voltage. That is, a slower clock can accommodate the increased delays that a lower voltage causes. Thus, if a designer decreases the clock frequency as voltage is decreased, performance will suffer but the circuit will operate correctly.

When both clock frequency and voltage are reduced, the resulting reduction in power can be dramatic. In one specific case, reducing the frequency to one-half the original rate allowed the voltage to be divided by 1.7. Because voltage is squared in the power equation (Equation 21.9), reducing the voltage allows the resulting power to be reduced dramatically. For the example, the resulting power was approximately 15% of the original power. Although the savings depend on the technology being used, the general idea can be summarized:

If a circuit can deliver adequate performance with a reduced clock frequency, power can be cut dramatically because reducing the clock frequency also allows voltage to be reduced.

Intel has invented an interesting twist on reduced clock frequency by permitting dynamic changes. The idea is straightforward. When the processor is busy, the operating system sets the clock frequency high. If the processor exceeds a preset thermal limit (i.e., overheats) or a power limit (e.g., would drain a battery quickly), the operating system reduces the clock frequency until the processor operates within the prescribed limits. For example, clock frequency might be increased or decreased dynamically by multiples of 100 MHz. If the processor is idle, the clock frequency can also be reduced to save energy. Instead of advertising the capability as dynamic speed reduction, Intel marketing turns the situation around and advertises the feature as *Turbo Boost*.

21.8.3 Slower Clock Frequency And Multicore Processors

In the early 2000s, at the same time power utilization was becoming a problem, chip vendors introduced *multicore processors*. On the surface, a shift to multicore architectures seems counterproductive because two cores will require twice as much power as a single core. Of course, the cores may share some of the circuitry (e.g., a memory or bus interface), which means the power consumption of a dual-core chip will not be exactly double the power consumption of a single core chip. However, a second core adds substantial additional power requirements.

Why would vendors introduce more cores if reducing power consumption is important? To understand, look carefully at clock frequency. Before multicore chips appeared, clock frequency increased every few years as new processors appeared. We know from the above discussion that slowing down a clock to one-half of its original speed allows voltage to be lowered and cuts power consumption significantly. Now consider a dual-core chip. Suppose that each core runs at one-half the clock frequency of a single-core chip. The computational power of the dual-core version is still approximately the same as a single core that runs twice as fast. In terms of power utilization, however, the voltage can be reduced, which means that each of the two cores takes a fraction, F, of the power required by the single-core version. As a result, the multicore chip takes approximately $2F$ as much power as the single core version. Provided F is less than 50%, the slower dual-core chip consumes less power. In the example above, F is 15%, which means a dual-core chip will provide equivalent computational power at only 30% of the original power requirements. We can summarize:

A multicore chip in which each core runs at a slower clock frequency and lower voltage can deliver approximately the same computational capability as a single core chip while incurring significantly lower power utilization.

Of course, the discussion above makes an important assumption about multicore processing. Namely, it assumes that computation can be divided among multiple cores. Unfortunately, Chapter 17 points out that experience with parallelism has not been promising. For computations where a parallel approach is not feasible, a slow clock can make the system unusable. Even in cases where some parallelism is feasible, memory contention and other inefficiencies can result in disappointing performance. When parallel processing is used to handle multiple input items at the same time, overall throughput from two cores can be the same as that of a single, faster core. However, latency (i.e., the time required to process a given item) is higher. Finally, one should remember that the discussion has focused on switching power — leakage can still be a significant problem.

21.9 Software Control Of Energy Use

Software on a system usually has little or no ability to make minor increases or decreases in the voltage used. Instead, software is often restricted to two basic operations:

- Clock gating
- Power gating

Clock Gating. The term refers to reducing the clock frequency to zero which effectively stops a processor. Before a processor can be stopped, a programmer must arrange for a way to restart it. Typically, the code image is kept in memory, and the memory retains power. Thus, the image remains ready whenever the processor restarts.

Power Gating. The term refers to cutting off power from the processor. A special solid-state device that has extremely low leakage current is used to cut off power. As with clock gating, a programmer must arrange for a restart, either by saving and then restoring a copy of the memory image or by ensuring that the memory remains powered on so the image is retained.

Systems that offer power gating capabilities do not apply gating across the entire system. Instead, the system is divided into *islands*, and gating is applied to some islands while others continue to operate normally. Memory cache forms a particularly important power island — if power is removed from a memory cache, all cached data will be lost. We know from Chapter 10 that caching is important for performance. Therefore, a memory cache can be placed in a power island that is not shut down when power is removed from other parts of the processor.

Some processors extend the idea to provide a set of *low-power modes* that software can use to reduce power consumption. Vendors use a variety of names to describe the modes, such as *sleep*, *deep sleep*, and *hibernation*. We will use the generic names *LPM0, LPM1, LPM2, LPM3*, and *LPM4*. In general, low-power modes are arranged in a hierarchy. LPM0 turns off the least amount of circuitry and has the fastest recovery. LPM4, the deepest sleep mode, turns off almost the entire processor. As a consequence, restarting from LPM4 takes much longer than other low-power modes.

21.10 Choosing When To Sleep And When To Awaken

Two questions must be answered: when should a system enter a sleep mode, and when should it awaken? Choosing when to awaken from sleep mode is usually straight-forward: wake up *on demand*. That is, the hardware waits until an event occurs that re-quires the processor, and the hardware then moves the processor out of sleep mode. For example, a screen saver restarts the display whenever a user moves a mouse, touches a touch-sensitive screen, or presses a key on a keyboard.

The question of when to enter a low-power mode is more complex. The motiva-tion is to reduce power utilization. Therefore, we want to *gate* power to a subsystem (i.e., turn it off) if the subsystem will not be needed for a reasonably long time. Be-cause we usually cannot know future requirements, most systems employ a heuristic to estimate when a subsystem will be needed: if a sufficiently long period of inactivity oc-curs, assume the subsystem will remain inactive for a while longer. Typically, if a pro-cessor or a device remains inactive for N seconds, the processor or device enters a sleep mode. The heuristic can also be applied to cause deeper sleep — if a processor remains in a light sleep state for K seconds, the hardware moves the processor to a deeper sleep state (i.e., additional parts of the processor are turned off).

What value of N should be used as a timeout for sleep mode? Subsystems that provide interaction with a human user typically allow the user to choose a timeout. For example, a screen saver allows a user to specify how long the input devices should remain idle before the screen saver runs. Allowing users to specify a timeout means that each user can tailor the system to their needs.

Choosing a timeout for a system that does not involve human preference requires a more careful analysis. A simplified model will help illustrate the calculation. For the model, we will assume two states: a *RUN* state in which the processor runs with full power and an *OFF* state in which all power is removed. When the processor makes a transition, some time elapses, which we denote $T_{shutdown}$ and T_{wakeup}. Figure 21.1 illus-trates the simplified model.

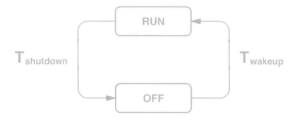

Figure 21.1 A simplified model of transitions among low-power modes.

Each transition uses power (i.e., hardware that saves state information or prepares I/O devices for the transition consumes power). To make calculations easier, we will assume that the power used during a transition remains constant. With the assumption of constant power use during a transition, we can calculate the energy required by multiplying the power used by the time that elapses during the transition:

$$E_{shutdown} \quad = \quad E_s \quad = \quad P_{shutdown} \times T_{shutdown} \tag{21.12}$$

and

$$E_{wakeup} \quad = \quad E_w \quad = \quad P_{wakeup} \times T_{wakeup} \tag{21.13}$$

Understanding the energy required for transitions and the energy used when the system runs and when it is shut down allows us to assess potential energy savings. In essence, shutting down is beneficial if shutdown, sleep, and later wakeup consume less energy than continuing to run over the same time interval.

Let t be the time interval being considered. If we assume the power used by the running system is constant, the energy consumed when the system remains running for time t is:

$$E_{run} \quad = \quad P_{run} \times t \tag{21.14}$$

The energy consumed if the system is put into sleep mode for time t consists of the energy required for each of the transitions plus P_{off}, the energy used (if any) while the processor is shut down:

$$E_{sleep} \quad = \quad E_s \ + \ E_w \ + \ P_{off} \ (\ t \ - \ T_{shutdown} \ - \ T_{wakeup} \ ) \tag{21.15}$$

Shutting down the system will be beneficial if:

$$E_{sleep} \quad < \quad E_{run} \tag{21.16}$$

By using Equations 21.12 through 21.15, the inequality can be expressed in terms of a single free variable, the time interval t. Therefore, it is possible to compute a *break-even point* that specifies the minimum value of t for which shutting down saves energy.

Of course, the analysis above is based on a simplified model. Power usage may not remain constant; the time and power required for transitions may depend on the state of the system. More important, the analysis focuses on energy consumed by switching and ignores leakage. However, the analysis does illustrate a basic point:

> *Even for a simplified model with only one low-power state, details such as the energy used during state transitions complicate the decision about when to move to low-power mode.*

21.11 Sleep Modes And Network Devices

Many devices have a low-power mode that is used to save energy. For example, a printer usually sleeps after N minutes of inactivity. Similarly, wireless network adapters can enter a sleep mode to reduce power consumption. For a network adapter, handling output (transmission) is trivial because the adapter can be awakened whenever an application generates an outgoing packet. However, input (reception) poses a difficult challenge for low-power mode because a computer cannot know when another computer will send a packet.

One approach uses low-power polling. For example, the Wi-Fi (802.11) standard includes a *Power Saving Polling* (*PSP*) mode. To save power, laptops and other devices using Wi-Fi shut down and only wake up periodically. We use the term *duty-cycle* to characterize the repeated cycle of a device running and then being shut down. A radio must be up when an access point transmits. A Wi-Fi base station periodically sends a beacon that includes a list of recipients for which the base station has undelivered packets. The beacon is frequent enough so a device is guaranteed to receive the beacon during the part of the duty cycle when they are awake. If a device finds itself on the recipient list, the device remains awake to receive the packet.

Two basic approaches have been used to allow a network adapter to sleep without missing packets indefinitely. In one approach, each device synchronizes its sleep cycles with the base station. In the other approach, a base station repeatedly transmits each packet multiple times until the receiver has time to wake up and receive it.

21.12 Summary

Power gives an instantaneous measure of the rate at which energy is used; energy is the total amount of power used over a given time. A digital circuit consumes dynamic or switching power when an output changes in response to the change of an input. In addition, unavoidable leakage power results from the physical properties of semiconductors. Leakage can account for 40 to 60 percent of the power a circuit consumes.

Power consumption can be reduced by making parts of a circuit inactive, reducing the clock frequency, and reducing the voltage. Reducing the voltage has the largest effect, but also increases delay. Power density refers to the concentration of power in a given space; power density is related to heat. The *power wall* refers to the limit of approximately 100 watts per cm^2 that gives the maximum power density for which heat can be removed from a silicon chip using current cooling technologies.

Clock gating and power gating can be used to turn off a circuit (or part of a circuit). For devices that use battery power, the overall goal of power management systems is a reduction in total energy use. Because moving into and out of a low-power (sleep) mode consumes energy, sleep mode is only justified if the energy required is less than the energy required to remain running. A simplified model shows that the computation involves the cost to shut down and the cost to wake up.

Devices can also use low-power modes. Network interfaces pose a challenge because the interface must be awake to receive packets and a computer does not always know when packets will arrive. The Wi-Fi standard includes a Power Saving Polling mode.

EXERCISES

21.1   Look on the Web to find the power required by the largest supercomputer in existence.

21.2   Suppose the frequency of a clock is reduced by 10% and all other parameters remain the same. How much is the power consumption reduced?

21.3   Suppose the voltage, V_{dd}, is reduced by 10% and all other parameters remain the same. How much is the power consumption reduced?

21.4   Use Equation 21.16 to find a break-even value for t.

21.5   Extend the model in Figure 21.1 to a three-state system in which the processor has both a *sleep* mode and a *deep sleep* mode.

Chapter Contents

22

Building Blocks: Transistors, Gates, And Clocks

22.1 Introduction

Previous chapters provide a high-level description of processors, memories, I/O devices, and other hardware units. The chapters focus on the functionality that each item provides without considering the underlying components and low-level details.

This chapter explains the building blocks used for all digital hardware. It introduces transistors, and shows how transistors can be used to build logic gates. Most important, it explains how a clock can transform a basic combinatorial circuit into a hardware mechanism that performs a sequence of steps.

22.2 The History Of Digital Technologies

Technologies for digital computation have changed dramatically. One of the earliest computational devices, known as an *abacus*, relied on humans to move beads to keep track of sums. By the early twentieth century, mechanical gears and levers were being used to create cash registers and adding machines. By the 1940s, researchers constructed the first electronic computers from vacuum tubes. Although they were much faster than mechanical devices, vacuum tubes (which require a filament to become red hot) were unreliable — a filament would burn out after a few hundred hours of use.

The invention of the transistor in 1947 changed computing dramatically. Unlike vacuum tubes, transistors did not require a filament, did not consume much power, did not produce much heat, and did not burn out. Furthermore, transistors could be produced at much lower cost than vacuum tubes. Consequently, modern digital computers are built from electronic circuits that use transistors.

22.3 Electrical Terminology: Voltage And Current

Electronic circuits rely on physical phenomena associated with electricity, including the flow of electrical current. Physicists have discovered ways to detect the presence of electrical charge and control its flow; engineers have developed mechanisms that can perform such functions quickly. The mechanisms form the basis for modern digital computers.

Engineers use the terms *voltage* and *current* to refer to quantifiable properties of electricity: the *voltage* between two points (measured in *volts*) represents the potential energy difference, and the *current* (measured in *amperes* or *amps*) represents the flow of electrons along a path (e.g., along a wire). A good analogy can be made with water: voltage corresponds to water pressure, and current corresponds to the amount of water flowing through a pipe at a given time. If a water tank develops a hole and water begins to flow through the hole, water pressure will drop; by analogy, if current starts flowing through a wire, voltage will drop.

The most important thing to know about electrical voltage is that voltage can only be measured as the difference between two points (i.e., the measurement is relative). Thus, a *voltmeter*, which is used to measure voltage, always has two probes; the meter does not register a voltage until both probes have been connected. To simplify measurement, we assume one of the two points represents zero volts, and express the voltage of the second point relative to zero. Electrical engineers use the term *ground* to refer to the point that is assumed to be at zero volts. The example digital circuits shown in this text assume that electrical power is supplied by two wires: one wire is a ground wire, which we assume to represent zero volts, and a second wire, which we assume to be at five volts.

Fortunately, we can understand the essentials of digital logic without knowing more about voltage and current. We only need to understand how electrical flow can be controlled and how electricity can be used to represent digital values.

22.4 The Transistor

The mechanism used to control flow of electrical current is a semiconductor device known as a *transistor*. At the lowest level, all digital systems are composed of transistors. In particular, digital circuits use a form of transistor known as a *Metal Oxide Semiconductor Field Effect Transistor* (*MOSFET*), abbreviated *FET*. A MOSFET can be formed on a crystalline silicon foundation by composing layers of P-type and N-type silicon, a silicon oxide insulating layer (a type of glass), and metal for wires that connect the transistor to the rest of the circuit.

The transistors used in digital circuits function as an on/off switch that is operated electronically instead of mechanically. That is, in contrast to a mechanical switch that opens and closes based on the mechanical force applied, a transistor opens and closes based on the voltage applied. Each transistor has three *terminals* (i.e., wires) that provide connections to the rest of the circuit. Two terminals, a *source* and *drain*, have a channel between them on which the electrical resistance can be controlled. If the resistance is low, electric current flows from the source to the drain; if the resistance is high, no current flows. The third terminal, known as a *gate*, controls the resistance and the flow of current through the transistor. In the next sections, we will see how switching transistors can be used to build more complex components that are used to build digital systems.

MOSFET transistors come in two types; both are used in digital logic circuits. Figure 22.1 shows the diagrams engineers use to denote the two types†.

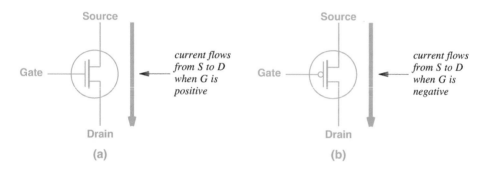

Figure 22.1 The two types of transistors used in logic circuits. The type labeled (a) turns on when the gate voltage is positive; transistor labeled (b) turns on when the gate voltage is zero (or negative).

In the diagram, the transistor labeled (a) turns on whenever the voltage on the gate is positive. To be precise, the voltage must exceed a minimum threshold. Thus, when the voltage on the gate is extremely small (e.g., .0001 volts), the transistor operates as if the voltage is zero. When the voltage on the gate exceeds the threshold required, a large current flows through the other two connections. When the voltage on the gate becomes zero (or close to zero), no current can flow from the source to the drain. The transistor labeled (b), which has a small circle on the gate, works the other way: a large current flows from the source to the drain whenever the voltage on the gate is zero (i.e., close enough to zero to be below the threshold), and the current stops flowing when the gate voltage becomes high (exceeds the threshold). The two forms of a transistor are known as *complementary*, and the overall chip technology is known as *CMOS (Complementary Metal Oxide Semiconductor)*. The chief advantage of CMOS arises because circuits can be devised that use extremely low power.

---

†Technically, the diagram depicts the *p-channel* and *n-channel* forms of a MOSFET.

22.5 Logic Gates

How are digital circuits built? A transistor has two possible states — current is flowing or no current is flowing. Therefore, circuits are designed using a two-valued mathematical system known as Boolean algebra. Most programmers are familiar with the three basic Boolean functions: *and*, *or*, and *not*. Figure 22.2 lists the possible input values and the result of each function.

A	B	A and B		A	B	A or B		A	not A
0	0	0		0	0	0		0	1
0	1	0		0	1	1		1	0
1	0	0		1	0	1			
1	1	1		1	1	1			

Figure 22.2 Boolean functions and the result for each possible set of inputs. A logical value of zero represents *false*, and a logical value of one represents *true*.

Boolean functions provide a conceptual basis for digital hardware. More important, it is possible to use transistors to construct efficient circuits that implement each of the Boolean functions. For example, consider the Boolean *not*. Typical logic circuits use a positive voltage to represent a Boolean *1* and zero voltage to represent a Boolean *0*. Using zero volts to represent 0 and a positive voltage to represent 1 means a circuit that computes Boolean *not* can be constructed from two transistors. That is, the circuit will take an input on one wire and produce an output on another wire, where the output is always the opposite of the input — when positive voltage is placed on the input, the output will be zero, and when zero voltage is placed on the input, the output will be positive†. Figure 22.3 illustrates a circuit that implements Boolean *not*.

The drawing in the figure is known as a *schematic diagram*. Each line on a schematic corresponds to a wire that connects one component to another. A solid dot indicates an electrical connection, and a small, open circle at the end of a line indicates an external connection. In addition to the two inputs and an output, the circuit has external connections to positive and zero voltages.

Electronic circuits that implement Boolean functions differ from a computer program in a significant way: a circuit operates automatically and continuously. That is, once power is supplied (the + voltage in the figure), the transistors perform their function and continue to perform as long as power remains on — if the input changes, the output changes. Thus, unlike a function in a program that only produces a result when called, the output of a circuit is always available and can be used at any time.

---

†Some digital circuits use 5 volts and some use 3.3 volts; rather than specify a voltage, hardware engineers write V_{dd} to denote a voltage appropriate for a given circuit.

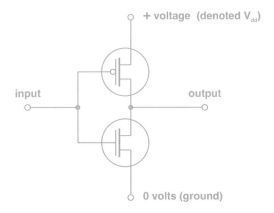

Figure 22.3 A pair of complementary transistors used to implement a Boolean *not*.

To understand how the circuit works, think of the transistors as choosing whether to connect the source to the drain or leave the two disconnected. In the figure, when the input is positive (i.e., corresponds to a logical 1), the top transistor turns off and the bottom transistor turns on. When a transistor is off, the source and drain are effectively disconnected, and no electrical current flows between them. With positive input, the bottom transistor turns on, connecting its source and drain. Because the drain connects to ground (zero volts), the output will be connected to ground, and the output will be zero volts. Conversely, when the input voltage is zero, the top transistor turns on and the bottom transistor turns off, which means the output connects to positive voltage. Thus, the output voltage represents the logical opposite of the input voltage.

A detail adds a minor complication for Boolean functions: because of the way electronic circuits work, it takes fewer transistors to provide the inverse of each function. Thus, most digital circuits implement the inverse of *logical or* and *logical and*: *nor* (which stands for *not or*) and *nand* (which stands for *not and*). In addition, some circuits use the *exclusive or* (*xor*) function. Figure 22.4 lists the possible inputs and the results for each function†.

A	B	A nand B		A	B	A nor B		A	B	A xor B
0	0	1		0	0	1		0	0	0
0	1	1		0	1	0		0	1	1
1	0	1		1	0	0		1	0	1
1	1	0		1	1	0		1	1	0

Figure 22.4 The *nand*, *nor*, and *xor* functions that logic gates provide.

_____

†A later section explains that we use the term *truth tables* to describe the tables used in the figure.

22.6 Implementation Of A Nand Logic Gate Using Transistors

For the remainder of the chapter, the details of transistors and their interconnection are unimportant. All we need to understand is that transistors can be used to create each of the Boolean functions described above, and that the functions are used to create digital circuits that form computers. Before leaving the topic of transistors, we will consider an example: a circuit that uses four transistors to implement a *nand* function. Figure 22.5 contains the circuit diagram. As described above, we use the term *logic gate* to describe the resulting circuit. In practice, a logic gate contains additional components, such as *diodes* and *resistors*, that are used to protect the transistors from electrostatic discharge and excessive electrical current; because they do not affect the logical operation of the gate, the extra components have been omitted from the diagram.

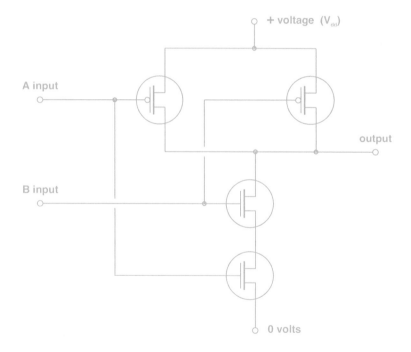

Figure 22.5 Example of four transistors interconnected in a circuit that implements a *nand* logic gate.

To understand how the circuit operates, observe that if both inputs represent logical one, the bottom two transistors will be turned on, which means the output will be connected to zero volts (logical zero). Otherwise, at least one of the top two transistors will be turned on, and the output will be connected to positive voltage (logical one). Of course, a circuit must be designed carefully to ensure that an output is never connected to positive voltage and zero volts simultaneously or the transistors will be destroyed.

The diagram in Figure 22.5 uses a common convention: two lines that cross do not indicate an electrical connection unless a solid dot appears. The idea is similar to the way vertices and edges are drawn in a graph: two edges that cross do not indicate a vertex is present unless a dot (or circle) is drawn. In a circuit diagram, two lines that cross without a dot correspond to a situation in which there is no physical connection; we can imagine that the wires are positioned so an air gap exists between them (i.e., the wires do not touch). To help indicate that there is no connection, the lines are drawn with a slight space around the crossing point.

Now that we have seen an example of how a gate can be created out of transistors, we do not need to consider individual transistors again. Throughout the rest of the chapter, we will discuss gates without referring to their internal mechanisms.

22.7 Symbols Used For Logic Gates

When they design circuits, engineers think about interconnecting logic gates rather than interconnecting transistors. Each gate is represented by a symbol, and engineers draw diagrams that show the interconnections among gates. Figure 22.6 shows the symbols for *nand*, *nor*, *inverter*, *and*, *or*, and *xor* gates. The figure follows standard terminology by using the term *inverter* for a gate that performs the Boolean *not* operation.

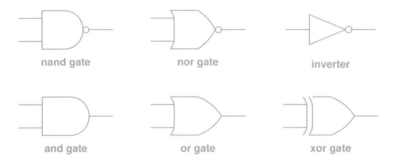

Figure 22.6 The symbols for commonly used gates. Inputs for each gate are shown on the left, and the output of the gate is shown on the right.

22.8 Example Interconnection Of Gates

The electronic parts that implement gates are classified as *Transistor-Transistor Logic* (*TTL*) because the output transistors in each gate are designed to connect directly to input transistors in other gates. In fact, an output can connect to several inputs†. For example, suppose a circuit is needed in which the output is true if a Wi-Fi interface is connected and the user presses a power-down button. Logically, the output is a Boolean *and* of two inputs. We said, however, that some designs are limited to *nand*, *nor*,

---

†The technology limits the number of inputs that can be connected to a single output; we use the term

and *inverter* gates. In such cases, the *and* function can be created by directly connecting the output of a *nand* gate to the input of an *inverter*. Figure 22.7 illustrates the connection.

Figure 22.7 Illustration of gate interconnection. The output from one logic gate can connect directly to the input of another gate.

As another example of gate interconnection, consider the circuit in Figure 22.8 that shows three inputs.

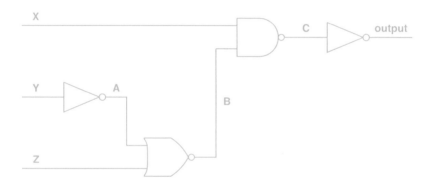

Figure 22.8 An example of a circuit with three inputs labeled *X*, *Y*, and *Z*. Internal interconnections are also labeled to allow us to discuss intermediate values.

What function does the circuit in the figure implement? There are two ways to answer the question: we can determine the Boolean formula to which the circuit corresponds, or we can enumerate the value that appears on each output for all eight possible combinations of input values. To help us understand the two methods, we have labeled each input and each intermediate connection in the circuit as well as the output.

To derive a Boolean formula, observe that input *Y* is connected directly to an inverter. Thus, the value at *A* corresponds to the Boolean function *not Y*. The *nor* gate takes inputs *not Y* (from the inverter) and *Z*, so the value at *B* corresponds to the Boolean function:

$$Z \; nor \; (not \; Y)$$

Because the combination of a *nand* gate followed by an inverter produces the Boolean *and* of the two inputs, the output value corresponds to:

$$X \text{ and } (Z \text{ nor } (not\ Y))$$

The formula can also be expressed as:

$$X \text{ and } not\ (Z \text{ or } (not\ Y)) \tag{22.1}$$

Although we have described the use of Boolean expressions as a way of understanding circuits, Boolean expressions are also important in circuit design. An engineer can start a design by finding a Boolean expression that describes the desired behavior of a circuit. Writing such an expression can help a designer understand the problem and special cases. Once a correct expression has been found, the engineer can translate the expression into equivalent hardware gates.

The use of Boolean expressions to specify circuits has a significant advantage: a variety of tools are available that operate on Boolean expressions. Tools can be used to analyze an expression, minimize an expression†, and convert an expression into a diagram of interconnected gates. Automated minimization is especially useful because it can reduce the number of gates required. That is, tools exist that can take a Boolean expression as input, produce as output an equivalent expression that requires fewer gates, and then convert the output to a circuit diagram. We can summarize:

> *Tools exist that take a Boolean expression as input and produce an optimized circuit for the expression as output.*

A second technique used to understand a logic circuit consists of enumerating all possible inputs, and then finding the corresponding values at each point in the circuit. For example, because the circuit in Figure 22.8 has three inputs, eight possible combinations of input exist. We use the term *truth table* to describe the enumeration. Truth tables are often used when debugging circuits. Figure 22.9 contains the truth table for the circuit in Figure 22.8. The table lists all possible combination of inputs on wires X, Y, and Z along with the resulting values on the wires labeled A, B, C, and output.

X	Y	Z	A	B	C	output
0	0	0	1	0	1	0
0	0	1	1	0	1	0
0	1	0	0	1	1	0
0	1	1	0	0	1	0
1	0	0	1	0	1	0
1	0	1	1	0	1	0
1	1	0	0	1	0	1
1	1	1	0	0	1	0

Figure 22.9 A truth table for the circuit in Figure 22.8.

The table in Figure 22.9 is generated by starting with all possible inputs, and then filling in the remaining columns one at a time. In the example, there are three inputs (X, Y, and Z) that can each be set to zero or one. Consequently, there are eight possible combinations of values in columns X, Y, and Z of the table. Once they have been filled in, the input columns can be used to derive other columns. For example, point A in the circuit represents the output from the first inverter, which is the inverse of input Y. Thus, column A can be filled in by reversing the values in column Y. Similarly, column B represents the *nor* of columns A and Z.

A truth table can be used to validate a Boolean expression — the expression can be computed for all possible inputs and compared to the values in the truth table. For example, the truth table in Figure 22.9 can be used to validate the Boolean expression (22.1) above and the equivalent expression:

$$X \text{ and } Y \text{ and } (not\ Z))$$

To perform the validation, one computes the value of the Boolean expression for all possible combinations of X, Y, and Z. For each combination, the value of the expression is compared to the value in the output column of the truth table.

22.9 A Digital Circuit For Binary Addition

How can logic circuits implement integer arithmetic? As an example, consider using gates to add two binary numbers. One can apply the technique learned in elementary school: align the two numbers in a column. Then, start with the least-significant digits and add each column of digits. If the sum overflows a given column, carry the high-order digit of the sum to the next column. The only difference is that computers represent integers in binary rather than decimal. For example, Figure 22.10 illustrates the addition of 20 and 29 carried out in binary.

```
        carry carry carry
          ⁱ   \ⁱ   \ⁱ
             1   0   1   0   0
       +     1   1   1   0   1
         ─────────────────────────
       1     1   0   0   0   1
```

Figure 22.10 Example of binary addition using carry bits.

A circuit to perform the addition needs one module for each column (i.e., each bit in the operands). The module for the low-order bits takes two inputs and produces two outputs: a *sum bit* and a *carry bit*. The circuit, which is known as a *half adder*, contains an *and* gate and an *exclusive or* gate. Figure 22.11 shows how the gates are connected.

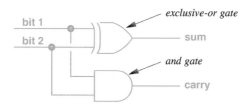

Figure 22.11 A half adder circuit that computes the sum and carry for two
input bits.

Although a half adder circuit computes the low-order bit of the sum, a more complex circuit is needed for each of the other bits. In particular, each successive computation has three inputs: two input bits plus a carry bit from the column to the right. Figure 22.12 illustrates the necessary circuit, which is known as a *full adder*. Note the
symmetry between the two input bits — either input can be connected to the *sum* of the
circuit for the previous bit.

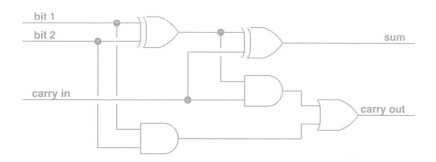

Figure 22.12 A full adder circuit that accepts a carry input as well as two input bits.

As the figure shows, a full adder consists of two half adder circuits plus one extra
gate (a logical *or*). The *or* connects the carry outputs from the two half adders, and
provides a carry output if either of the two half adders reports a carry.

Although a full adder can have eight possible input combinations, we only need to
consider six when verifying correctness. To see why, observe that the full adder treats
bit 1 and *bit 2* symmetrically. Thus, we only need to consider three cases: both input
bits are zeros, both input bits are ones, and one of the input bits is one while the other is
zero. The presence of a carry input doubles the number of possibilities to six. An exercise suggests using a truth table to verify that the full adder circuit does indeed give
correct output for each input combination.

22.10 Multiple Gates Per Integrated Circuit

Because the logic gates described above do not require many transistors, multiple gates that use TTL can be manufactured on a single, inexpensive electronic component. One popular set of TTL components that implement logic gates is known as the *7400 family*†; each component in the family is assigned a part number that begins with *74*. Physically, many of the parts in the 7400 family consist of a rectangular package approximately one-half inch long with fourteen copper wires (called *pins*) that are used to connect the part to a circuit; the result is known as a *14-pin Dual In-line Package* (*14-pin DIP*). More complex 7400-series chips require additional pins (e.g., some use a 16-pin DIP configuration).

To understand how multiple gates are arranged on a 7400-series chip, consider three examples. Part number 7400 contains four *nand* gates, part number 7402 contains four *nor* gates, and part number 7404 contains six inverters. Figure 22.13 illustrates how the inputs and outputs of individual logic gates connect to pins in each case.

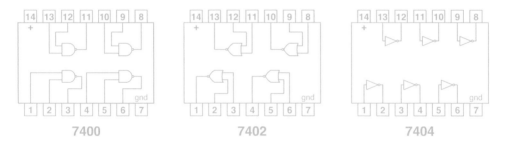

Figure 22.13 Illustration of the pin connections on three commercially available integrated circuits that implement logic gates.

Although the figure does not show gates connected to pins 14 and 7, the two pins are essential because they supply power needed to run the gates — as the labels indicate, pin 14 connects to plus five volts and pin 7 connects to ground (zero volts).

22.11 The Need For More Than Combinatorial Circuits

An interconnection of Boolean logic gates, such as the circuits described above, is known as a *combinatorial circuit* because the output is simply a Boolean combination of input values. In a combinatorial circuit, the output only changes when an input value changes. Although combinatorial circuits are essential, they are not sufficient — a computer requires circuits that can take action without waiting for inputs to change. For example, when a user presses a button to power on a computer, hardware must perform a sequence of operations, and the sequence must proceed without further input from the user. In fact, a user does not need to hold the power button continuously — the startup

---

†In addition to the logic gates described in this section, the 7400 family also includes more sophisticated

sequence continues even after the user releases the button. Furthermore, pressing the same button again causes the hardware to initiate a shutdown sequence.

How can a power button act to power down as well as power up a system? How can digital logic perform a sequence of operations without requiring the input values to change? How can a digital circuit continue to operate after an input reverts to its initial condition? The answers involve additional mechanisms. Sophisticated arrangements of logic gates can provide some of the needed functionality. The rest requires a hardware device known as a *clock*. The next sections present examples of sophisticated circuits, and later sections explain clocks.

22.12 Circuits That Maintain State

In addition to electronic parts that contain basic Boolean gates, parts are also available that contain gates interconnected to maintain *state*. That is, electronic circuits exist in which the outputs are a function of the sequence of previous inputs as well as the current input. Such logic circuits are known as *sequential circuits*.

A *latch* is one of the most basic of sequential circuits. The idea of a latch is straightforward: a latch has an input and an output. In addition, a latch has an extra input called an *enable line*. As long as the enable line is set to logical one, the latch makes its output an exact copy of the input. That is, while the enable line is one, if the input changes, the output changes as well. Once the enable line changes to logical zero, however, the output freezes at its current value and does not change. Thus, the latch "remembers" the value the input had while the enable line was set, and keeps the output set to that value.

How can a latch be devised? Interestingly, a combination of Boolean logic gates is sufficient. Figure 22.14 illustrates a circuit that uses four *nand* gates to create a latch. The idea is that when the enable line is logical zero, the two *nand* gates on the right remember the current value of the output. Because the outputs of two *nand* gates feed back into each other's input, the output value will remain stable†. When the enable line is logical one, the two gates on the left pass the data input (on the lower wire) and its inverse (on the higher wire) to the pair of gates on the right.

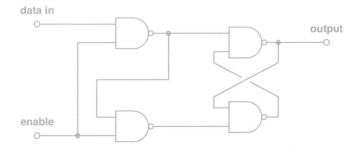

Figure 22.14 Illustration of four *nand* gates used to implement a one-bit latch.

22.13 Feedback And Propagation Delay

A latch uses *feedback*, which means that the output from a circuit connects back to one of the inputs. To understand how feedback works in a latch, one must know that each gate has a *propagation delay*. That is, a delay occurs between the time an input changes and the output changes. During the propagation delay, the output remains at the previous value. Of course, transistors are designed to minimize delay, and the delay can be less than a microsecond, but a finite delay exists. To see how propagation delay affects a circuit that uses feedback, consider the circuit in Figure 22.15.

Figure 22.15 An inverter with the output connected back to the input.

As the figure shows, the output of an inverter is connected back to the input. It does not seem that such a connection makes sense because an inverter's output is always the opposite of its input. The Boolean expression for such a circuit is:

$$output = not(output)$$

which is a mathematical contradiction.

Propagation delay explains that the circuit works. At any time, if output is 0, the input to the inverter will be 0. After a propagation delay, the inverter will change the output to 1. Once the output becomes 1, another propagation delay occurs, and the output will become 0 again. Because the cycle goes on forever, we say that the circuit *oscillates* by generating an output that changes back and forth between 0 and 1 (known as a *square wave*). The concept of propagation delay explains the operation of the latch in Figure 22.14 — outputs remain the same until a propagation delay occurs.

22.14 Using Latches To Create A Memory

We will see that processors include a set of *registers* that serve as short-term storage units. Typically, registers hold values that are used in computation (e.g., two values that will be added together). Each register holds multiple bits; most computers have 32-bit or 64-bit registers. The circuit for a register illustrates an important principle of digital hardware design:

> *A circuit to handle multiple bits is constructed by physically replicating a circuit that handles one bit.*

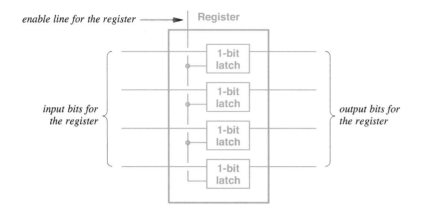

Figure 22.16 A 4-bit register formed from four 1-bit latches.

To understand the principle, consider Figure 22.16 which shows how a 4-bit register circuit can be constructed from four 1-bit latches†. In the figure, the enable lines of all four latches are connected together to form an enable input for the register. Although the hardware consists of four independent circuits, connecting the enable lines means the four latches act in unison. When the enable line is set to logical one, the register accepts the four input bits and sets the four outputs accordingly. When the enable line becomes zero, the outputs remain fixed. That is, the register has stored whatever value was present on its inputs, and the output value will not change until the enable line becomes one again.

The point is:

> *A register, one of the key components in a processor, is a hardware mechanism that uses a set of latches to store a digital value.*

22.15 Flip-Flops And Transition Diagrams

A *flip-flop* is another circuit in which the output depends on previous inputs as well as the current input. There are various forms. One form acts exactly like the power switch on a computer: the first time its input becomes *1*, the flip-flop turns the output on, and the second time the input becomes *1*, the flip-flop turns the output off. Like a push-button switch used to control power, a flip-flop does not respond to a continuous input — the input must return to *0* before a value of 1 will cause the flip-flop to change state. That is, whenever the input transitions from 0 to 1, the flip-flop changes its output from the current state to the opposite. Figure 22.17 shows a sequence of inputs and the resulting output.

---

†Although the diagram only shows a 4-bit register, the registers used in typical processors store 32 bits or 64 bits.

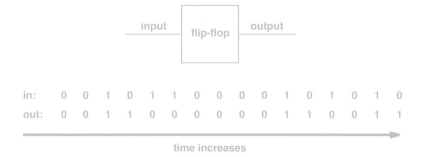

Figure 22.17 Illustration of how one type of flip-flop reacts to a sequence of
             inputs. The flip-flop output changes when the input transitions
             from 0 to 1 (i.e., from zero volts to five volts).

Because it responds to a sequence of inputs, a flip-flop is not a simple combinatorial circuit. A flip-flop cannot be constructed from a single gate. However, a flip-
flop can be constructed from a pair of latches.

To understand how a flip-flop works, it is helpful to plot the input and output in
graphical form as a function of time. Engineers use the term *transition diagram* for
such a plot. In most digital circuits, transitions are coordinated by a clock, which
means that transitions only occur at regular intervals. Figure 22.18 illustrates a transition diagram for the flip-flop values from Figure 22.17. The line labeled *clock* in Figure 22.18 shows where clock pulses occur; each input transition is constrained to occur
on one of the clock pulses. For now, it is sufficient to understand the general concept;
later sections explain clocks.

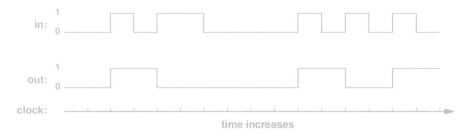

Figure 22.18 Illustration of a transition diagram that shows how a flip flop
             reacts to the series of inputs in Figure 22.17. Marks along the
             x-axis indicate times; each corresponds to one clock tick.

We said that a flip-flop changes output each time it encounters a one bit. In fact,
the transition diagram shows the exact details and timing that are important to circuit
designers. In the example, the transition diagram shows that the flip-flop is only trig-

gered when the input *rises*. That is, the output does not change until the input transitions from zero to one. Engineers say that the output transition occurs on the *rising edge* of the input change; circuits that transition when the input changes from one to zero are said to occur on the *falling edge*.

In practice, additional details complicate flip-flops. For example, most flip-flops include an additional input named *reset* that places the output in a 0 state. In addition, several other variants of flip-flops exist. For example, some flip-flops provide a second output that is the inverse of the main output (in some circuits, having the inverse available results in fewer gates).

22.16 Binary Counters

A single flip-flop only offers two possible output values: 0 or 1. However, a set of flip-flops can be connected in series to form a binary *counter* that accumulates a numeric total. Like a flip-flop, a counter has a single input. Unlike a flip-flop, however, a counter has multiple outputs. The outputs count how many input pulses have been detected by giving a numerical total in binary†. We think of the outputs as starting at zero and adding one each time the input transitions from 0 to 1. Thus, a counter that has three output lines can accumulate a total between 0 and 7. Figure 22.19 illustrates a counter, and shows how the outputs change when the input changes.

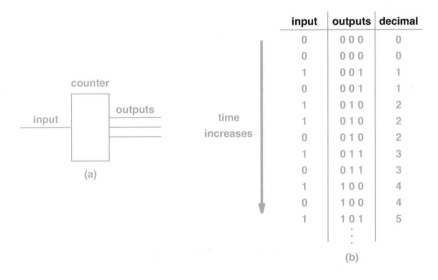

input	outputs	decimal
0	0 0 0	0
0	0 0 0	0
1	0 0 1	1
0	0 0 1	1
1	0 1 0	2
1	0 1 0	2
0	0 1 0	2
1	0 1 1	3
0	0 1 1	3
1	1 0 0	4
0	1 0 0	4
1	1 0 1	5

(b)

Figure 22.19 Illustration of (a) a binary counter, and (b) a sequence of input values and the corresponding outputs. The column labeled *decimal* gives the decimal equivalent of the outputs.

---

†Chapter 3 considers data representation in more detail. For now, it is sufficient to understand that the outputs represent a number.

In practice, an electronic part that implements a binary counter has several additional features. For example, a counter has an additional input used to reset the count to zero, and may also have an input that temporarily stops the counter (i.e., ignores the input and freezes the output). More important, because it has a fixed number of output pins, each counter has a maximum value it can represent. When the accumulated count exceeds the maximum value, the counter resets the output to zero and uses an additional output to indicate that an *overflow* occurred.

22.17 Clocks, Feedback, And Sequences

Although we have seen the basic building blocks of digital logic, one additional feature is absolutely essential for a digital computer: automatic operation. That is, a computer must be able to execute a sequence of instructions without any inputs changing. The digital logic circuits discussed previously all use the property that they respond to changes in one or more of their inputs; they do not perform any function until an input changes. How can a digital logic circuit perform a series of steps?

The answer lies in a combination of feedback and a mechanism known as a *clock* that allows hardware to take action without requiring the input to change. In fact, most digital logic circuits are said to be *clocked*, which means that the clock signal, rather than changes in the inputs, controls and synchronizes the operation of individual components and subassemblies to ensure that they work together as intended (e.g., to guarantee that later stages of a circuit wait for the propagation delay of previous stages).

What is a clock? Unlike the common definition of the term, hardware engineers use the term *clock* to refer to an electronic circuit that oscillates at a regular rate; the oscillations are converted to a sequence of alternating ones and zeros. Although a clock can be created from an inverter†, most clock circuits use a quartz crystal, which oscillates naturally, to provide a signal at a precise frequency. The clock circuit amplifies the signal and changes it from a sine wave to a square wave. Thus, we think of a clock as emitting an alternating sequence of 0 and 1 values at a regular rate. The speed of a clock is measured in *Hertz (Hz)*, the number of times per second the clock cycles through a 1 followed by a 0. Most clocks in high-speed digital computers operate at speeds ranging from one hundred Megahertz (100 MHz) to several Gigahertz (GHz). For example, at present, the clock used by a typical processor operates at approximately 3 GHz.

It is difficult for a human to imagine circuits changing at such high rates. To make the concept clear, let's consider a clock that operates at an extremely slow rate of 1 Hz. Such a clock might be used to control an interface for a human. For example, if a computer contains an LED that flashes on and off to indicate that the computer is active, a slow clock is needed to control the LED. Note that a clock rate of 1 Hz means the clock completes an entire cycle in one second. That is, the clock emits a logical 1 for one-half cycle followed by a logical zero for one-half cycle. If a circuit arranges to turn on an LED whenever the clock emits a logical 1, the LED will remain on for one-half second, and then will be off for one-half second.

†See Figure 22.15 on page 420.

How does an alternating sequence of 0 and 1 values make digital circuits more powerful? To understand, we will consider a simple clocked circuit. Suppose that during startup, a computer must perform the following sequence of steps:

- Test the battery
- Power on and test the memory
- Power on the Wi-Fi radio
- Power up the screen
- Read the boot sector from SSD into memory
- Start the CPU

To simplify the explanation, we will assume that each step requires at most one second to complete before the next step can be started. Thus, we desire a circuit that, once it has been started, will perform the six steps in sequence, at one-second intervals with no further changes in input.

For now, we will focus on the essence of the circuit, and consider how it can be started later. A circuit to handle the task of performing six steps in sequence can be built from three building blocks: a clock, a binary counter, and a device known as a *decoder/demultiplexor†*, which is often abbreviated *demux*. We have already considered a counter, and will assume that a clock is available that generates digital output at a rate of exactly one cycle per second. The last component, a decoder/demultiplexor, is a single integrated circuit that uses a binary value to map an input to a set of outputs. We will use the decoding function to select an output. That is, a decoder takes a binary value as input, and uses the value to choose an output. Only one output of a decoder is on at any time; all others are off — when the input lines represent the value i in binary, the decoder selects the ith output. Figure 22.20 illustrates the concept.

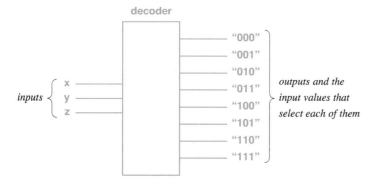

Figure 22.20 Illustration of a decoder with three input lines and eight output lines. When inputs x, y, and z have the values 0, 1, and 1, the fourth output from the top is selected.

---

†An alternate spelling of *demultiplexer* is also used.

When used as a decoder, the device merely selects one of its outputs; when used as a demultiplexor, the device takes an extra input which it passes to the selected output. Both the decoder function and the more complex demultiplexor function can be constructed from Boolean gates.

A decoder provides the last piece needed for our simplistic sequencing mechanism. When we combine a clock, counter, and decoder, the resulting circuit can execute a series of steps. For example, Figure 22.21 shows the interconnection in which the output of a clock is used as input to a binary counter, and the output of a binary counter is used as input to a decoder.

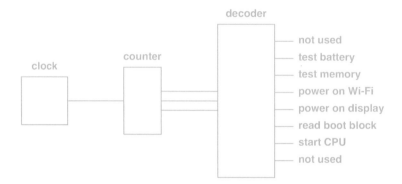

Figure 22.21 An illustration of how a clock can be used to create a circuit that performs a sequence of six steps. Output lines from the counter connect directly to input lines of the decoder.

To understand how the circuit operates, assume that the counter has been reset to zero. Because the counter output is 000, the decoder selects the topmost output, which is not used (i.e., not connected). Operation starts when the clock runs and changes from logical 0 to logical 1. The counter accumulates the count, which changes its output to 001. When its input changes, the decoder selects the second output, which is labeled *test battery*. Presumably, the second output wire connects to a circuit that performs the necessary test. The second output remains selected for one second. During the second, the clock output remains at logical 1 for one-half second, and then reverts to logical 0 for one-half second. When the clock output changes back to logical 1, the counter output lines change to 010, and the decoder selects the third output, which is connected to circuitry that tests memory.

Of course, details are important. For example, some decoder chips make a selected output 0 and other outputs 1. Electrical details also matter. To be compatible with other devices, the clock must use five volts for logical 1, and zero volts for logical 0. Furthermore, to be directly connected, the output lines of the binary counter must use the same binary representation as the input lines of the decoder. We will assume that the output wires from the counter have been connected to the correct input wires of the decoder.

22.18 The Importance Of Feedback

The simplistic circuit in Figure 22.21 lacks a key feature: there is no way to control operation (i.e., to start or stop the sequence). Because a clock runs forever, the counter in the figure counts from zero through its maximum value, and then starts again at zero. As a result, the decoder will repeatedly cycle through its outputs, with each output being held for one second before moving on to the next.

Few digital circuits perform the same series of steps repeatedly. How can we arrange to stop the sequence after the six steps have been executed? The solution lies in adding feedback†. Feedback lies at the heart of complex digital circuits because it allows the results of processing to affect the way a circuit behaves. In the computer start-up sequence, feedback is needed for each of the steps. If the SSD cannot be started, for example, the boot sector cannot be read.

We have already seen feedback used to maintain a data value in the latch circuit of Figure 22.14 because the output from each of the right-most *nand* gates feeds back as an input to the other gate. For another example of feedback, consider how we might use the final output of the decoder, which corresponds to input 111, to stop the sequence. An easy solution consists of using the output to prevent clock pulses from reaching the counter. That is, instead of connecting the clock output directly to the input of the counter, we insert logic gates that only allow the counter input to continue when F has the value 0. In terms of Boolean algebra, the counter input should be:

$$\text{CLOCK } and \text{ } (not \text{ F})$$

That is, as long as the final output is false, the counter input should be equal to the clock; however, when the final output becomes true, the counter input changes to (and remains) zero. Figure 22.22 shows how two inverters and a *nand* gate can be used to implement the necessary function.

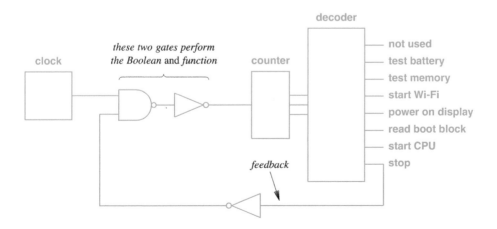

Figure 22.22 A modification of the circuit in Figure 22.21 that includes feedback to stop processing after one pass through each output.

The feedback in Figure 22.22 is fairly obvious because the last output of the decoder connects to a combinatorial circuit on the input side. The figure also makes it easy to see why feedback mechanisms are sometimes called *feedback loops*†.

22.19 Starting A Sequence

Figure 22.22 shows that it is possible to use feedback to terminate a process. However, the circuit is still incomplete because it does not contain a mechanism that allows the sequence to start. Fortunately, adding a starting mechanism is trivial. To understand why, recall that a counter contains a separate input line that resets the count to zero. All that is needed to make our circuit start is another input (e.g., from a button that a user pushes) connected to the counter reset.

When a user pushes the button, the counter resets to zero, which causes the counter's output to become 000. When it receives an input of all zeros, the decoder turns on the first output, and turns off the last output. When the last output turns off, the *nand* gate allows the clock pulses through, and the counter begins to run.

Although it does indeed start the sequence, allowing a user to reset the counter can cause problems. For example, consider what happens if a user becomes impatient during the startup sequence and presses the button a second time. Once the counter resets, the sequence starts again from the beginning. In some cases, performing an operation twice simply wastes time. In other cases, however, repeating an operation causes problems (e.g., some disk drives require that only one command be issued at a time). Thus, a production system uses complex combinatorial logic to prevent a sequence from being interrupted or restarted before it completes.

Although it only contains a few components, the example demonstrates an important concept: a set of Boolean logic gates and a clock are sufficient to allow the execution of a sequence of logical steps. The point is:

> *The example circuit shows that Boolean logic gates and a clock make it possible to build a circuit which, when started, performs a logical sequence of steps and then halts.*

We can now understand the feedback loop that a processor uses to advance the program counter, as illustrated in Figure 15.4‡. On each clock cycle, the processor increments the current program counter by four (the number of bytes in an instruction), and then places the result back in the program counter. Using a program counter and instructions in memory adds a key feature that shows how the digital logic gates described in this chapter can be used to build a *programmable* processor. The basic hardware performs a fixed sequence of two steps: fetch an instruction from memory and execute the instruction. The power of a computer arises from its ability to follow a sequence of instructions in memory, where each instruction can perform an arbitrary operation.

---

†A feedback loop is also present among the gates used to construct a flip-flop.
‡Figure 15.4 can be found on page 291.

22.20 Iteration In Software Vs. Replication In Hardware

The most significant difference between the way software and hardware engineers organize systems arises from the way they handle the situation of performing an operation on multiple items. In software, a fundamental paradigm for handling multiple items consists of *iteration* — a programmer writes code that repeatedly finds the next item in a set and applies the operation to the item. Because the underlying system only applies the operation to one item at a time, a programmer must specify the number of items. Iteration is so essential to programming that most programming languages provide statements (e.g., a *for loop*) that allow the programmer to express the iteration clearly.

Although hardware can be built to perform iteration, doing so makes the design more complex and the resulting hardware clumsy. The fundamental hardware paradigm used to handle multiple items consists of *replication* — a hardware engineer creates multiple copies of a circuit, and allows each copy to act on one item. All copies perform at the same time. For example, to compute a Boolean operation on a pair of thirty-two-bit values, a hardware engineer designs a circuit for a pair of bits, and then replicates the circuit thirty-two times. Thus, to compute the Boolean *exclusive or* of two thirty-two-bit integers, a hardware designer can use thirty-two *xor* gates.

Replication can be difficult for programmers to appreciate because replication is antithetical to good programming practices — we teach programmers to avoid duplicating code. In the hardware world, however, replication has three distinct advantages: elegance, speed, and correctness. Elegance arises because replication avoids the extra hardware needed to select an individual item, move it into place, and move the result back. In addition to avoiding the delay involved in moving values and results, replication increases performance by allowing multiple operations to be performed simultaneously. For example, thirty-two inverters working at the same time can invert thirty-two bits in exactly the same amount of time that it takes one inverter to invert a single bit. Such speedup is especially significant if a computer can operate on sixty-four bits at the same time.

The third advantage of replication focuses on high reliability. Replication increases reliability by making hardware easier to validate. For example, to validate that a thirty-two-bit operation works correctly, a hardware engineer only needs to validate the circuit for a single bit — the remaining bits will work the same because the same circuit is replicated. As a result, hardware is much more reliable than software. Even the legal system holds product liability standards higher for hardware than for software — unlike software that is often sold "as is" without a warranty, hardware (e.g., an integrated circuit) is sold within a legal framework that requires fitness for the intended purpose. We can summarize:

> *Unlike software, which uses iteration, hardware uses replication. The advantages of replication are increased elegance, higher speed, and increased reliability.*

22.21 Gate And Chip Minimization

We have glossed over many engineering details. For example, once they choose a general design and the amount of replication that will be used, hardware engineers seek ways to minimize the amount of hardware needed. Two aspects arise: minimizing gates and minimizing integrated circuits. To minimize gates, one uses general rules of Boolean algebra. For example, consider the Boolean expression:

$$not \ (not \ z)$$

A circuit to implement the expression consists of two inverters connected together. Of course, we know that two *not* operations are the identity function, so the expression can be replaced by z. That is, a pair of directly connected inverters can be removed from a circuit without affecting the result.

As another example of Boolean expression optimization, consider the expression:

$$x \ nor \ (not \ x)$$

Either *x* will have the value 1, or *not x* will have the value 1, which means the *nor* function will always produce the same value, a logical 0. Therefore, the entire expression can be replaced by the value 0. In terms of a circuit, it would be foolish to use a *nor* gate and an inverter to compute the expression because the circuit resulting from the two gates will always be logical zero. Thus, once an engineer writes a Boolean expression formula, the formula can be analyzed to look for instances of subexpressions that can be reduced or eliminated without changing the result.

Fortunately, sophisticated design tools exist that help engineers minimize gates. Such tools take a Boolean expression as an input. The design tool analyzes the expression and produces a circuit that implements the expression with a minimum number of gates. The tools do not merely use Boolean *and*, *or*, and *not*. Instead, they understand the gates that are available (e.g., *nand* and *nor*), and define the circuit in terms of available electronic parts.

Although Boolean formulas can be optimized mathematically, further optimization is needed because the overall goal is minimization of integrated circuits. To understand the situation, recall that many integrated circuits contain multiple copies of a given type of gate. Thus, minimizing the number of Boolean operations may not optimize a circuit if the optimization increases the types of gates required. For example, suppose a Boolean expression requires four *nand* gates, and consider an optimization that reduces the requirements to three gates: two *nand* gates and a *nor* gate. Unfortunately, although it reduces the total number of gates, the optimization increases the number of integrated circuits required because a single 7400 integrated circuit contains four *nand* gates, but introducing a *nor* gate requires an extra integrated circuit.

22.22 Using Spare Gates

To understand the concept of spare gates, consider the circuit in Figure 22.22 carefully†. Assuming the clock, counter, and decoder each require one integrated circuit, how many additional integrated circuits will be required? The obvious answer is two:

one is needed for the *nand* gate (e.g., a 7400) and another for the two inverters (e.g., a 7404). Surprisingly, it is possible to implement the circuit with only one additional integrated circuit. To see how, observe that although the 7400 contains four *nand* gates, only one is needed. How can the spare gates be used? The trick lies in observing that *nand* of 1 and 0 is 1, and *nand* of 1 and 1 is 0. That is,

$$1 \; nand \; x$$

is equivalent to:

$$not \; x$$

The point is: a spare *nand* gate can be used as an inverter by connecting one of the two inputs to logical one (i.e., five volts).

22.23 Power Distribution And Heat Dissipation

In addition to planning digital circuits that correctly perform the intended function and minimizing the number of components used, engineers must contend with the underlying power and cooling requirements†. For example, although the diagrams in this chapter only depict the logical inputs and outputs of gates, every gate consumes power. The amount of power used by a single integrated circuit is insignificant. However, because hardware designers tend to use replication instead of iteration, complex digital systems contain many circuits. An engineer must calculate the total power required, construct the appropriate power supplies, and plan additional wiring to carry power to each chip.

The laws of physics dictate that any device that consumes power will generate heat. The amount of heat generated is proportional to the amount of power consumed, so an integrated circuit generates a minimal amount of heat. Because a digital system uses hundreds of circuits that operate in a small, enclosed space, the total heat generated can be significant. Unless engineers plan a mechanism to dissipate heat, high temperatures will cause the circuits to fail. For small systems, engineers add holes to the chassis that allow hot air to escape and be replaced by cooler air from the surrounding room. For intermediate systems, such as personal computers, fans are added to move air from the surrounding room through the system more quickly. For the largest digital systems, cool air is insufficient — a refrigeration system with liquid coolant must be used (e.g., circuits in the Cray 2 supercomputer were directly immersed in a liquid coolant).

22.24 Timing And Clock Zones

Our quick tour of digital logic omits another important aspect that engineers must consider: *timing*. A gate does not act instantly. Instead, a gate takes time to *settle* (i.e., to change the output once the input changes). In our examples, timing is irrelevant be-

---

†The previous chapter considers power in more detail.

cause the clock runs at the incredibly slow rate of 1 Hz and all gates settle in less than a microsecond. Thus, the gates settle long before the clock pulses.

In practice, timing is an essential aspect of engineering because digital circuits are designed to operate at high speed. To ensure that a circuit will operate correctly, an engineer must calculate the time required for all gates to settle.

Engineers must also calculate the time required to propagate signals throughout an entire system, and must ensure that the system does not fail because of *clock skew*. To understand clock skew, consider Figure 22.23 that illustrates a circuit board with a clock that controls three of the integrated circuits in the system.

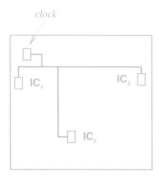

Figure 22.23 Illustration of three integrated circuits in a digital system that are controlled by a single clock. The length of wire between the clock and an integrated circuit determines when a clock signal arrives.

In the figure, the three integrated circuits are physically distributed (presumably, other integrated circuits occupy the remaining space). Unfortunately, a finite time is required for a signal from the clock to reach each of the circuits, and the time is proportional to the length of wire between the clock and a given circuit. As a result, the clock signal will arrive at some of the integrated circuits sooner than it arrives at others. As a rule of thumb, a signal requires one nanosecond to propagate across one foot of wire. Thus, for a system that measures eighteen inches across, the clock signal can reach locations near the clock a nanosecond before the signal reaches the farthest location. Obviously, clock skew can cause a problem if parts of the system must operate before other parts. An engineer needs to calculate the length of each path and design a layout that avoids the problem of clock skew.

As a consequence of clock skew, engineers seldom use a single global clock to control a system. Instead, multiple clocks are used, with each clock controlling one part of the system. Often, clocks that run at the highest rates are used in the smallest physical areas. We use the term *clock zone* to refer to the region that a given clock controls. The idea is not limited to physically large systems — integrated circuits, such as CPUs, have become so large and complex that multiple clock zones are used on a chip.

Although using multiple clock zones avoids the problems of clock skew, multiple clocks introduce another problem, *clock synchronization*: digital logic at the boundary between two clock zones must be engineered to accommodate both zones. Usually, such accommodation means the circuit slows down and takes multiple clock cycles to move data.

22.25 Clockless Logic

As chips increase in size and complexity, the problem of clock skew and the division of a system into clock zones has become increasingly important. In many systems, the boundary between clock zones forms a bottleneck because logic circuits at the boundary must wait multiple clock cycles before the output from one clock zone can be forwarded to another clock zone. The problem of zone synchronization has become so important that researchers have devised an alternative approach: *clockless logic*. In essence, a clockless system uses two wires instead of one to represent a Boolean value. The use of two wires means that an output can indicate the end of a bit unambiguously without depending on a clock. Figure 22.24 lists the four possible combinations of values on two wires and their meanings.

Wire 1	Wire 2	Meaning
0	0	Reset before starting a new bit
0	1	Transfer a 0 bit
1	0	Transfer a 1 bit
1	1	Undefined (not used)

Figure 22.24 Meaning of signals on two wires when clockless logic is used to transfer bits from one chip to another.

The idea is that the sender sets both wires to zero volts between each bit to *reset* the receiver. After the reset, the sender transfers a logical 0 or a logical 1. A receiver knows when a bit arrives because exactly one of the two wires is high (e.g., 5 volts).

Why use clockless logic? In addition to eliminating the problem of clock zone coordination and allowing higher-speed data transfer among chips, the clockless approach can use less power. Clocked circuits need to propagate the clock signal continuously, even when parts of the circuit are inactive. Clockless logic can avoid the overhead of propagating clock signals.

Does the clockless approach work in practice? Yes. By designing an entire processor that uses clockless logic, ARM, Inc. has demonstrated that the approach scales to large, complex circuits. Thus, the clockless approach has potential. Currently, most chip designers still use the clocked approach.

22.26 Circuit Size And Moore's Law

Most digital circuits are built from *Integrated Circuits* (*ICs*), a technology that permits many transistors to be placed on a single silicon chip along with wiring that interconnects them. The idea is that the components on an IC form a useful circuit.

ICs are often created by using CMOS technology. Silicon is doped with impurities to give it negative or positive ionization. The resulting substances are known as *N-type silicon* or *P-type silicon*. When arranged in layers, N-type and P-type silicon form transistors.

IC manufacturers do not create a single IC at a time. Instead, a manufacturer creates a round *wafer* that is between twelve and eighteen inches in diameter and contains many copies of a given IC design. Once the wafer has been created, the vendor cuts out the individual chips, and packages each chip in a plastic case along with pins that connect to the chip.

ICs come in a variety of shapes and sizes; some have only eight external connections (i.e., *pins*), and others have hundreds of pins†. Some ICs contain dozens of transistors, others contain millions.

Depending on the number of transistors on the chip, ICs can be divided into four broad categories that Figure 22.25 lists.

Name	Example Use
Small-Scale Integration (SSI)	Basic Boolean gates
Medium-Scale Integration (MSI)	Intermediate logic, such as counters
Large-Scale Integration (LSI)	Small, embedded processors
Very Large-Scale Integration (VLSI)	Complex processors

Figure 22.25 A classification scheme used for integrated circuits.

For example, integrated 7400, 7402, and 7404 circuits described in this chapter are classified as SSI. A binary counter, flip-flop, or demultiplexor is classified as MSI.

The definition of VLSI keeps changing as manufacturers devise new ways to increase the density of transistors per square area. Gordon Moore, a cofounder of Intel Corporation, is attributed with having observed that the density of silicon circuits, measured in the number of transistors per square inch, would double every year. The observation, known as *Moore's Law*, was revised in the 1970s, when the rate slowed to doubling every eighteen months.

As the number of transistors on a single chip increased, vendors took advantage of the capability to add more and more functionality. Some vendors created *multicore* CPU chips by placing multiple copies of their CPU (called a *core*) on a single chip, and then providing interconnections among the cores. Other vendors took a *System on Chip* (*SoC*) approach in which a single chip contains processors, memories, and interfaces for I/O devices, all interconnected to form a complete system. Finally, memory manufac-

---

†Engineers use the term *pinout* to describe the purpose of each pin on a chip.

turers have created chips with larger and larger amounts of main memory called *Dynamic Ram* (*DRAM*).

In addition to general-purpose ICs that are designed and sold by vendors, hardware engineers can build special-purpose, customized ICs. Known as *Application-Specific Integrated Circuits* (*ASICs*), the ICs are designed by a private company, and then the designs are sent to a vendor to be manufactured. Designing an ASIC can be both expensive and time-consuming. It can take up to two years and over one million dollars to produce an ASIC mask for a high-end fabrication technology. Once a design has been completed, many copies of the ASIC chip can be produced at low cost. Thus, companies choose ASIC designs for products where standard chips do not meet the requirements and the company expects a large volume of the product to be produced.

22.27 Circuit Boards And Layers

Most digital systems are built using a *Printed Circuit Board* (*PCB*) that consists of a fiberglass board with thin metal strips attached to the surface and holes for mounting integrated circuits and other components. In essence, the metal strips on the circuit board form the wiring that interconnects components.

Can a circuit board be used for complex interconnections that require wires to cross? Interestingly, engineers have developed *multilayer* circuit boards that solve the problem. In essence, a multilayer circuit board allows wiring in three dimensions — when a wire must cross another, the designer can arrange to pass the wire up to a higher layer, make the crossing, and then pass the wire back down.

It may seem that a few layers will suffice for any circuit, and many designs only need six layers. However, large complex circuits with thousands of interconnections may need additional layers. It is not uncommon for engineers to design circuit boards that have twenty layers; the most advanced boards can have fifty layers.

22.28 Levels Of Abstraction

As this chapter illustrates, it is possible to view digital logic at various levels of abstraction. At the lowest level, a transistor is created from silicon. At the next level, multiple transistors are used along with components, such as resistors and diodes, to form gates. At the next level, multiple gates are combined to form intermediate scale units, such as flip flops. Earlier chapters discuss more complex mechanisms, such as processors, memory systems, and I/O devices, that are each constructed from multiple intermediate scale units. Figure 22.26 summarizes the levels of abstraction.

The important point is that moving up the levels of abstraction allows us to hide more details and talk about larger and larger building blocks without giving internal details. When we describe processors, for example, we can consider how a processor works without examining the internal structure at the level of gates or transistors.

Abstraction	Implemented With
Computer	Circuit board(s)
Circuit board	Processor, memory, and bus adapter chips
Processor	VLSI chip
VLSI chip	Many gates
Gate	Many transistors
Transistor	Semiconductor implemented in silicon

Figure 22.26 An example of levels of abstraction in digital logic. An item at one level is implemented using items at the next lower level.

An important consequence of abstraction arises in the diagrams architects and engineers use to describe digital systems. As we have seen, schematic diagrams can represent the interconnection of transistors, resistors, and diodes. Diagrams can also be used to represent an interconnection among gates. Earlier chapters use high-level diagrams that represent the interconnection of processors and memory systems. In such diagrams, a small rectangular box will represent a processor or a memory without showing the interconnection of gates. When looking at an architectural diagram, it will be important to understand the level of abstraction and to remember that a single item in a high-level diagram can correspond to an arbitrarily large number of items at a lower-level abstraction.

22.29 Summary

Digital logic refers to the pieces of hardware used to construct digital systems such as computers. As we have seen, Boolean algebra is an important tool in digital circuit design — there is a direct relationship between Boolean functions and the gates used to implement combinatorial digital circuits. We have also seen that Boolean logic values can be described using truth tables.

A clock is a mechanism that emits pulses at regular intervals to form a signal of alternating ones and zeros. A clock allows a digital circuit output to be a function of time as well as of its logic inputs. A clock can also be used to provide synchronization among multiple parts of a circuit.

Although we think of digital logic from a mathematical point of view, building practical circuits involves understanding the underlying hardware details. In particular, besides basic correctness, engineers must contend with problems of power distribution, heat dissipation, and clock skew.

EXERCISES

22.1 Use the Web to find the number of transistors on a VLSI chip and the physical size of the chip. If the entire die was used, how large would an individual transistor be?

22.2 Digital logic circuits used in smart phones and other battery-powered devices do not run on five volts. Look at the battery in your smart phone or search the Web to find out what voltage is being used.

22.3 Design a circuit that uses *nand*, *nor* and *inverter* gates to provide the *exclusive or* function.

22.4 Write a truth table for the full adder circuit in Figure 22.12.

22.5 Use the Web to read about flip-flops. List the major types and their characteristics.

22.6 Create the circuit for a decoder from *nand*, *nor*, and *inverter* gates.

22.7 Look at Web sources, such as Wikipedia, to answer the following question: when a chip manufacturer boasts that it uses a seven-nanometer chip technology, what does the manufacturer mean?

22.8 What is the maximum number of output bits a counter chip can have if the chip has sixteen pins? (Hint: the chip needs power and ground connections.)

22.9 If a decoder chip has five input pins (not counting power and ground), how many output pins will it have?

22.10 Design a circuit that takes three inputs, A, B, and C, and generates three outputs. The circuit would be trivial, except that you may only use two inverters. You may use arbitrary other chips (e.g., *nand*, *nor*, and *exclusive or*).

22.11 Assume a circuit has a spare *nor* gate. Can any useful functions be created by connecting one of the inputs to logical one? To logical zero? Explain.

22.12 Read about clockless logic. Can you find an example of a clockless logic circuit being used in practice?

Chapter Contents

23

Hardware Modularity

23.1 Introduction

Earlier chapters give an overview of hardware architectures without discussing design or implementation details. This brief chapter considers designs that employ modularity. The chapter begins by contrasting hardware modularity with software modularity, and explaining why familiar programming abstractions do not apply to hardware. The chapter then considers two examples of hardware modularity, and uses an example to illustrate how a basic hardware module can be designed that is flexible, and how replication of a basic module allows a designer to form a scalable hardware design.

23.2 Motivations For Modularity

Modular construction offers both intellectual and economic advantages. From an intellectual perspective, a modular approach allows a designer to break a large complex problem into smaller pieces. Using smaller pieces makes the design easier to understand and less prone to errors. The use of small pieces makes it easier to test corner cases for each piece. Furthermore, a designer can analyze and optimize individual pieces.

The economic motivation for modularity arises from the cost of designing and testing products. In many cases, a company creates a set of related products. For example, a company might offer a set of products that range from a low-cost model with minimal performance to a high-priced model with ultra-high performance. Alternatively, a company may offer a series of products that supply the same basic functionality, but where each product has special features. Modularity allows the company to produce related products without designing each product in isolation. In fact, savings occur whenever a company can design a basic hardware module and then reuse the module in multiple products — once a basic module has been tested thoroughly, successive designs that use the module can assume it works without further testing.

23.3 Software Modularity

Since the early days of computer software, modularity has played a key role in software design. The most common abstraction consists of a *function* (also known as a *procedure*, *subprogram* or *subroutine*). Instead of repeating sections of code at multiple places throughout the program, a single copy of the function resides in memory when the program executes, and then the copy is *called* (*invoked*) repeatedly.

Like hardware modularity, the use of functions offers two important advantages. First, using functions allow a programmer to divide a large, complex problem into small pieces. Second, once an expert builds a function, other programmers can use and trust the function, thereby lowering the cost of building software. For example, once experts implement trigonometric functions, such as *sine* and *cosine*, other programmers can use the functions without learning how to structure floating point computations for accuracy and precision.

23.4 Parameterization

Software functions use *parameters* to increase generality. When creating a function, a programmer specifies a set of *formal parameters*, and when invoking the function, a caller specifies actual arguments to be substituted in place of formal parameters. The key point is:

> *Modularized software uses a single copy of each subprogram with actual arguments supplied for each invocation of the subprogram.*

23.5 Forms Of Hardware Modularity

Many hardware designs employ modularity. We will consider two examples that illustrate basic forms of hardware modularity.

- Modular chip construction (SoC design and chiplet technology)
- Replication and parallelism

23.6 Modular Chip Construction

23.6.1 SoC Design

Consider a small embedded system, such as the remote-control used for a television. Such systems contain a processor, memory, storage, and basic I/O devices (e.g., a keypad and an RF or IR transmitter). Thus, the system meets our definition of a computer. In terms of hardware, a small embedded device typically consists of a single computer chip. Hardware engineers use the term *System on Chip* (*SoC*) to describe a chip that contains all the key components on a single chip.

How does a hardware engineer construct an SoC chip? In most cases, the engineer uses a graphical design system that offers many pre-built modules. For example, the engineer starts by selecting a CPU module, a memory module, a storage module, and a set of I/O interface modules. The engineer then uses the design system to interconnect the modules. Once the interconnections have been completed, the design system can simulate the resulting SoC, allowing the engineer to test for correctness. Finally, after thorough testing, the design system produces a set of masks, and sends the masks to a fabrication facility that produces a physical chip.

Using pre-designed hardware modules makes it faster and safer to build chips. A module can be large enough to hold an entire CPU or an entire bus interface. It can take weeks or months for an engineer to build and test a large module from scratch. Using modules that have already been designed and tested means that the resulting chip is less likely to contain errors.

23.6.2 Chiplet Technology

Industry has created another modular technology used to construct chips. Known as *chiplets*, the technology creates a chip by interconnecting small, pre-defined functional pieces. The chiplet approach differs from the systems described above because chiplets use *late-binding*. During the design process, a hardware engineer chooses chiplets to place on the chip, but does not configure the interconnections among them. Instead, the chip contains an interconnection mechanism that can be configured after a chip has been fabricated. In particular, the interconnection mechanism allows hardware interconnections to be installed. That is, once a chip has been fabricated, the manufacturer can choose which of the chiplets to use, and can configure how the chiplets interconnect to form a system.

Important motivations for chiplet designs arise from economics. An SoC chip can be designed that has multiple chiplets, where each chiplet corresponds to a specific I/O interface. For example, a chip for a remote-control device might contain one chiplet for a Bluetooth interface and another for an infrared interface. The vendor can manufacture many copies of the chip without choosing which interfaces to include. Then, as customers order the chips, the vendor can choose whether to configure a chip to have an infrared interface, a Bluetooth interface, or both. Because the chiplet technology allows the vendor to leave some chiplets unconnected, the resulting chips do not draw power unnecessarily. The point is:

The late-binding feature of chiplet technology allows a vendor to wait until a chip has been manufactured before choosing which chiplets to include and how to interconnect them. Thus, the vendor can satisfy customer demand without overproducing some versions of the chip and underproducing other versions.

23.6.3 Chiplets And Fabrication Flaws

Another motivation for chiplet technology arises from the physics and chemistry of chip fabrication. Because physical processes introduce imperfections, chip manufacturers face a major challenge: flaws. Even in the best of conditions, a few small flaws occur when silicon forms crystals (e.g., a few atoms do not connect to the crystal correctly). Although the probability of a flaw is small, the probability of at least one flaw in a chip can be high if the chip contains billions of transistors. In a multicore processor, a flaw may make one of the cores unusable. With conventional chip technology, an unusable core forces the manufacturer to sell the chip as having fewer cores.

The chiplet approach helps by allowing a chip vendor to select the number of cores after the chip has been created. To use the approach, a vendor defines each core to be a chiplet, and includes a few extra cores when building the chip. Once a chip has been fabricated, the vendor tests cores, and configures the interconnections among them. If a particular chiplet contains a flaw, the chip can be configured to ignore the failed unit and substitute one of the spares, allowing the vendor to choose the maximum number of viable cores without incurring unnecessary power drain.

23.7 Replication And Parallelism

Although it works well for software, parameterized invocation does not work well with hardware. Unlike software that invokes a function repeatedly over time, hardware designs use separate physical instantiations that iterate in space to achieve parallelism. If a software engineer designs code that handles a set of N items, the engineer will likely store the items in an array and write code that iterates through the array, performing the necessary computation on each item. Accommodating more items means using a larger array.

When a hardware engineer creates a system to handle a set of items, the engineer designs a separate piece of hardware for each item. Accommodating more items means adding more copies of the hardware. In other words, scaling a hardware design always requires adding additional pieces of hardware. As a consequence:

When hardware designers think about a modular design, they look for ways to make it possible to add additional hardware to a design, not for ways to invoke a given piece of hardware iteratively.

23.8 Basic Block Replication

The fundamental technique used to make it possible to scale hardware consists of defining a basic hardware block that can be replicated as needed. We have already seen trivial examples. For instance, a latch circuit can be replicated N times to form an N-bit register, and a *full adder* is replicated $N-1$ times and combined with a *half adder* to build a circuit to compute the sum of two N-bit integers.

In the trivial cases described above, replication involves a small circuit (i.e., a few gates), and a designer knows how many replications will be needed. Although replication of a small circuit is an important aspect of design, the approach can be applied to significantly larger circuits and used to scale a design. Replication is especially important in designs where the number of inputs or outputs visible to a user varies across a series of products.

23.9 An Example Modular Design: A Rebooter

An example will clarify the idea. Rather than choose a hypothetical design, we will consider a piece of hardware used in the author's lab. The lab, which is used for operating system and networking research, has a large set of *backend* computers that are available for researchers and students in classes. The lab facilities allow a user to create an operating system, allocate a backend computer, download the operating system into the backend computer's memory, and start the computer running. The user then can interact with the backend computer.

Unfortunately, experimental work on operating systems often results in crashes or leaves the computer hardware in a state that cannot respond to further input. In such situations, the backend computer must be power-cycled to regain control. Therefore, we created a special-purpose hardware system that can power-cycle individual backend computers as needed. We call the system a *rebooter*. Several generations of rebooter hardware have been used in the lab; we will review one design.

23.10 High-Level Rebooter Design

In principle, the rebooter hardware follows a straightforward approach. The rebooter has a set of outputs that each supply power to a backend computer. The inputs to the rebooter consist of a binary value that specifies one of the outputs to reboot and an *enable input* that tells the rebooter to act. To use the rebooter, the interface circuit must place a binary value on the input lines that specify one of the outputs, and then set the *enable* input to 1, which causes the rebooter to power-cycle the specified output†. Figure 23.1 illustrates the inputs and outputs.

---

†The exact details of how the rebooter circuit is used are irrelevant to the discussion that follows; it is only important to understand the basics.

power connections for
2^N backend computers

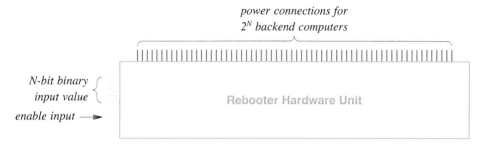

N-bit binary
input value
enable input ⟶

Figure 23.1 The conceptual organization of rebooter hardware.

How many outputs should a rebooter have? The question is important because the rebooter needs a physical connection for each computer in the lab. Initially, the lab had only one backend, but the size evolved quickly to two and then eight. To plan for the future, we needed a rebooter circuit to accommodate at least 40 backends, and perhaps 100. The situation illustrates a standard hardware dilemma:

- A design with too few outputs will not accommodate future needs
- A design with too many outputs is wasteful

23.11 A Building Block To Accommodate A Range Of Sizes

Rather than choose a specific size, we chose to use a modular approach. That is, we chose a basic hardware building block and devised a way to replicate the basic block to form larger and larger rebooters. The modular approach allowed us to construct a small rebooter, and then add additional outputs as needed.

Our basic building block consists of a sixteen-output rebooter as Figure 23.2 illustrates.

power connections for
16 backend computers

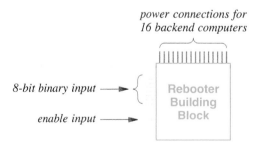

8-bit binary input ⟶
enable input ⟶

Figure 23.2 Illustration of the basic building block used for the rebooter.

Look carefully at the figure. The binary input value consists of eight bits, but the unit only has sixteen output lines. Only four bits are needed to select one of the outputs. Why are extra input bits present? We will see that they allow us to scale the design to a larger size by replicating multiple copies of the building block.

23.12 Parallel Interconnection

Our design uses a parallel approach common to many hardware systems. That is, the design allows us to connect multiple copies of the basic block and send all inputs to all copies in parallel. To make replication possible, each building block must pass a copy of its inputs (the binary value and the enable input) to the next building block. Figure 23.3 illustrates the idea.

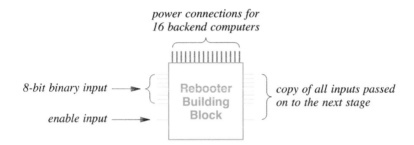

Figure 23.3 Illustration of a basic building block passing all inputs to the next stage of the rebooter.

We think of each block as a module; Figure 23.4 shows how inputs pass in parallel across four modules.

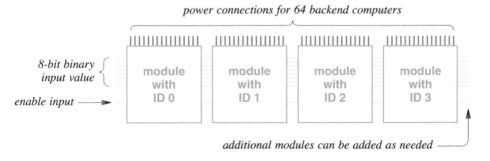

Figure 23.4 An example interconnection of four copies of the basic building block that provides 64 outputs.

23.13 Module Selection

As Figure 23.4 shows, all inputs pass in parallel to all modules. A question arises: if the input specifies power-cycling computer number 5, does each module power-cycle its fifth output? The answer is no. Only the fifth output on module 1 is affected.

To understand how modules respond to inputs, it is necessary to know that each module is assigned a unique ID (0, 1, 2, and 3 in our example). A module includes hardware that checks the four high-order bits of the input to see if they match the assigned ID. If the input does not match the ID, the module ignores the input. In other words, the hardware interprets the four high-order bits as *module selection* bits, and interprets the four low-order bits as an *output selection*.

As an example, Figure 23.5 illustrates how the hardware interprets the input value 5 as module 0 and output 5.

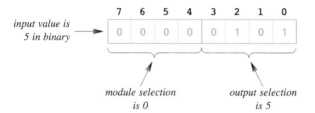

Figure 23.5 The interpretation of input 5 by the rebooter in Figure 23.4.

As Figure 23.5 shows, input 5 means the four high-order bits contain 0000 and the four low-order bits contain 0101. The high-order bits match the ID assigned to module 0, but none of the other modules. Therefore, only module 0 responds to the input.

Using the high-order bits of the input to select a module makes the hardware extremely efficient. The module selection bits can be passed to a *comparator chip* along with the ID of the module. As the name implies, a comparator compares two sets of inputs, and sets an output line high if the two are equal. Thus, very little additional hardware is needed to perform module selection.

23.14 Summary

Both hardware and software engineers use modularity. Modular chip technologies allow a designer to build a chip from predefined modules. Chiplet technology permits modules to be selected and interconnected after a chip has been fabricated. Many modular hardware designs use replication of a basic building block.

One method used to accommodate a range of hardware sizes consists of structuring a module (i.e., a building block) to accept a set of N input lines that control a set of 2^N

outputs. When building blocks are replicated, each is assigned a unique ID. Additional input lines are added to the design, which means the high-order bits of the input can be used to select one of the modules, and the low-order bits can be used to select an output on the module.

EXERCISES

23.1   In engineering, what is the relationship between *modularity* and *reuse*?

23.2   How does the ability to pass arguments to functions help programmers control the complexity of software?

23.3   When a software engineer and a hardware engineer think about the design of a crypto system that processes 128-bit integers, they each start with a bias. A software engineer might imagine an algorithm that iterates through the integers, working on 32 bits at a time. What will a hardware engineer envision?

23.4   Read about SoC designs and chiplet technologies. How does placing a memory on an SoC improve performance?

23.5   Mathematically, one can have an arbitrary number of outputs from a module and use arithmetic to extract a module number and an input for the module (e.g., for seven outputs per module divide the input value by 7 to get a module number and use the remainder to select an output within the module). However, hardware engineers always choose to make outputs a power of two. Explain.

23.6   What are the tradeoffs to consider when choosing how many outputs a piece of hardware should have?

23.7   Suppose a basic building block contains 4 outputs, and a design must scale to 64 outputs. How many building blocks will be used?

23.8   If each building block contains 8 outputs and the input has 16 bits, how many total outputs can be controlled, and how many building block chips will be used?

23.9   In the previous exercise, draw a diagram similar to the one in Figure 23.5 that shows how bits of the input are interpreted.

23.10   Consider the four-module interconnection that Figure 23.4 illustrates. Are all possible combinations of the 8-bit input value valid? Why or why not?

23.11   In Figure 23.4, which output line(s) on which module(s) will be selected if the binary input value is 00100101?

23.12   Look up comparator chips. How many pairs of inputs does a single comparator have?

23.13   In the previous exercise, suppose a comparator chip can compare K pairs of inputs and a designer needs to compare $2K$ pairs. How can multiple chips be used?

Appendix 1

Rules For Boolean Algebra Simplification

A1.1 Introduction

Boolean expressions can be simplified by applying the rules of Boolean algebra. Specifically, there are rules that cover associative, reflexive, and distributive properties. From an engineering perspective, the motivation for simplification is that an implementation requires fewer gates. For example, consider a *logical or*. We know that if either of the two expressions is *true*, the *logical or* will also be *true*. Thus, the expression *X or true* can be replaced by *true*.

A1.2 Notation Used

In Figure A1.1, a dot ($\cdot$) denotes *logical and*, a plus sign ($+$) denotes *logical or*, an apostrophe ($'$) denotes *logical not*, *0* denotes *false*, and *1* denotes *true*. Using the notation, the expression:

$$(X + Y) \cdot Z'$$

represents:

$$(X \; or \; Y) \; and \; (not \; Z)$$

A1.3 Rules Of Boolean Algebra

Figure A1.1 lists nineteen rules of Boolean algebra. Although many of the initial rules may seem obvious, they are included for completeness.

$$x + 0 = x$$
$$x + 1 = 1$$
$$x \cdot 0 = 0$$
$$x \cdot 1 = x$$
$$x + x = x$$
$$x + x' = 1$$
$$x \cdot x = x$$
$$x \cdot x' = 0$$
$$(x')' = x$$
$$x \cdot y = y \cdot x$$
$$x + y = y + x$$
$$x \cdot (y \cdot z) = (x \cdot y) \cdot z$$
$$x + (y + z) = (x + y) + z$$
$$x \cdot (y + z) = (x \cdot y) + (x \cdot z)$$
$$x + (y \cdot z) = (x + y) \cdot (x + z)$$
$$x \cdot (x + y) = x$$
$$x + (x \cdot y) = x$$
$$(x \cdot y)' = x' + y'$$
$$(x + y)' = x' \cdot y'$$

Figure A1.1 Rules of Boolean algebra that can be used to simplify Boolean expressions.

Appendix 2

A Quick Introduction To x86 Assembly Language

A2.1 Introduction

Engineers use the term *x86* to refer to a series of processors that use an architecture created by Intel Corporation†. Each processor in the Intel series was more powerful than its predecessor. Over time, the design changed from a 16-bit architecture to a 32-bit architecture. During the transition, Intel enforced *backward compatibility* to guarantee that newer chips in the series could execute code written for earlier chips. Thus, the fundamentals remain the same.

The x86 has undergone another transition, this time from a 32-bit architecture to a 64-bit architecture; the change was led by AMD, an Intel competitor. Once again, backward compatibility is a key part of the transition. In this brief chapter, we will discuss the 32-bit version first, and then describe 64-bit extensions.

Because it follows a CISC approach, an x86 processor has a large, complex instruction set. In fact, the instruction set is huge — the vendor's manuals that document the instructions comprise nearly 3000 pages. An x86 can contain special instructions for high-speed graphics operations, trigonometric functions, and the large set of instructions an operating system uses to control processor modes, set protection, and handle I/O. In addition to the 32-bit instructions used by applications running on recent processors, an Intel x86 processor retains hardware that supports previous versions. Consequently, we cannot review the entire instruction set in a brief appendix. Instead, we provide an overview that introduces basics. Once a programmer masters a few fundamentals, learning new instructions is straightforward.

---

†The name arises because Intel assigned part numbers such as 8086, 80286, 80386, and 80486.

A2.2 The x86 General-Purpose Registers

As a result of extensions, the x86 architecture suffers from confusing and unexpected inconsistencies. For example, the architecture includes eight *general-purpose registers*, and inconsistencies are especially apparent in the way the general-purpose registers are named and referenced. In particular, the initial design used four general-purpose 16-bit registers, and the assembly language provided names for individual bytes of each register. When the registers were extended to thirty-two bits, each extended register was given a name, and the architecture mapped each of the original 16-bit registers onto the low-order sixteen bits of the corresponding extended register. Thus, the assembly language provides a set of names that allows a programmer to reference an entire 32-bit register, the low-order 16-bit region of the register, or individual bytes within the 16-bit region. Unfortunately, the names are confusing. Initially, registers were assigned specific purposes, and the names reflect the historical use. Figure A2.1 illustrates the eight general-purpose registers, lists their historical purpose, and gives names for the registers as well as each subpart†.

Figure A2.1 The eight general-purpose registers on an x86 processor, their historical purpose, and the names used to reference a register and the subparts.

---

†Because most assemblers do not distinguish between uppercase and lowercase, names *eax* and *EAX* refer

Although most of the registers are no longer restricted to their original purpose, the *stack pointer* (*ESP*) and *base pointer* (*EBP*) still have special meaning. The use of the base and stack pointers during a procedure call is explained below.

A2.3 Allowable Operands

Operands specify the values to be used in an operation and a location for the result. An operand can specify one of the registers, a location in memory, or a constant. Each instruction specifies the combinations that are allowed. For example, a *mov* instruction copies data from one location to another. *Mov* can copy a constant to a register or to memory, or can copy a data value from a register to memory, from memory to a register, or from one register to another. However, *mov* cannot copy data from one memory location directly to another. Thus, to copy data between two memory locations, a programmer must use two instructions. First, a programmer uses a *mov* to copy the data from memory to a register, and second, a programmer uses a *mov* to copy the data from the register to the new memory location.

Figure A2.2 lists the nomenclature used to describe the set of operands that are allowed for a given instruction.

Name	Meaning
\<reg32\>	Any 32-bit register, such as EAX, EBX, ...
\<reg16\>	Any 16-bit register, such as AX, BX, ...
\<reg8\>	Any 8-bit register, such as AH, AL, BH, BL...
\<reg\>	Any 32-bit, 16-bit, or 8-bit register
\<con32\>	Any 32-bit constant
\<con16\>	Any 16-bit constant
\<con8\>	Any 8-bit constant
\<con\>	Any 32-bit, 16-bit, or 8-bit constant
\<mem\>	Any memory address

Figure A2.2 Nomenclature used to specify allowable operands.

A later section explains how a memory address can be computed. For now, it is sufficient to understand that we will use the terminology from Figure A2.2 to explain instructions. As an example, consider the *mov* instruction, which copies a data item specified by a *source* operand into the location specified by a *target* operand. Figure A2.3 uses the nomenclature in Figure A2.2 to list the allowable operand combinations for *mov*.

Source Operand	Target Operand
\<reg\>	\<reg\>
\<mem\>	\<reg\>
\<reg\>	\<mem\>
\<con\>	\<reg\>
\<con\>	\<mem\>

Figure A2.3 Allowable operand combinations for a *mov* instruction.

A2.4 Intel And AT&T Forms Of x86 Assembly Language

Before we examine instructions, it is important to know a few assembly language basics. For example, assembly language employs a fixed statement format with one statement per line:

label   opcode   operands...

The *label* on a statement, which is optional, consists of a name used to identify the statement. If the statement defines a data item, the label specifies a name for the item; if a statement contains code, the label is followed by a colon, and can be used to pass control to the statement. The *opcode* field defines the type of data item or specifies an instruction; zero or more *operands* follow the opcode to give further details for the data or operation.

Unfortunately, many x86 assemblers have been created, and each has features that distinguish it from the others. Rather than examining each individual assembler, we will focus on two major categories. The first category employs a syntax that was originally defined by Intel and adopted by Microsoft; it is known informally as *Intel assembly language* or *Microsoft-Intel assembly language*. The second category employs a syntax originally defined by AT&T Bell Labs for Unix and adopted by the open source community for use in Linux; it is known as *AT&T assembly language* or *GNU assembly language* (*gas*).

Assemblers in either category are functionally equivalent in that they allow a programmer to code an arbitrary sequence of x86 instructions and to declare arbitrary data items in memory. Despite overall similarities, the two types of assemblers differ in many details. For example, the order in which operands are listed, the way registers are referenced, and the comment syntax differ. Although either type can be used, a programmer may find that one type is more intuitive, more convenient, or helps catch more programming errors. Because both types of assemblers are widely used in industry, we will examine examples for each.

A2.4.1 Characteristics Of Intel Assembly Language

An Intel assembler has the following characteristics:

- Operand order is right-to-left, with the source on the right and the target on the left
- Comments begin with a semicolon (;)
- Register names are coded without punctuation (e.g., eax)
- Immediate constants are written without punctuation
- The assembler deduces opcode type from the operand(s)

To remember the operand order, a programmer can think of an assignment statement in a high-level language: the expression is on the right and the value is assigned to the variable on the left. Thus, in Intel assembly language, a data movement operation is written:

```
mov    target, source
```

For example, the following code adds two to the contents of register EBX and places the result in register EAX:

```
mov    eax, ebx+2
```

The x86 hardware has *implicit* operand types, which means that at run-time, the opcode specifies the types of the operands. For example, instead of one *mov* instruction, the hardware contains an opcode for each possible operand type. That is, the x86 has an opcode to move a byte, another opcode to move a word, and so on. The hexadecimal values are 88, 89, 8A, 8B, 8C, and so on. When it produces binary code, an Intel assembler *deduces* the correct opcode from the operand types. If the target is a single byte, the assembler chooses the opcode that moves a byte, if the target is a sixteen-bit register, the assembler chooses the opcode that moves a sixteen-bit value, and so on. Each instruction follows the same pattern — although a programmer uses a single mnemonic in the program (e.g., *add* for addition or *sub* for subtraction), the processor has a set of opcodes for each operation, and the Intel assembler chooses the opcode that is appropriate for the operands the programmer specifies.

A2.4.2 Characteristics Of AT&T Assembly Language

An AT&T assembler has the following characteristics:

- Operand order is left-to-right, with the source on the left and the target on the right
- Comments are enclosed in /*... */ or begin with a hash mark (#)
- Register names are preceded by a percent sign (e.g., %eax)
- Immediate constants are preceded by a dollar sign ($)
- The programmer chooses a mnemonic that indicates the type as well as the operation

The operand order is the exact opposite of that used by an Intel assembler. Thus, in AT&T assembly language, a data movement operation is written:

        mov   source, target

For example the following code adds two to the contents of register EBX and places the thirty-two-bit result in register EAX.

        movl %ebx+2, %eax

A2.5 Arithmetic Instructions

Addition And Subtraction. Many arithmetic and logical operations on the x86 take two arguments: a *source* and a *target*. The *target* specifies a location, such as a register, and the *source* specifies a location or a constant. The processor uses the two operands to perform the specified operation, and then places the result in the target operand. For example, the instruction:

Intel: add   eax,ebx

AT&T: add   %ebx,%eax

causes the processor to add the values in registers EAX and EBX, and then place the result in register EAX. In other words, the processor changes EAX by adding the value in EBX. Figure A2.4 lists the allowable combinations of operands for addition and subtraction.

Source Operand	Target Operand
<reg>	<reg>
<mem>	<reg>
<reg>	<mem>
<con>	<reg>
<con>	<mem>

Figure A2.4 The allowable combinations of operands for add or subtract.

Increment And Decrement. In addition to *add* and *sub*, the x86 offers increment and decrement instructions that add or subtract one. The instructions, which have opcodes *inc* and *dec* (followed by a designator on the AT&T assembler), each take a single argument that can be any register or any memory location. For example, the instruction:

Intel: inc   ecx

AT&T: incl %ecx

increments the value of register ECX by one. A programmer must decide whether to use *inc* or *add*.

The inclusion of increment and decrement instructions in the instruction set illustrates an important principle about the architecture:

> *A CISC architecture, such as the one used with x86, often provides more than one instruction to perform a given computation.*

Multiplication And Division. Integer multiplication and division pose an interesting challenge for computer architects. The product that results when a pair of registers are multiplied can exceed a single register. In fact, the product can be twice as long as a register. Most computers also permit the dividend used in integer division to be larger than a single register.

The x86 includes many variations of integer multiplication and division. Some of the variations of multiplication allow a programmer to restrict the result to a specific size (e.g., restrict the product to thirty-two bits). To handle the case where the product will exceed one register, the x86 uses a combination of two registers to hold the result. For example, when multiplying two thirty-two-bit values, the x86 places the sixty-four-bit result in the EDX and EAX registers, with EDX holding the most significant thirty-two bits and EAX holding the least significant thirty-two bits.

The x86 also permits integer division to have a sixty-four-bit operand, stored in a pair of registers. Of course, integer division can also be used with small items. Even if the dividend does not occupy sixty-four bits, an x86 can use two registers to hold the result of an integer division: one holds the quotient and the other holds the remainder. Having a way to capture a remainder makes computations such as hashing efficient.

An x86 offers two basic forms of multiplication. The first form follows the same paradigm as addition or subtraction: the multiplication instruction has two arguments, and the result overwrites the value in the first argument. The second form takes three arguments, the third of which is a constant. The processor multiplies the second and third arguments, and places the result in the location specified by the first argument. For example,

Intel: imul   eax,edi,42

AT&T: imul   %edi,42,%eax

multiplies the contents of register EDI by 42, and places the result in register EAX.

A2.6 Logical Operations

The x86 processors offer *logical* operations that treat data items as a string of bits and operate on individual bits. Three of the logical operations perform bit-wise operations on two operands: logical *and*, *or*, and *xor*. The fourth logical operation, *not*, per-

Logical and, or, xor
Source Operand	Target Operand
<reg>	<reg>
<mem>	<reg>
<reg>	<mem>
<con>	<reg>
<con>	<mem>

Logical not
Target Operand
<reg>
<mem>

Figure A2.5 The allowable combinations of operands for *and*, *or*, *xor*, and *not* instructions.

forms bit inversion on a single operand. Figure A2.5 lists the operand types used with logical operations.

In addition to bit-wise logical operations, an x86 supports bit *shifting*. Shifting can be applied to a register or memory location. In essence, a shift takes the current value, moves bits left or right by the amount specified, and places the result back in the register or memory location. When shifting, the x86 supplies zero bits to fill in when needed. For example, when shifting left by K bits, the hardware sets the low-order K bits of the result to zero, and when shifting right by K bits, the hardware sets the high-order K bits of the result to zero. Figure A2.6 lists the allowable operands used with left and right shift operations.

shift left (shl) and shift right (shr)
Source Operand	Target Operand
<con8>	<reg>
<con8>	<mem>
<cl>	<reg>
<cl>	<mem>

Figure A2.6 Allowable operand combinations for shift instructions. The notation *<cl>* refers to the 8-bit register CL.

A2.7 Basic Data Types

Assembly language for an x86 allows a programmer to define initialized and uninitialized data items. Data declarations must be preceded by a *.data* assembler directive, which tells the assembler that the items are to be treated as data. A programmer can define each individual data item or can define a sequence of unnamed data items to occupy successive memory locations. Figure A2.7 lists the basic data types available; the figure assumes the AT&T assembler is set to produce code for a thirty-two-bit processor.

Intel Name	AT&T Name	Size In Bytes
DB (Data Byte)	.byte (single byte)	1
DW (Data Word)	.hword (half word)	2
DD (Data Double)	.long (long word)	4
DQ (Data Quad)	.quad (quad word)	8

Figure A2.7 Basic data types used by Intel and AT&T assemblers.

Each type of assembler permits a programmer to assign an initial value to data items. In Intel assembly program, a label starts in column 1, the data type appears next, and an initial value for the item follows the data type. An Intel assembler uses a question mark to indicate that the data item is uninitialized. In an AT&T assembly program, a label ends in a colon, and is followed by the type and an initial value; if the initialization is omitted, zero is assumed. Figures A2.8 and A2.9 illustrate declarations for the two types of assemblers.

```
        .DATA           ; start of data declarations  (Intel assembler)
z       DD      ?       ; four bytes that are uninitialized
y       DD      0       ; four bytes that are initialized to zero
x       DW      -54     ; two bytes initialized to -54
w       DW      ?       ; two bytes that are uninitialized
v       DB      ?       ; one byte that is uninitialized
u       DB      6       ; one byte initialized to 6
```

Figure A2.8 Examples of data declarations when using an Intel assembler.

An assembler places successive data items in adjacent bytes of memory. In the figures, the item named u is placed in the byte following the item named v. Similarly, y is placed just beyond z; because z is four bytes long, y starts four bytes beyond the location at which z starts.

```
        .data           ; start of data declarations  (AT&T assembler)
z:      .long           ; four bytes that are initialized to zero
y:      .long   0       ; four bytes that are initialized to zero
x:      .hword  -54     ; two bytes initialized to -54
w:      .hword          ; two bytes that are initialized to zero
v:      .byte           ; one byte that is initialized to zero
u:      .byte   6       ; one byte initialized to 6
```

Figure A2.9 Examples of data declarations when using an AT&T assembler.

A2.8 Data Blocks, Arrays, And Strings

Although it does not provide data aggregates, such as structs, x86 assembly languages do allow a programmer to declare multiple occurrences of a data item that occupy contiguous memory locations. For example, to declare three sixteen-bit items that are initialized to 1, 2, and 3, a programmer can write three separate lines that each declare one item or can list multiple items on a single line:

```
Intel:              q      DW     1, 2, 3
AT&T:               q:     .hword 1, 2, 3
```

The Intel assembler uses the modifier *K DUP(value)* to repeat a data value multiple times; the AT&T assembler uses *.space* to fill a specified size of memory with a value. For example, to declare one thousand repetitions of a data byte that is initialized to the numeric value 220, one writes:

```
Intel:              s      DB     1000 DUP(220)
AT&T:               s:     .space 1000, 220
```

The AT&T assembler provides a *.rept* macro to declare repetitions of larger items, such as a dozen occurrences of four-byte zero:

```
Intel:                     DD     12 DUP(0)

AT&T:                      .rept  12
                           .long  0
                           .endr
```

In addition to numeric values, x86 assembly language allows a programmer to use ASCII characters as initial values. The Intel assembler encloses character constants in single quotation marks, and allows multiple characters to be used to form a *string*. The assembler does not add a trailing zero (null termination). An AT&T assembler surrounds a string of characters with double quotation marks, and uses the directive *.ascii* or *.asciz* to declare a string; *.ascii* does not add a null termination byte, and *.asciz* does. For example, a programmer can declare a byte in memory that is initialized to the letter *Q* or a string that contains the characters *hello world*, with or without null termination.

```
Intel:              c      DB     'Q'
                    d      DB     'hello world'
                    e      DB     'hello world', 0

AT&T:               c:     .ascii "Q"
                    d:     .ascii "hello world"
                    e:     .asciz "hello world"
```

A2.9 Memory References

As we have seen, many x86 instructions permit an operation to reference memory, either to fetch a value for use in the instruction or to store a result. The x86 hardware offers a complex mechanism that a programmer can use to compute a memory address: an address can be formed by adding the contents of two general-purpose registers plus a constant. Furthermore, one of the registers can be multiplied by two, four, or eight. A few examples will illustrate some of the possibilities.

Data Names. The most straightforward form of memory reference consists of a reference to a named data item. Intel assemblers use square brackets to enclose the name of a memory item, and AT&T assemblers precede the name by a dollar sign. In either case, the assembler computes the memory address assigned to the item, and substitutes the constant in the instruction. For example, if an assembly program contains a declaration for a 16-bit data item named *T*, the following instructions are used to move the 16-bit value from the memory into register DX:

Intel: mov   dx, [T]

AT&T: movw $T, %dx

Indirection Through A Register. A programmer can compute a numeric value, place the value in a register, and then specify that the register should be used as a memory address. For example, the instruction:

Intel: mov   eax, [ebx]

AT&T: movl   (%ebx), %eax

uses the contents of register EBX as a memory address, and moves four bytes starting at that address into register EAX.

Expressions that compute an address are permitted, provided they adhere to the rule of adding at most two registers and a constant, with the option of multiplying one of the registers by two, four, or eight. For example, it is possible to form a memory address by adding the contents of EAX, the contents of ECX, and the constant 16, and then using the address to store the value of register EDI. In Intel notation, the operation is written:

                          mov   [eax+exb+16], edi

The rules for addresses can be difficult to master at first because they seem somewhat arbitrary. Figure A2.10 lists examples of valid and invalid memory references.

Valid references

```
mov    eax, [lab1]        ; move 4 bytes from label lab1 in memory to EAX
mov    [lab2], ebx        ; store 4 bytes from EBX to label lab2 in memory
and    eax, [esi-4]       ; and EAX with 4 bytes at address given by ESI - 4
not    [edi+8]            ; invert 32 bits at location given by EDI + 8
mov    [eax+2*ebx],0      ; store zero in 4 bytes at address given by EAX+2*EBX
mov    cl, [esi+4*ebx]    ; move byte from ESI+4*EBX into register CL
```

Invalid references

```
mov    eax, [esi-ebx]     ; cannot subtract two registers
mov    [eax+ebx+cl], 0    ; cannot specify more than two registers
```

Figure A2.10 Examples of valid and invalid memory references using Intel
notation.

A2.10 Data Size Inference And Explicit Size Directives

Because a memory address can be calculated at run time, an address merely consists of an unsigned thirty-two-bit integer value. That is, an address by itself does not
specify the size of an item in memory. An x86 assembler uses heuristics to *infer* the
data size whenever possible. For example, because the following instruction moves a
value from memory into register EAX, which is four bytes long, an assembler will infer
that the memory address refers to a four-byte value. For example, in Intel notation, the
instruction is written:

```
mov    eax, [ebx+esi+12]
```

Similarly, if a name has been assigned to a data item that is declared to be a single byte,
an assembler infers that a memory reference to the name refers to one byte. In some
cases, however, a programmer must use an explicit *size directive* to specify the size of a
data item. For example, suppose a programmer wishes to store −1 in a sixteen-bit word
in memory. The programmer computes a memory address, which is placed in register
EAX. An assembler cannot know that the programmer thinks of the address as pointing
to a sixteen-bit (i.e., two-byte) data item, and will infer that it refers to a four-byte item.
Therefore, a programmer must add a size directive before the memory reference, as in
the following example that uses Intel notation:

```
mov    WORD PTR [eax], -1
```

It is good programming practice to use a size directive to make the intention clear
if there is any doubt, even in cases where the inference rules of the assembler produce
the correct result. Figure A2.11 summarizes the three size directives available.

Directive	Meaning
BYTE PTR	The address refers to a single byte in memory
WORD PTR	The address refers to a 16-bit value in memory
DWORD PTR	The address refers to a 32-bit value in memory

Figure A2.11 Size directives that can be prepended to memory references for the Intel assembler.

A2.11 Computing An Address

We said that an integer value can be computed, placed in a register, and then used as a memory address. However, most address computation begins with a known location in memory, such as the initial location of an array. For example, for the Intel assembler, suppose an array of four-byte integers has been declared using the name *iarray* and initialized to zero:

```
iarray    DB    1000 DUP(0)
```

The memory location of the ith element can be computed by multiplying i by four (because each element is four bytes long) and adding the result to the address of the first byte of the array.

How can a running program obtain the address of the first byte of an array? More generally, how can a program obtain the memory address of an arbitrary variable? The answer lies in a special instruction that loads an address into a register rather than a value. Specified by the name *load effective address* and the mnemonic *lea*, the special instruction takes a register and a memory location as operands. Unlike the *mov* instruction, *lea* does not access an item in memory. Instead, *lea* stops after it computes the memory address, and places the address in the specified register. For example,

```
lea    eax, [iarray]
```

places the memory address of the first byte of item *iarray* in register EAX.

Observe that computing the offset of the ith element of an array of four-byte integers is straightforward. First, place i in a register, for example, EBX. Once the index is in the register, the memory location corresponding to that element of the array can be computed with a single *lea* instruction:

```
mov  ebx, [i]              ; obtain index from variable i in memory
lea  eax, [4*ebx+iarray]   ; place address of ith element in EAX
```

A2.12 The Stack Operations Push And Pop

The x86 hardware includes instructions that manipulate a memory *stack*. The stack operates as a *Last-In-First-Out* (*LIFO*) data structure, with the most recently added item being accessed first. Like the stack on other processors, an x86 stack grows downward, with new items being added at successively lower memory addresses. Despite growing downward in memory, we say that the most recently added item is on the "top" of the stack.

When an item is added to a stack, we say the item is *pushed* onto the stack, and the top of the stack corresponds to the new item. When the top item is removed from the stack, we say that the stack has been *popped*.

An x86 stack always uses four-byte items — when an item is pushed onto a stack, four additional bytes of memory are used. Similarly, when an item is popped from a stack, the item contains four bytes, and the stack occupies four fewer bytes of memory.

In an x86, the ESP register (stack pointer) contains the current address of the top of the stack. Thus, although ESP does not appear explicitly, stack manipulation instructions always change the value in ESP. The names of stack instructions reflect the generic terminology described above: *push* and *pop*. Figure A2.12 lists the allowable argument types.

```
push   <reg32>              pop    <reg32>
push   <mem>                pop    <mem>
push   <con32>
```

Figure A2.12 Operands allowed with the *push* and *pop* instructions.

Once register ESP has been set, adding items to the stack is trivial. For example, the instruction:

```
push   eax
```

pushes the value of register EAX onto the stack, and the instruction:

```
pop    [qqqq]
```

pops the top of the stack and places the value in the memory location with name *qqqq*. Similarly, the instruction:

```
push   -1
```

pushes the constant -1 onto the stack. The x86 hardware does not have a stack bound, which means that a programmer must plan stack use carefully to avoid situations in which a stack grows downward into a memory area used for other variables.

A2.13 Flow Of Control And Unconditional Branch

Normally, after a statement is executed, the processor proceeds to the next statement. An x86 supports three types of instructions that change the flow of control:

- unconditional branch
- conditional branch
- procedure call and return

An *unconditional branch* instruction is the easiest to understand: the opcode is *jmp* (for "jump"), and the only operand is the label on a statement. When it encounters a *jmp* instruction, the processor immediately moves to the specified label and continues execution. For example,

```
jmp     prntname
```

means the next instruction the processor will execute is the instruction with label *prntname*. The programmer must have placed the label on an instruction (presumably the first instruction in a sequence that prints a name). In Intel notation, the programmer writes:

```
prntname: mov     eax, [nam]
                .
                .
                .
```

A2.14 Conditional Branch And Condition Codes

Each arithmetic instruction sets an internal value in the processor known as a *condition code*. A *conditional branch* instruction uses the value of the condition code to choose whether to branch or continue execution with the next sequential statement. A set of conditional branch instructions exists; each instruction encodes a specific test. Figure A2.13 summarizes.

Opcode	Meaning
jeq	jump if equal
jne	jump if not equal
jz	jump if zero
jnz	jump if not zero
jg	jump if greater than
jge	jump if greater than or equal
jl	jump if less than
jle	jump if less than or equal

Figure A2.13 Conditional branch instructions and the meaning of each.

For example, the following code in Intel notation decrements register EBX and jumps to label *atzero* if the resulting value is zero.

```
dec   ebx        ; subtract 1 from ebx
jz    atzero     ; jump to label atzero if EBX reaches zero
```

Some of the instructions in Figure A2.13 require a programmer to compare two items. For example, *jge* tests for greater-than-or-equal. However, conditional branch instructions do not perform comparisons — they have a single operand that consists of a label specifying where to branch. As with arithmetic tests, conditional branches involving a comparison rely on the condition code. Various instructions set the condition code, which means that a conditional branch can be executed immediately after the condition code has been set. If a conditional branch does not immediately follow the instruction that sets the condition code, a programmer must code an extra instruction that sets the condition. The x86 architecture includes two instructions used to set a condition code: *test* and *cmp*. Neither of the two modifies the contents of registers or memory. Instead, they merely compare two values and set the condition code. The *cmp* instruction checks for equality. In essence, a *cmp* performs a subtraction and then discards the answer, keeping only the condition code. For example, the following code in Intel notation tests whether the four-byte value in memory location *var1* has the value 123, and jumps to label *bb* if it does.

```
cmp  DWORD PTR [var1], 123   ; compare memory item var1 to 123
jeq   bb                     ; jump to label bbb if they are equal
```

The *test* instruction is more sophisticated: it performs a bit-wise *and* of the two operands, and sets various condition code bits accordingly. As a result, *test* sets conditions such as whether a data value contains odd or even parity.

A2.15 Subprogram Call And Return

The x86 hardware supports *subroutine invocation* (i.e., the ability to call a subprogram and have the subprogram return to its caller). Subroutine invocation forms a key part of the run-time support needed for a high-level procedural language.

Figure A2.14 summarizes the two x86 instructions that make subprograms possible: one instruction is used to invoke a subprogram and the other is used by a subprogram to return to its caller.

```
call    <label>
ret
```

Figure A2.14 Instructions used to invoke a subprogram: *call* invokes a subprogram, and *ret* returns to the caller.

Subprogram call and return use the run-time stack. For example, a *call* instruction
pushes a return address on the stack. The next section discusses details.

A2.16 C Calling Conventions And Argument Passing

The term *calling conventions* refers to rules that calling and called programs use to
guarantee agreement about details, such as the location of arguments. Calling conventions assign responsibilities to the calling program and the called subprogram. For example, the conventions specify exactly how a calling program pushes arguments on the
stack for the subprogram to use, and exactly how a subprogram can return a value for
the calling program to use.

Each high-level language defines a set of calling conventions. We will use the popular C calling conventions in examples. Although the conventions are intended to allow C or C++ programs to invoke an assembly language program and an assembly
language program to invoke C functions, C calling conventions can also be used when
an assembly language program invokes an assembly language subprogram. Thus, our
examples are general.

The easiest way to understand calling conventions is to visualize the contents of a
run-time stack when a subprogram is invoked. Our example consists of a call that
passes three integer arguments (four bytes per argument) with values 100, 200, and 300
to a subprogram that has four local variables, each of which is thirty-two bits. The calling conventions specify the following during a call:

- *Caller Actions*. The caller pushes the values of registers EAX, ECX, and
  EDX onto the stack to save them. The caller then pushes arguments onto
  the stack in reverse order. Thus, if the arguments are 100, 200, and 300,
  the caller pushes 300, pushes 200, and then pushes 100. Finally, the caller
  invokes the *call* instruction, which pushes the *return address* (i.e., the address immediately following the *call* instruction) onto the stack and jumps
  to the subprogram.

- *Called Subprogram Actions*. The called subprogram pushes the EBP register onto the stack, and sets the EBP to the current top of the stack. The
  caller pushes the EBX, EDI, and ESI registers onto the stack, and then
  pushes each local variable onto the stack (or merely changes the stack
  pointer to allocate space if a local variable is uninitialized).

Figure A2.15 illustrates the stack immediately after a subprogram call has occurred (i.e., after both the caller and called subprogram have followed the conventions outlined above). To understand the figure, remember that a stack grows downward in memory. That is, a *push* operation decrements the stack pointer and a *pop* operation increments the pointer.

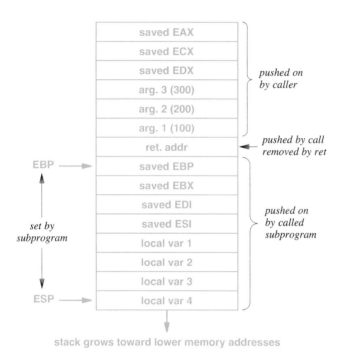

Figure A2.15 Illustration of the run-time stack after a subprogram has been called with three arguments and the subprogram has reserved space for four local variables.

When it finishes, the called subprogram must undo actions taken during the call and return to its caller. The following specifies steps the subprogram and caller take during a return.

- *Called Subprogram Return Actions.* The called subprogram deallocates local variables from the stack. To do so, the subprogram adds *4N* bytes to the stack pointer, where *N* is the number of local variables (each local variable is assumed to be four bytes long). The subprogram then restores the ESI, EDI, EBX, and EBP registers by popping their saved values off the stack. Finally, the subprogram executes a *ret* instruction to pop the return address from the stack and jump back to the caller.

- *Caller Return Actions*. When a called subprogram returns, the caller deal-locates the arguments (e.g., by adding a constant to the stack pointer equal to four times the number of arguments). Finally, the caller restores the values of EDX, ECX and EAX.

A2.17 Function Calls And A Return Value

Technically, the above set of calling conventions applies to a *procedure call*. In the case of a *function call*, the subprogram must return a value to the caller. By convention, the return value is passed in register EAX. Therefore, when a function is invoked, the above calling conventions are modified so the caller does not restore the saved value of EAX.

Does it make sense for a caller to save EAX on the stack before calling a function? Once the function returns, EAX will contain the returned value. However, there are two reasons why EAX should be saved. First, a symbolic debugger will expect the stack to have the same layout for each procedure or function that has been called. Second, a caller may choose to continue computation after saving the result from a function. For example, suppose a compiler has used EAX to hold an index variable for a loop. If the loop contains a statement such as:

$$r = f(t);$$

the compiler may generate code to save the value of EAX before the call, store the return value in memory location r immediately after function f returns, and then restore EAX and allow the loop to continue.

A2.18 Extensions To Sixty-Four Bits (x64)

The x86 architecture has been expanded to a sixty-four-bit version. Interestingly, AMD Corporation defined an extension scheme that was eventually adopted by Intel and other vendors. Known as *x86-64*, and often shortened to *x64*, the architecture includes many changes. For example, arithmetic and logical instructions, instructions that involve two registers, instructions that involve a register and memory location, and instructions that involve two memory locations have all been extended to operate on sixty-four-bit quanti-ties. The stack operations have been changed so they push and pop sixty-four bits (eight bytes) at a time, and pointers are sixty-four-bits wide. The two changes most pertinent to our discussion involve general-purpose registers:

- Each general-purpose register has been extended to make it sixty-four-bits long.

- Eight additional general-purpose registers have been added, making a total of sixteen general-purpose registers.

As in the x86, the x64 architecture attempts to preserve backward compatibility. For example, the lower half of each sixty-four-bit register can be referenced as a thirty-two-bit register. Furthermore, it is possible to reference the sixteen-bit and eight-bit parts of the first four registers exactly as in the x86. Figure A2.16 illustrates the general-purpose registers available in the x64; readers should compare the figure with Figure A2.1 on page 454.

A2.19 Summary

We reviewed x86 fundamentals, including data declarations, registers, operand types, basic instructions, arithmetic and logical instructions, memory references, stack operations, conditional and unconditional branch, and subprogram invocation. Because the x86 architecture provides many instructions, a programmer may have a choice of multiple mechanisms to perform a given task. A sixty-four-bit extension has been designed that is known by the name *x64*.

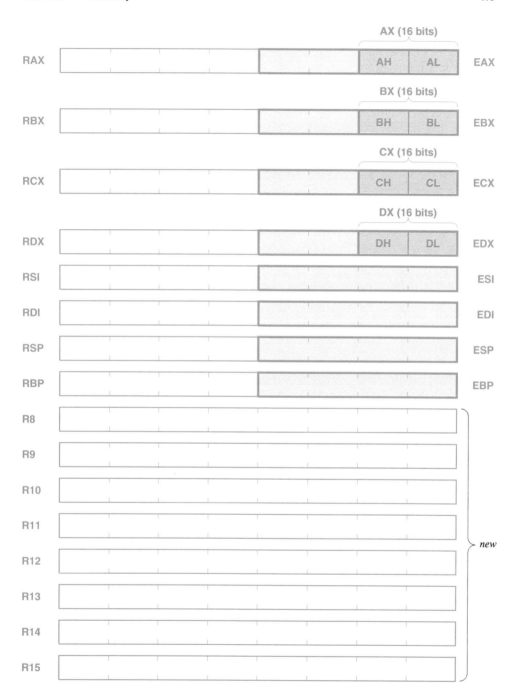

Figure A2.16 General-purpose registers in the x64 architecture.

Appendix 3

ARM Register Definitions
And Calling Sequence

A3.1 Introduction

The previous appendix presents an overview of the x86 and x64 architectures. As we have seen, the x86 is a canonical example of a CISC instruction set. This appendix continues the discussion by providing information about the ARM architecture. ARM provides a canonical example of a RISC architecture.

Although ARM has defined a set of processors, this appendix focuses on features that are common to most of the thirty-two-bit ARM products. The reader is referred to ARM documentation for details about specific models.

A3.2 Registers On An ARM Processor

An ARM processor has 16 general-purpose registers numbered 0 through 15, and generally denoted with names *r0* through *r15*. Registers r0 through r3 are used to pass arguments to a called subroutine and to pass results back to the caller. Registers r4 through r11 are used to hold local variables for the subroutine that is currently being run. Register r12 is an *intra-procedural call scratch register*. Register r13 is the *stack pointer*. Register r14 is a *link register*, and is used in a subroutine call. Finally, register r15 is the *program counter* (i.e., an instruction pointer). Thus, loading an address into r15 causes the processor to branch to the address. Figure A3.1 summarizes the purpose of the registers, and gives alternate names used by the gcc assembler.

Register	Name	Purpose
r15	pc	Program counter
r14	lr	Link register during function call
r13	sp	Stack pointer
r12	ip	Intra-procedural scratch
r11	fp	Frame or argument pointer
r10	sl	Stack limit
r9	v6	Local variable 6 (or real frame pointer)
r8	v5	Local variable 5
r7	v4	Local variable 4
r6	v3	Local variable 3
r5	v2	Local variable 2
r4	v1	Local variable 1
r3	a4	Argument 4 during a function call
r2	a3	Argument 3 during a function call
r1	a2	Argument 2 during a function call
r0	a1	Argument 1 during a function call

Figure A3.1 The general-purpose registers in an ARM architecture, the alternate name used in assembly language, and the meaning assigned to each register.

In addition to general-purpose registers, each ARM processor has a thirty-two-bit *Current Program Status Register* (*CPSR*). The CPSR is divided into many fields, including fields that control the processor mode and operation, control interrupts, report the condition code after an operation, report hardware errors, and control the endianness of the system. Figure A3.2 summarizes the bit fields in the CPSR.

A3.3 ARM Calling Conventions

Programming languages support a call mechanism in which a piece of code calls a subroutine, the subroutine executes, and control passes back to the point at which the call occurred. In terms of the run-time environment, subroutine calls are pushed onto the run-time stack. We say that code becomes a *caller* when it invokes a subroutine, and use the term *callee* to refer to the subroutine that is invoked. In the C Programming Language, a subroutine is known as a *function*; we will use the term throughout the remainder of the appendix.

Although the hardware places constraints on function invocation, a programmer or a compiler is free to choose some of the details. Throughout this chapter, we will describe the calling conventions that *gcc* follows, which have become widely accepted.

Name	Bit Range	Purpose
N	31	Negative/less than
Z	30	Zero
C	29	Carry/borrow/extend
V	28	Overflow
Q	27	Sticky overflow
J	24	Java state
DNM	20 – 23	Do not modify
GE	16-19	Greater-than-or-equal-to
IT	10 – 15 and 25 – 26	The if-then state
E	9	Data endianness
A	8	Imprecise data abort disable
I	7	IRQ disable
F	6	FIQ disable
T	5	Thumb state
M	0 – 4	Processor mode

Figure A3.2 Bits in an ARM CPSR and the meaning of each.

The argument passing conventions for ARM have the following characteristics:

- Allow a caller to pass zero or more arguments to a callee
- Optimize access for the first four arguments
- Allow a callee to return a set of results to the caller
- Specify which registers the callee can change and which must be unchanged when the call returns
- Specify how the run-time stack is used when a function is called and returns

Many functions have four or fewer parameters. To optimize access for the first four arguments, the values are passed in general-purpose registers r0 through r3†. Additional arguments are placed on the stack in memory. Because a callee can access the first four arguments merely by referencing a register, access is extremely fast.

A callee can use registers r0 through r3 to return a result to the called program. In most programming languages, a function only returns one result, which is found in register r0. If an argument or a result is larger than 32 bits, the value is placed in memory and the address is passed in an argument register.

Figure A3.3 shows an example of the stack layout immediately after a function call. The example will clarify the calling conventions and explain how register values are preserved during a function call.

---

†To distinguish using the first four registers for argument passing rather than for general-purpose computation, some literature uses the names *a1* through *a4* instead of r0 through r3.

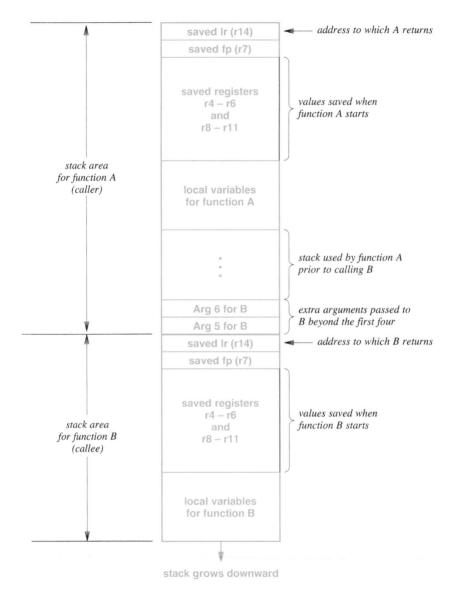

Figure A3.3 Layout of items on the run-time stack just after function A calls
function B with six arguments.

In the figure, function *A* was executing and has called function *B*, which takes six
arguments. The first four arguments are passed in registers†, which means they do not
appear on the stack. However, arguments beyond the first four must be passed on the

---

†Recall that the first four arguments are passed in registers r0 through r3.

stack. Therefore, function A pushes arguments 5 and 6 onto the runtime stack in reverse order before calling function B. As the figure shows, the extra arguments are the last two items on the stack when the call occurs.

A caller expects that values in most of the general-purpose registers will be *preserved* during a function call. That is, a caller expects the called function will not disturb register values. Of course, most functions need to use registers. Therefore, a called function saves the register contents upon entry and restores them before returning. As the figure illustrates, the prelude code in function B pushes the link register (r14), the frame pointer (r7), registers r4 through r6, and registers r8 through r11 onto the stack. The prelude code in function B then reserves space on the stack for its local variables (if any). Once local storage has been allocated, function B is ready to run. Before function B returns, postlude code in the function runs. The postlude code restores the registers from the saved values on the stack, and leaves the stack exactly as it was before the call.

Appendix 4

Lab Exercises For A Computer Architecture Course

A4.1 Introduction

This appendix presents a set of lab exercises for an undergraduate computer architecture course. The labs are designed for students whose primary educational goal is learning how to build software, not hardware. Consequently, most of the labs focus on programming rather than on building digital circuits.

In terms of hardware, the facilities required for the lab are minimal: a small amount of specialized hardware is needed for the digital circuit labs; the rest can be performed on a computer running a version of the Unix operating system (e.g., Linux) and a C compiler. A RISC architecture works best for the assembly language labs because instructors find that CISC architectures absorb arbitrary amounts of class time on assembly language details.

One lab asks students to write a C program that detects whether an architecture is big endian or little endian. Few additional resources are needed because most of the coding and debugging can be performed on one of the two architectures, with only a trivial amount of time required to port and test the program on the other.

A4.2 Hardware Required for Digital Logic Experiments

The labs that cover digital logic require each student to have the following:

- Solderless breadboard
- Wiring kit used with breadboard (22-gauge wire)
- Five-volt power supply
- Light-Emitting Diode (used to measure output)
- NAND and NOR logic gates

None of the hardware is expensive. To handle a class of 70 students, for example, Purdue University spent less than $1000 on hardware. Smaller classes or sharing in the lab can reduce the cost further. As an alternative, it is possible to institute a lab fee or require students to purchase their own copy of the hardware.

A4.3 Solderless Breadboard

A *solderless breadboard* is used to rapidly construct an electronic circuit without requiring connections to be soldered. Physically, a breadboard consists of a block of plastic (typically three inches by seven inches) with an array of small holes covering the surface.

The holes are arranged in rows with a small gap running down the center and extra holes around the outside. Each hole on the breadboard is a socket that is just large enough for a copper wire — when a wire is inserted in the hole, metal contacts in the socket make electrical contact with the metal wire. The size and spacing of the sockets on a breadboard are arranged to match the size and spacing of pins on a standard integrated circuit (technically an IC that uses a standard DIP package), and the gap on the breadboard matches the spacing across the pins on an IC, which means that one or more integrated circuits can be plugged into the breadboard. That is, the pins on an IC plug directly into the holes in the breadboard.

The back of a breadboard contains metal strips that interconnect various sockets. For example, the sockets on each side of the center in a given row are interconnected. Figure A4.1 illustrates sockets on a breadboard and the electrical connections among the sockets.

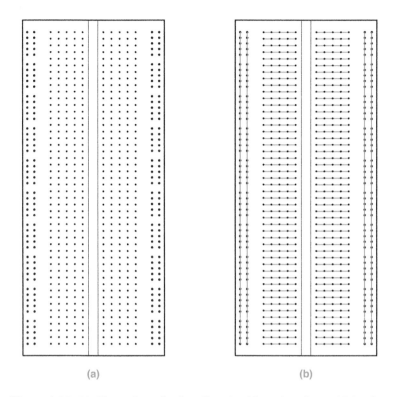

(a)   (b)

Figure A4.1 (a) Illustration of a breadboard with sockets into which wires can be inserted, and (b) blue lines showing the electrical connections among the sockets.

A4.4 Using A Solderless Breadboard

To use a breadboard, an experimenter plugs integrated circuits onto the breadboard along the center, and then uses short wires to make connections among the ICs. A wire plugged into a hole in a row connects to the corresponding pin on the IC that is plugged into the row. To make the connections, an experimenter uses a set of pre-cut wires known as a *wiring kit*. Each individual wire in the wiring kit has bare ends that plug into the breadboard, but is otherwise insulated. Thus, many wires can be added to a breadboard because the insulated area on a wire can rub against the insulation of other wires without making electrical contact.

Figure A4.2 illustrates part of a breadboard that contains a 7400 IC, with wires connecting some of the gates on the IC.

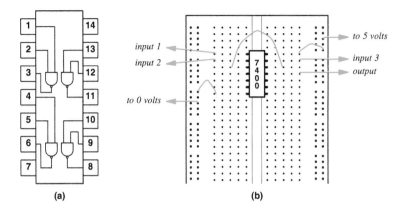

Figure A4.2 Illustrations of (a) the internal connections on a 7400 chip, and (b) part of a breadboard with blue lines indicating wires connecting a 7400 chip. Using a set of sockets to connect power and ground wires allows additional connections to be added.

A4.5 Power And Ground Connections

When multiple chips are plugged into a breadboard, each chip must have connections to *power* and *ground* (i.e., five volts and zero volts). To ensure that the power and ground connections are convenient and to keep the wires short, most experimenters choose to devote the outer sets of sockets on both sides of the breadboard to power and ground.

The wires used to connect power and ground are semi-permanent in the sense that they can be reused for many experiments. Thus, experimenters often use the color of a wire to indicate its purpose, and choose colors for power and ground that are not used for other connections. For example, red wires can be used for all power connections, black wires can be used for all ground connections, and blue wires can be used for other connections. Of course, the wires themselves do not differ — the color of the insulation merely helps a human understand the purpose of the wire. When disassembling a breadboard after an experiment is finished, the experimenter can leave the power and ground connections for a later experiment.

A4.6 Building And Testing Circuits

The easiest approach to building a digital circuit consists of constructing the circuit in stages and testing each stage of the circuit as building proceeds. For example, after connecting power and ground to a chip, a gate on the chip can be tested to verify that the chip is working as expected. Similarly, after a particular gate has been connected, the input(s) and output(s) of the gate can be measured to determine whether the connections are working.

Although it is possible to use a voltmeter to measure the output of a digital circuit, most experimenters prefer an easy and inexpensive alternative: a *Light Emitting Diode* (*LED*). The idea is to choose an LED that can be powered directly†. The LED glows when it is connected to logical one (i.e., five volts), and is off when its input wire connects to logical zero (i.e., zero volts). For example, to test the circuit in Figure A4.2, an LED can be connected to the output (pin 11 of the integrated circuit).

A4.7 Lab Exercises

The next pages contain a series of lab exercises. Although each writeup specifies the steps to be taken in lab, additional details that pertain to the local environment or computer system must be supplied by the lab instructor. For example, the first lab asks students to establish their computer account, including environment variables. Because the set of directories to be included on the path depend on the local computer system, the set of actual paths must be supplied for each environment.

---

†Warning: the LED must have electrical characteristics that are appropriate for the circuit — an arbitrary LED can draw so much electrical power that it will cause a 7400-series integrated circuit to burn out.

Lab 1

Introduction And Account Configuration

Purpose

To learn about the lab facilities and set up a computer account for use in the lab during the semester.

Background Reading And Preparation

Read about the *bash shell* available with Linux, and find out how to set Linux environment variables.

Overview

Modify your lab account so your environment will be set automatically when you log in.

Procedure And Details (Check off as each item is completed)

_____ 1. Modify your account startup file (e.g., *.profile* or *.bash_profile*) so your PATH includes directories as specified by your lab instructor.

2. Log out and log in again.

_____ 3. Verify that you can reach the files and compilers that your lab instructor specifies.

Lab *2*

Representation: Testing Big Endian Vs. Little Endian

Purpose

To learn how the integer representation used by the underlying hardware affects programming and data layout.

Background Reading And Preparation

Read Chapter 3 to learn about big endian and little endian integer representations and the size of an integer.

Overview

Write a C program that examines data stored in memory to determine whether a computer uses big endian or little endian integer representation.

Procedure And Details (Check off as each item is completed)

_____ 1. Write a C program that creates an array of bytes in memory, fills the array with zero, and then stores integer 0x04030201 in the middle of the array.

_____ 2. Examine the bytes in the array to determine whether the integer is stored in big endian or little endian order.

_____ 3. Compile and run the program (without changes to the source code) on both a big endian and little endian computer, and verify that it correctly announces the integer type.

_____ 4. Add code to the program to determine the integer size (hint: start with integer 1 and shift left until the value is zero).

_____ 5. Compile and run the program (without changes to the source code) on both a thirty-two-bit and a sixty-four-bit computer, and verify the program correctly announces the integer size.

Optional Extensions (Check off as each item is completed)

_____ 6. Find an alternate method of determining the integer size.

_____ 7. Implement the alternate method to determine integer size, and verify that the program works correctly.

_____ 8. Extend the program to announce the integer format (i.e., one's complement or two's complement).

Notes

Lab *3*

Representation: A Hex Dump Function In C

Purpose

To learn how values in memory can be presented in hexadecimal form.

Background Reading And Preparation

Read Chapter 3 on data representation, and find both the integer and address sizes for the computer you use†. Ask the lab instructor for an exact specification for the output format.

Overview

Write a C function that produces a hexadecimal dump of memory in ASCII. The lab instructor will give details about the format for a particular computer, but the general form is as follows:

```
Address          Words In Hexadecimal           ASCII characters
--------- -------- -------- -------- -------- --------------------

aaaaaaaa xxxxxxxx xxxxxxxx xxxxxxxx xxxxxxxx cccccccccccccccc
```

In the example, each line corresponds to a set of memory locations. The string *aaaaaaaa* denotes the starting memory address (in hexadecimal) for values on the line, *xxxxxxxx* denotes the value of a word in memory (also in hexadecimal), and *cccccccccccccccc* denotes the same memory locations when interpreted as ASCII characters. Note: the ASCII output only displays printable characters; all other characters are displayed as blanks.

Procedure And Details (Check off as each item is completed)

_____ 1. Create a function, *mdump*, that takes two arguments that each specify an address in memory. The first argument specifies the address where the dump should start, and the second argument specifies the highest address that needs to be included in the dump. Test to ensure that the starting address is less than the ending address.

---

†On most computers, the address size equals the integer size.

2. Modify each of the arguments so they specify an appropriate word address (i.e., an exact multiple of four bytes). For the starting address, round down to the nearest word address; for the ending address, round up.

3. Test the function to verify that the addresses are rounded correctly.

4. Add code that uses *printf* to produce headings for the hexadecimal dump, and verify that the headings are correct.

5. Add code that iterates through the addresses and produces lines of hexadecimal values.

6. To verify that function *mdump* outputs correct values, declare a *struct* in memory, place values in the fields, and invoke the *mdump* function to dump items in the struct.

7. Add code that produces printable ASCII character values for each of the memory locations, as shown above.

8. Verify that only printable characters are included in the output (i.e., verify that a non-printable character such as 0x01 is mapped into a blank).

Optional Extensions (Check off as each item is completed)

9. Extend *mdump* to start and stop on a byte address (i.e., omit leading values on the first line of output and trailing values on the last line).

10. Modify *mdump* so that instead of printing bytes in ASCII, it displays the values of words in decimal.

11. Modify *mdump* so that instead of printing ASCII values, the function assumes the memory corresponds to machine instructions and gives mnemonic opcodes for each instruction. For example, if the first word on the line corresponds to a *load* instruction, print *load*.

12. Add an argument to function *mdump* that selects from among the various forms of output (ASCII characters, decimal, or instructions).

Lab 4

Processors: Learn A RISC Assembly Language

Purpose

To gain first-hand experience with an assembly language and understand the one-to-one mapping between assembly language instructions and machine instructions.

Background Reading And Preparation

Read Chapters 4, 5, and 6 to learn the concepts of instruction sets and operand types. Read about the specific instruction set available on your local computer. Consult the assembler reference manual to learn the syntax conventions needed for the assembler. Also read the assembler reference manual to determine the conventions used to call an external function.

Overview

Write an assembly language program that shifts an integer value to the right and then calls a C function to display the resulting value in hexadecimal.

Procedure And Details (Check off as each item is completed)

_____ 1. Write a C function, *int_out*, that takes an integer argument and uses *printf* to display the argument value in hexadecimal.

_____ 2. Test the function to ensure it works correctly.

_____ 3. Write an assembly language program that places the integer 4 in a register and shifts the contents of the register right one bit.

_____ 4. Extend the program to pass the result of the previous step as an argument to external function *int_out*.

_____ 5. Verify that the program produces 0x2 as the output.

6. Load integer 0xBD5A into a register and print the result to verify that sign extension works correctly.

7. Instead of shifting the integer 4 right one bit, load 0xBD5B7DDE into a 32-bit register, shift right one bit, and verify that the output is correct.

Optional Extensions (Check off as each item is completed)

8. Rewrite the external function *int_out* and the assembly language program to pass multiple arguments.

Notes

Lab 5

Processors: Assembly Function That Can Be Called From C

Purpose

To learn how to write an assembly language function that can be called from a C program.

Background Reading And Preparation

Read Chapter 7 to learn about the concept of subroutine calls in assembly languages, and read the C and assembler reference manuals to determine the conventions that C uses to call a function on your local computer.

Overview

Write an assembly language function that can be called from a C program to perform the *exclusive or* of two integer values.

Procedure And Details (Check off as each item is completed)

_____ 1. Write a C function *xor* that takes two integer arguments and returns the exclusive-or of the arguments.

_____ 2. Write a C main program that calls the *xor* function with two integer arguments and displays the result of the function.

_____ 3. Write *axor*, an assembly language version of the C *xor* function that behaves exactly like the C version. (Do not merely ask the C compiler to generate an assembly file; write the new version from scratch.)

_____ 4. Add a *printf* call to the *axor* function and use it to verify that the function correctly receives the two values that the C program passes as arguments (i.e., argument passing works correctly).

_____ 5. Arrange for the C main program to test *axor* to verify that the code returns correct results for a reasonable range of inputs. Hint: generate values randomly.

Optional Extensions (Check off as each item is completed)

_____ 6. Modify the C program and the *axor* function so that the C program passes a single structure as an argument instead of two integers. Arrange for the structure to contain two integer values.

Notes

Lab 6

Memory: Row-Major And Column-Major Array Storage

Purpose

To understand storage of arrays in memory and row-major order and column-major order.

Background Reading And Preparation

Read Chapters 8 through 10 to learn about basic memory organization and the difference between storing arrays in row-major order and column-major order.

Overview

Instead of using built-in language facilities to declare two-dimensional arrays, implement two C functions, *two_d_store* and *two_d_fetch*, that use linear storage to implement a two-dimensional array. Function *two_d_fetch* takes six arguments: the base address in memory of a region to be used as a two-dimensional array, the size (in bytes) of a single entry in the array, two array dimensions, and two index values. For example, instead of the two lines:

```
int  d[10,20];
x = d[4,0];
```

a programmer can code:

```
char  d[200*sizeof(int)];
x = two_d_fetch(d, sizeof(int), 10, 20, 4, 0);
```

Function *two_d_store* has seven arguments. The first six correspond to the six arguments of *two_d_fetch*, and the seventh is a value to be stored. For example, instead of:

```
int  d[10,20];
d[4,0] = 576;
```

a programmer can code:

```
char   d[200*sizeof(int)];

two_d_store(d, sizeof(int), 10, 20, 4, 0, 576);
```

Procedure And Details (Check off as each item is completed)

_____ 1. Implement function *two_d_store*, using row-major order to store the array.

_____ 2. Create an area of memory large enough to hold an array, initialize the entire area to zero, and then call *two_d_store* to store specific values in various locations. Use the hex dump program created in Lab 6 to display the result, and verify that the correct values have been stored.

_____ 3. Implement function *two_d_fetch*, using row-major order to match the order used by *two_d_store*.

_____ 4. Verify that your implementations of *two_d_store* and *two_d_fetch* work correctly.

_____ 5. Test *two_d_store* and *two_d_fetch* for boundary conditions, such as the minimum and maximum array dimensions.

_____ 6. Rewrite *two_d_store* and *two_d_fetch* to use column-major order.

_____ 7. Verify that the code for column-major order works correctly.

Optional Extensions (Check off as each item is completed)

_____ 8. Verify that functions *two_d_store* and *two_d_fetch* work correctly for an array that stores: characters, integers, or double-precision items.

_____ 9. Extend *two_d_store* and *two_d_fetch* to work correctly with any range of array index. For example, allow the first index to range from –5 to +15, and allow the second index to range from 30 to 40.

Lab 7

Input / Output: A Buffered I/O Library

Purpose

To learn how buffered I/O operates and to compare the performance of buffered and unbuffered I/O.

Background Reading And Preparation

Read Chapter 12 to learn about I/O and buffering.

Overview

Build three C functions, *buf_in*, *buf_out*, and *buf_flush* that implement buffered I/O. On each call, function *buf_in* delivers the next byte of data from file descriptor zero. When additional input is needed from the device, *buf_in* reads sixteen kilobytes of data into a buffer, and allows successive calls to return values from the buffer. On each call, function *buf_out* writes one byte of data to a buffer. When the buffer is full or when the program invokes function *buf_flush*, data from the buffer is written to file descriptor one.

Procedure And Details (Check off as each item is completed)

_____ 1. Implement function *buf_in*.

_____ 2. Verify that *buf_in* operates correctly for input of less than sixteen kilobytes (i.e., less than one buffer of data).

_____ 3. Redirect input to a file that is larger than thirty-two kilobytes, and verify that *buf_in* operates correctly for input that requires *buf_in* to fill a buffer multiple times.

_____ 4. Implement functions *buf_out* and *buf_flush*.

5. Verify that *buf_out* and *buf_flush* operate correctly for output of less than one buffer (i.e., less than sixteen kilobytes).

6. Verify that *buf_out* and *buf_flush* operate correctly for output that spans multiple buffers.

Optional Extensions (Check off as each item is completed)

7. Compare the performance of functions *buf_in*, *buf_out*, and *buf_flush* to the performance of unbuffered I/O (i.e., *read* and *write* of one byte) for various size files. Plot the results.

8. Measure the performance of *buf_in*, *buf_out*, and *buf_flush* for various size buffers when copying a large file. Use buffers that range in size from 4 bytes to 100 Kbytes, and plot the results.

Notes

Lab 8

A Hex Dump Program In Assembly Language

Purpose

To gain experience coding assembly language.

Background Reading And Preparation

Review Chapters 7, 8, and 9, as well as assembly language programs written in earlier labs.

Overview

Rewrite the hex dump program from Lab 3 in assembly language.

Procedure And Details (Check off as each item is completed)

_____ 1. Rewrite the basic hex dump function from Lab 3 in assembly language.

_____ 2. Verify that the assembly language version gives the same output as the C version.

Optional Extensions (Check off as each item is completed)

_____ 3. Extend the assembly language dump function to start and stop on a byte address (i.e., omit leading values on the first line of output and trailing values on the last line).

_____ 4. Change the function to print values in decimal instead of ASCII character form.

_____ 5. Modify the dump function so instead of printing ASCII values, the function assumes the memory corresponds to machine instructions and gives mnemonic opcodes for each instruction. For example, if the first word on the line corresponds to a *load* instruction, print *load*.

6. Add an argument to the dump function that selects from among the various forms of output (ASCII characters, decimal, or instructions).

Notes

Lab 9

Digital Logic: Use Of A Breadboard

Purpose

To learn how to wire a basic breadboard and use an LED to test the operation of a gate.

Background Reading And Preparation

Read Chapter 22 to learn about basic logic gates and circuits, and read the beginning sections of this appendix to learn about breadboards. Attend a lecture on how to properly use the breadboard and related equipment.

Overview

Place a 7400 chip on a breadboard, connect power and ground from a five-volt power supply, connect the inputs of a gate to the four possible combinations of zero and one, and use an LED to observe the output.

Procedure And Details (Check off as each item is completed)

_____ 1. Obtain a breadboard, power supply, wiring kit, and parts box with the necessary logic gates. Also verify that you have a data sheet that specifies the pins for a 7400, which is a quad, two-input NAND gate. A copy of the pin diagram can also be found in Figure 22.13 of the text, which can be found on page 418.

_____ 2. Place the 7400 on the breadboard as shown in Figure A4.2b on page 484.

_____ 3. Connect the two wires from a five-volt power supply to two separate sets of sockets near the edge of the board.

_____ 4. Add a wire jumper that connects pin 14 on the 7400 to five volts.

5. Add a wire jumper that connects pin 7 on the 7400 to zero volts. NOTE: be sure not to reverse the connections to the power supply or the chip will be damaged.

6. Add a wire jumper that connects pin 1 on the 7400 to zero volts.

7. Add a wire jumper that connects pin 2 on the 7400 to zero volts.

8. Connect the LED, from the lab kit, between pin 3 on the 7400 and ground (zero volts). NOTE: the LED must be connected with the positive lead attached to the 7400.

9. Verify that the LED is lit (it should be lit because both inputs are zero which means the output should be one).

10. Move the jumper that connects pin 2 from zero volts to five volts, and verify that the LED remains lit.

11. Move the jumper that connects pin 2 back to zero volts, move the jumper that connects pin 1 from zero volts to five volts, and verify that the LED remains lit.

12. Keep the jumper from pin 1 on five volts, move the jumper that connects pin 2 to five volts, and verify that the LED goes out.

Optional Extensions (Check off as each item is completed)

13. Wire the breadboard as shown in Figure A4.2b (pin 3 connected to pin 12, and pin 13 acting as an additional input).

14. Connect the LED between pin 11 and ground.

15. Record the LED values for all possible combinations of the three inputs.

16. What Boolean function does the circuit represent?

Lab 10

Digital Logic: Building An Adder From Gates

Purpose

To learn how basic logic gates can be combined to perform complex tasks such as binary addition.

Background Reading And Preparation

Read Chapter 22 about basic logic gates and circuits, and read the beginning sections of this appendix to learn about breadboards.

Overview

Build a half adder and full adder circuit using only basic logic gates. Combine the circuits to implement a two-bit binary adder with carry output.

Procedure And Details (Check off as each item is completed)

_____ 1. Obtain a breadboard, power supply, wiring kit, and parts box with the necessary logic gates as well as lab writeups that describe both the chip pinouts and the logic diagram of an adder circuit.

_____ 2. Construct a binary half adder as specified in the logic diagram that your lab instructor provides.

_____ 3. Connect the outputs to LEDs, the inputs to switches, and verify that the results displayed on the LED are the correct values for a one-bit adder.

_____ 4. Construct a binary full adder as specified in the logic diagram that your lab instructor provides.

_____ 5. Connect the outputs to LEDs, the inputs to switches, and verify that the results displayed on the LED are the correct values for a full adder.

_____ 6. Chain the half adder circuit to the full adder circuit to make a two-bit adder. Verify that the circuit correctly adds a pair of two-bit numbers and the carry out value is correct.

Optional Extensions (Check off as each item is completed)

_____ 7. Draw the logic diagram for a three-bit adder.

_____ 8. Draw the logic diagram for a four-bit adder.

_____ 9. Give a formula for the number of gates required to implement an n-bit adder.

Notes

Lab *11*

Digital Logic: Clocks And Decoding

Purpose

To understand how a clock controls a circuit and allows a series of events to occur.

Background Reading And Preparation

Read Chapter 22 to learn about basic logic gates and clocks. Concentrate on understanding how a clock functions.

Overview

Use a switch to simulate a clock, and arrange for the clock to operate a decoder circuit (informally called a *demultiplexor circuit*).

Procedure And Details (Check off as each item is completed)

_____ 1. Obtain a breadboard, power supply, wiring kit, and parts box with the necessary logic gates as well as lab writeups that describe both the chip pinouts and the logic diagram of a decoder.

_____ 2. Use a switch to simulate a slow clock.

_____ 3. To verify that the switch is working, connect the output of the switch to an LED, and verify that the LED goes on and off as the switch is moved back and forth.

_____ 4. Connect the simulated clock to the input of a four-bit binary counter (a 7493 chip).

_____ 5. Use an LED to verify that each time the switch is moved through one cycle, the outputs of the counter move to the next binary value (modulo four).

_____ 6. Connect the four outputs from the binary counter to the inputs of a decoder chip (a 74154).

_____ 7. Use an LED to verify that as the switch moves through one cycle, exactly one output of the decoder becomes active. Warning: the 74154 is counterintuitive because the active output is low (logical zero) and all other outputs are high (logical one).

Optional Extensions (Check off as each item is completed)

_____ 8. Use a 555 timer chip to construct a 1-Hz clock, and verify that the clock is working.

_____ 9. Replace the switch with the clock circuit.

_____ 10. Use multiple LEDs to verify that the decoder continually cycles through each output.

Notes

Index

Printed and bound by CPI Group (UK) Ltd, Croydon, CR0 4YY

17/10/2024

01775666-0001